Navigating the Research University

a guide for first-year students

THIRD EDITION

BRITT ANDREATTA, PH.D.

University of California, Santa Barbara
Antioch University Santa Barbara

WADSWORTH
CENGAGE Learning

Australia · Brazil · Japan · Korea · Mexico · Singapore · Spain · United Kingdom · United States

**Navigating the Research University
a guide for first-year students
Third Edition**

Britt Andreatta

Senior Sponsoring Editor: Shani Fisher

Assistant Editor: Daisuke Yasutake

Editorial Assistant: Cat Salerno

Media Editor: Amy Gibbons

Senior Marketing Manager: Kirsten Stoller

Marketing Coordinator: Ryan Ahern

Marketing Communications Manager:
Courtney Morris

Content Project Manager: Jessica Rasile

Senior Art Director: Pam Galbreath

Production Technology Analyst: Jeff Joubert

Print Buyer: Julio Esperas

Senior Rights Acquisition Specialist, Image:
Jennifer Meyer Dare

Senior Rights Acquisition Specialist, Text:
Katie Huha

Production Service/Compositor: Integra

Text Designer: Patti Hudepohl

Cover Designer: Grannan Graphic Design

Cover Image: Image of University of
Washington campus, © Danita Delimont/
Alamy

Illustrations: Britt Andreatta

For product information and technology assistance, contact us at
Cengage Learning Customer, & Sales Support, 1-800-354-9706

For permission to use material from this text or product, submit all requests online at **www.cengage.com/permissions**.
Further permissions questions can be emailed to
permissionrequest@cengage.com.

Library of Congress Control Number: 2010939879

ISBN-13: 978-0-495-91378-8

ISBN-10: 0-495-91378-2

Wadsworth
20 Channel Center Street
Boston, MA 02210
USA

Cengage Learning is a leading provider of customized learning solutions with office locations around the globe, including Singapore, the United Kingdom, Australia, Mexico, Brazil and Japan. Locate your local office at **international.cengage.com/region**

Cengage Learning products are represented in Canada by Nelson Education, Ltd.

For your course and learning solutions, visit **www.cengage.com.**

Purchase any of our products at your local college store or at our preferred online store **www.cengagebrain.com.**

Instructors: Please visit **login.cengage.com** and log in to access instructor-specific resources.

Printed in the United States of America
2 3 4 5 6 7 14 13 12 11

Contents

Preface

New to This Edition

This edition focuses more deeply on the unique features of the research university and how the research mission shapes every aspect of the student experience. The text explores academic, social, and personal areas that a first-year student is likely to experience, providing practical activities and strategies. Through connecting student experience with current theories and empirical data, both freshmen and transfer students will gain an appreciation for both the value of cutting-edge research as well as the privilege of learning from some of the world's leading minds.

A new feature titled **@myU** discusses how a variety of topics are likely to materialize in the daily experience of the student. This feature includes space for personal reflection so students can personalize the content. A new **Scenic Route** feature appears in the margin that directs students to related websites and tools via this text's companion website found at www.cengagebrain.com. This edition also includes the following new information:

+ New Student Stories from the Path from universities across the United States
+ New material on critical thinking and higher order thinking skills
+ New material on note-taking and test-taking strategies
+ New material on the Holland Career Typology, Myers-Briggs Type Indicator®, and the Strong Interest Inventory®
+ New material on motivation and the imposter phenomenon
+ New material on stress management and sleep hygiene
+ New material on programs created by student leaders including Teach For America and Invisible Children

Features

Each chapter of this text includes the following features:

+ Statistics, studies, and theories representing the latest research on the college student experience
+ "Scenic Route" feature with links to websites and related materials and tools for students
+ "@myU" feature that discusses how the various topics are likely to materialize in the daily experience of the student—this feature includes space for personal reflection
+ "Point of Interest" feature offering suggestions and strategies for how students can make the most of their educational experience
+ "Stories from the Path" feature, where current students share their advice and suggestions for success
+ The author donates 10 percent of her royalties to nonprofit organizations that support education.

The Research University

The first year of college is an important time in a young adult's life. It is a time filled with transition as the student adjusts to the academic demands of higher education while simultaneously dealing with social and personal issues associated with young adulthood. This is true whether the student is attending a local community college, a private liberal arts institution, or a premiere research university. However, the experiences associated with each type of institution can be quite different. While many guides and texts exist that discuss the college experience, texts that explore and describe issues associated with undergraduate education at a **research university** have been nonexistent. Many instructors, like myself, have been forced to compile readers from a wide variety of sources, often with large gaps in specific content or perspective.

Additionally, the transition for many high school and transfer students to the academic rigor of a research institution can be difficult. While students are expected to adapt to their university's demands, few texts provide them with guidance in how to do so. Students often gain skills in academic inquiry via a slow progression through discipline-based courses with little understanding of how to accelerate or maximize their academic performance. While many fine texts exist that introduce students to "skills for college success," many of these are not appropriately targeted for the student at a research university with its unique academic focus. Furthermore, few texts do justice to the social and personal development students face, which can also be impacted by the unique nature of a research university.

Navigating the Research University: a guide for first-year students seeks to address the issues stated above by providing first-year students (both freshmen and transfers) with a comprehensive introduction to education at a research university. While orientation sessions and other first-year programs are designed to *orient* the student to the many aspects of university life, this text will help the student *navigate* the university on a daily basis. It is written primarily for the first-year student, both freshman and transfer, and is suited for use in a variety of settings, including:

+ Orientation programs
+ Summer reading programs
+ Introductory writing courses
+ First-year experience courses
+ Freshman seminars
+ Freshman interest groups
+ Transfer preparation courses

Families of first-year students might also find it helpful in understanding their student's experience. It has a broad scope and is applicable to most research institutions in the United States, yet will leave students and instructors the ability to make appropriate connections to their particular university. Utilizing my 20 years of experience as a faculty member and administrator, I hope to provide students with valuable information based on empirical research, student experiences, and the expertise of university staff and administrators.

Ancillary Materials

This text has a companion website for students. Visit www.cengagebrain.com to access additional resources. Available materials include: exercises for students to complete, glossary of terms, Scenic Route links to websites, more Stories from the Path, and recommended readings.

The Instructor's Companion Site includes an *Instructor's Manual & Test Bank*. Matching the organization of the main text, these materials offer additional classroom activities, learning tools, sample syllabi, and quiz questions. The instructor's resources can be accessed at login.cengage.com. In addition, the author maintains a host of teaching materials and classroom activities for instructors on her website at www.brittandreatta.com.

If you're looking for more ways to assess your students, Cengage Learning has resources to consider:

- College Success Factors Index 2.0
- Noel-Levitz College Student Inventory
- The *Myers-Briggs Type Indicator® (MBTI®) Instrument*[1]

You can also package this textbook with the College Success Planner to assist students in making the best use of their time both on and off campus.

An additional service available with this textbook is support from **TeamUP Faculty Program Consultants**. For more than a decade, our consultants have helped faculty reach and engage first-year students by offering peer-to-peer consulting on curriculum and assessment, faculty training, and workshops. Consultants are available to help you establish or improve our student success program and provide training on the implementation of our textbooks and technology. To connect with your TeamUP Faculty Program Consultant, call 1-800-528-8323 or visit www.cengage.com/teamup.

For more in-depth information on any of these items, talk with your sales rep, or visit www.cengagebrain.com.

Acknowledgments

I would not have been able to write this book without the effort and support of many people. I wish to offer special thanks to the following wonderful colleagues and friends.

The Publishing Team: Many terrific folks at Wadsworth dedicated long hours and hard work to bring this edition to fruition. My thanks goes to Annie Todd, Director of College Success and Developmental English; Shani Fisher, Senior Sponsoring Editor; Daisuke Yasutake, Assistant Editor; Cat Salerno, Editorial Assistant; Jessica Rasile, Content Project Manager; and Kirsten Stoller, Marketing Manager. I'm grateful for the work of Linda Ireland, Copy Editor, and Amrin Sahay, Project Manager. Thanks also go to Sean Wakely, Executive Vice President of Academic Solutions—Arts & Sciences; Lyn Uhl, Publisher; and PJ Boardman, Editor-in-Chief.

The Chapter Contributors: Many thanks to Miles Ashlock, Joanna Hill, Sabrina Kwist, Monica Lenches, Don Lubach, Garrett Naiman, Cedric Walker, and the wonderful researchers at the Higher Education Research Institute at UCLA. Their expertise and experience contributed greatly to this book.

The Reviewers: My heartfelt thanks go to the reviewers, whose comments helped shape this edition: Geoff Cohen, University of California, Riverside; Adrianna Guram, University of Wisconsin at Madison; Beth McCoy, University of Oklahoma; Alice Lanning, University of Oklahoma; Holly T. Moses, University of Florida; Rachael Orr, University of Missouri at Columbia; Mary Jo Parker, University of Houston—Downtown; Paul S. Voakes, University of Colorado—Boulder; Catrina L. Wagner, University of California, Davis; Toni Woolfork-Barnes, Western Michigan University. Special thanks to Chris Wyckoff of Auburn University and Kimberly Little of Southern Illinois University, Carbondale, for their additional feedback and the wonderful contributions of their students' stories.

The Users: Finally, I wish to acknowledge all first-year students who are tackling the sometimes challenging but wonderful process of attending a research university. I also honor the dedicated faculty and staff who support students and their success.

About the Author

Britt Andreatta, Ph.D., is currently the Chair of the Bachelor's Program at Antioch University Santa Barbara. In this role, she oversees all aspects of the bachelor's degree program from

---

[1] MBTI and Myers-Briggs Type Indicator are registered trademarks of Consulting Psychologists Press, Inc.

admissions criteria and orientation to graduation requirements and commencement. She hires and trains all faculty, ensuring an engaging and supportive learning environment for students who prefer a smaller setting. Britt also teaches the transitions course for new students as well as the capstone seminar for graduating seniors along with a variety of other topics.

Prior to that, she served as the Assistant Dean of Students and a faculty member at the University of California at Santa Barbara where she worked for 21 years. She was responsible for designing and teaching all of the student success courses well as coordinating programming and mentoring efforts for all 4,000 freshmen students and 1,500 new transfer students. Additionally, she coordinated UCSB's various leadership development programs. You will find many references in this text to "my university" where the author discusses her work at UCSB, a top research university.

She serves as an educational consultant and diversity educator, providing training on a variety of issues to students, staff, and faculty at college and universities. Dr. Andreatta has an M.A. in Communication, and a Ph.D. in Education. Her dissertation was titled "The Effects of Social and Academic Integration on the Retention of First-Year University Students" and she continues to explore issues related to student success. She has received numerous awards including UCSB's prestigious Getman Service to Students Award, Professor of the Year, and the national Outstanding Experienced Professional by the American College Personnel Association (ACPA).

Dr. Andreatta has created several exciting programs for parents of first-year students including two workshops entitled "Your Student's First Year" and "Parents in Transition," both of which have been adapted to over 250 colleges and universities in the United States, Canada, and Australia.

She lives with her husband, Chris Sneathen, and daughter Kiana, in Santa Barbara along with various critters. In her spare time, she enjoys surfing, reading, yoga, singing in a band, hanging out with friends, fly fishing, and the many fine flavors of Ben & Jerry's ice cream.

She donates 10 percent of her royalties from this book to nonprofit organizations that support education. Learn more about her at www.brittandreatta.com.

Introduction

Why This Book

As the author, I am assuming that you currently are, or soon will be, attending a research university as either a freshman or a transfer student. I also attended a research university as an undergraduate, and I have worked at one for over 20 years, as both the assistant dean of students (overseeing First-Year Programs and Leadership Education) and a faculty member in two academic departments. In my experiences in working with students over the years, from freshmen to graduating seniors, it has become clear to me that many do not fully understand the nature of a research university and the degree to which it affects every aspect of their college experience. The qualities that are unique to a research university shape everything about your daily experience as a college student, including:

+ Who teaches you
+ The content of your courses
+ The focus of your majors
+ The resources available to you at your campus
+ The expectations faculty have for your academic performance
+ The quality of your classmates
+ The nature of your social experiences
+ Your career choices
+ Your development as a future leader

In addition, college students in general face transition issues such as separating from their family, making choices involving alcohol and other drugs, living in a diverse community, getting involved, and developing leadership skills. The purpose of this book is to give you a clear understanding of what a research university is and to offer some suggestions about how you can successfully navigate your college experience. While orientation programs are designed to orient you to the various aspects of the institution you are attending, this book will serve as your travel guide, helping you to *navigate* the sometimes rocky and confusing path.

In this book, I will explain many things that are often understood by the faculty and staff at a research university but that are rarely clearly communicated to, or comprehended by, students. Most new students do not understand how attending a research university really affects their daily lives. In response to this, I have created @MyU sections throughout each chapter in which I will connect the information you have just read to more concrete examples of student experiences. This feature also includes areas for you to write in information about you and your university. In addition, I will provide you with some of my best tips and suggestions for ways to succeed at a research university. These sidebars are called Point of Interest and are things I often say to students who meet with me for assistance during their first year. You will also find advice from current students in a feature called Stories from the Path. Finally, the Scenic Route feature indicates that there are useful links to online resources at the companion website found at www.cengagebrain.com. The companion site also includes more Stories from the Path, glossary, and student activities.

I have organized this book into nine chapters, with each focusing on a different, yet equally important, aspect of your university experience. It is important that you read Chapter 1 first, as it provides the information and background you will need to understand the remaining material. However, at that point, you can read the chapters in the order of importance or necessity to you, knowing that together, they will provide a complete guide to a successful university experience.

The content of each chapter mirrors many aspects of education at a research university. Each topic will include current statistics from empirical studies about college students as well as theories and models that illuminate important aspects of the college experience or student development. This book is interdisciplinary, in that it draws from a wide range of disciplines to form a more complete understanding of the research university experience of first-year students.

If your classes are beginning soon, I recommend reading the Quick Start Guide starting on page xivi. This will give you a quick overview of the various things you need to know to immediately navigate your campus and get you ready for the first week of classes.

Information for Students and Instructors

This book has been written to provide all first-year students, both freshmen and transfer students, with useful information for making the most of their experience at a research university. Freshmen and transfer students often have very different needs, so where appropriate, I have provided advice that is specific to each population. However, there are also many places of overlap between the experiences of freshmen and transfer students. In these areas, your own experience as a member of those populations will guide your interpretation of the material. Finally, this text is written to cover the broader themes and issues that are relevant to students at a research university. However, you will need to take this information and put it in the context of your specific university. In this way, you can customize the material to suit your specific needs.

A Word to Freshmen

If you have been admitted to a research university, it means that you have demonstrated a strong performance in high school, which indicates that you are prepared to begin a university-level education. Your admission is a reflection of your *potential*, but your choices as a university student will ultimately determine your performance and success. With this in mind, it is important to remember that this is not "high school, the sequel"—it is an entirely new level of education that you have neither seen nor experienced. Your ability to successfully adjust to this new experience greatly depends on your willingness to let go of how you used to do things and enthusiastically embrace being a beginner again. Your first year in college will be somewhat similar to your first year in high school. There will be a new and unfamiliar environment, higher expectations for your performance, and also many students who are older and more experienced than you. This can be disconcerting after you have worked so hard to achieve so much success in your high school. You definitely bring many strengths to your university experience, and you were selected from thousands of other applicants because of the promise you have demonstrated. Feel good about your past accomplishments and also embrace the attitude of being a new learner again. You will eventually gain the skills and experience you need to master this environment as well. I hope this book will guide you in making the most of your university experience from your first day to your graduation ceremony.

A Word to Transfer Students

If you have been admitted to a research university, it means that you have demonstrated a strong performance in college (most likely a two-year community college), which indicates that you are prepared to begin a university-level education. Your admission does not guarantee that you will automatically be as successful as you were at your previous institution—it is an entirely new level of education that you have neither seen nor experienced (unless you were already attending a research university). You do have a distinct advantage over the freshmen, which is to say that you have a lot of experience with some aspects of higher education such as choosing classes, going to office hours, and writing research papers. However, all of these aspects change as you transfer from your previous institution to a research university. In some cases, the changes are minor; others will bear no resemblance to your previous experiences. In addition, transfer students have much less time to adjust to the new environment than freshmen do, as you have to get going on your major and graduation requirements immediately.

The greatest error that transfer students make is to think, "I know how to do this already" and not seek the assistance they need or utilize the support that is offered, such as orientation, advising, and counseling. This choice can have a negative impact on both your academic and social transition to your new campus. You definitely bring many strengths to your university experience, and you were selected from hundreds of other applicants because of the promise you have demonstrated. Feel good about your past accomplishments and also embrace the attitude of being a new learner again. You will eventually gain the skills and experience you need to master this environment as well. I hope this book will guide you in making the most of your university experience from your first day to your graduation ceremony.

Quick Start Guide

This Quick Start Guide is designed to help you navigate the first few days of attendance at your university. Below are typical issues or questions that new students need to address before the start of classes. Many of these issues are addressed in much more depth in subsequent chapters, but this guide will provide you with the essential information to get started.

Academic Issues

Advising, Registration, and Orientation

Before you can start attending classes, you need to select and enroll in classes for your first term. Most universities provide some kind of orientation program to present students with important information on academic requirements and the registration process. It is strongly recommended that both freshmen and transfer students have assistance in selecting courses their first term, as inappropriate choices can have negative consequences for both progress and performance. If you have not already attended, contact your university to find out the options that are still available. Even if formal orientation programs have concluded, you can still arrange an individual appointment with an academic advisor in your college.

Resources: orientation, registrar's office, academic advisors, schedule of classes, general catalog

Finding Your Classes

Before the first day of classes, it is a good idea to walk around campus to find and confirm the location of each class. That way, you will not find yourself lost on campus or late for your classes. Often, locations and times of classes can change from what was published when you enrolled. Always double-check the times and locations using the most up-to-date information, such as an online schedule of classes.

Resources: campus map, schedule of classes

First Classes

The first day of classes will include full lectures, so come to class prepared to take notes and to stay the entire time. You will also receive a syllabus in each class that gives you valuable information. It will tell you the books and readers that are required for your class and also when assignments will be due. It's always a good idea to review all your syllabi together the first couple of days of the term. That way, if you discover that you will have four final exams on one day, you have time to drop or switch one of your classes before the deadline.

Resources: school supplies, syllabi

Adding and Dropping Classes

Your campus should have a publication that explains the process for adding and dropping classes, including the deadlines for doing so and any fees that are affiliated with the process. It's a good idea to write these dates in your planner so that you don't miss them. If you know that you need to adjust your schedule, be sure to do so right away. If you have any questions or concerns, see an advisor in your college as soon as you can. If you do not plan on completing a course, be sure you officially drop it from your schedule—lack of attendance does *not* guarantee that you will be dropped by the instructor.

Resources: *registrar's office, schedule of classes*

Books and Readers

Your syllabus for each course will tell you the books and readers that you will need. It's a good idea to purchase these as soon as possible, as sometimes the supply runs out and students have to wait a week or so before new ones arrive. You will have a full reading schedule the first week, so it's important to get started right away. Books will be found in the campus bookstore and also at many online bookstores. Most bookstores have some kind of organizational system that allows you to look up a particular course and instructor to find the books assigned. You might have the choice to buy a new copy or a previously owned copy (which will be cheaper but will also have someone else's highlighting and notes). Used books can be problematic because you may end up with the wrong edition of the book or you might find that the previous owner's comments hinder your own learning process. In addition, neither the author nor the publisher receive any compensation for the purchase of a used book. You might find that your instructor also lists optional books. Ask your instructor whether they are truly optional or whether there is an expectation that students will utilize these materials in some fashion. There is probably a short period of time in which books can be returned to the place of purchase. Be sure you pay attention to these deadlines if you decide to drop that course.

A reader is a compilation of articles and other readings that the instructor has put together in a packet or book. The syllabus will usually tell you where the reader can be purchased. Readers are usually not returnable once purchased, so make sure you plan to stay enrolled in the course before you buy the reader. Finally, ask your instructor whether or not you are expected to bring the books and readers to class. Unlike high school, most university classes do *not* require students to bring materials to each class. For this reason, you will find that very few campuses have lockers for students' things. Students typically carry the items they need for that day's classes in a backpack or tote bag.

Resources: *campus bookstore, syllabi*

Notebooks, Computers, and Other Supplies

Very little guidance is provided to students regarding notebooks and other supplies. You might occasionally find a reference to a certain calculator that you need or a specific type of folder in which to submit papers, but those specifications are pretty rare. As a result, you really have the freedom to purchase the types of school supplies that best suit your needs. Some students prefer three-ring binders; others like spiral-bound notebooks. Some students like to keep the notes for all of their classes in one place; others like a separate notebook for each course. Since university-level note taking is very different from that in high school, you may change your previous preferences. It's really up to you to discover the system that keeps you the most organized.

As for computers, wait until you begin classes before making a new purchase. First, many financial aid rebates and scholarships require that the purchase date occur after classes begin (check your campus for details). Second, campus bookstores often have excellent packages with special discounts for education. Finally, each academic discipline has its own standard for computers and software that align with related careers. Be sure your purchase will meet these standards.

Resources: *campus bookstore, office supply store*

Meeting Your Instructors

You will find that instructors can have many different titles. Not all instructors are professors, so calling an instructor by that title might be incorrect. Until your instructors clarify this for you, the best term for your primary instructor (the one leading the lectures) is "Doctor." Most of your primary instructors have Ph.D.s, so this title is the most accurate and respectful. You will also have secondary instructors who lead discussion sections or labs. These instructors are usually graduate students, so the appropriate title is "Mr." or "Ms." until you are told otherwise. Some instructors are comfortable with your using their first name, but do so only if they give you permission. Most faculty are listed by department in the general catalog and the schedule of classes should list the name of the instructor for each course.

Resources: general catalog, schedule of classes, syllabi

Paying Tuition

If you have not already paid your tuition for your first term, you will need to take care of this right away. You should have received some type of billing statement from the university regarding the payment deadline and forms of payment they will accept. Be sure you pay attention to this deadline, which can creep up on you quickly during the hectic first days of the term. Also, sometimes the deadline is at 12 noon rather than the end of the day. Missing the deadline may have some penalties, such as being dropped from your classes and/or having to pay a late fee. Sometimes deadlines are adjusted for students who are receiving financial aid.

Resources: billing office, financial aid award letter

Receiving Financial Aid

If you are receiving financial aid, you would have received some information from your financial aid office regarding when and where you will receive these funds. Again, there may be deadlines you need to adhere to or documents you need to process. Review the materials and make sure you follow the instructions. Failing to do so can bring about penalties and may delay the disbursement of your funds.

Resource: financial aid award letter

Attending Convocation and Other Events

Your campus probably has organized a series of events and programs to welcome new students to campus. These will be published in a calendar or announcement that either was sent to you at home or is available once you arrive on campus. An important event to look for is an official induction ceremony, often called convocation. Attendance at this event is usually mandatory and is a great way to learn some important information you need to know as a new student. Also, there may be mandatory meetings for your college or major department, and your attendance will be expected. Be sure you keep track of the dates and times of these events so that you don't miss them. There will also be many optional events that you might find it useful to attend, such as study skills workshops or orientations to the library. Read through the calendar of events and plan to attend as many as you can.

Resources: calendar of events, campus map, campus newspaper, fliers

Social and Personal Issues

Moving to Campus

If you are moving to campus, you will want to make sure to allow yourself enough time to move in your belongings and get settled before classes begin. If you are moving into a university-owned residence hall or apartment, you will receive an informative packet about when to move in and what to bring. Read through this carefully and follow the instructions. This packet should also tell you about utilities that are included, how to receive mail and packages, and any meal services that are available to you.

If you are moving into housing that is independent of the university, you probably signed a lease or contract of some kind that outlines important information that you should be familiar with. Most likely, you will need to arrange for basic utilities such as phone, electricity, gas, and cable. Contact your local utility companies to set up these services. Many require deposits, so you might want to discuss this with roommates. Finally, ask whether there are any student discounts or specials that are available to you.

Resources: *housing information packet, local phone directory*

Living with Roommates

If you will be living with others, it is important to establish some guidelines early on about how you will live together in a way that respects each person's preferences. It is a good idea to have a meeting in the first week that you live together to establish some ground rules that each person agrees to follow. That way, you won't have to worry about these issues later on or figure out how to confront someone if they are doing something that bothers you. Some typical issues to discuss are:

+ How will shared bills be handled?

+ Who will put the various utilities in his or her name?

+ How will costs be split or shared?

+ What happens if someone doesn't pay his or her share on time?

+ How do people feel about sharing belongings, such as clothing, cars, and computers? Can people borrow without asking?

+ Will food be shared or does each person have a separate supply? If so, how is that indicated?

+ When and how much do they need to study?

+ What kind of study environment does each person need?

+ How will noise, such as music and TV, be addressed if someone needs quiet for studying?

✦ How do people feel about overnight guests? Do the others need to be notified in advance or asked for permission?

✦ Is there a limit to how many overnight guests a person can have in a term or a limit to the number of consecutive nights?

✦ Who will ensure that the guest adheres to the ground rules?

✦ When people share bedrooms, are there any special considerations needed for romantic or sexual relationships?

✦ How will cleaning duties be shared?

✦ How will people know what needs to be done, and by when?

✦ What if someone doesn't do his or her share?

✦ What happens if people have different comfort levels with messiness or cleanliness?

✦ How do people feel about hosting parties?

✦ Do others need to be notified in advance or asked for permission?

✦ What about buying and serving alcohol?

✦ If this violates campus or state laws, how does that affect everyone?

✦ Are there special considerations for minors?

✦ What about having or using other drugs in the living space?

These are only a few of the items to discuss but you will want to create a shared understanding of how you will live together. You might also want to establish periodic meetings to see if anything needs to be discussed or addressed. Your campus may have some handouts or guidebooks on successful roommate relationships that would be helpful to utilize.

Resources: *roommate handbooks, local phone directory, housing contract*

Bank Accounts

Conducting business is generally easier if you have an account with a bank that is local to your university community. Many local businesses do not take out-of-town checks, and it is certainly easier to make deposits and withdrawals if there are branches or ATMs on or near campus. For this reason, many local banks offer student specials to start a checking account, and you might want to explore these options. If your family will be making deposits to your bank account, choose a bank that also has a branch in your hometown.

Resource: local banks

Transportation and Parking

If parking is not affiliated with your living arrangements, you will need to contact the university's parking office to find out options available to you. Some campuses have ample parking and students are able to purchase parking permits easily. Other campuses with limited parking often have additional stipulations regarding eligibility for parking, such as how far from campus a person lives. In addition, campus parking may be zoned for different groups, such as students, staff, and faculty. Parking rates can range from free to very expensive. Many campuses work with local government agencies to provide students with access to public transit systems at low or no cost. You may find that you don't really need a car at college, especially during the first year.

Resources: parking office, local public transit schedules

Health Records

Most universities require new students to supply health records to the campus health center. You should have received information about this from your campus with instructions about where and when to send these files. In addition, many campuses now require that students show proof of certain immunizations, such as those for hepatitis B or meningitis, in order to stay enrolled. Be sure that you take care of these items by the deadlines. Also, if you have been under the care of a psychiatrist for mental health issues, it is important that these records be included. The stresses of the first year of college can often affect mental health, so make sure your doctor is in communication with campus health officials in order to guarantee the best care for you.

Resources: student health center, counseling center

Attending Events

In addition to academic events, your campus will probably host many social events to help students get to know each other as well as the campus. Some of these are designed for certain populations, such as students living in a residence hall or students pursuing a certain major; others are open to everyone. Some are educational in nature; others are purely social. Again, read through the calendar of events and take note of the ones that interest you. These special events are usually not repeated throughout the year, so take advantage of them while you can. These events can be a great way to help you meet new friends, become familiar with various opportunities and activities at your campus, and feel comfortable with the new environment.

Resources: calendar of events, campus newspaper, campus map, fliers

Important Contacts:

Department	Location	Website	Phone
College			
Academic advisors			
Major			
Registrar			
Billing			
Financial aid			
General catalog			
Schedule of classes			
Academic skills/tutoring			
Bookstore			
Housing			
Student health			
Counseling			
Career center			
Student life/activities			
Campus escort			

CHAPTER 1

Research and the Research University

Image copyright © Tomasz Szymanski. Used under license from Shutterstock.com

Southern Illinois University at Carbondale

If you are, or soon will be, attending a research university, it is important for you to grasp the nature of research to fully understand how this affects you as a student. The research mission affects every aspect of an undergraduate student's education, including what you learn in your classes, the majors from which you can choose, who teaches your classes and the quality of their teaching, the makeup of the student body, various opportunities available to you, and your future options after college. Most students apply to research universities because of their prestige, but don't really understand the nature of the research mission.

This chapter will provide you with an overview of what research is, how faculty conduct research and share it with the world, the ways in which research affects almost every aspect of the university environment, and the various members of the campus community. Whether you are a freshman or a transfer student, this knowledge will give you an important base from which to understand the information presented in the remaining chapters as well as your own daily experiences as a university student.

CHAPTER OVERVIEW

YOUR UNIVERSITY'S MISSION

According to the Carnegie Foundation for the Advancement of Teaching (2010), there are nearly 4,400 institutions of higher education in the United States, ranging from two-year community colleges to Ivy League private universities. The Merriam-Webster OnLine Dictionary (2010) defines a **college** as "an independent institution of higher learning offering a course of general studies leading to a bachelor's degree." A **university** is defined as "an institution of higher learning providing facilities for teaching and research and authorized to grant academic degrees; specifically one made up of an undergraduate division which confers bachelor's degrees and a graduate division which comprises a graduate school and professional schools each of which may confer master's degrees and doctorates." As a result, a university may house several colleges and schools.

A **research university** is a university that has a mission to produce research, and there are approximately 285 research universities located throughout the United States, Puerto Rico, and Canada. The primary goal or mission of a research university is to bring together a group of the best minds in the world to do their research. These people, the faculty, are hired and promoted largely on the basis of their research skills—in other words, a primary focus of their jobs is to produce new knowledge and share it with the world through publications. In addition, these faculty members disseminate known knowledge in a process called teaching. Both aspects are important in a student's educational experience at a research university.

The Purpose of Research

Research is the process of discovering and creating *new* knowledge—that which has not been known before. This is very different from **teaching,** which is the dissemination of known knowledge. Research is very important to human society because it has allowed us to develop almost every aspect of what surrounds us. From turning on a light switch, to the medicines you take, to eating microwave popcorn, to cell phones that take pictures, research has played a role in bringing these things to society.

Research also plays a role in making our society a better place by allowing us to understand how people function in the world and how they interact with and influence each other. You are surrounded by research every day. Look at any form of media and you will find examples like these articles from popular news sources:

> *When you go to the gym, do you wash your hands before and after using the equipment? Bring your own regularly cleaned mat for floor exercises? Shower with antibacterial soap and put on clean clothes immediately after your workout? Use only your own towels, razors, bar soap, water bottles? If you answered "no" to any of the above, you could wind up with one of the many skin infections that can spread like wildfire in athletic settings. Recreational athletes as well as participants in organized sports are prone to fungal, viral and bacterial skin infections. Sweat, abrasion and direct or indirect contact with the lesions and secretions of others combine to make every athlete's skin vulnerable to a host of problems. While MRSA may be the most serious skin infection, athlete's foot, jock itch, boils, impetigo, herpes simplex and ringworm, among others, are not exactly fun or attractive. Steven M. Zinder, from the University of North Carolina at Chapel Hill and chief author of the study, said in an interview that these recommendations are not esoteric. "You need to keep yourself and your equipment clean. You never know who last used the equipment in a gym. It can be a great breeding ground for these bugs, some of which are pretty nasty," he said.*

Brody, New York Times, August 2, 2010

Babies whose mothers are attentive and caring tend to grow into happy, well-adjusted children. But the psychological benefits of having a doting mother may extend well beyond childhood. According to a new study, which followed nearly 500 infants into their 30s, babies who receive above-average levels of affection and attention from their mothers are less likely than other babies to grow up to be emotionally distressed, anxious, or hostile adults. The findings make a strong case for policies that would help foster positive interactions between infants and parents, such as paid parental leave, says Joanna Maselko, Ph.D., assistant professor of psychiatry and behavioral sciences at Duke University. The findings add to a large body of psychological research on mother-child attachment that suggests that healthy bonds between young children and parents are crucial to a child's emotional development.

Gardner, CNN, July 26, 2010

New knowledge can come about in a variety of ways, from happy accidents such as the one in which researchers at 3M created the nonstick glue that makes Post-It notes so useful, to following a hunch, as many inventors have done. Through a process of trial and error, Ben Franklin discovered electricity and the Wright brothers discovered how to fly.

There is also the process of formal research, which is done in a detailed and very structured way to search for new answers. For example, scientists systematically test various chemicals and the impact they have on cancer cells. This requires a steady and slow process of trying something new and recording the results, making an infinitesimally small adjustment, and then trying again and recording the results. This process allows researchers to chart their progress and to recreate findings should they prove to be successful.

Research can happen in all kinds of places and can be done by all kinds of people. Some prominent places in which research is conducted are corporations as they work to develop "new and improved" products to sell, government offices and labs, private "think tanks," hospitals, and educational institutions of all kinds. While all of these places for research are important, we will focus on research as it occurs in a university setting and how this affects the education of undergraduate students. See "Point of Interest: Participating in Research."

In the United States, the **Carnegie Foundation for the Advancement of Teaching** classifies all institutions of higher education. Research universities are classified based on the number of doctoral degrees awarded per year and the amount of research generated, as well as whether they are a public or private institution. In addition to the Carnegie Foundation's classification system, research universities can distinguish themselves by becoming members of the prestigious **Association of American Universities** (AAU). Currently, membership consists of sixty-one U.S. universities and two Canadian universities, both public and private (AAU, 2010).

The AAU was founded in 1900 by a small group of Ph.D.-granting universities in the United States to strengthen and standardize doctoral programs. But today, the purpose of the AAU is broader, focusing on a range of issues related to research, education of students (both undergraduate and graduate), funding, and policies related to research. If you look at your campus's website or promotional materials, you will most likely find references to both of these important organizations.

Visit www.cengagebrain.com to find the companion website containing links to:

- Carnegie Classifications of Institutions of Higher Education
- Current listing of AAU member institutions
- National Center of Education Statistics

Who Conducts Research

Conducting research requires a set of specific and well-honed skills, as does flying a large commercial plane. Just as a pilot goes through extensive training and years of practice to become a qualified and excellent pilot, so does a researcher. Some of the specific skills and abilities that a person needs to excel at research include critical thinking, reading, analyzing, creative thinking, and writing, to name a few. In addition, researchers must be very knowledgeable about the

PARTICIPATING IN RESEARCH   If you are like most freshmen, you probably didn't understand what a research university was when you applied to one, and you may not be particularly interested in a career as a researcher or a professor. That's okay. Since you are attending a research university, you should take advantage of this unique educational setting. The best part about attending a research university is the research, so I strongly recommend getting involved in research during your college experience. Not to do so is like going to the Hershey's Chocolate Factory and not tasting the chocolate. Sure, there are other things to do, but you miss out on the whole point of the place.

At a research university, you have the amazing opportunity to participate in research by working with faculty in their labs, classrooms, and even far away from the campus on research sites. Students at my campus have been involved with the following:

◆ Traveling to Tibet and recording the unwritten languages of mountain tribes
◆ Documenting and coding violence in television programs
◆ Photographing the annual fashion shows in Milan, Italy
◆ Testing how a new medicine affects the symptoms of drug addiction
◆ Deep-sea diving to document the mating patterns of a newly discovered fish
◆ Taking samples from the ice core in Antarctica to chart global warming

You could participate in groundbreaking research as an undergraduate student and even publish or present your work as a scholar. It's an opportunity not to be missed!

There are several ways to get involved in research. First, you can approach faculty members whose classes you enjoy and ask whether they have any positions open in their research projects. Second, you can visit the department to see whether there are any postings for jobs or positions. Finally, there might be an office on your campus that coordinates student involvement in research. Check with your college or major department to find out more. And don't be discouraged if you have to start out with less-than-glamorous work. Often, faculty members expect you to work a bit before they give you access to the truly interesting stuff, so be patient.

area or topic they are researching. A person would need to know chemistry very well to research aspects of it, and another person would need to know history in order to conduct historical research.

Not all people are good at, or interested in, doing research—just as not all people want to fly planes. Research is a career that certain people are drawn to and must spend years of study to prepare for. **Faculty** who are hired as researchers must have an advanced degree in their field. Types of advanced degrees include a Doctorate of Philosophy (Ph.D.), a Doctorate of Medicine (M.D.), a Doctorate of Education (Ed.D.), a Doctorate of Psychology (Psy.D.), a Master's in Business Administration (M.B.A.), and a Juris Doctor (J.D.) or law degree. These advanced degrees signify that after completing an undergraduate degree in college, the person completed more schooling to become an expert in a particular field. Many of these degrees require several years of graduate study; for example, a Ph.D. in anthropology takes five to seven years to complete, and an M.D. requires four years of medical school followed by a lengthy residency program.

Most faculty members at research universities have a Ph.D. in a particular discipline, such as physics or literature. A **discipline** is a field or area of study, such as history, biology, mathematics, philosophy, dramatic arts, sociology, electrical engineering, or music. A large part of the degree is learning and mastering the research skills that are required for that particular discipline, as well as conducting an original research project. This research project focuses on a narrow topic within the larger discipline and culminates in a **doctoral dissertation,** which is a very long final paper (often 100–200 pages) exemplifying original research, and analytical and writing skills. Every Ph.D. program around the globe requires doctoral students to do extensive study in their discipline and then to choose a very narrow area in which to focus their research.

Today's most famous theorists were once doctoral students and were required to follow this standard process. Let's look at an example. Dr. Stephen Hawking, the world-renowned physicist who, among other things, proposed the existence of black holes, attended the University College at Oxford University as an undergraduate, where he studied physics and graduated with a degree in natural science (Hawking, 2010). He went on to earn his Ph.D. at Trinity Hall at Cambridge University, where he narrowed his interests to cosmology, which is the study of the universe as a whole and the basic laws that govern it. After earning his Ph.D., he worked at Cambridge University. Dr. Hawking's research led to the groundbreaking work of combining the theory of general relativity with quantum theory, which is considered one of the great developments in science. Throughout his astonishing career, Dr. Hawking has published articles and books on a wide range of topics within his field. If you visit his website at www.hawking.org.uk, you will find a list of his 195 publications from 1965 to 2010.

Although not all research university faculty are as famous as Stephen Hawking, most have a similar history. They have all completed intense academic study and are motivated by a desire to learn that is so strong that they pursued it as a career. Many faculty members are also motivated by the desire to teach. You can find out more about your faculty's research history and publications by looking them up in your campus library's database, reviewing your campus website, or by visiting your professors during office hours and asking about their work.

Needless to say, attending a research university means you are taking classes from some of the best minds in the world who are truly experts in what they study and teach. This is an amazing opportunity for you to explore your own passion for learning (see "Juan Carlos's Story from the Path").

JUAN CARLOS'S STORY FROM THE PATH

Assisting with academic research led to the most fulfilling experiences of my undergraduate career. It began during my second year after completing a course about U.S. legal history that I really enjoyed. I visited my history professor to talk about her other courses, the subjects she studied, and whether I could work with her through an independent study. She agreed, and soon I was working with her as a research assistant, checking footnotes, reviewing court cases, and evaluating scholarship. The experience initiated a new way of thinking and created many undergraduate and professional career opportunities.

This research added to all of my undergraduate work because it provided an in-depth starting point from which to look at different subjects. Whether I was studying the Renaissance, racial theory, or higher education, the lessons I learned as a research assistant encouraged a critical-thinking approach to new subjects. Working as an assistant also improved my relationships with other professors. Because we shared an interest in research, I was more comfortable speaking in class. Even outside the classroom, as a student activist, I used many academic theories and concepts to help me shape stronger arguments when fighting to save student outreach programs and facilitating community dialogues about social justice and diversity.

What was most interesting about research was the way working with my professors repositioned me from a place of *learning from* my professors to *helping them* acquire new knowledge. From an insider's perspective, I was able to understand how individual experiences and ideas determined what my professors chose to teach. Similarly, the research process taught me new ways to ask questions about my own life. It forced me to think about where my ideas come from and how those ideas shape my everyday choices. In this way, research introduced me to a new way of thinking that influenced how I make decisions about my life.

Assisting professors ultimately motivated me to do my own research. Using the research tools I learned as a research assistant, I examined issues that I found personally relevant, which included an affirmative action policy history, an evaluation of diversity facilitation models, and a study of "access to justice" in the state's court system. In doing so, the relationships I developed with my professors were essential, as they shared valuable feedback and advice. Later, my professors also helped me when I needed undergraduate and career advice, letters of recommendation, and information about job opportunities. Because they knew my work and we shared a common passion, they were more than happy to help me further my career.

At its most basic, research is about curiosity. If you are a curious person and you want to learn how to ask better questions, then research is for you. Beyond that, like anything else, research presents its own challenges and rewards: from the research process itself to what you get when the project is over.

At your research university, you will have the opportunity to interact with some of the best minds in the world. You will enjoy your experience more if you get to you know your faculty and learn more about their experiences as researchers and educators. Choose a professor and e-mail him/her to arrange an interview time. Do a bit of background research by looking the person up on your campus's website to learn more about his/her research and teaching interests. Of course, be on time and present yourself professionally. Ask a few of the following questions, feeling free to adjust as needed during the interview:

1. What motivated you to pursue a career in academia? What influenced this interest?

2. What was your undergraduate experience like? Why did you choose to go to [*institution*] as an undergrad, or [*institution*] for your graduate work?

3. What percent of your time is spent on teaching, research, and service?

4. What is your teaching philosophy?

5. What advice would you give me, and other first-year students, about how to succeed in your classes?

6. What research are you currently doing? Why is this research important or how does it contribute to the field of [*discipline/subject*]?

7. What opportunities exist for students to be part of your research?

8. What advice would you give undergraduates who want to prepare for graduate school?

9. What do you like the most and least about being a faculty member here?

10. Why did you choose to come to this research university? How does it compare to other institutions you have attended or worked at?

11. How do you balance your personal life with the demands of being a professor? Do you have family commitments? What do you like to do for fun?

12. If you were not in academia, is there another career choice you would have considered?

The Academic Disciplines

There are literally hundreds of academic disciplines in the world, and it would not be very efficient or cost-effective for every campus to do research in every discipline. As a result, each college or university chooses to offer a certain set of disciplines in which students can earn a degree. You can discover the disciplines that exist at your institution by looking at the academic departments that are listed in the general catalog. Each department will indicate the particular disciplines that are offered.

If your institution has a biology department, this means that your university has a group of faculty who specialize in research in the **academic field** of biology and will offer one or more majors within the biological sciences. Within that field of biology, each faculty member will specialize in a very narrow subfield of that discipline.

If you explore your general catalog, you will find that each major department lists the areas of study that are available at your school. For example, at the University of California at Santa Barbara, six subfields of biology are offered: molecular, cellular, developmental, ecological, evolutionary, and marine. This means that students here can find several faculty members who are nationally recognized for their work in each of these areas, as well as ample courses to choose from on these topics.

Likewise, the department of communication specializes in three subfields: mass media, interpersonal communication, and organizational communication. The faculty that are here specialize in one of these major areas and are engaged in research and teaching classes on topics related to these areas. As a result, a student at this school could focus on one of these areas in his or her own choice of classes while completing a major in this field. There are obviously many more areas within this field, such as rhetoric and intercultural communication, which are not offered at this institution. However, you will find rhetoric programs at Purdue University, the University of Nebraska at Lincoln, Ohio State University, Carnegie Mellon University, and many others. Programs in intercultural communication can be found at Pennsylvania State University, Pepperdine University, the University of Wisconsin, and the University of Kansas, to name a few.

Essentially, a **department** consists of a group of faculty members who are experts in their subfields and who offer a set of courses that satisfy a bachelor's degree and often master's and doctoral degrees. Each university must decide which fields it will offer and then build a strong department by hiring faculty members who are renowned researchers in that field. It is generally better for a department to focus on a smaller set of subfields than to try to offer a wider range of subfields.

It's important to remember that the primary mission of the institution is to conduct research, so these decisions are made from the perspective of carrying out that mission to the highest degree possible. Each institution makes informed choices about being very strong in certain areas, knowing that other areas will become the hallmark of another campus.

All of these various **academic disciplines** can be a bit unwieldy, so they are often clustered with similar disciplines that share general philosophies or practices. According to Compton and Tait (1994), these clusters can be defined in the following ways:

+ The **humanities** are the academic disciplines that study human thought and experience through the written record of what people have thought, felt, or experienced in a variety of cultures. Subject areas include languages, literature, philosophy, history, and religion.
+ The **social sciences** are the academic disciplines that study people and their behavior from a variety of perspectives: as individuals (psychology), within social groups (sociology, ethnic studies), within cultures (anthropology), within social structures (education), or even as economic and political entities (economics, political science, global studies).
+ The **arts** are the academic disciplines that explore and represent human thought and behavior in creative works. Creating works of art is a way of both coming to understand and expressing ideas and feelings. Subject areas include studio art, dramatic art, film studies, dance, and music.
+ **Quantitative studies** are the academic disciplines that create systems for describing the physical world or human behavior in abstract or mathematical terms. Subject areas include mathematics, statistics, and computer science.
+ The **physical and biological sciences** are the academic disciplines that study the physical world, its inhabitants, and the symbolic relationships within. Subject areas include biology, ecology, physics, geology, chemistry, and environmental studies.
+ The **engineering sciences** are the academic disciplines that study how scientific knowledge can be applied to practical uses for society. Subject areas include civil, electrical, mechanical, computer, and chemical engineering.

Not all campuses organize their departments in these exact groupings, but the general categories are fairly consistent. These categories are not distinct, and aspects of our world can overlap several disciplines. For example, poverty is a topic that can be explored and

MAKING CONNECTIONS BETWEEN CLASSES

Even though you might be taking classes in a wide variety of disciplines, there will be some connections among them. Students gain the most from their education when they can draw connections and see similarities among the various courses they are taking. Instead of approaching your history class as a separate entity unto itself, see how what you are learning in that history class might be relevant to your biology class or your language class. Look for the bigger picture and the interdisciplinary nature of things whenever you can. You might even find that this allows you to bring a unique and critical analysis to a course you are taking and ultimately improves your performance in that course.

researched in all of these disciplines. An economist might explore the relationship between minimum wage jobs and the number of people living in poverty. A sociologist might research the relationship between the quality of a poorer community's public high school education and the college success of its graduates. A biologist might study the effects that inadequate nutrition has on bone density. An ethnomusicologist would be interested in the forms of music that have their roots in poorer communities. A mathematician might want to create a statistical model of how long it would take a family on welfare to rise above the poverty level on the basis of different salaries. As you can see, the possibilities are endless. See "Point of Interest: Making Connections between Classes."

@*myU* SO HOW DOES THIS AFFECT YOU?

One assumption that faculty and administrators make is that students have "done their homework" in looking at what a school has to offer. We assume that you looked at the various types of universities available to you and specifically chose to attend a research university because you wanted this particular type of education. We also assume that you explored which majors were offered before you applied to each university. If you did not check these things out before applying or if you were undecided at that time, you might discover that your institution does not offer what you want. If so, you can consider choosing from the majors that are offered or transferring to a different institution that does offer what you are looking for. You can receive helpful advice from academic and career advisors, as well as the faculty, at your campus. Many disciplines overlap, so you might be able to find a field comparable to the one you were hoping to study. Look through your campus catalog and list three majors that interest you:

1.

2.

3.

Some students are disappointed to find the research emphasis at a research university. They were hoping to find classes that prepared them for specific careers. While there are very few classes that do this, the majority of students that graduate from research universities go on to successful jobs and careers in nonresearch areas. The prestige of their degree has value in the workplace even though the content of their courses might not have given them specific job skills. It is true that to be competitive in today's job market, students need to gain important job skills while in college. The best way to do this is through **internships,** which provide students with preprofessional work opportunities and experience. Some internships are paid and some are not, but all provide valuable job training as well as a chance to "try on" a career before committing to it. To learn more, visit the office on your campus that provides career advising. It is never too early to secure an internship, and many career advisors recommend completing at least three before you graduate. Based on your interests, list three places where you would like to complete an internship:

1.

2.

3.

How Research Is Conducted

Discussing research in a general sense is a bit challenging to do because each discipline has a unique approach. There are sets of prescribed processes, called **research methods,** that researchers use to best address the topic they are exploring. For example, a biologist might be interested in what causes a healthy cell to become cancerous and multiply out of control. To learn more about that process, the researcher will need to work with cells and do a variety of tests in a lab. Obviously, a biologist could not ask the cells to fill out a survey about why they multiply. On the other hand, an economist who is interested in how the unemployment level of a neighborhood is related to crime rates would not find it useful to look at skin samples of criminals under the microscope. In this case, looking at police records and employment data would be far more useful.

The more creative disciplines such as music or art focus on the creation or production of new works, so "research" in these fields is often focused on the work associated with writing an innovative composition or creating a specific sculpture. However, there are also subfields in these disciplines that might use more traditional research methods. For example, ethnomusicology is the study of how music relates to the expression of a specific culture, so a researcher in this field might analyze sound patterns of a certain regional genre or conduct surveys to ask people in a particular tribe about the ceremonial purpose of their songs.

Each field has its own way of conducting research, and there are certain methods of inquiry that are appropriate for getting answers. One of the things you will learn during your university education is how these fields differ from each other and the various ways in which research is conducted in each field. Once you select a major, you will be introduced to the methods that are appropriate to the field you selected to study. In chemistry, you will learn how researchers precisely measure and control various experiments. In anthropology, you will be introduced to how researchers observe and document aspects of a culture without interfering with it. These introductions will allow you to better understand and evaluate the various material you will learn in your courses for a particular major. Should you choose to pursue research as a career, you will be taught research methods and procedures in much more depth in your graduate studies.

HOW KNOWLEDGE IS SHARED

Academic Publications

Recall that the purpose of research is finding and creating new knowledge—as a result, it is important that this knowledge is shared with others. This sharing of knowledge is another primary aspect of being a researcher and it is done through **publishing** results of scholarly studies. Faculty must continually engage in writing and speaking about their research as a way to add what they have learned to the body of knowledge of their field. This is most often done in writing in the form of journal articles and books. The way most research is shared with other researchers is through something called a **scholarly journal,** which is a monthly or quarterly publication that features write-ups of the latest studies that have been done in a particular field. Each discipline has several of these journals, with each journal focusing on a certain aspect of that discipline. Most researchers subscribe to several of these journals to stay current on the latest findings, and the campus library subscribes to hundreds of journals so that they are accessible to faculty and students alike.

For example, in the field of education, some of the scholarly journals are the *Journal of Higher Education*, the *Journal of College Student Development*, *Higher Education Review*, and the *American Educational Research Journal*. Some journals for the field of marine science are the *Journal of Marine Biology and Ecology*, *Marine Ecology Progress Series*, *Ecological Monographs*, *Oecologia*, and *Marine Biology*. In order to contribute new knowledge, it is important for a

@myU   SO HOW DOES THIS AFFECT YOU?

Faculty research affects your daily experience as a student because your faculty members pass along expectations for this level of reading to you. We are used to reading large amounts of material, so faculty rarely think we are assigning too much. When we put together our books and readers for your classes, we are truly assessing what we think you need to know—and for faculty, it's hard for us to eliminate material because so much of it seems relevant. In addition, we will ask you to read about relevant research and studies from their original sources, or scholarly journals. In all of your classes, you will be required to look up studies published in scholarly journals and use what you learn to complete various assignments, most commonly research papers. It is important for you to become familiar with your campus library and the process for finding specific articles.

Complete this exercise to help you learn more. First, visit your library and ask for assistance in looking up your current professors. You want to find out what they have published recently. Your librarian will be able to show you how to do a search for a particular author and to find the journal using the library's system of cataloging material. Once you have the article in hand, write down the following:

1. In which journal was the article published?

2. Were there other authors? If so, who?

3. What is the title of the article?

4. Read the article. What is the study about?

5. What did the authors find?

6. What confused you or was difficult to understand?

Finally, visit your professor during office hours and ask him/her more about the study and questions you have about the article. This is an excellent way to get to know your faculty.

researcher to stay up on the latest developments in his or her field, so reading journals is a big part of a researcher's job. Your faculty members will often be reading several books and journals simultaneously. The ability to read and comprehend copious amounts of material on a consistent basis is a trademark skill for the research profession.

While your faculty are in the process of learning about others' research, they are engaging in their own research with the ultimate goal of also sharing it with their professional colleagues. The type of research that faculty members conduct varies greatly and is guided by their discipline. Once a researcher completes his or her work, it is time to share the new knowledge by having it published. Studies are generally shared in the form of a paper or journal article, while other research lends itself more to being a book chapter or an entire book. You will find that, in general, writing a series of journal articles is more affiliated with the sciences, whereas writing a book or book chapters is more affiliated with the humanities.

Research takes a lot of time. Depending on the field, it can take several months to years to initiate, plan, conduct, complete, and publish a study. For this reason, most researchers are simultaneously working on several research projects, each in a different stage of completion. For example, Dr. Tania Israel, an associate professor in clinical psychology, is currently working on the following projects:

+ Four studies in which she is preparing to collect data
+ Three studies in which she is collecting and analyzing data
+ Six manuscripts she is preparing for submission to be published
+ Four articles submitted for publication and awaiting reviews from editors
+ Two proposals for grant funding
+ Three proposals submitted for book chapters in other editors' books
+ One book she is coediting and providing feedback to the authors who are submitting chapters

This particular faculty member is engaged in several research and writing projects simultaneously; many of your faculty members will be just as busy working on one book rather than several articles. This workload is typical, and it does not include the work of teaching several classes a year as well as holding office hours and serving on campus and nationwide committees. These responsibilities also take up a lot of time. It is common for most faculty to work fifty to sixty hours per week—more than is required for the average full-time job.

Scholarly Standards for Publication

It would be very chaotic if every person writing up research did so in his or her own unique way. It would be difficult to review and analyze the work in any kind of consistent or fair manner. As a result, some professional standards have been created for **academic writing** that all researchers and scholarly publishers follow. One aspect of this standardization has to do with writing style, and there are several manuals and guides that faculty use based on their discipline. Another aspect of this standardization has to do with format. There is no one standard format for books or book chapters as each project is different. However, **empirical studies** do have a specific format with which they need to be written, and they are usually published as articles in scholarly journals.

Essentially, every article needs to include the following sections in the following order; because you will no doubt read hundreds of journal articles before you graduate, it's important for you to understand these sections:

1. An **abstract,** which is a very brief summary of the study and the primary findings.
2. An **introduction** to the general topic being studied.
3. A review of all that is currently known about that topic—this is known as the **literature review** and is an overview of all (yes, all) relevant past research, most of which has been published in journals and books.
4. From the literature review comes a discussion of what makes this study different from that which has already been done—in other words, a justification of what makes it new knowledge and an answer to the question "Why should this study be done?"
5. A detailed list of specific **research questions** this study attempts to answer—this often includes educated guesses about what the researcher thinks will be found, which are called **hypotheses.**
6. A detailed description of how the study was conducted, or the **research methods** that were used and how these were implemented—this includes the who, what, where, and when of the study.
7. An overview of how the data were analyzed (quantitatively or qualitatively) and what the **results** were with regard to the specific research questions—essentially, the researcher has to address whether the hypotheses were right or wrong and to what degree (using statistical indicators).
8. A **discussion** of what the researcher thinks the results mean with regard to the hypotheses and the general topic—this is essentially the author's interpretations of what the study indicates in the bigger picture of that topic or discipline.

9. A list of all literature that was reviewed or mentioned in the course of the study with all the information that another person would need to look up those references—this is called the **bibliography.**
10. Finally, throughout the paper, there may be relevant charts and graphs that illustrate aspects of the study or the results.

All of this has to be written in a formal way that is objective and factual. The only place where the researcher's opinion is allowed is in the discussion section, and even there, that opinion must flow logically from the results of the study and the topic at hand. In addition, a researcher is held to the utmost ethical standard that everything written is true, is authentic, and represents the work of the person who wrote it.

Once the researcher has written up the study and has edited and proofread it numerous times to ensure that it is of the highest possible quality, the researcher submits the paper to a specific journal to be considered for publication. Other researchers in the same field review the article extensively and anonymously, which is called the **blind review** process. The reviewers do not know the identity of the author, and the author does not know the identities of the reviewers. The reviewers evaluate the paper on the basis of the quality of research that was done, the extent to which it contributes new knowledge to the field, and the quality of the writing. If there are any problems, the submission can be rejected outright and the author cannot resubmit it to that journal, or it can be sent back for revisions and the author can resubmit it.

Eventually, if the researcher did a good study and has good writing skills, the paper will be published in the journal in the form of an article, thereby contributing to the knowledge of that field. This whole process can take many months, and even years, from the date a study was completed to the date it is published. Books take even longer; getting a book published is often a multiyear process.

The Cutting Edge

This is all important for you to know because it illustrates one of the main benefits of attending a research university. While researchers are conducting their research, writing their articles and books, and spending hours in the library, they often share their newly discovered knowledge with students in the classroom that same day—long before others will read about it. This is known as the **cutting edge,** and it refers to the fact that the new knowledge that is being discovered every moment at a research university is woven into the education of the students who are currently enrolled. You will hear information in your classes that will not even be published for at least three to four years and will not reach a textbook until later still. This makes a degree from a research university very valuable because graduates not only know the most recent information about a field but also have the skills to stay current for a lifetime.

Let's look at this book as an example. Although it is more of a text or reference book than a research-related book, the publishing process is similar for most books. I wrote this original sentence for the first edition on October 10, 2003, while sitting in my home office in Santa Barbara, California. I spent many hours writing, editing, researching, and rewriting the chapters. Each chapter was sent out to several anonymous reviewers, who offered suggestions. I utilized their feedback to make changes and the entire book was sent to more reviewers, who read the entire text and offered more suggestions. Finally, the book was entrusted to the good people at Cengage, who did some more editing, designed the layout, created a cover design, and sent it to the printing press to be printed and bound. I received my copy of the first edition in April 2005.

I am now working on the third edition and am writing this sentence on May 15, 2010. All of the chapters have significant changes from the previous editions, based on the reviews that were completed by instructors who used the book in their classes. It will again go through the editing, design, and printing process so that the third edition can be completed by January 2011. If you are reading this page, it means that the whole process worked

@myU   SO HOW DOES THIS AFFECT YOU?

Being at a research university means that you are now at a very different type of educational institution than any you have experienced before. There is an excitement to being at a research university because you are surrounded by brilliant faculty who are creating new knowledge every day. The graduate students and faculty whom you see sitting in the campus eatery could be talking about how close they are to finding a cure for cancer, or shifting what we know about gravity, or understanding the intersection of racial identity and gender. Your campus library is filled with journals containing information that the general public won't know for months or even years. Most campuses keep track of the groundbreaking work of their faculty and publicize it in some way. Peruse your campus's website to answer the following questions (note: this information is often found on the webpages for the departments of admissions, public relations, and/or research):

How many National Science Foundation (NSF) awards are on your campus?

Are there any Nobel Prize winners among your faculty?

What national or international institutes are housed on your campus?

List three recent noteworthy discoveries made by your faculty:

	FACULTY A	FACULTY B	FACULTY C
Name/Dept			
Discovery			
Classes s/he teaches			

and these words made their way from my computer in California in 2003 to your hands on today's date.

As I was writing this book, I shared all of these ideas with my students in my class lectures. That means that freshmen at my university began hearing about these ideas in the fall of 2000. Even if you are the first person to buy the current edition of this book, you will be reading these words more than eleven years later. So listen carefully in your lectures this week—you might hear something the rest of the world will not know for a few years.

NEW WAYS OF KNOWING

Epistemology, the study of knowledge, is a word you'll often hear at a research university. In essence, it explores what knowledge is and is not, and how people gain knowledge. The processes of discovering new knowledge, disseminating it to others, and learning it are all activities that occur at a research university on a daily basis. More specifically, there are certain levels that both faculty and students go through in gaining an understanding or knowledge of a certain topic.

Higher Order Thinking Skills

In 1956, Benjamin Bloom created a taxonomy, or hierarchy, of various levels of knowledge. This new way of thinking about thinking brought about a significant change to the field of education and how instructors teach. Essentially, Bloom identified that there are six different levels of thinking that employ increasingly complex ways of processing information or content. Table 1.1 shows **Bloom's Hierarchy of Knowledge** along with associated skills, question cues, and sample exam questions. The first two levels, Knowledge and Comprehension, focus on learning and memorizing the material as well as understanding it. The third level, Application, requires applying or using that knowledge. While these first three levels are often the hallmark of K–12 education, you will find that this is not the case at a research university. Remember, a research university places more emphasis on discovering new knowledge, which includes looking at things in new ways. As a result, the first three levels of Bloom's Hierarchy serve as the background or base from which the new levels of knowledge are reached. The highest three levels of analysis, synthesis, and evaluation are more directly related to the research process in that they require a person to take a set of known information and transform it in some way to create something that was not present before. These upper levels are also known as **higher order thinking skills.**

Table 1.1 highlights the levels of Bloom's Hierarchy, provides an overview of the kinds of skills students would be asked to demonstrate for each level, and gives examples of question cues and student behaviors. See "Point of Interest: How to Study Better."

Critical Thinking

The top three levels of Bloom's Hierarchy (analysis, synthesis, and evaluation) are all part of another concept called **critical thinking.** You will hear this term frequently at research universities because it is a primary goal of your faculty to teach you how to engage in critical thinking. In fact, based on a 2007–08 study of more than 22,000 faculty members at 372 institutions of higher learning, 99.6 percent of all faculty state that developing their students' ability to think critically is very important or essential (DeAngelo, et al., 2009). Critical thinking is essentially the process of suspending your beliefs and authentically looking at other options. This is a crucial skill for researchers because the search for new knowledge must be committed to finding the "truth" and not just confirming what one already believes. The processes of analysis, synthesis, and evaluation require us to let go of the material as we know it and to become open to altering it through taking it apart, putting it together, or assessing it in some new way.

Dr. Clark Kerr, former President of the University of California system of research universities, once said, "The University is not engaged in making ideas safe for students. It is engaged in making students safe for ideas" (Conrad, 2009). This statement exemplifies the power of an education at a research university and the training you will receive as a student. The search for truth requires powerful thinking, groundbreaking analysis, and creative solutions. Students need to adjust their relationship to learning from that of being a passive receiver of information that they memorize for exams to being an active consumer and producer of knowledge using these higher order thinking skills.

Critical thinking requires you to do more than just know the material; you need to examine it critically and from more than one perspective. The critical-thinking process will form the basis of not only your academic work in college but your professional life and role as a responsible citizen as well. There are several aspects of critical thinking and you will want to practice and hone your skills with each one. It is quite common for first-year students to lack critical-thinking skills because the focus of learning during K-12 education has been at the lower levels of Bloom's Hierarchy. And students agree; of the 26,758 college freshmen who participated in the 2009 Your First College Year study, more than three-quarters (76 percent) rated their critical-thinking skills as stronger or much stronger than when they began college (Ruiz, et al., 2010).

The first and most important aspect of critical thinking is you must be willing to suspend your original beliefs or opinions and consider other possibilities. Adopting an attitude of

TABLE **1.1** BLOOM'S HIERARCHY OF KNOWLEDGE

COMPETENCE	SKILLS DEMONSTRATED	QUESTION CUES	SAMPLE QUESTIONS
Knowledge (Memorizing)	Student remembers or recognizes information, ideas, and principles in the approximate form in which they were learned. ✦ observation and recall of information ✦ knowledge of dates, events, places ✦ knowledge of major ideas, mastery of subject matter	Write, list, label, name, state, define, tell, show, describe, identify, recognize, quote, examine, tabulate, who, when, what, where	Define the six levels of Bloom's Hierarchy of Knowledge. Describe the factors that indicate global warming.
Comprehension (Understanding)	Student explains, comprehends, or interprets information based on prior learning. ✦ understand information ✦ grasp meaning ✦ translate knowledge into new context ✦ interpret facts, compare, contrast ✦ order, group, infer causes ✦ predict consequences	Explain, illustrate, exemplify, predict, summarize, infer, paraphrase, interpret, associate, distinguish, estimate, differentiate, discuss, extend	Provide examples that illustrate the differences between the analysis and evaluation levels of Bloom's Hierarchy. Estimate the earth's population in 2030 and discuss the impact this will have on global climate.
Application (Using)	Student selects, transfers, and uses data and principles to complete a problem or task with a minimum of direction. ✦ use information ✦ use methods, concepts, theories in new situations ✦ solve problems using required skills or knowledge	Use, compute, solve, implement, demonstrate, apply, construct, calculate, complete, illustrate, examine, modify, relate, change, classify, experiment, discover	Write an instructional objective for each level of Bloom's Hierarchy. Calculate how many U.S. citizens would have to switch to hydrogen-based vehicles to stop the rise of carbon dioxide in the atmosphere.
Analysis (Taking Apart)	Student differentiates, classifies, and relates the assumptions, hypotheses, evidence, or structure of a statement or question. ✦ seeing patterns ✦ organization of parts ✦ recognition of hidden meanings ✦ identification of components	Analyze, compare, contrast, organize, order, categorize, separate, connect, authenticate, classify, arrange, divide, select, deconstruct	Classify the following ten questions by the level of Bloom's Hierarchy they illustrate. Compare the cost/benefit ratio of ethanol to fossil fuels in terms of production costs and CO_2 emissions.
Synthesis (Creating)	Student integrates and combines ideas to create a product, plan, or proposal that is new to him or her. ✦ use old ideas to create new ones ✦ generalize from given facts ✦ relate knowledge from several areas ✦ predict, draw conclusions	Create, design, invent, produce, hypothesize, develop, combine, integrate, modify, rearrange, construct, substitute, plan, compose, formulate, prepare, generalize, rewrite	Design a syllabus for a freshman history class that utilizes all levels of Bloom's Hierarchy. Formulate a plan for reducing student use of fossil fuels by 50 percent on this campus.
Evaluation (Judging)	Student appraises, assesses, or critiques on a basis of specific standards and criteria or justifies a decision or course of action. ✦ compare and discriminate between ideas ✦ assess value of theories, presentations ✦ make choices based on reasoned argument ✦ verify value of evidence ✦ recognize subjectivity	Judge, recommend, critique, justify, assess, decide, rank, grade, test, measure, convince, select, support, discriminate, conclude, summarize	Critique the effectiveness of Bloom's Hierarchy from the perspectives of three different academic disciplines. Using the standards of the Kyoto Treaty, rank the top three nations in terms of reducing greenhouse gas emissions. Justify your position with specific evidence.

POINT OF INTEREST

HOW TO STUDY BETTER When you study, focus on applying the material you are learning to all six levels of Bloom's Hierarchy. Study in such a way that you could answer the kinds of question cues listed in Table 1.1. Also, don't assume that topics will be presented one at a time; you might be expected to apply these levels to two or more topics simultaneously. For example, in an introductory sociology class, you might have started the class learning about the modern sociological theories, including symbolic interactionism, later read information on the civil rights movement of the 1960s, and a few weeks later heard a lecture on the effects of globalization on today's world economy. A faculty member might then ask you to analyze the civil rights movement and the effects of globalization from the perspective of a symbolic interactionist. Clearly, this question would test your knowledge and comprehension of those three seemingly separate pieces of information, but it would also require you to apply the theory to the two situations and analyze them from that theoretical perspective. Needless to say, many new students could walk into this exam feeling ready and yet walk out feeling blindsided.

It is a common mistake for students to spend a lot of time studying and memorizing the data but be unprepared for the higher levels of analysis that faculty will expect. Be prepared—faculty can and do utilize the whole range of Bloom's Hierarchy to assess your mastery of the material. You will excel in your classes if you plan accordingly. When you are studying for any class, keep this chart on Bloom handy and create questions for yourself at each of the six levels. Or better yet, work with a study group and have each person create one question per level. Between all of you, you will most likely simulate what the instructor will ask.

curiosity and a willingness to consider that you might not know about something makes engaging in critical thinking easier. It is also the first premise of doing great research and it means that, ultimately, you must be willing to change your mind. The goal of critical thinking is to identify and analyze evidence in order to make good decisions. This is true whether it is applied at a university for designing a research study or at a corporation for designing a new product.

The critical thinker looks at existing data or evidence, and also at existing arguments, and critiques their validity. As a result, critical thinkers must be skilled at first understanding and then analyzing both data and arguments, and separating them from opinions. This means that they don't just assume what they are reading or hearing is accurate and/or true but rather they question *everything,* including authority. University students should not only learn the material presented in a course but also question it, even if the source is their world-renowned professor or a scientific textbook.

STEPS OF THOROUGH CRITICAL THINKING

1. Understand the data or argument. You must understand it before you can critique it, and this includes making sure that you understand the definition of terms or concepts utilized by the author of that material.
2. Distinguish opinions from facts. Every author has a bias, even the most seasoned researcher. Search for clues about the author's opinion, especially those that are unsupported by the evidence presented. Determine what issue or question the author is addressing and see if you can identify the author's purpose.
3. Analyze the sources used for both accuracy and validity. This is where an understanding of both logical reasoning and research methods can be helpful. There may be a flaw in the logic and/or the way the data was collected or analyzed. Either of these can nullify an argument.
4. Explore alternative explanations. Are there other arguments and different conclusions that can be drawn from the same data? Is there other data that would lead to different conclusions? Identify the assumptions the author made as a way to find other possibilities.
5. Form your own conclusion about the issue at hand and support it with your own data or evidence. This last step is something you will do in university exams and papers as a way

to demonstrate your critical-thinking skills to your instructors. Your performance will rest on the strength of your critical-thinking skills and your ability to convey your process.

You will be trained on these steps and receive ample opportunities to practice them in every class. It is important that you understand that the goal is to have you *engage with* the material in an analytic way, as opposed to just learning it. Becoming a strong critical thinker is one of the major benefits of an education at a research university and one that many employers value. Many research universities even have stated goals about developing their students' critical-thinking skills. One example is Dartmouth College, where the Writing Program has developed several online resources to help faculty assist their students in becoming strong critical thinkers. This website (2010) states: "We want students to be able …:

THE SCENIC ROUTE

Visit www.cengagebrain.com to find the companion website containing links to:

- Dartmouth University's guide on argument formation
- Criticalthinking.org's tools, assessments, and articles on critical thinking
- Study Guides & Strategies' info on thinking critically

+ To know the difference between reliable and unreliable observations;
+ To be persistent enough to observe objectively and thoroughly, and to collect sufficient factual or textual evidence;
+ To see patterns or relationships in what they have observed or discovered in their reading;
+ To infer and to assume carefully;
+ To form opinions even while keeping an open mind;
+ To create arguments understanding that these arguments are not the last word, but part of an ongoing debate in a scholarly process."

No matter which research university you attend, your faculty will have similar expectations for you to develop and hone your critical-thinking skills.

THE IMPORTANCE OF ACADEMIC INTEGRITY

Because the primary mission of the research university is to create and discover new knowledge, you can probably understand that **academic integrity** is an essential element of the entire research process. The whole value of research would collapse if it could not stand on the notion that people do honest work and represent their research accurately and completely.

One of the worst violations a researcher can commit is to manipulate or misrepresent his or her findings; this invalidates the entire search for the truth. Faculty are fired for this. With that said, academic integrity is a value that is woven deeply into every element of your institution. As students you are expected to do your own work and stand by the quality of that work. Needless to say, cheating and plagiarism are serious violations of the essence of a research university. For this reason, it is important that you become very familiar with your campus's definitions and regulations regarding these offenses. You will most likely find that these issues are treated far more seriously than what you experienced in high school. In fact, a typical high school book report would be considered plagiarism at most universities because it summarizes the words of another without giving appropriate credit.

Typical forms of **plagiarism** (using another's words or ideas without giving him or her credit) include using material from any source (e.g., books, lectures, the Internet) without giving the proper credit, purchasing a paper from the Internet or another source, turning in another student's work (even if it is several years old), using your own work from one class in another (you need permission from both instructors to do so), turning in papers with similar sections as another student (even if they are worded differently, similarly organized thoughts and arguments can constitute plagiarism), and stealing another student's work and turning it in. Even if you do not engage in cheating or plagiarism directly, you can be held responsible for aiding in another student's **academic dishonesty.**

My freshman year was totally ruined because I was accused of cheating. Halfway through the year, I got called in to my political science professor's office. He told me that my paper was almost identical to another student's in the class. I was shocked because I had worked really hard on that paper and I had written it myself. Apparently, the other student told him the same thing, so he had to accuse both of us of cheating because he didn't know who was lying. The class had 700 students in it, and I didn't even know the other guy. We were both sent to the Office of Judicial Affairs, where we were assigned a hearing, which didn't occur until over a month later. In the meantime, I still had to go to all my classes, including poli sci, and try to focus, but I was stressed out so it was hard. The hearing was scary because there were twelve people in the room, and I had to prove my innocence.

It turns out that he lived in my hall and kind of knew my roommate. He had asked to use my roommate's computer one night when I was out. My roommate was working on another assignment, so he let the guy use mine. The guy found my paper and he copied it. I guess he just rearranged the paragraphs and turned it in. Luckily, my roommate was able to testify on my behalf because the other guy kept swearing that I stole his paper! I was found innocent, and he was suspended for three terms. But the whole thing was really stressful and made that whole quarter hell. Since then, I put a password on my computer, and no one is allowed to use it that I don't personally know. Even then, I have another password on my homework files.

Some common forms of **cheating** include copying answers from a classmate on an exam, bringing to and using unapproved notes and resources during an exam, having another person take an exam in your place, changing answers on an already graded exam and resubmitting it for credit, and stealing exam materials from department offices.

When an instructor suspects a student of cheating or plagiarism, several actions can be taken. At some universities, instructors have the power to fail a student on that particular assignment or even in the entire course without consulting anyone. All universities have some office or governing body that deals with cases of academic dishonesty; it might be called something like the Office of Judicial Affairs or the Committee on Student Conduct that oversees the enforcement of campus regulations and issues punishments to those who violate them. In some cases, faculty have the option to turn the student over to this agency, and in some cases, faculty are required to do so. This agency usually engages in a **judicial process** in which all evidence is presented to an impartial group of people, usually comprising faculty, staff, and students, who hear the case and render a decision. If found innocent, the student is let go without penalty. However, if found guilty, the student faces serious consequences that can include **suspension** from the university for a term or two, or even permanent **expulsion** from a university or system of campuses (including graduate school). In addition, a guilty finding forces the creation of a **conduct record** for that student that exists for five to seven years. All universities are required to divulge if a student has a conduct record, and this can damage a student's future admission to other institutions and many jobs. See "Justin's Story from the Path."

YOUR CAMPUS COMMUNITY

The campus community is made up of many, many individuals. There are undergraduate students, graduate students, faculty, staff, and administrators as well as people from the local community in which the campus is located. Each of these groups plays some integral role in the daily functioning of the research university and is part of what is known as the **community of scholars.**

As we have discussed, the role of the faculty is primarily to conduct research. Faculty also are charged with teaching both graduate and undergraduate students in order to prepare future researchers as well as to provide the courses needed to satisfy graduation requirements. Staff

@myU SO HOW DOES THIS AFFECT YOU?

Be forewarned that the consequences for cheating and plagiarism are usually quite severe. At my campus, a first-time infraction typically results in a two-quarter suspension after a hearing. This means that the student must move out of the residence hall, lose financial aid, drop out of classes, and stop attending for the length of the punishment. With such steep consequences, it is important that you know what your campus's policies are. They are most likely published in a printed version and online, and a simple search at your campus's website will likely yield them. However, you can always speak to your instructors or academic advisors if you have any questions.

In addition, if you participate in the process of another student's cheating, either intentionally or not, you can be held accountable. You have to be very careful about how you share your work with other students. For example, if you let another student see your paper, it is up to you to make sure that he or she does not use it to cheat. For this reason, it is important to be clear with your peers how, and to what extent, they can utilize any materials you are sharing with them. In addition, it is your responsibility to keep your hard copies and computer files secure. If you let a friend use your computer and he or she copies your paper and turns it in, you can both be accused of academic dishonesty.

My campus's policy is located at:

The name of the judicial agency is:

Penalty for cheating:

Penalty for plagiarism:

and administrators play pivotal roles in ensuring that every aspect of the university runs smoothly and efficiently. In addition, people who live near the university often interact with and/or are affected by the university community in a variety of ways. Each of these groups has different responsibilities, needs, goals, and ways of working. As a result, it is important for you to learn more about these different communities and how they affect your daily experience as an undergraduate student.

Undergraduate Students

The part of the community of scholars of which you are a member is the **undergraduate student** body. This ranges from freshmen to graduating seniors—any student who is currently enrolled in a bachelor's degree program. In addition, you will find yourself a member of the freshman or transfer class or the "Class of [*graduation year*]." On some campuses, class identity is quite strong, and you will find yourself identified by your group and familiar with many people in your class. On larger campuses, this is often not the case. At the University of Georgia, there are more than 25,000 undergraduate students and a freshman class of 5,000 students, and the only time the freshmen are seen as a group is during the first week of school at **convocation,** the official induction ceremony. Because not all students graduate in exactly four years, the entire freshman class is usually not together at **commencement,** the ceremony for graduation.

The role that an undergraduate plays in the community of scholars is to be both a consumer of knowledge and a producer of knowledge. As you take classes, your instructors will teach you information about particular topics, and you will learn/consume the latest research findings and theories. Once you select a major, you will begin to receive more specific training in how to conduct research for that particular discipline. This is where you also begin to be a producer of knowledge, as many of your assignments in these and other major classes will require you to write research papers and conduct small research projects.

If you show academic promise in your major, you might be invited to conduct a senior research project or to be involved in a faculty member's research. You can also seek out these opportunities on your own. If you aspire to continue on to graduate school, these are excellent opportunities to pursue, as they give you a chance to build your research résumé early, which gives you an edge when applying to graduate schools. In addition to their academic work, undergraduate students contribute to the campus community in a variety of ways including community service, student government, and other important leadership roles.

Graduate Students

Most research universities have both graduate and undergraduate students. **Graduate students** applied for, and were admitted to, an advanced degree program (usually master's or doctorate) in a specific discipline at your campus. That means that, just like you, they have courses to take and papers to write in order to graduate. Depending on the program they are in, they will be graduate students for one to three years if they are pursuing a master's degree or four to seven years if they are pursuing a doctoral degree. You might not always recognize graduate students because they may be close in age to undergraduates.

Graduate students play some key roles in the workings of a research university. First, they are researchers-in-training. In their courses, they are learning the theories and research methods that are used in their disciplines (usually in much greater depth than that which is presented to undergraduates). They must also become producers of knowledge by engaging in the type of research that is common in their discipline. Before they can graduate, they must produce original research under the close scrutiny of the faculty in their department.

The most likely place where you will encounter graduate students is in your classes, as they often serve as **teaching assistants,** or TAs. TAs work with faculty members to help teach courses to undergraduate students—and frankly, the university could not run without them. They usually are responsible for running discussion sections, teaching additional material in those sections, and grading some, if not most, of your work. All of these duties are done under the close supervision of the instructor of record for a particular course. Serving as a TA usually provides the graduate student with two important resources: money for school (as these positions are paid) and valuable teaching experience as they prepare for their own careers as faculty members.

Get to know your TAs and other graduate students on your campus. They were all very successful as undergraduate students, and they probably have some useful pointers for you. Graduate students can assist you with the assignment they might be grading, provide advice on how to balance academics with a social life, and give you useful strategies for various academic skills.

In some cases, very advanced graduate students may be promoted to a **teaching associate** position and given a course of their own to teach as hands-on job training; that is, they would serve as the instructor of record and have primary responsibility for that course. These advanced students are close to graduating and becoming an entry-level faculty member somewhere else.

Faculty

There are different types of faculty members at a research university. A **faculty member** is any person who has a contract with the university to provide teaching, research, or both. These titles may vary slightly from institution to institution, but they are generally similar across universities in the United States and Canada. The length of the contract may also vary; some faculty members have temporary or short-term appointments while others have long-term or permanent contracts. This distinction between the lengths of the contract is very important and essentially creates two categories of faculty.

WHO FACULTY ARE   If you think about it, faculty members are people who liked school so much that we never left. Ponder that for a moment. We were perhaps the top students in our high schools, and we went on to become the top students in our undergraduate colleges. We then chose to pursue a Ph.D. or other advanced degree that requires several more years of schooling. Once we graduated, we intentionally chose a career that requires hours of reading, writing, studying, and research. Generally, we are truly excited about learning and we find the material we research and teach to be fascinating. And we think our students do too.

We often assume that you intentionally chose a research university because you want to become a researcher yourself and are interested in the material we have to teach. This assumption can create a disconnection between students and faculty because we believe that you have a passion for learning, just like us, when in reality, students may be focused more on getting a good grade or a good job after graduation instead. Nothing slights our academic passion more than to have a student seem uninterested or bored, or worse, only focused on finding out what is on the test. Those kinds of priorities, and the attitudes that accompany them, are offensive to your faculty. Think carefully about how you interact with these passionate educators and what you convey about yourself with your words and actions.

LONG-TERM CONTRACTS   The first category of faculty is people with long-term contracts, and it includes those with "professor" titles. The **professorial titles** are the most prestigious faculty titles at a research university. These positions focus most on the person's research skills, although teaching is important as well. Because the primary job responsibility is research, the teaching loads for professors are lower than those of lecturers (described next). For example, a professor might teach four to five courses per year that can range from large undergraduate courses to small graduate seminars. These positions are paid the highest of the faculty titles and have many levels for growth and promotion. See "Point of Interest: Who Faculty Are."

The professorial titles are also known as **ladder-rank** faculty because they are "on the ladder" to tenure. **Tenure** is closely tied to the process of research and is the way in which academic freedom is guaranteed for every faculty member. Tenure is job security, and it means that a person has a job for life and cannot be fired except under extreme circumstances. Tenure is based on a person's contributions in four main areas:

1. Research, usually assessed by examining the quality and quantity of scholarly contributions (such as publications or creative works)
2. Teaching, usually assessed primarily by examining teaching evaluations from students
3. **Community service** to the home campus, usually assessed by examining the amount of participation in campus programs, on campus committees, and so on
4. **Professional service** to the discipline, usually assessed by examining the amount and level of involvement in national or international professional organizations

Every faculty member with the title of professor goes through frequent comprehensive performance evaluations in which these four areas are assessed. These periodic reviews involve faculty from the same department, other departments on the same campus, professional colleagues from around the world, and various administrators up the chain of command all the way to the president or chancellor.

By far the most heavily weighted factor at a research university is the faculty member's research skills, which are determined by examining the quantity and quality of the person's scholarly contributions, such as publications or creative works. The quantity of contributions indicates that the person is a competent researcher who regularly contributes to the new knowledge of the field and is respected by colleagues around the world. Therefore, this person will be a valuable addition to a university and will help fulfill its research mission. In fact, research is so important that every few years, professors earn a **sabbatical,** which is paid time away from teaching and community service to focus solely on their research.

Visit www.cengagebrain.com to find the companion website containing links to:

- Comparison of student experiences in high school versus the research university
- Professor Dutch's response to typical student complaints
- Professor Dorn's response to Professor Dutch

Tenure is used to guarantee faculty members **academic freedom,** which is an important concept at research universities. Academic freedom means that every faculty member has the right to research and teach what she or he wants without fear of retribution or punishment. This means that a researcher can actively pursue controversial topics without fear of losing his or her job. For example, a political scientist could research and publish things that were critical of the state or federal government, or a biologist could explore an unpopular theory about AIDS transmission.

Academic freedom is a core value of a research institution and is held in the same sacred way that freedom of speech is held in the United States. In fact, the concept of academic freedom was born during the McCarthy era in the 1940s and 1950s when scholars were routinely harassed and persecuted for holding views that the government did not agree with. Academic freedom and the tenure that guarantees it were specifically designed to ensure that McCarthyism could never be repeated in the United States.

There are four levels within the ladder-rank or professor titles: assistant, associate, full, and emeritus professors.

Assistant Professors

These are faculty members who have just completed a Ph.D. and have been hired by the university for a specified period of time, usually up to seven years. They do not have tenure and are given a period of time in which to earn it. During this time period, assistant professors are trying to demonstrate their research and teaching skills—in other words, their usefulness to both their field and their institution. Assistant professors have just a few years to produce a professional file of publications and teaching evaluations that shows them to be worthy of tenure. When assistant professors are granted tenure, they earn a permanent position at that university. If tenure is not granted, the temporary contract is ended; in other words, they are fired. The phrase **"publish or perish"** refers to this process and is often the mantra of stressed young faculty who are trying to gain tenure. Some campuses tie together tenure and promotion to the next level of associate professor; others keep these two processes separate.

Associate Professors

These faculty members are more advanced than assistant professors in the career of academia. Once tenure is earned, associate professors have job security for life, but the university's expectations that they continue to produce new knowledge also last for a lifetime, so associate professors by no means reduce their publishing goals. But they do probably feel less pressure and stress because they cannot be fired, and this frees up some of their time for involvement in university and professional service. What motivates associate professors to continue researching is their passion for learning and teaching. At some campuses, future promotions and salary increases may be based on their research skills and the quantity and quality of new contributions.

Full Professors

These faculty members also have tenure but have now achieved the highest level possible within this career in academia. They have been promoted from associate professor and granted the esteemed title of full professor. Again, full professors are motivated because of their intellectual passion. At some campuses, future promotions and raises may depend on their production of research. Full professors tend to be older because of the length of time it takes to reach the status of full professor. They are also the highest-paid members of the faculty, but salaries vary greatly across disciplines. Once faculty members achieve full professor status, they might also take on more administrative duties at their campus by becoming the administrative leader, or chair, of their department or by serving as an academic dean.

Outside of their campus, they might become a leading officer in a professional organization or become an editor of a scholarly journal. If a professor chooses to stop or slow his or her research production, the result is career stagnation. Although the person will continue to have job security for life, there is a cost in that colleagues might not view that person as highly as before, and this can lead to fewer opportunities within the department or campus.

Emeritus Professors

These faculty members have served as full professors for many years and have now retired. They no longer have an active contract, although some emeritus professors are asked to teach an occasional course in their specialty.

SHORT-TERM CONTRACTS The second category of faculty is people with short-term contracts. This includes teaching assistants and teaching associates, who were described earlier in the section about graduate students. In addition, there are lecturers, visiting titles, and acting titles.

Lecturers

These are faculty members who have been hired on the basis of their teaching skills. As a result, they have the heaviest teaching loads and are expected to teach nearly twice as many courses per year as tenured faculty. These courses may be introductory courses for freshmen or advanced courses for seniors. Occasionally, lecturers might be asked to teach a course for graduate students. Lecturers' contracts tend to have a specific time limit after which the contract is ended, no matter how good the lecturer was at the job. These faculty positions are paid less than the professor titles, even though most lecturers also hold a Ph.D.

Visiting Titles

These are faculty members who have a Ph.D. and have been invited to be part of the faculty for a specified, and usually short, period of time. The term *visiting* can be attached to both lecturer and professor titles; it indicates that although the person is working at this particular institution for a short period of time, she or he has a position at another institution elsewhere in the state, country, or world. Visiting faculty often are invited because they bring a perspective or background that is not found among the regular faculty at that particular campus.

Acting Titles

The term *acting* can also be used with all the faculty titles; it indicates that the person is in a temporary position with specified beginning and ending dates. It also might indicate that the person does not hold a similar title but does have the appropriate academic qualifications.

Regardless of the titles your instructors hold, it is important for you to use their assistance as you do your academic work. All instructors are required to have weekly office hours, the minimum being about two hours a week. The purpose of **office hours** is to be sure that students have regular and easy access to their instructors for the purpose of doing well in that particular class. Nearly 90 percent of all freshmen who participated in the Your First College Year survey (Ruiz, et al., 2010) interacted with faculty during office hours with 28 percent indicating that they visited office hours one to two times per month. Seventy-five percent interacted with faculty outside of class or office hours. More than half (52 percent) of students said they occasionally or frequently received "emotional support or encouragement" from their faculty and 43 percent said they received critical feedback on their academic work. More than two-thirds, 68 percent, were satisfied or very satisfied with their amount of contact with faculty. See "Point of Interest: Dos and Don'ts of Office Hours."

POINT OF INTEREST

DOS AND DON'TS OF OFFICE HOURS

Many students are intimidated by office hours because they are not sure what they are supposed to do during them. Generally, office hours are a time when you can DO the following:

- Ask questions about the week's lectures or readings—either because you did not understand the material and would like it explained further or because you have new questions about what it means in the bigger picture.

- Ask questions about your academic skills and get some advice—to show your instructor your lecture notes or chapter outlines and see whether you are capturing the right material and to the level of detail she or he would expect.

- Ask questions about an upcoming exam or assignment—to make sure that you understand it correctly and/or are approaching it in the correct way. For papers, you might also be able to have your instructor read outlines or even completed drafts and give you feedback.

- Ask questions about your past performance in order to improve—to find out why you received a certain grade for the purpose of learning how you can better prepare for future exams or papers.

- Bring something to your instructor's attention—such as an error on the syllabus or a test question that might have multiple interpretations.

- Ask for an extension on an assignment—but be sure you have a good and documented excuse, and even then, your instructor is not obliged to accommodate you.

- If you are a student with a diagnosed disability, speak to your instructor about any special accommodations that you might be able to access.

- Ask questions about the major or the academic discipline—to learn more about the wider scope of the field.

- Ask questions about the faculty's research—to learn more about his or her work or to find out whether there is an open student position on the project.

- Seek advice about future classes to take, graduate programs to apply for, and the like.

- Request a letter of recommendation for graduate school or a professional job.

Remember, you are attending a research university, where the faculty are charged with discovering new knowledge and, in general, are people who love to learn. With that said, there are definitely things that you DON'T do in office hours:

- Ask for copies of lecture notes. It is your job to take your own notes. If you were absent, you need to make arrangements with a fellow student to get a copy. It is okay to request copies of handouts, but it might be easier to ask the student from whom you are getting the notes to pick up a set for you.

- Ask questions that might be offensive to your instructor as a professional scholar—things like "Did I miss anything important?," "Will this be on the test?," or "Are we expected to know this stuff?" These questions indicate that you are trying to do the minimum and are not dedicated to your work.

- Go over an assignment with the instructor for the purpose of arguing about the feedback you received or making a statement like, "But I always get As on papers." Your faculty have years of experience teaching and grading, so they have a few things to teach you about performing at the university level. Trust that you have been assessed accurately and fairly, and seek to learn how you can do better next time. However, faculty do make mistakes occasionally (e.g., we might have added a score incorrectly or misgraded a question), and it is fine to point these things out to us—just be mindful of doing it respectfully.

Remember that each instructor is free to schedule the hours at his or her convenience, so they might conflict with your other classes, job, and so on. To address this, most faculty members are also available by appointment, which means that you can request a one-on-one meeting with your faculty or teaching assistant. You can do this either in person before or after class, by phone, or by e-mail. However, it is important that you have your schedule handy or give your instructor some options that work in your schedule. Once you have made an appointment, it is imperative that you show up. Your faculty member has taken time out of her or his busy schedule to be available to you, so missing an appointment is very unwise.

Staff and Administrators

While faculty and students represent the main producers and consumers of knowledge on a university campus, their daily lives would not be possible without the work of the hundreds of staff and administrators who work there as well. Many staff and administrators have chosen to work at research universities because they believe in the power of education and discovery. They work in ways that enable and facilitate the research and learning process of both faculty and students. Of the 26,758 freshmen who participated in the 2009 Your First College Year survey, 94 percent had interacted with academic advisors/counselors with 60 percent doing so once or twice per term. Nearly three-fourths (78 percent) interacted with other college personnel at a minimum of one or two times per term (32 percent) or per month (20 percent).

Without their efforts, many important aspects of the university would fail or falter. Since it is impossible to provide an overview of all that staff and administrators do, let's focus on how many people are involved every time an instructor wants to offer a class: It is the work of several people to schedule all classrooms, publish a document that lists all available courses, order books for students to purchase, assist in the making and copying of syllabi and exams, ensure that the classroom is heated and cleaned properly, process the grades and post them to students records, and process the instructor's paycheck every month.

And that's just a small taste of what is needed from the faculty's perspective. Think about some of other things that need to be done to help you be successful in school: advise you on how to choose and register for classes; counsel you when you are going through a difficult time; medically treat you when you are sick; process the payment of your tuition and provide you with financial aid when needed; talk to your family when they have questions; provide you with cocurricular activities such as campus events, clubs, and organizations; and encourage your success.

Staff and administrators are involved with every aspect of the operations of campus, so their work affects your experience every day. Obviously, these positions range from the person who mows the grass to a medical doctor in the health center. Because of this variety, it is hard to make concrete statements that represent all of these positions, but in general, tenure or job security is not something that is extended to staff and administrators at most research universities. It is also important to distinguish between staff and administrators.

Generally, **administrators** serve in leadership roles as the director or coordinator of a department or program, such as dean, provost, director, vice president, or chancellor. They must provide guidance and leadership to the staff who work under them in that particular department or program and to the department itself, ensuring that it functions at its best. This includes setting goals, overseeing the annual budget, hiring and supervising all staff, responding to unexpected crises, reacting to government or state mandates, and various other duties. In addition, administrators report to another administrator who is above them in the university's hierarchy.

In contrast, **staff members** are generally people who work in a department or program and report to the administrator who serves as the director or coordinator. Larger departments often have organizational hierarchies so that not every person reports to the head administrator but maybe to a manager or assistant director instead.

It is important to note that staff members often work very hard and do not receive the same prestige or status that is awarded to the faculty at a research university. On some campuses and in some departments, staff are considered "second-class citizens" compared to faculty and experience daily frustrations that stem from that attitude, such as lower salaries, less favorable parking spots, cubicles instead of offices, and all kinds of other privileges that they experience in less quantity or quality than those provided to the faculty. In general, any staff members with whom you interact will greatly appreciate being treated with respect and thanked for the service provided.

As with any community of people, sometimes problems or conflicts can arise between or among various members. Should this happen to you, seek information on the best way to get your grievance resolved. Either the office of the dean of students or the ombuds office would be a good place to start. See "Point of Interest: A Word about Grievance Procedures."

POINT OF INTEREST

A WORD ABOUT GRIEVANCE PROCEDURES

Every once in a while, things can go wrong at a university, and a student's rights or safety is compromised. Unfortunately, sometimes an instructor or staff member treats students unfairly or inappropriately. Examples can include minor situations that can cause problems for the student, such as an instructor grading an exam incorrectly or a staff member being rude. In addition, more serious problems can occur, such as a faculty member who drastically changes the assignments or grading procedures during the term or who treats some students very differently from others in ways that negatively affect their ability to perform well. Faculty or staff might even make offensive comments or sexually harass a student. There is generally a standard procedure that students should follow if they have experienced a problem in which their rights or safety have been violated.

In less serious situations, the general procedure to follow is to start with the person with whom you are having the problem and determine whether it is a communication issue. State what you are requesting in clear and polite terms. You would be surprised at how many situations can be resolved with simple and direct communication. If this does not bring the results you would like, then you can take the situation up to the next level at the university. For a staff member, you would make an appointment with his or her supervisor; for a faculty member, you would make an appointment with the chair of that department. It is usually a good idea to write down a summary of what has happened so far, including dates and specific comments. Also, state what you are requesting in terms of a solution. Be sure you arrive on time; a missed appointment will not make you look very credible. At this meeting, you might learn about campus policies or procedures that could influence the situation and any processes that exist,

such as petitions or grievance forms that you can fill out and submit.

If this meeting does not bring satisfaction, you have the option of continuing to the next level of the organization. For staff, it might be the director or the dean, or possibly the vice chancellor or vice president, who oversees the division in which that department is located. For faculty, it would be the dean or provost for the college in which the academic department is housed. Again, make an appointment and be on time. Bring written documentation and make your request clear. If this final level does not bring the results you were hoping for and you still feel strongly that you have been wronged, you can work with the office that addresses student concerns, often called the **ombuds office,** the dean of students office, or the office of student complaints and mediation. You also have the option of seeking legal counsel.

In serious situations such as sexual harassment or threats of violence, you should immediately speak to someone who can help. If the situation is urgent or obviously illegal, call your local police. If not, you may be able to pursue various options at your campus. Most universities have staff and administrators who assist students with these kinds of problems and can also protect them from retribution. Often, there is a complaint officer or an ombudsperson who handles these situations, but if you are not sure, contact your dean of students office. You would want to make an appointment with this person as soon as possible. It is usually very helpful when a written summary of what has happened so far is prepared in advance. This person can talk to you about a range of options and assist you in resolving the situation. These can include removing you from the situation in a way that keeps your academic record in good standing, to assisting you in filing a formal complaint and following a grievance process in which the offending party's behavior can be evaluated and possibly punished.

The Surrounding Community

Every campus is located in or near a community of some sort, whether it is a small rural town, a large city, or something in between. The presence of a university, along with its many members, has a very real impact on the surrounding community. Some of the ways in which the surrounding community is affected by a university are employment opportunities, housing costs and availability, parking costs and availability, student behavior, general safety, economic growth, availability of resources, and space planning and development. These impacts can be positive—for example, the availability of jobs with good benefits or resources such as an extensive library or lectures and performing arts events that are open to the public. And some of these impacts can be negative, such as local emergency rooms being clogged with alcohol-poisoning cases or the damage some students do to apartments and other personal or public property.

@myU SO HOW DOES THIS AFFECT YOU?

You are now a member of your university's community of scholars as well as a citizen of the local area for the duration of your college experience. Your actions and choices do have an impact on those around you, and only you can choose whether these will be positive or negative. Your behavior as a member of these communities is an important part of your education, and it prepares you for your future roles as an employee, a neighbor, a parent, and a partner. Look up how many people comprise the following groups in your new community:

undergrads:

graduate students:

faculty:

staff and administrators:

population of town:

population of county:

Many communities are involved with the local university in the form of beneficial formal and informal partnerships. One example on our campus is the adoption of a local elementary school. We provide additional funding to the school, and many of our students volunteer there as tutors. Sometimes faculty share their expertise with the local community. For example, Drs. Robert and Lynn Koegel have done groundbreaking research on children with autism. They share their work with local families by providing free consultations and treatment programs. They are not alone. A study done in 2007–08 of more than 22,000 faculty at 372 colleges and universities found that 88 percent of faculty believe that colleges "have a responsibility to work with their surrounding communities to address local issues" (DeAngelo, et al., 2009). This same percentage felt that students should be encouraged to participate in community service. Many local businesses have also created preprofessional internships in which our students can gain valuable work experience while still in college. These beneficial relationships go both ways and represent collaboration in its truest sense.

WHO DOES WHAT

Research universities tend to be larger campuses, which means that they are big structures organizationally. Most organize themselves into various **divisions** and then have more departments and programs within those larger divisions. Each division represents a different function of the university, and these divisions are combined differently on each campus. As you navigate your education, you will deal with many different offices across all of the divisions. The following is a brief description of some typical functions and/or divisions that you might encounter as an undergraduate.

The primary head of your university, either a **president** or **chancellor,** supervises the entire campus and has responsibilities to the county and state as well as other universities if yours is part of a statewide system. Each division is run by a **vice president** or **vice chancellor.** Within each division, there are a variety of departments and programs, each one run by another administrator and supported by various staff members. A look at your campus's general catalog, central phone directory, or website will give you an overview of your campus's organizational structure. Although this might seem irrelevant to you, it will help you know which department to visit for a particular issue and who is in charge. As a student, the academic, student affairs, and housing divisions will most likely directly affect you, so more details are offered on those three areas.

The Academic Division

The **academic division** is designed to provide the structure, policies, and services needed to assist students in successfully obtaining an academic degree. This aspect of your university will have the largest and most direct impact on your experience because it will eventually award your bachelor's degree. Again, because of size, some organizational structure will be in place, and you will want to find out what it is like on your specific campus. You will probably find that your university has a few colleges and/or schools that are different in terms of the types of majors they offer. One might offer several degrees in the engineering disciplines, while another might offer a liberal arts education with a wide range of majors.

For example, the University of Florida has seven schools and eighteen colleges ranging from the fine arts to business administration to education to nursing, whereas the University of Arizona has more than 300 degree programs organized into twelve schools and eighteen colleges. A **school** is a subdivision of the college and may house one or more academic programs or disciplines.

COLLEGES In general, a **college** awards a range of bachelor's degrees in a variety of majors. The college typically has certain graduation requirements in addition to those you must satisfy for your major. As a result, the college usually maintains student records on these requirements and has staff members who provide academic advising about them. Typically, these staff members are familiar with all the majors and can provide advice about the majors offered in the college as well as advice for undeclared students. Your college might also boast an **honors program** and can provide you with information about how to qualify for, and the benefits associated with, membership. Your college has certain policies and procedures for its students (e.g., withdrawals, repeated courses), and there are staff who oversee and administer these policies. Most likely, the college has some kind of committee or administrative structure that oversees all of the major departments to ensure that they are operating in a similar and fair fashion. A main administrator known as a **provost** or **dean** typically runs a college, and depending on the size, there may be several associate or assistant administrators in charge of various elements.

ACADEMIC MAJORS/DEPARTMENTS An academic or major **department** is a collection of faculty in a certain discipline, such as education or chemistry. These faculty members are located together in a specific building where they have office space. They determine the requirements you will need to fulfill to obtain a bachelor's degree in that particular field, that is, your major. You can be sure that these major requirements will include the theoretical and/or research traditions of that particular discipline. In addition, you will begin to see the specific research specialties of that particular group of faculty reflected in the courses offered. The faculty range from lecturers to full professors and are active and respected researchers and educators in that particular discipline. Your major department might also offer advanced degrees or graduate programs for students to pursue a master's or doctoral degree in that same discipline.

An academic department is run by a **department chair.** The chair is a current faculty member who has taken on specific administrative duties of running the department for a specified period of time. Usually, chairs are full professors who have achieved tenure and are at the highest level of their career path. Being a chair takes a lot of time and energy, which decreases research productivity, so these positions rotate through the faculty of the department. Duties include overseeing faculty meetings, supervising faculty in terms of classroom conduct and performance, scheduling courses, overseeing the review process for faculty, the graduate student admission process, funding and grants, producing various reports, and responding to any requests from the overseeing college or high-level administrators.

ENROLLMENT AND ACADEMIC SUPPORT SERVICES Besides colleges and major departments, you will discover a plethora of other departments, services, and programs that support you in being successful in your academics. Most of these entities provide a specific service and are usually run by an administrator or director and supported by staff. Note that not all of these are housed within the academic division on every campus; some are found in the division of student affairs. Some examples include the following (for detailed definitions of each, visit the companion website for this text at www.cengagebrain.com):

+ Academic skills center
+ Judicial affairs
+ Library
+ Information systems
+ Admissions
+ Orientation
+ Registration
+ Financial aid
+ Education abroad programs
+ International students
+ Disabled students support

The Student Affairs Division

The Division of Student Affairs is designed to provide the support services needed to keep students healthy and functioning so that they can perform well academically. This division is home to many services and programs that directly support the success of students, both academically and personally. These services can vary greatly at each campus, but most research universities provide some version of the following services (for a detailed description, visit the companion website for this text at www.cengagebrain.com):

+ Student health
+ Counseling
+ Dean of students
+ Career advising
+ Athletics and recreation
+ Cocurricular activities
+ Educational opportunity program
+ Multicultural programs

The Housing Division

If your campus owns and runs residence halls or apartments that students live in, then it will most likely have a division that operates and maintains the living spaces. This division also hires and trains a staff of professionals and student members who live in the building(s) and oversee the daily functioning and safety of the living community. In addition, they provide mediation services and respond in emergencies. On many campuses, housing and student affairs are combined in the same division. Some typical services include the following (visit the companion website for this text at www.cengagebrain.com for more information):

+ Contracts and assignments
+ Food services
+ Facilities and maintenance
+ Residential life
+ Judicial affairs
+ Student government and leadership

Other Divisions

As a student, you might not have much contact with these remaining areas, but they are still central to the running of a research university. In addition, they represent a variety of potential careers that you might wish to explore, and they may offer opportunities for student employment internships:

+ *Research affairs:* This entity is responsible for overseeing all research that is conducted, making sure that all studies and experiments are held to impeccably high ethical standards and that all human and animal subjects' rights are protected. In addition, this office manages a vast amount of grant and contract funding, and may also address copyright and intellectual property issues in terms of determining how much of a faculty's work (research results, patents, publications, courses, etc.) belongs to the university versus the individual faculty member. A research university also often houses independent research units that operate outside of academic departments and are not involved with offering academic credit for a bachelor's degree.

+ *Business affairs:* A university is a large business and this division maintains the various contracts and purchases for the campus. This includes addressing insurance and liability issues, arranging utilities like electricity and water, and negotiating discount prices with vendors for office supplies, printing, and so on. You might also find any campus businesses such as the bookstore or dining establishments based here, along with all the various departments that keep the physical aspect of the campus clean and functioning (groundskeepers, carpenters, electricians, etc.).

+ *Budget and planning:* This division often focuses on managing the various funding streams that come into and go out of the university. It also is primarily responsible for managing future growth in terms of new buildings, and meeting local codes and county ordinances.

+ *Human resources:* This area is responsible for the employment aspect of the university. It is where people apply for and get hired for all university jobs. In addition, this department manages the benefits (health insurance, dental plans, etc.) for all employees as well as any labor disputes, union contracts, mediation services, training and development, and sometimes professional counseling.

+ *Institutional advancement:* This division fosters positive relationships with the local community, alumni, potential donors, and government offices at the local, state, and federal levels. This area might also work on media relations as well as large public events.

The Academic Senate and Faculty Committees

Every university is a large organization and operates in many ways like a large corporation. When decisions need to be made, it is often a complex process that involves many constituencies and many layers of the university. Because of the research mission, faculty members play a strong role in the running of the university. From admissions standards to budget cuts to parking to academic requirements, every major decision must involve the faculty in some way. This is also known as **shared governance.** At some universities, the faculty play an integral role in the governing of most aspects of the campus; at others, the faculty are involved only with academic matters. All tenured faculty are members of a governing entity, sometimes called the **academic senate,** academic council, or faculty board. Each campus has its own academic senate, and in larger state universities that have many campuses, an additional system-wide academic senate is composed of representatives from all the campuses.

Because there may be several hundred faculty members on a campus, the academic senate can be quite large, and it would be inefficient to have the entire faculty debate and discuss each issue. As a result, the academic senate usually splits itself into several ongoing **committees** that meet regularly to discuss campus issues. For example, there might be a committee on general education requirements and another committee on tenure review. In addition, new, short-term committees may be created to address a specific issue such as hiring a new vice president or responding to a current situation such as a formal reaccreditation process. There may even be a committee on committees to determine who will serve on which committees and for how

POINT OF
INTEREST

SERVING ON COMMITTEES Students who are interested can contact their campus's academic senate office to learn more about which committees are in need of student participation. The student voice is very important in these meetings, and students often find themselves educating faculty on the "real" student experience.

Needless to say, this can also be a very positive experience for students in that it provides them with professional training experience and also the chance to make a difference at their campus. In addition, it creates the strong possibility that several faculty would be willing to write a letter of recommendation for the student.

long. Faculty, as part of their professional duties, are required to serve on committees and provide community service to the institution throughout their career. As was stated before, this level of involvement is part of the tenure review process.

Most of this faculty governance will be unseen to the student eye, as committee meetings occur in small conference rooms across campus. Most academic senate meetings are open to students. Student involvement is very much needed in the governance of the university, and a few spots are usually reserved on these committees for undergraduate or graduate student representatives. See "Point of Interest: Serving on Committees."

RELATED MATERIALS

For Scenic Route websites, more Stories from the Path, glossary, and student activities, access the study tools for *Navigating the Research University* at www.cengagebrain.com.

@myU SO HOW DOES THIS AFFECT YOU?

The most obvious way in which students are affected by faculty governance is that the faculty are primarily responsible for setting the academic requirements for all degrees awarded, including unit requirements, general education, and so on. For these broader campuswide decisions, faculty committees composed of tenured faculty from across the various disciplines are convened to create, implement, review, and revise requirements, policies, and procedures. This process is usually hidden to students and requires not only the approval of the specific committee involved but also the approval of other, related committees, and finally, it must be voted on by the entire faculty population, that is, the academic senate. As a result, changes can take years.

In addition, the faculty determines the requirements that are specific to each major, but this process is limited to the faculty in that particular department; the premise is that only psychology faculty, for example, would know best what a bachelor's degree in psychology should consist of. However, each major must be in alignment with the workload and difficulty of other majors at the same institution, so even department-specific requirements and policies will need to receive the approval of some college or campuswide committee. Search your campus website to find:

The location of the academic senate office:

The next academic senate meeting:

List three committees on which you might wish to serve:

1.

2.

3.

REFERENCES

Andreatta, B. (2010, January 6). *The research university*. Lecture for Education 20, Introduction to the research university. University of California at Santa Barbara.

Association of American Universities (AAU). (2010). *AAU membership: Public and private*. Retrieved from http://www.aau.edu/about/default.aspx?id=4020.

Bloom, B. S. (Ed.). (1956). *Taxonomy of educational objectives: The classification of educational goals: Handbook I, cognitive domain*. New York: Longmans: Green.

Brody, J. (2010, August 2). Be sure exercise is all you get at the gym. *New York Times*. Retrieved from http://www.nytimes.com/2010/08/03/health/03brod.html?ref=health.

Carnegie Foundation for the Advancement of Teaching. (2010).

Compton, H. T., & Tait, F. E. (1994). The liberal arts and critical thinking. In J. Gardner & A. Jewler (Eds.). *Your college experience: Strategies for success* (1st ed.). Belmont, CA: Wadsworth.

Conrad, E. (2009, Summer). A towering anniversary. *UC Santa Barbara Today*. Santa Barbara, CA: Alumni Association.

DeAngelo, L., Hurtado, S. H., Pryor, J. H., Kelly, K. R., Santos, J. L., & Korn, W. S. (2009). *The American college teacher: National norms for the 2007–2008 HERI faculty survey*. Retrieved from http://www.heri.ucla.edu/publications-brp.php.

Gardner, A. (2010, July 26). Can a mother's affection prevent anxiety in adulthood? *Cable News Network (CNN)*. Retrieved from http://www.cnn.com/2010/HEALTH/07/26/mother.affection.anxiety/index.html.

Hawking, S. (2010). *A brief history of mine*. Retrieved from http://www.hawking.org.uk/index.php/about-stephen.

Ruiz, S., Sharkness, J., Kelly, K., DeAngelo, L., & Pryor, J. (2010). *Findings from the 2009 administration of Your First College Year (YFCY): National aggregates*. Retrieved from http://www.heri.ucla.edu/publications-brp.php.

CHAPTER 2

The First-Year Experience at the Research University

Auburn University

© Jeff Greenberg/Alamy

Being a first-year student is a unique experience because of various transition issues, which are discussed in this book. An enormous amount of personal growth and development occurs in college that will shape your entire life. The first year is also very important because the choices you make during that year will often determine the level of success you can achieve both while in college and after graduation.

This chapter will help you understand the major themes affiliated with the first-year experience, for both freshmen and transfer students at a research university. It includes national statistics, so you can see how your experiences compare to those of other students. You will see the many common themes and issues of first-year students across North America, which have served as the guide for writing this book.

This chapter will also provide you with a bigger picture of the first-year experience by utilizing four student development theories created by researchers who have studied the college experience. These theories provide additional ways in which to explore and understand your own experiences.

WHAT TO EXPECT YOUR FIRST YEAR

As you move through your first year at your research university, you will have a host of experiences. Some will be positive and some will be challenging. They will involve your academic experiences, the interactions you have socially with your peers, and issues that affect your personal life. This section highlights common themes found in the lives of first-year college students.

Common Themes in the First-Year Student Experience

To put your own experience in context, let's turn to some national data on college attendance. The National Center for Education Statistics (NCES) houses a plethora of useful reports and current statistics on education that can be accessed at http://nces.ed.gov. According to the NCES, in 2009 approximately 18.4 million students were enrolled in degree-granting undergraduate institutions; 13.7 million of them attended a public institution and the remaining 4.6 million attended a private institution. The NCES did a study over six years (1995–2001) tracking students' college attendance. One-third of the students had transferred at some point in their college career; 42 percent of students at two-year colleges had transferred compared to 23 percent of students at four-year colleges. Interestingly, only 28 percent of all adults in the United States have completed four years of college. More than one-quarter (26 percent) of college freshmen do not return for their second year (some transfer), and about one-third of students who begin college do not finish their degree. Most high school graduates (three-quarters) do not attend college at all, and about 12 percent of K–12 students drop out of school before earning their high school diploma (NCES, 2010).

Two more primary sets of data will be used in this section to highlight common themes in the first year. One is from a survey conducted by UCLA's Higher Education Research Institute. In 2009, the institute conducted its annual national study of college freshmen asking them about their experiences during their first year of college. Called Your First College Year (YFCY), the survey sampled 26,758 first-time, full-time students at 457 four-year institutions in the United States, not all of which were research universities (Ruiz, et al., 2010). Results of this study indicated that 77 percent of students were satisfied or very satisfied with their overall college experience.

A second source of data is a doctoral study done on the academic and social integration of freshman students. This study utilized both surveys and in-depth interviews, and all quotes in the following section are from real students who spoke in depth about their experiences (Andreatta, 1998).

The following represents a compilation of these data sets, as well as general trends noticed in recent research and common themes discussed at national conferences and in higher education online discussions. Some of these issues affect both freshmen and transfer students; others are more likely to be associated only with freshmen. An additional set of issues is unique to the transfer population.

Table 2.1 provides an overall summary of the general categories (academic, social, general campus environment, and personal) and the specific issues listed within each. In addition, the table provides a place for you to rate how much that particular issue is affecting your success from not at all (1) to very much (5). As you read each section, fill in this chart. Finally, for each issue, there is an indication of which student development theories (explained later in this chapter) are related in some way.

ACADEMIC ISSUES   Depending on the university and the student, factors within the academic system can contribute to either a positive or a negative experience. Following is a brief summary of some of the most commonly mentioned issues.

TABLE **2.1** OVERVIEW OF FIRST-YEAR EXPERIENCES CORRELATED BY STUDENT DEVELOPMENT THEORY

Rate yourself on a scale of 1 (not affecting my success at all) to 5 (very much affecting my success). (Theories are indicated with a C for Chickering, P for Perry, T for Tinto, and K for Kohlberg.)

	Specific Issues	Relevant Theories	Rating 1–5
Academic Issues	Reputation of campus	T	
	Previous preparation	C, P, T	
	Pace of the academic term	T	
	Academic success skills	C, P, T	
	Academic performance	C, P, T	
	Intellectual self-confidence	C, T	
	Academic dishonesty	C, T, K	
	Contact with faculty	C, T	
	Approachability of faculty	C, T	
	Use of office hours	T	
	Experiences with specific departments	P, T	
	Use of academic services	T	
	Majors and programs offered	T	
	Level of students	T	
	Level of competitiveness	C, T	
Social Issues	Living situation	C, T, K	
	Social/friend networks	C, T	
	Activities offered	C, T	
	Impact of working and other commitments	C, T, K	
	Party/social scene	C, T, K	
	Impact of athletic involvement	C, T	
	Being in the minority	C, T, K	

(Continued)

TABLE **2.1** (CONTINUED)			
General Campus Environment	Physical environment	T	
	Emotional environment	T, K	
	Distance from home	C, T	
Personal Issues	Family separation process	C, T, K	
	First-generation status	C, P, T, K	
	Personal crises	C, T, K	
	Mental health	C, T, K	
	Money and credit management	C, T, K	
	Burnout	C, T, K	
Issues Unique to Transfer Students	Academic differences between institutions	P, T	
	Transferability of previous work	T	
	Transferability of GPA	T	
	Progress in major	T	
	Social networks	C, T, K	
	Nontraditional/re-entry students	C, T	
	Veterans	C, T	

Reputation of Campus

Students refer most often to either the academic reputation of the school or the social or party reputation. Whether this affects a student positively or negatively has to do with how well the student feels matched to the reputation. For example, a student who is not into partying will tend to feel out of place at a campus with a big party reputation, but another student might feel perfectly happy.

> *"I want to be a part of a program that is a more prestigious school in both academics and sports. I don't want to go to a school that when I tell someone where I go, they refer to it as a 'party school.'"*

Previous Preparation

Some students enter college and find themselves well prepared by their previous educators. They can jump right in and are able to understand the material in most of their courses and perform at a satisfactory level. Other students find that their preparation is sorely lacking—they are missing important content or skills that their fellow classmates possess and often feel behind and have to work harder to perform well. According to the 2009 Your First College Year (YFCY) study, only 21 percent of students said they found it "very easy" to adjust to the academic demands of college; 36 percent found it to be "somewhat difficult" or "very difficult." The quality of a student's previous academic preparation can create a positive or negative transition to the university's academic environment.

"I felt my grades were adequate and I am up to the level of education needed to participate in the university setting."

"I was completely unprepared. It seemed like most of the students knew what the professor was talking about and I was totally lost. I didn't pass that class."

Pace of the Academic Term

This refers to the overall quantity and quality of work expected in the amount of time allowed. Most university students find that they often cover in one term what took a year to cover in their previous school. The pace of the students' workload is faster and more intense than they previously experienced, especially if the campus is on the quarter system. First-year students struggle the most with this as they are adjusting, but it eventually gets easier and more comfortable.

Academic Success Skills

Students need to master several skills to succeed at a research university. For example, critical thinking is a cornerstone of the research university. Some first-year students find that they do not have well-developed critical-thinking skills and may struggle a bit in their classes while they are developing and honing them. This is especially challenging for freshmen who come from high schools where academic work was conducted in the lower levels of Bloom's Hierarchy. In addition, time management, writing, and other important skills might also need developing.

Academic Performance

It is quite common for first-year students to experience a 1.0 drop in their GPA from their previous institution. This is obviously due to the transition to a more challenging academic environment and the lack of the success skills necessary for an education at a research university. Most students learn from their experiences and are able to improve their skills and performance during the latter part of the first year and on through college to graduation.

"My first quarter GPA was a shock. I had been the valedictorian from my high school and came here with a 4.3 GPA and several scores of 5 on AP exams, so I thought I was pretty well prepared. However, I ended up getting a 1.8 GPA and was on academic probation. I knew I could have studied harder but I certainly didn't feel like I was bombing my classes. That was a wakeup call and I got my act together after that."

Intellectual Self-Confidence

One negative consequence of the above-mentioned academic issues is that they often have the combined effect of undermining a student's academic self-esteem. Most university students come from schools where they were among the strongest students, and many take these initial challenges as an indication that they are not "university material." Students can doubt their abilities and often perceive themselves to be the only one struggling. According to the 2009 YFCY study, 40 percent of the students rated their intellectual self-confidence as "average" or "below average" at the beginning of college, and 17 percent saw themselves in the "highest 10 percent."

"I learned that I might not necessarily be a top student and that I have to accept that. I took an anthropology class and was in the honors section. I really loved the class—it was great, and we had a terrific section. I had full understanding of the material, the book, etc., but for some reason, everyone who was in my study group for that class got As on the paper and I got a D-minus. I talked to the professor but I didn't get any specifics on what I needed to change. He let me rewrite it, which I did, and then I got a C+. The experience really affected my perception. It

gave me a more negative perception of my abilities but I guess it made me more realistic about myself."

It is important to note that a serious decline in a student's self-confidence can lead to the onset of depression. Symptoms of depression are quite common among college students and can be alleviated through assistance from campus student health or counseling professionals. See more information at the end of this chapter.

Academic Dishonesty

As a result of some of the issues discussed above, some students turn to cheating as a way to improve their performance or to at least keep from failing. Research universities take academic integrity very seriously, so students might find themselves facing suspension or expulsion for cheating, even for a first-time offense. Even if students successfully cheat, they shortchange themselves in terms of the preparation that particular assignment or course provided for their future academic performance.

Contact with Faculty

This is often an area of complaint for students at larger universities, where classes may include several hundred students, compared to both high school and community college environments, where classes were smaller. Some courses might not even be taught by professors but rather by graduate students. While the 2009 YFCY study indicated that 68 percent of students were satisfied or very satisfied with their amount of contact with faculty, some students found their interactions with faculty to be unsatisfactory.

Approachability of Faculty

Many first-year students find that the approachability of their faculty is a very important factor in determining whether or not they seek help. Students comment on watching how an instructor treats other students in the classroom, and this becomes a primary basis for whether or not they choose to seek help from that instructor. Faculty who seem distant or even mean to students are avoided, while faculty who are perceived to be caring and approachable are thought of highly and sought after. Sadly, many students will not seek help from faculty who seem unapproachable even if they are struggling in a class. According to the 2009 YFCY study, 81 percent of students occasionally or frequently asked a professor for advice after class, and 52 percent said they occasionally or frequently received emotional support from their professor.

"I feel very welcomed and comfortable here. The professors and tutors have been very helpful."

"I tend to like TAs and professors who are more friendly because they don't seem like they are on a 'power trip' and then are more likely to explain things better. For example, my math professor treated everyone like a number and seemed to like to intimidate the students. I think most professors are not kind to students."

Use of Office Hours

Not surprisingly, students' use of office hours is often directly connected to how they perceive their instructor in terms of approachability and helpfulness. Many students who go to office hours find it extremely helpful and are able to improve their performance through seeking this additional support. The YFCY data indicated that while 36 percent of students attended faculty office hours one to two times per term and another 28 percent attended one to two times per month, 9 percent never attended faculty office hours. One-quarter of students never interact with faculty outside of class or office hours.

"I didn't interact with my faculty because I felt intimidated. I thought they would think I was asking stupid questions."

"Going to office hours was the best thing I did. My professor looked over the draft of my paper and I was able to use her comments to rework it and get an A."

Experiences with Specific Departments

Many students comment on experiences with certain departments, especially as first-year students are often required to take a number of courses from certain key departments such as math, chemistry, writing/English, and foreign language. In some cases, key required classes are designed to eliminate many students. For example, if the campus cannot accommodate all those who wish to pursue biology or premed majors, the math and chemistry classes might be set at a difficult level to weed out many of those students. In these classes, students often do not feel that they were supported to do their best, which can be both discouraging and frustrating.

"In my calculus class, 75 percent of the students got less than a C on the midterm. I'm sorry, but that seems really unfair."

"My writing teacher was awesome. He spent a ton of time helping us work on our writing. He even let me change the assigned paper topic to another one that really interested me."

Use of Academic Services

Using academic services is often necessary for first-year students to achieve academic success. Many students find that utilizing the academic skills and tutoring services as well as assistance from instructors is what helps them to succeed, or at least not fail. Such students credit these experiences as crucial to their academic survival the first year, and it is clear that the most successful students actively choose to use these services.

"I really liked my chemistry tutor at the Skills Center. I couldn't have survived Chem 1 without her. She really helped me improve my performance, which increased my confidence. I also used the writing lab and it was really great."

Majors and Programs Offered

This issue is directly related to whether or not a student thoroughly understood the nature of a research university before applying or accepting admission. Many students assume that all universities offer the same majors and may not explore if what they are looking for is offered at their particular institution. In addition, universities offer a range of academic programs that can enhance the intellectual engagement of its students.

"I would like to change my major to animal science but this university does not have that major."

"The honors program catered to my academic needs and helped stimulate my intellectual growth, which I would not have gained otherwise."

Level of Students

Students attend a university amid thousands of their peers. Some find that they are in sync with those around them in terms of academic focus and abilities, and some discover that they are not.

"I feel that I belong here because I'm surrounded by individuals who are hard working, intelligent, and motivated like me."

"I have been in several situations in which I take school/studying more seriously than the other students here seem to."

Level of Competitiveness

Every campus harbors a different atmosphere in terms of the competitiveness among its students. For some a competitive environment is motivating and an indicator of intellectual stimulation, while others find a less competitive environment to be more supportive of their college experience.

> *"Everyone here does not revolve their life around grades, which is something that fits me well. I cannot just be a student. I need other activities to have my mind be at peace and this campus offers those to me."*

SOCIAL ISSUES Within the social experience of college, several factors can affect the overall nature of a student's experience. Although often these are not controlled or provided by the university specifically, they still have a very powerful effect on the overall quality of a student's experience.

Living Situation

Students' living situations have a strong impact on their university success because these situations affect the students every day. If they live with others with whom they get along, and the overall living environment is conducive to their academic and personal goals, then students tend to have a positive experience. However, roommate conflicts or environments that are too noisy or too crowded can create a negative experience. Even in the best of circumstances, most college living situations require students to share small spaces with other people, which can be quite unnerving, especially since most students need some private and/or quiet time. The YFCY study indicated that 30 percent of students had difficulty getting along with roommates or housemates.

> *"My roommate and I get along great. We talk about everything and do stuff together all the time."*

> *"My roommate was a challenging experience because he was not talkative and we had minimal communication. We didn't fight or anything and we worked out a 'live and let live' philosophy. It was basically a neutral situation but I'd hoped for a more positive experience. I ended up hanging out a lot in the hall since it was uncomfortable in our room."*

> *"I hated my residence hall. My roommate was Japanese and the two of us and our suitemates were really close because we were the only minorities in the whole building. Everyone on our floor was only into partying. We were close to each other but felt separated from the whole hall so we stuck to ourselves."*

Social/Friend Networks

The quantity and quality of a student's friendships can greatly affect the overall social experience. Creating a satisfying network of friends often takes time and depends on the student being outgoing enough to seek out venues where she or he can meet others and find those who share common goals, values, and experiences. Once friendships begin to form, time provides the truest test as people weather the ups and downs of the academic year together. Most friendship networks that are formed in the fall are rarely still intact by June because some kind of "drama" occurs that causes tension and distance among the group. For a student who has invested all of his or her energy into one network, this dissolution can be very stressful because he or she might now need to find new connections in the middle of the year. Students who have more than one network tend to fare the best. More than three-quarters (78 percent) of the freshmen in the 2009 YFCY survey stated that they were satisfied or very satisfied with the interaction they had with other students, and 81 percent said that they interacted daily with friends at their campus. Sixty-eight

Visit www.cengagebrain.com to find the companion website containing links to:
- Tips on college roommate relationships
- UCLA's latest research on college students
- Practicalmoneyskills.com's tools for college students

percent felt satisfied or very satisfied with the overall sense of community among students, and 76 percent spent more than 5 hours per week socializing with friends.

> *"I started working at the campus radio station where I met a lot of people. I developed 8 to 10 solid friends from the station and that's mainly who I hung out with."*

> *"I am having trouble adjusting. I haven't made any good friends yet and my roommate situation is not a good one but I will stick it out through the year."*

Activities Offered

This refers to the amount and type of cocurricular activities that are offered at the campus. Some students find that there is a good match between their interests and the school's offerings; other students experience a lack of options that meet their needs. This can affect a student's overall sense of social connection to the campus. Generally, students eventually find things they enjoy because universities tend to offer such a wide range of options. Nearly two-thirds (63 percent) of students in the 2009 YFCY study said that they participated in student clubs or groups, and 70 percent said that they were satisfied or very satisfied with the campus's social activities.

Impact of Work and Other Commitments

Most students will work at some time during their undergraduate experience, whether it is a casual part-time job to earn some extra spending money, a preprofessional internship to prepare for a future career, or even near full-time hours to put themselves through school. Working, or any kind of involvement, up to 20 hours per week has been shown to have a positive impact on students because it improves their time management skills and provides another avenue for social connections. However, full-time students who have to work more than 20 hours per week usually find that this has a negative impact on both their academic performance and their social connections because they just do not have the time for studying or casual social interactions. This is also true for any nonacademic commitment, including clubs such as Greek organizations, athletic teams, and hobbies. The YFCY data showed that 30 percent of students had a paying job (17 percent worked on campus and 13 percent had an off-campus job). Of these students who were working, 60–80 percent indicated that their job frequently or occasionally interfered with their coursework, with the greatest impact on students who worked more than 20 hours per week at a job off campus.

> *"The money strain is really putting the burden on my family and my school work is hard to juggle with my job where I work thirty-five hours a week."*

> *"None of my roommates have to work so they have a lot more time to hang out in our suite or go to campus events. I work more than forty hours a week and am putting myself through school. I get resentful when they get on my case for not doing my share of the dishes, etc. I mean, couldn't they just cut me some slack once in a while?"*

Party/Social Scene

Socializing and partying are obviously a cornerstone of the college experience and a main component of the overall social experiences a student has at his or her university. Ideally, there is a match between the types of social events and parties offered and the student's personal interests. If the school has a reputation as a party school, the students who enjoy drinking and partying will probably feel comfortable with the focus on alcohol, but this can be quite a negative experience for students who are not interested in those activities. Students who feel a strong disconnection with the overall social atmosphere might choose to transfer to a different type of school. The respondents in the 2009 YFCY study indicated that their alcohol consumption increased over the first year. One-third (34 percent) said they occasionally or frequently drank beer at college entry and this number rose to 46 percent by the end of the first year. Likewise, consumption of wine/liquor went from 41 to 53 percent. More than two-thirds (68 percent) said that their social life frequently or occasionally interfered with their schoolwork.

"The atmosphere around here is boring, and there are no alternatives for people who don't like to get drunk."

"I love to party with my friends. We get wasted every Thursday, Friday, and Saturday nights. My parents say that as long as I am getting good grades, it's OK for me to have fun so it's not a problem."

Impact of Athletic Involvement

Student athletes have extraordinary responsibilities and pressures compared to nonathletes at the same campus. Student athletes have lengthy daily trainings that are rigorous and mandatory. The scheduling of these training sessions often prevents student athletes from taking certain classes, which can even eliminate the possibilities of entire majors. In addition, student athletes in their competitive season have to travel frequently, missing classes and exams while still needing to perform academically at a successful level. This can be quite stressful, and many first-year student athletes are not able to maintain their grades and their athletic performance. As a result, some first-year student athletes leave their team, and this creates additional negative experiences, as the team is most likely their primary social network. Furthermore, many student athletes have been doing their sport their whole lives, so they often experience an identity crisis of sorts as they lose one of their primary senses of self. The YFCY data indicated that 15 percent participated in intercollegiate athletics and another 42 percent played club, intramural, or recreational sports.

Being in the Minority

The term **minority** here does not necessarily refer to ethnicity, although people of various ethnic backgrounds certainly are in the minority on many campuses. It refers to any student who feels that she or he is in the minority compared to the overall student body. Although a whole host of issues can cause a student to feel this way, these feelings are most prevalent for students who are in the minority in terms of a primary component of their identity such as race, economic class, age, region, sexual orientation, religion, and political affiliation. These students often face daily challenges in a place where they may not feel comfortable or even safe, and they certainly feel conspicuous and conscious of their identity because of being "the only one" in a classroom or a residence hall. Needless to say, this can have a negative impact on a student's social experience and create challenges that are not experienced by the students in the majority. Interestingly, the 2009 YCFY study asked students how often they had "guarded or cautious" interactions from a racial group other than their own. Less than 7 percent of White students indicated this happened often or very often, while each minority group experienced more of these interactions, from 11 percent for Native Americans and 17 percent each for Asian Americans and Latino/a students, to 20 percent for African American/Black students.

"This campus is not diverse—it's predominately White or upper class and I can't relate to the people here. Those who do not fall into these categories have to build their own cliques."

"I feel very comfortable here—I love the diversity of the campus—everyone fits in."

"My roommate and I were the only African Americans on our hall. It seemed like whenever we would come around, the only topics the White students would bring up would be about rap music, basketball, and women. There was never anything else. At first,

I didn't see it at all but after a while it started to get repetitive. Sometimes, you know, I wanted to talk about how to do better on my chemistry test, and it would be turned back around to my music or whatever. Maybe they really did like rap music and basketball but it was the only conversations we had with them."

GENERAL CAMPUS ENVIRONMENT When a student goes to college, she or he spends a significant amount of time on the physical campus. This can be a source of experiences that either positively or negatively affect a student's overall college experience.

Physical Environment

This refers to the actual physical environment of the campus and the surrounding community. If the environment is similar to the student's home community, then the student will often feel a sense of overall comfort in the environment. However, students who come from a different environment might feel overwhelmed and uncomfortable, maybe even unsafe, on their college campus. Some specific examples include students from a busy urban/city environment feeling uncomfortable on a quiet, rural campus, and vice versa. A student usually adjusts to this over time, but if the experience represents frequent challenges to the student in terms of overall comfort, as well as the availability of certain services and experiences, she or he might choose to transfer.

"I love being near the mountains, and surrounded by kids my own age. It's fun, but most of all I love the really beautiful atmosphere."

"I missed home and the big city. Being on campus all the time is very confining and I missed living in a huge city and community."

"My culture is not represented in this community so I have to drive two hours to the nearest city to find someone who can cut my hair or a store that carries the food I like."

Emotional Environment

Most campuses have a certain kind of feel or vibe to them that is conveyed in the actions, words, and nonverbal communication of its students. Some campuses feel very competitive, while others are laid-back. Some campuses feel very progressively focused, and others are more conservative. It goes without saying that a good match between the student and the student body will lead to positive experiences, while a poor match will cause some level of disconnection and even tension.

Distance from Home

This refers to the physical distance the student's campus is from his or her community. Although this can certainly be measured in miles, most students refer to a more emotional factor of whether it is the *right amount* of distance from home. Students who are close to their families often want to visit home frequently, so the right amount of distance will be that which is convenient in terms of both time and modes of transportation. For students who seek more independence from their family or who do not wish to be surprised by unannounced visits, the right amount will tend to be farther—still close enough to visit a couple of times per term but not much more than that. Some students consider this distance factor when selecting their university; others discover its relevance after the term has begun. Extreme homesickness can contribute to a choice to transfer to another college closer to home.

"I'm getting a good education. I got a car so that eliminated my problem of being too far away from home."

"I am from out of state and everyone I know, including all of my friends, family, and boyfriend, are there so I wanted to go home. I'll be transferring back at the end of the year."

PERSONAL ISSUES Personal issues, especially problems, often impede a student's academic success and sometimes social success as well. Although many campus services and counselors are available to help students address personal issues, students need to let people know they are struggling and seek out support. Some of the common personal issues that affect college students include the following.

Family Separation Process

The details of this complex process are discussed in Chapter 4. Students who are given appropriate levels of distance and support from their families report increasingly positive interactions and relationships with family members and often develop better relationships with family members than ever before. However, this is not the case for all students.

"Before I left for college, it seemed like I was fighting with my folks all the time. But now we are closer than ever before. I think I needed to get away before I could really appreciate them and they could see me as more of an adult."

"When I came out to my parents as being gay, they freaked out and cut off all contact with me. I'm now putting myself through college and I'm pretty stressed out most of the time."

First-Generation Status

College students are considered **first generation** if they are the first in their family to either attend or complete college. First-generation students have much to be proud of, especially if they are attending a top research university, but they also face some unique challenges, like having family members who do not necessarily understand the college experience and therefore might not be able to provide the same kinds of suggestions or support that other students receive from their families. In addition, first-generation students' families are often immigrants, so the family might not speak the language in which the university conducts its official business via orientation, forms, parent newsletters, and the like. The English-speaking students often find themselves not only taking care of all of their university business by themselves, but also having many responsibilities serving as the family's interpreter. Many students in this situation travel home frequently to carry out this role and this can detract from their academic and social success. For these reasons, many campuses provide support to first-generation students and their families.

Personal Crises

Many students experience personal crises during the year that can seriously impede their success if they are not able to seek or secure the appropriate support. Some examples include a parent battling a serious illness or dying; a parent losing a job; the family's home or business being damaged in a fire; the student developing a serious illness such as cancer, depression, or an eating disorder; the student experiencing a physical debilitation such as a broken back and being unable to attend classes; and the student being the victim of a crime such as sexual assault. Here are some descriptions of crises that students in this author's study faced during their first year at college:

* One male student confided that his father had died two weeks prior to school beginning. He was completely overwhelmed and unable to study or focus but could not go home because his father told him to "stay in school" just prior to his death. However, this student did not inform anyone of his situation because he did not want to receive any "special treatment."

* A male student was a member of a gang and tried to maintain his membership throughout fall quarter. Midway through the fall, his cousin, who was sixteen years old, was shot twelve times and killed in a gang shooting. Over winter break, the student

negotiated with his gang and received "permission" to leave, but he found that home was not the same after that.

✦ One female student developed a severe eating disorder during fall quarter because of the pressure she felt on the campus to be attractive and thin (she had no prior history of eating disorders). This caused major difficulties with her roommate and her friends who tried to help her. Finally, she sought counseling (through student health) in the middle of winter quarter, which she found very helpful.

✦ A male student was incredibly shy and introverted. This caused problems with his roommate and others, so he felt more and more socially isolated. He had a series of very negative academic experiences and he ended up on academic probation. However, he could not tell his parents because of the pressure from his father to follow in his foot-steps as an engineer. These and some other negative experiences at college led him to feel suicidal.

Mental Health

Quite a few first-year students develop depression or an anxiety disorder for the first time in college. This is not surprising because students experience the change of familiar environment along with the loss of support systems coupled with the addition of overwhelming stress and the pressure to succeed. According to the 2009 YFCY survey, 12 percent of students indicated that they frequently felt depressed, while another 41 percent felt overwhelmed. See "Miles's Story from the Path." A study at Kansas State University found that the number of depressed students had doubled over the past ten years and the number of students who had thought about suicide had tripled (Benton, et al., 2003).

It is important to recognize the symptoms of depression and anxiety so that you can seek help or encourage another to do so. The following is from *Responding to Distressed Students* (University of California, 2010). **Depression** has specific symptoms of significant duration and severity. The most common features of depression are the subjective experi-ence of feeling empty, hopeless, helpless, worthless and unloved; a deep sense of sadness and emotional pain; the inability to experience pleasure in many activities; irregular sleep and eating patterns; difficulty concentrating, retaining information, and making decisions; and fatigue and social isolation. Some depressed students experience agitation, anxiety, and intense anger. Some have recurrent thoughts of destruction and are preoccupied with death. Some desire to escape the pain through suicide. Fortunately, depression responds to treatment, and 80–90 percent of those treated show improvement. Research supports the use of both medication and psychotherapy for the most effective treatment of major depression.

Anxiety disorders are the most common psychiatric conditions in the United States, affecting more than 23 million people. Anxiety disorders are grouped into twelve distinct diag-nostic categories, among which are generalized anxiety, social anxiety, panic disorder, obsessive-compulsive disorder, post-traumatic stress disorder, and phobias. Some features of anxiety that may be noted in students are intense tension or fear when there is no danger, feelings of losing control and a sense of doom, confusion, ruminations, excessive worry, irratio-nal thoughts, catastrophic thinking, avoidance behavior, hypervigilance, physical agitation, and inability to sleep and eat. Students may suffer from a wide range of anxious conditions. Some may have a generalized anxiety, which can impact their ability to perform academically by affecting concentration, memory, the processing of information, the ability to recall informa-tion, and the ability to comprehend. Others may struggle with a specific type, such as perfor-mance anxiety, which can affect an oral presentation, or test-taking anxiety, which impacts the ability to perform on a test. Research suggests that when treating persons with high levels of anxiety, the most effective treatment is the combination of psychotherapy and psychotropic medication.

MILES'S STORY FROM THE PATH

By the middle of college, I was not taking adequate care of myself physically or emotionally. I had a very inconsistent sleep schedule, I was overcommitted and dissatisfied with my work, and I had set my social and emotional well-being as my lowest priorities. Stress and anxiety had taken the best of me so that even the most basic daily activities were overwhelming. I knew something was wrong—it was all I could think of anymore!

Even after I came to realize that I was having a problem with anxiety and depression, I refused to consider medication as an option, whether as an adjunct or alternative to counseling. I found the counseling staff to be very helpful and accommodating. The counselor I met with regularly was a graduate student and clearly experienced and knowledgeable. Furthermore, my desire to attempt to relieve my anxiety without medication was respected. Most importantly, I was always welcomed back to the center and received weeks of counseling for free.

After several months, I found that the problem was getting worse instead of better. Counseling had allowed me to look seriously at my situation and to start purging my emotions regularly—it also allowed me to accept the fact that I was having a difficult time. Being unable to live life as usual was nothing short of terrifying, but I was assured that my progression of experiences was normal and that my life could, in fact, have a bright future.

Eventually I felt that I could not continue in school—it was time to deal with my anxiety head-on. My decision to withdraw from school during my junior year was one of the hardest decisions I have ever made. In retrospect, though, it was one of the best decisions I have ever made! The staff in the dean of students office were very helpful in assisting me with the logistics of my withdrawal and eased my feelings of shame for leaving my studies mid-year.

Still, I sensed that I was nearing the end of my rope. At student health, I was able to make an urgent appointment to see a physician about trying medication. My plea was met with reassurance, and I felt that I was given very thoughtful medical evaluation. Despite the fact that I had so vehemently denied the possibility of taking medication, it eventually proved to be a necessary tool for me to lift my overwhelming anxiety and depression.

The combination of counseling and medication made me—for the first time in years, perhaps—start to feel somewhat normal again. The time that followed was not easy, but I was determined to work through my anxiety and get back to my real life. With the support of those campus resources, I was able to do just that. In fact, the act of saying, "I can't," and "please help," was the most therapeutic experience I had that year.

My return to school was not easy, but it was a great success. I took classes the next four consecutive quarters earning nearly straight As before graduating. I began working part-time in retail and found a social life much more satisfying than what I had created before. I came to think of my personal well-being as essential, and as a result, my other commitments benefited as well. Just a year after my return to school, I began work as a staff member at the dean of students office, the very place that had been instrumental in connecting me with campus support services and facilitating my time off from school. Now I am able to provide support to students as they face challenges in their own college careers, and I can say with confidence, "Let me tell you, I know how you feel."

In addition to developing depression or anxiety while at college, many students have been *previously* diagnosed with another **mental illness** (e.g., bipolar disorder, schizophrenia, borderline personality disorder, etc.) that requires medication and the supervision of health care professionals. Stresses of college life, such as erratic sleeping and eating patterns, and possible increased consumption of alcohol and other drugs, can exacerbate a mental health illness beyond the effectiveness of the medication. Since most university students move away from home, they are no longer being regularly monitored by their parents, who know them well and can get them to their doctor when needed. Some students even stop taking their medications because they want to "be like the other students." It is important for such students to monitor their health carefully and to seek support if they notice a change in their own feelings or behavior. Family, friends, and roommates may also be in a position to notice changes and should encourage the student to seek medical evaluation. All should stay aware until the student's condition improves.

Students without mental health issues can also be significantly affected by the mental health issues of their family and friends, which can negatively impact their university experience. It's important for these students to seek support from campus departments and counselors as well. Mental health can be a threat to campus safety if students become homicidal, as in the tragedy that occurred on the campus of Virginia Tech on April 16, 2007.

"I found my roommate cutting herself in the bathroom. It really scared me because she's always talking about how depressed she is. I know she's working with a therapist but it's really stressful living with her. I wish I could move to another apartment."

"During fall, my younger brother developed schizophrenia. He was always running away from home so I went home every weekend to help out my parents. He was eventually put into a home for troubled teens. This has been really hard on me because I'm very close with my brother."

Money and Credit Management

Many students do not have well-developed money management skills, also known as **financial literacy**, when they move away from home. They might not know how to establish a reasonable monthly budget and then live within it. In addition, they might not be skilled at balancing their checking account or keeping track of bills and late fees, or they may feel peer pressure to have certain things. Needless to say, students can get in trouble financially if they have not learned money management skills before college begins. Furthermore, a growing trend on college campuses across North America is for students to accrue unacceptable amounts of both loan and credit card debt. Nationally, 76 percent of undergraduate students have credit cards with the average number of cards per student being four. The average outstanding balance is $2,169, but nearly one-quarter have a balance of more than $3,000 (Nellie Mae, 2010).

Students who receive financial aid are especially susceptible if their aid amount does not cover their annual expenses. However, even financially secure students are in danger because of the ease with which they can qualify for credit cards. Students are turning to credit cards as a way to solve their money management problems instead of learning to create a budget and live within their means. Many students are unaware of how interest rates work and are lured by the temptation to "charge" their way out of a jam. The Center for Student Credit Card Education, Inc. (Carolan, 2002) determined if a student with a balance of $2,327 stopped using the card and then paid the minimum monthly payment (at an APR of 18 percent), it would take more than thirty-three *years* to pay off the debt. In addition, the student would pay $5,912 in interest—that's *more than twice* the actual amount charged. Because students are adults at 18 years of age, credit card companies specifically target college campuses to sign up new customers.

"I have gotten in trouble with credit cards because it's just so easy to charge the things I want to have like clothes, music, beer, or whatever. My parents have no idea but I already owe $1,800."

Burnout

This seems to haunt first-year students and to diminish with each subsequent year. It refers to the student's ability to withstand the academic and social experiences for the length of the entire academic year. The increased pace and demand in the academic sphere paired with interactions with hundreds, if not thousands, of peers can be tiring, and students often report feeling burned out by spring. This burnout often causes students to lose focus academically before they complete their courses. In addition, many students say that they are tired of the social scene on their campus and/or in their living environment and look forward to the summer break.

@myU SO HOW DOES THIS AFFECT YOU?

Ideally, after reading about the typical experiences that first-year students have, you realize two things. One, you are normal! There are lots of other students who are struggling with the same issues you are, and all of you can still be very successful in the university environment even if you are facing some big challenges. Two, the students around you might be having a really different experience from the one you are having. Many of the issues listed in this chapter might be affecting someone you know, and you might not know it unless he or she chooses to tell you or you choose to ask. Not everyone will read this book, so you could prove to be invaluable to someone else's success by checking in with and encouraging him or her to seek support.

Review what you wrote in Table 2.1. Focus on the higher numbers first and seek out assistance in addressing those issues. A general campus advisor or someone in the office of the dean of students can point you in the right direction. It's important to address any issues that are negatively affecting your experience early on so that

you can have a good first year, both academically and socially. List your top five issues and where you can seek support on your campus:

1.

2.

3.

4.

5.

"I was looking forward to going home because I was tired of school, tired of partying, and tired of people always interrupting me and dragging me out to do something."

"Spring finals are the worst! I have a really hard time getting psyched, again, for that last batch of exams and papers. And with the great weather, well, just forget it."

ISSUES UNIQUE TO TRANSFER STUDENTS   Transfer students can and do experience many of the issues previously listed, especially if they were living at home and have now moved away to attend the new institution. In addition, there are some issues that are unique to transfer students. These days, there are many types of **transfer students:** the traditional transfer, who starts at a two-year school and transfers to a four-year institution; the reverse transfer, who starts at a four-year institution and transfers to a two-year school; the lateral transfer, who transfers from one institution to another of the same type; and even the "swirling" transfer, who is enrolled in more than one institution simultaneously. For the purposes of this book, we will focus on the traditional transfer student because that is the most common type of transfer student found at research universities.

According to the American Association of Collegiate Registrars and Admissions Officers (2004), there are more than 1,200 two-year community colleges in the United States, and together they enroll approximately 10 million students each year (although not all of these students are working toward a degree). Almost half (46 percent) of first-time college students begin at a two-year college, compared to 26 percent at four-year institutions. Community colleges are typically more diverse, with students of color making up 48 percent of their student population. Community college students are typically older as well: 30 percent are between the ages of 22 and 29, and 27 percent are over 30. Many of these older students attend part-time while also working and having families.

Many students attend community colleges because these schools are much more affordable than universities. Tuition per term is approximately half that of four-year schools and students can complete many of their requirements while keeping costs down. In addition,

POINT OF INTEREST

ADVICE FOR TRANSFER STUDENTS The most important thing a transfer student can do is to take advantage of the services that are provided. Most transfer students could avoid problems by treating their new campus as a brand-new experience instead of approaching it with an attitude of "been there, done that." It is definitely worth your time to attend orientation, meet with advisors, and become quickly acclimated to your new university. Sure, some of it will be somewhat repetitive, but that is a small price to pay to ensure that you don't miss out on some crucial information.

If you find that your work did not transfer as you had planned, don't give up. Many institutions are not able to fully evaluate all the courses you took simply by looking at the course name and number on your transcript. If there is any doubt, the evaluator tends to deny credit first and leave it up to students to appeal. There are advisors who specialize in transfer issues, and they can help you sort things out. They can also help you with the appeal process if you feel that your previous work has not been adequately evaluated. Typically, the appeal process goes more smoothly when you can provide more detailed information, such as catalog descriptions, the actual syllabus from the course you took, and even the papers you wrote. You will want to provide as much information as you can to help the evaluators correctly assess your work.

Also, you need to become involved. It will be important for you to find a few social networks to join, though it might take a little effort to find ones that you connect with. Most universities have clubs and organizations that are affiliated with certain majors and careers, and there might even be a transfer student club. Join those right away. Also look for a way to meet students who share similar hobbies and interests because you won't want all of your social connections to be academically based. Take a swing dancing class, go on organized hikes or bike rides, attend film festivals—whatever it is that suits your interests.

Finally, if you are finding the transition particularly challenging, don't get discouraged. Even if you are experiencing the kind of problems that will delay graduation, remember that you will still be getting your degree from a research university, the most prestigious type of institution of higher learning in the country. But in the meantime, be sure to get support. The advisors who specialize in transfer students are aware of and sensitive to your experiences. You are paying for their services, so be sure to utilize them.

many students find that community colleges can be a gateway to a prestigious school to which they might not have been admitted after high school graduation.

Following is a summary of issues that first-year transfer students often face, especially when moving from a community college to a research university.

Academic Differences between Institutions

Transfer students have already proven themselves to be quite successful in the college environment; otherwise, their GPA would not be sufficient to support their admission to a research university. This often leads transfer students to feel overconfident in their abilities and, as a result, to not take advantage of the services provided to assist them in their transition, such as orientation and academic advising. The truth is that transfer students often struggle during their first term or two until they become accustomed to the new level of performance expected by the faculty and the faster pace (especially if they are moving from the semester to the quarter system). Even simple things such as where offices are located and procedures for filing forms can be new and confusing to the transfer student. This can cause a first-term transfer student not to perform as well as she or he had hoped. A poor performance in the first term can be quite disheartening to transfer students and might lead them to doubt either their abilities or their choice of university. See "Point of Interest: Advice for Transfer Students."

Transferability of Previous Work

Unless a student transferred within campuses of the same university system, his or her previous work will need to be evaluated and deemed transferable by the new institution. Some transfer students receive excellent academic advising, and all courses transfer as they expected. However, every year, thousands of college transfers are surprised to learn that certain courses did not transfer as expected. This can be quite frustrating and can affect the student's ability to graduate in two years. Students may have to utilize an appeal process to correct the situation. Vocational-prep courses that are commonly found at community colleges are rarely offered at research universities so transferability of these courses is very limited.

Transferability of GPA

Again, if the student is not transferring within the same system, it is probable that the previous GPA will not transfer to the new campus. While it will always be part of a student's overall academic record, the student might find that he or she is starting the first term with a 0.0 GPA. This puts pressure on a transfer student to do well the first term because an average to poor GPA can be difficult to raise in only two years.

Progress in Major

Depending on the situation, some students will find that they are on track for their major and can jump right into appropriate classes at the university and expect to complete the degree in two years. However, some universities admit transfer students on the basis of their academic performance and not necessarily their major. Every fall, many transfer students arrive at their new campus erroneously believing that all their previous work was approved by their new major department when that is not actually the case.

"I was really frustrated when I transferred. I applied as a psych major and had taken a lot of psych classes at my community college, where my advisor said I was in good shape. Once I got here, I found out that most of my classes didn't transfer because the major doesn't offer counseling psych, only experimental. I also only had 'premajor' status and had to get As in two courses before I could be admitted to the major. I will be here at least three years because of this mess."

Social Networks

Transfer students sometimes do not develop social networks at the new campus. This is usually attributed to two factors. First, some students feel that they are "only here two years" and so do not make much of an effort to meet students through the range of available venues. Second, the majority of the campus community has already been attending together since their freshman year, so many students have settled into well-established friendship networks. These networks might or might not be open to new members, a situation that can present a challenge to the newly arrived transfer student. More often than not, transfer students who leave a university do so for social rather than academic reasons. See "Scott's Story from the Path."

Nontraditional and Re-Entry Students

Nationally, the age of the average college student is 26 (NCES, 2010), but many students are older and have professional jobs as well as families. This reflects a large population of older students who are earning their degree or returning to complete a degree that was begun years ago. Although every research university has nontraditional/re-entry students in its freshman population, they are much more commonly transfer students. This group of students is usually older than the typical college student for that campus and might even be older than many of their instructors. In addition, they often continue to hold jobs and might have a spouse or partner to support and/or children to care for. These students have extraordinary responsibilities that they must manage while also competing with the traditional student population in their courses.

"It's definitely challenging being a parent and a student. When my daycare calls and says that my son is sick, I have to drop everything and go get him. Luckily, I have

SCOTT'S STORY FROM THE PATH
As I began my journey at my university as a new transfer student, I had no idea how much would happen during those two short years. It took me several years to get there (I transferred at 25), but once I did I was proud of the work I had done and I was happy that I didn't have very many requirements to finish. I started my first term thinking, "I just need these classes and I will finally be done with college!" Well, that is where the fun began; I had no idea that my university experience would be about much more than finishing my degree.

During my first quarter I applied to be resident assistant in the halls because a friend, who I met at a Week of Welcome social, encouraged me to apply. Before I knew it I was hired to be the RA for the Rainbow House. This was the first time I realized the leadership qualities I have and I really felt like I was making a difference in people's lives.

While my first year as a transfer student was going well, I also went through a pretty difficult breakup with my partner. It hit me really hard during winter quarter and I got Cs in all my classes, which hurt my GPA. Things weren't looking very good for a while but my friends and my campus therapist helped me get through it. At the same time I got connected with someone who worked in student affairs and she soon became my mentor. I was surprised to find someone who worked at the university who actually cared about me outside of the classroom.

In my second and final year, I really had a great time! I was RA again, this time for transfer students. I also got involved with a campus group called Men Against Rape, got hired to be an advisor with orientation staff, and co-led an introduction to the university course. I also did an independent research project with a faculty member.

While all of those exciting things were happening, I started to freak out about what I was going to do after I graduated. I started going to the career center and worked with a career counselor, Lily, who helped me apply to graduate school. My mentor and Lily were really instrumental in helping me decide what the next step would be for me, and I am now finishing my master's degree.

Looking back I know that I was lucky to have great experiences come to me, but I also know it took my effort to create the great relationships and experiences. I really encourage other transfer students to do the same and look beyond the classroom for opportunities and support.

found that the faculty and staff here are really supportive and I also connect with other student parents through the Re-Entry Student Services Center."

Veterans

Although veterans of the armed services have always been part of university campuses, their numbers are gradually increasing as a result of the U.S. wars in Iraq and Afghanistan since September 11, 2001, and the 2008 update to the GI Bill. While veterans can certainly attend universities as freshmen, most arrive as transfer students or return to campus after leaving to serve their country. They tend to be older than the general undergraduate population, usually in their late 20s. This group faces unique challenges as they transition to research universities. First, many find the academic culture of questioning authority to be counter to the military tradition in which they are steeped. Second, some suffer from post-traumatic stress syndrome and some have physical injuries, including brain trauma which is not visible to others. Third, many experience insensitive comments or questions from students and faculty alike. All of these issues combined mean that veterans need to seek out support to ensure their success. Many campuses have an office for veterans' affairs.

"My biggest frustration as a veteran on this campus is how my peers treat me. Whenever I share that I am a vet, the first question I get is, 'Did you kill anybody?' I mean, come on! Do you actually think that is a topic for casual conversation when I just met you? And did you consider that you are asking me to recall traumatic memories? I avoid socializing with the regular students. It's just easier to hang out with the vets."

HOW YOU'LL CHANGE IN COLLEGE

As the common themes above indicate, the college experience is rich with varied opportunities and challenges. Each student has a unique experience only known to him or her, but elements of it may be shared by a wide range of students who are also attending college for the first time. We now shift our attention to research done on college students that attempts to explain the ways in which students change or develop.

Theories of College Student Development

The experiences of college students have been researched for decades. Scholars have looked at a variety of issues, such as what benefits a college education brings, how and in what ways students develop and mature in college, which kinds of college experiences tend to be positive or negative, and what leads to a person dropping out or leaving college, to name a few. Many of the staff and administrators at your campus have gone to graduate school to learn more about these issues and may have completed a master's or doctoral degree in which they focused on higher education or student development, which is why they hold the positions that they do.

Several theories have emerged over the years that illuminate various aspects of the college experience. Each of them can contribute to your overall understanding of the experience you are having in college as well as help you appreciate the experiences of your peers. Four theories in particular are very useful in exploring the first-year experience: Chickering's Seven Vectors of College Student Development, Perry's Nine Positions of Cognitive Development, Tinto's Model of Institutional Departure, and Kohlberg's Six Stages of Moral Development. These four theories, in combination, provide a well-rounded understanding of the general college experience. As you read them, consider how they relate to your daily life at your university and how they might assist you in maximizing your success, both academically and socially. Note that a few more theories that focus on identity development are discussed in Chapter 7.

CHICKERING'S SEVEN VECTORS OF COLLEGE STUDENT DEVELOPMENT   Arthur Chickering researched college students at a variety of schools in the Northeast. He was interested in mapping a holistic view of all the ways in which students develop over the course of their college years. On the basis of this research, he proposed a theory that outlines seven different areas, or vectors (Chickering & Reisser, 1993). Although the theory is not linear, Chickering found that students develop simultaneously in the first four vectors and that sufficient development is needed in the fifth vector to be able to fully develop in the last two. See Figure 2.1.

Vector 1: Developing Competence

This vector focuses on developing skills or competence in three areas. The first is intellectual skills, such as critical thinking and writing and the repertoire of skills found in Bloom's Hierarchy. The second is interpersonal skills, which focus on a person's ability to get along with others, and include listening, cooperating, and communicating clearly as well as responding to the needs of others and helping a relationship grow. Finally, manual and physical skills are a measure of basic health and fitness and include athletic and artistic achievements as well as self-discipline.

Vector 2: Managing Emotions

Chickering argues that this vector first focuses on a student experiencing and being able to acknowledge his or her feelings. Once this has been accomplished, the student can look for ways to express (not suppress) those feelings in healthy ways. Chickering would argue that a student who is angry should not suppress that emotion but rather should explore what the anger is about and then find healthy and appropriate ways to express it, such as going for a run or talking to friends. This vector also focuses on becoming comfortable with a whole range of emotions, even those that cause some level of discomfort such as boredom or nervousness, and developing the ability to manage the impulse of wanting instant gratification, which directly relates to saying "no" to distracting temptations and choices such as alcohol and other drugs.

FIGURE 2.1 Timeline of Chickering's Seven Vectors of College Student Development

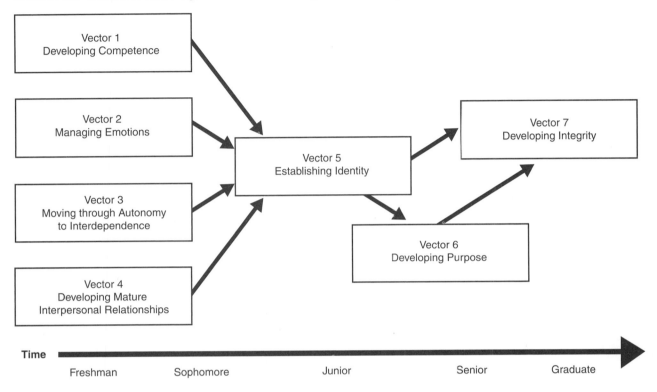

Vector 3: Moving through Autonomy to Interdependence

While students focus a lot on the independence and freedom of college, this vector is really about moving *through* that to another stage of interdependence, that is, realizing that your words and actions have an impact on those around you just as their words and actions have an impact on you. Chickering believes that this vector consists of two types of independence. There is both emotional independence, which is a freedom from the need for continual reassurance or approval, and instrumental independence, or the ability to solve problems in a self-directed way.

Vector 4: Developing Mature Interpersonal Relationships

This is a more advanced level than the interpersonal skills achieved in the first vector. There are two aspects here: (1) tolerance or acceptance of differences, and appreciation for those differences, which becomes relevant when interacting with those who are different from you (e.g., racially); and (2) capacity for intimacy in relationships, such as the extent to which you can trust or open up to others. Relationships become an interconnection between equals and therefore have more depth than previous relationships.

Vector 5: Establishing Identity

Chickering argues that one cannot truly succeed at Vector 5 (establishing identity) without significant development in Vectors 1 through 4. He also states that the last two vectors are dependent on success in Vector 5. This vector focuses on the person's self-concept and self-esteem with regard to several aspects of his or her identity. Development here reflects acceptance of and comfort with a variety of personal issues, including body and appearance; gender identity and sexual orientation; sense of self in social, historical, and cultural contexts (i.e., understanding the experiences of cultural groups, such as ethnic or religious, to which you belong); self-concept through roles and lifestyle; sense of self in light of feedback from valued others; overall self-esteem and ability to accept aspects of one's self; and overall personal stability. All of these require some amount of self-exploration and reflection and depend on the competencies that are developed in the first four vectors. This process takes time and some students have done more self-reflection prior to college than others. Some research actually indicates that establishing identity occurs in the mid-twenties.

Vector 6: Developing Purpose

This vector actually comes later in a person's development and can be achieved only after the identity has been appropriately established. Ironically, however, this is often the first priority for most students and their parents: the idea of choosing a major and a future career. Chickering states that developing purpose focuses on three areas: vocational or career plans (which stem from finding a passion), personal interests in terms of lifestyle, and future commitments for family and other significant relationships. Balancing these three might require compromises.

Vector 7: Developing Integrity

This last vector reflects the person's overall alignment with his or her values and subsequent behaviors. There are three stages, which occur in the following order: (1) humanizing values, or a shift from rigid beliefs to balancing one's own self-interest with the interests of others; (2) personalizing values, or being able to affirm personal values and beliefs while respecting others'; and (3) developing congruence, which means that values and behaviors match (i.e., "walking your talk").

It is important to realize that development in these vectors occurs over several years, and not only in the first year. Although all students are different, the general time frame shown in Figure 2.1 is applicable to most students. Freshmen would be working on the first four vectors during their first and second years at a research university; transfer students would most likely be addressing issues of identity during their first year. See "Point of Interest: Chickering and You." Note that Chickering's research has been criticized for not having a racially representative sample, and as a result, the vectors might not accurately map the development of all groups.

PERRY'S NINE POSITIONS OF COGNITIVE DEVELOPMENT William Perry (1970, 1981) explored a completely different side of college students: their **cognitive development.** Essentially, Perry researched in detail the intellectual competence development that Chickering identifies in Vector 1. Perry looked at how people learn and make sense out of information that is presented to them. Unlike Chickering's vectors, Perry's Nine Positions of Cognitive Development are linear, and you must complete one to move on to the next. Students start off wanting to believe that information is very concrete and that experts know the "truth." Perry identified how students move from that belief to one that acknowledges multiple perspectives as well as multiple truths. This requires students to shift, both in their beliefs about what "truth" is and in their perceptions of what experts know and can teach them. Each of Perry's nine positions has unique attributes, but for the purpose of this chapter, we will look at them in three clusters: dualism, relativism discovered, and commitment to relativism.

Dualism

This cluster contains the first three positions that Perry identified. At the beginning of this cluster, students see the world dualistically, meaning that everything can be sorted into dichotomous categories such as good/bad, right/wrong, and better/worse. Authorities are believed to know the "truth" and are always correct, so learning is about gaining the truth from the experts. A student might start this cluster thinking, "My professors know the truth, and I can learn the right answers." As students move through the first three positions, they begin to realize that the "right" answer is not always easy to determine because all authorities do not always agree with one another. At first, a student might discount an authority figure if that person does not seem to know the "right" answer. However, as students have more of these experiences, they begin to adjust their perception of what "truth" means and the role of

POINT OF INTEREST

➡️ **CHICKERING AND YOU** You can be attentive to your own development and actively focus on developing maximally in all areas. Understanding Chickering's model will help you to be more aware of how your college experiences are shaping your development, and you can even guide your own development. Your university will have resources, services, and opportunities aligned with each of the vectors. For example, if you know that you are not comfortable with your body image, one of the primary areas of Vector 5, you can focus some time and energy in that area. Resources and opportunities that might help you include personal counselors (to assist you in accepting your body), nutritionists (to help you make good choices amid a plethora of junk food), and activities such as intramural sports or the recreation center (to assist you in exercising and caring for your body in a healthy way). There are even specialists who can assist with eating disorders and other issues that plague both male and female college students.

I recommend that once a year, you read through Chickering's vectors and rate yourself on a scale of 1–10 (1 being "not at all" and 10 being "maximized") for how developed you feel in each of the vectors and subvectors. Don't worry if your numbers are lower in your first year or two—they are supposed to be. After doing the assessment, pick a few vectors to work on and seek the experiences and services that will help you do so. Each year, reassess yourself, set new goals, and seek out new opportunities. This process will guarantee that you will make the most of your college experience. It will also give you something concrete to use in your graduate school applications and job interviews in terms of reflecting on your college experience.

	1	2	3	4	5	6	7	8	9	10
Vector 1: Developing Competence • Intellectual competence/academic skills • Interpersonal skills • Making healthy choices										
Vector 2: Managing Emotions • Acknowledging emotions • Correctly identifying emotions • Expressing emotions in a healthy manner										
Vector 3: Autonomy to Interdependence • Emotional independence • Independence from need for approval										
Vector 4: Mature Interpersonal Relationships • Tolerance and acceptance of difference • Capacity for intimacy										
Vector 5: Establishing Identity • Body and appearance • Gender identity • Sexual orientation • Self in cultural contexts (race, religion) • Self-esteem and personal stability										
Vector 6: Developing Purpose • Selecting major • Choosing career • Personal interests and lifestyle plans										
Vector 7: Developing Integrity • Balancing self-interests with others' • Affirming own values while respecting others' • Values and behaviors consistently match										

authority figures. A student might complete this cluster thinking, "Experts know the 'truth,' but different experts might have different perspectives. I can learn the right answer for this particular situation."

Relativism Discovered

This cluster contains the next three positions, where a student makes sense out of increased complexity of information and responds by swinging away from dualism to the other extreme of total relativism, that is, thinking that everything is relative. Students believe that they might have to choose from several experts' opinions and that there is no one "truth" because there are so many variables. The student is now reluctant to evaluate concepts as right/wrong or correct/incorrect, and is in fact wary of authority figures who do, because that does not allow for relativism. Students in this cluster might think, "All knowledge is really contextual, so nobody really knows the 'truth,' and all possibilities are acceptable."

Commitment to Relativism

The final three positions of Perry's model see the student moving back from relativism to a middle ground that allows for commitment to certain views or beliefs as correct or true within a specific context. The student sees that people have to make choices based on what they know, or find new information that is relevant to the current situation. While the "truth" is essentially impossible to learn, a person can make choices based on what is right for him or her in this context while allowing others the right to have different views. In essence, evaluation of concepts as right/wrong or correct/incorrect becomes appropriate as long as it occurs with a certain context and is not indiscriminately applied as was done in the dichotomous phases. A student might think, "I know what my values are, and I think this is what is right for me. However, it is okay if someone else has different values and makes different choices."

Some research indicates that the majority of college students do not move out of the second cluster by graduation. And we certainly all know older adults who have not achieved the stages in the third cluster, so there is still a lot of individual variance with regard to these positions. Note that Perry did his research on male college students attending Ivy League universities, so his sample has been criticized for not being representative of women and people of color.

TINTO'S MODEL OF INSTITUTIONAL DEPARTURE   Many universities are worried about a concept called **retention,** which refers to the number of college students who are retained, that is, who continue their education at the same institution through to graduation. This is also known as **persistence.** Universities want to have high retention or persistence rates because they indicate that the school is doing a good job of meeting its students' needs. In fact, if you are reading this book in affiliation with some campus course or program for first-year students, it was most likely developed out of this national concern.

In the 1970s, Vincent Tinto began to research this issue and explored the things that affect a student's decision to stay in or leave college (in other words, to drop out). His research led to the development of a model that describes the factors that affect and influence a student's ultimate decision to depart. Tinto has revised this model over the years, and his current model (1993) is a longitudinal (i.e., over time) look at the influences of the student's background characteristics, intentions and commitments, external commitments, the external community, and institutional experiences involving persistence. See Figure 2.2.

According to Tinto, students arrive at an institution with a certain set of background characteristics, such as family background, skills and abilities, and previous education, in addition to their individual intentions, goals, and institutional commitments. Through a variety of campus experiences over time, both formal and informal, students can become integrated into the academic and social systems of the college. In addition, the student's external commitments and the external community, namely, family and friends, affect the student.

Most K–12 education is aligned with the dualism cluster—students are expected to learn the correct answers from their teachers. At research universities, the focus on the discovery of new knowledge and on thinking critically is more aligned with the last cluster. The college curriculum in general is designed to help students develop along Perry's positions. You will naturally become more relativistic over the course of your four years in college, but it can be a bit challenging at first. Most first-year students experience frustration in their classes because they have been used to thinking and studying in a dualistic way. This has earned them good grades in the past and is the system they know, so it is what many students cling to at the beginning of college. Freshman and sophomore students in particular expect the faculty to know the "right" answers and communicate them clearly so that the students can learn the information for exams. Your adjustment to university-level work will be smoother if you can accept that college will ask you to utilize new and different ways of thinking. Review your current syllabi and identify some lectures, readings, and assignments that indicate that relativistic thought is taught by the instructor and/or expected to be demonstrated by the student.

CLASS	EVIDENCE

There are many causes of withdrawal and/or dismissal from the college environment. First are individual characteristics, such as the student's skills and abilities, as well as the student's intentions (or goals) and commitments (or motivation/effort)—the goal of earning a college degree and the commitment to doing the work needed to accomplish this goal. This also relates to the desire the student has to attend and graduate from a particular institution. Second, the model focuses on the experiences a student has at an institution, as Tinto believes that they are the most important in terms of influencing a student's decision to stay or leave.

The academic system of the university environment consists of the student's academic performance and his or her interactions with faculty, whereas the social system is formed by cocurricular activities and the student's interactions with his or her peers. Tinto acknowledges that the systems are interconnected and can affect each other: Students might not feel equally comfortable in both systems, and the student's social life can undermine or support his or her academic experience, and vice versa. Full integration into both systems is not required for persistence, but students usually need to meet minimum academic criteria to stay enrolled, such as a minimum GPA or number of credits completed.

The model includes elements of external forces and communities. Forces outside of the campus, including family, home community, state and national organizations, natural disasters, and work commitments, play a role in the decisions of students who depart from college. When the demands from these external sources are greater than those of the academic and social systems, the student can be pulled away from college attendance.

The key of Tinto's model is a concept he coined **integration**, or a student's overall sense of belonging. Tinto found that students need to be sufficiently integrated into both the academic and social systems of the campus in order to stay. Most notably, Tinto's model focuses on the importance of the *student's perception* of his or her own integration, which largely affects

FIGURE 2.2 Tinto's Model of Institutional Departure (1993)

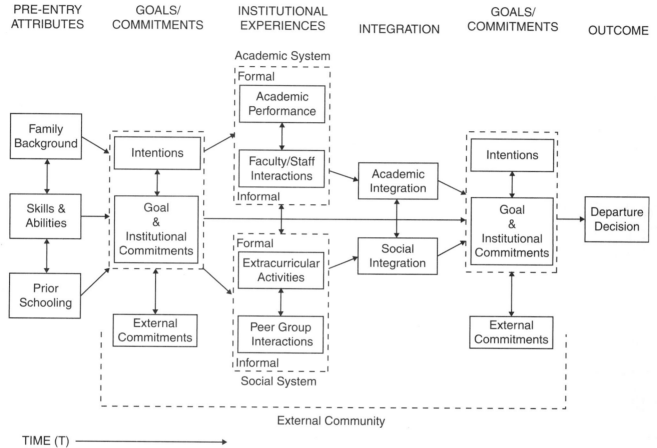

the student's decision to continue or leave. Any campus counselor can share accounts about students who appear to be popular yet feel isolated and alone and therefore are prime candidates for withdrawal. It is clear that only students' perceptions matter in the ultimate evaluation of their integration.

Tinto claims that there are four main categories of experiences that can hinder a student's integration: adjustment, difficulty, incongruence, and isolation. **Adjustment** refers to the time when the student is becoming familiar and comfortable with the new environment. Problems with adjustment usually arise from either the student's inability to separate from his or her previous community or the challenges imposed by the new and often tougher demands of the college environment (both academic and social). **Difficulty** refers to the academic standards of the institution and the student's ability to meet them. This is where students from poorer schools can find themselves unable to compete with their more privileged peers and unable to perform at satisfactory levels. **Incongruence** occurs when the student's needs and interests generally do not match those of the campus, because she or he either does not wish to be in college or is at the "wrong" institution for a variety of reasons, such as academic major, location, or other criteria of importance to the student. Finally, **isolation** refers to the lack of connections and interactions with other members of the campus community. Tinto states that when students are unable to become integrated into both the intellectual and social communities of the college environment, these students leave the institution.

As a result, Tinto states that programs and experiences that address these four categories of experiences can increase students' perceptions of both academic and social integration, and therefore are likely to increase student retention as well. Tinto's model has had a large impact on college campuses around North America. Many have taken his model to heart and intentionally attempt to affect students' integration process by providing programs, courses, counseling, and support so that students feel more integrated, both academically and socially. See "Point of Interest: Tinto and You." Note that a weakness of Tinto's model is that it weights academic and social integration equally. Although both are certainly important, research suggests that students' social experiences have more impact on their ultimate decision to stay or leave a university, as long as they have not been academically dismissed (Andreatta, 1998).

KOHLBERG'S SIX STAGES OF MORAL DEVELOPMENT Our final theory is about how people learn to make and support moral decisions, which relates to Chickering's seventh vector. You will find that as you move away from home, you will be faced with daily opportunities to make choices that have moral implications. These choices range from academic integrity to underage drinking, premarital sex, and treating others equally and respectfully. Moral development is a hallmark of the maturation process as young adults leave home, which is why this next theory is useful in exploring the college student experience.

Lawrence Kohlberg (1976) developed his theory by posing ethical dilemmas to his male subjects and then examining the criteria and justification they used for recommending a specific course of action. His research utilized the Heinz Dilemma, which is a story about Heinz, whose wife is dying from a rare form of cancer. A certain drug can save her, but the scientist who created it refuses to sell it at a price Heinz can afford, even though the scientist is making a substantial profit on it. A series of questions are posed about whether Heinz should steal the drug, and whether or not he should be punished if he does and is caught. After analyzing his subjects' answers, Kohlberg concluded that people have six stages of moral reasoning that are grouped into three levels. See Table 2.2.

Kohlberg found that this model is linear and that everyone goes through the stages in order without skipping one. However, he learned that a person only moves on to the next stage if she or he is faced with some kind of problem that cannot be adequately addressed by his or her current moral reasoning. If a challenge is not presented, a person can stay in a certain stage for many years, if not a lifetime. Also, people can only conceive of the next stage but not beyond because they do not have the perceptions or beliefs that would support considering more complex moral questions.

The first two stages comprise the **pre-conventional morality** level. Stage 1 is the punishment-obedience orientation. In this first stage, a person only sees something as morally wrong if there is a punishment attached to it. Further, actions are seen as more or less wrong based on the punishments associated with them. This person believes that everyone holds the same view and there is no room for multiple or different perspectives. A person decides to "do right" only out of fear of punishment. For example, a person in this stage would argue that Heinz should not steal the drug because it is against the law and he could go to prison.

Stage 2 is called the instrumental relativist orientation. There is recognition now that everyone might have different needs and that sometimes these needs are in conflict. In this stage, a person focuses on self-interests and only does what serves him or her the most. Rules are followed when they meet the person's needs or are considered fair or equal. If a person in this stage considers others, it is only in the form of equal exchange, that is, "I'll do something for you if you do something for me." In this stage, the Heinz Dilemma could be addressed by arguing either that Heinz should steal the drug because he would be happier if his wife lived, or that he should not steal the drug because he could suffer in prison.

TINTO AND YOU This model suggests that your feelings about college will fluctuate many times throughout the year and will depend on the kinds of experiences you are having academically and socially. If those experiences become more negative than positive, you might begin to feel that you don't belong or don't want to stay. Just knowing that there will be days that you love your campus and days that you don't can help you get through the more difficult ones.

It's also important to look at what, specifically, is contributing to the bad days so that you can address those issues and improve your own integration and persistence.

I suggest that you assess yourself in each area of Tinto's model so that you know which areas might need your attention. Take some time to consider the topics in the table below, and rate yourself in each area on a scale of 1 to 5, with 1 being "not at all" or "very poor," and 5 being "very much" or "very strong."

	1	2	3	4	5
Extent that your family background supports your university success					
Extent to which your prior schooling prepared you for success at your university					
Your overall academic skills and abilities like critical thinking, math, analytical writing, etc.					
The strength of your commitment to earning a college degree					
Your level of commitment to graduating from your current university					
The quality of your academic experiences at your university					
Your sense of integration or belonging to the academic system at your university					
The quality of your social experiences at your university					
Your sense of integration or belonging to the social system at your university					
The level of external commitments/communities that detract from your university experience					
The extent to which you want to leave this university					

When you identify an area that could be improved, actively work on it. You can contribute to your own success by working to increase your own integration. For example, academically, a student could visit office hours to interact with faculty, meet with an academic advisor, and use services that help increase study skills. Socially, a student could attend various campus events, join a campus club, and meet with a counselor. It's important to get help if you are struggling. There are many staff and faculty who are trained in student transition issues and can help you assess what's not working, help you develop a plan, and support you in achieving it. These folks are paid to help you, so take advantage of their assistance.

TABLE **2.2 KOHLBERG'S STAGES OF MORAL DEVELOPMENT**			
	STAGE AND ORIENTATION	WHAT IS RIGHT	REASONS FOR DOING RIGHT
Level One: Pre-Conventional Morality	1 Punishment-Obedience	Obeying rules and laws.	I do not want to be punished.
	2 Instrumental Relativist	Meeting own needs.	I have to worry about me and let others worry about themselves.
Level Two: Conventional Morality	3 Good Boy–Nice Girl	Meeting others' expectations of what is good and right.	I care about others and I want them to think highly of me.
	4 Law and Order	Obeying rules and laws. Contributing to society.	The good of society is more important than my own needs.
Level Three: Post-Conventional Morality	5 Social Contract	Honoring human rights. Laws should reflect the greatest good for the most people.	When in conflict, I will place human rights over laws.
	6 Universal Ethical Principle	Honoring universal human principles of justice, equality, and autonomy.	I only do what is just, and I will not abide by an unjust law.

The level of **conventional morality** includes Stages 3 and 4. Stage 3 is known as the good boy–nice girl orientation. This stage brings in the view of society and a person's desire to conform to social expectations. In other words, people like to be seen as "good" and "nice" by others. The focus shifts to examining the impact a choice will have on interpersonal relationships, and the concept of the Golden Rule (do unto others as you would have them do unto you) is illustrative of this focus. The Heinz Dilemma illustrates that there is more than one society norm to address; it could be argued that Heinz should save his wife because he is a "good" husband, and it could also be argued that Heinz should not steal the drug because he is not a "bad" person or a criminal.

Stage 4 is titled the law and order orientation. In this stage, society plays an even more central role in that laws, rules, and social norms are seen as crucial for creating a functioning society. Now, instead of considering interpersonal relationships, a person looks at contributing to the greater benefit of society as more important than individual needs. If a person goes against societal rules, then he or she should be accountable for his or her actions. As such, a person in this stage would argue either that Heinz should not steal the drug, since people cannot break laws just because they have needs, or that he should steal the drug but then accept the punishment for doing so and go to prison.

The final two stages make up the level of **post-conventional morality**, also known as the principled level. Stage 5, the social contract orientation, introduces the concept that society's rules should benefit the most people, and that rules and laws are a social contract entered into by people for the greatest good of the majority. If rules are no longer serving the majority of society, they should be changed. The belief in a democratic government is based in this stage and is responsive to the needs of the people. However, an individual's needs may still be in conflict with the greater good, and this stage allows for an individual to view his or her own needs before society's. Although this sounds similar to Stage 2, the difference is that the individual's needs in Stage 5 are seen as part of human rights and are justified in this light. The concept of the Platinum Rule fits here—do unto others as they would want done unto them. A person in this stage could argue either that Heinz should steal the medicine because the right to life is more important than the law, or that he should not steal the medicine because the scientist deserves to make a profit.

Finally, Stage 6 is known as the universal ethical principle orientation. This stage focuses on the overarching human rights principles upon which laws or rules are built. If there is a conflict between the principles and the laws, the principles take precedence. Universal ethical principles include justice, equality, and respect for individual autonomy. A person in this stage would make moral choices based on whether the action supported these ethical principles, rather than laws. In fact, a moral person would not abide an unjust law because it violates the more important principle of justice. As a result, at this stage one could argue that Heinz should steal the medicine because saving a human life is more important than financial gain. Alternatively, one could argue that Heinz should not steal the medicine because doing so might deny the medicine to others whose lives are equally as valuable as his wife's.

Interestingly, Kohlberg could not find people in his research who consistently operated from Stage 6, which suggests that few people actually achieve this level of moral reasoning. In addition, Kohlberg's work has been criticized for overemphasizing justice as a moral value when other values, such as caring, are significant as well. Further, Kohlberg's sample did not include women, begging the question of whether women's ways of making moral decisions differ from those of men.

RELATED MATERIALS

For Scenic Route websites, more Stories from the Path, glossary, and student activities, access the study tools for *Navigating the Research University* at www.cengagebrain.com.

REFERENCES

American Association of Collegiate Registrars and Admissions Officers. (2004). *The college transfer student in America: The forgotten student.* Washington, DC: Author.

Andreatta, B. J. (1998). *The effects of social and academic integration on the retention of first year university students: A quantitative and qualitative study.* (Doctoral dissertation, University of California at Santa Barbara, 1998). *Dissertation Abstracts International, 59(07),* 2375.

Andreatta, B. (2010, January 13). *The first-year student experience.* Lecture for Education 20, Introduction to the research university. University of California at Santa Barbara.

Benton, S. A., Robertson, J. M., Tseng, W., Newton, F. B., & Benton, S. L. (2003). Changes in counseling center client problems across 13 years. *Professional psychology: Research and practice, 34*(1), 66–72.

Carolan, C. (2002). *The ABCs of credit card finance: Essential facts for students.* Burlingame, CA: Center for Student Credit Card Education, Inc.

Chickering, A. W., & Reiser, L. (1993). *Education and identity.* San Francisco: Jossey-Bass.

Kohlberg, L. (1976). Moral stages and moralization: The cognitive-developmental approach. In T. Lickona (Ed.). *Moral development and behavior: Theory, research and social issues.* New York: Holt: Rinehart & Winston.

National Center for Education Statistics (NCES). (2010). *Digest of education statistics, 2005.* Retrieved from http://nces.ed.gov/programs/digest/d08/.

National Center for Education Statistics (NCES). (2010). *Fast facts*. Retrieved from http://nces.ed.gov/fastfacts/#.

Nellie Mae. (2010). *College students get wise about credit cards*. Retrieved from http://www.nelliemae.com/aboutus/collegestudentswise052505.html.

Perry, W. (1970). *Forms of intellectual and ethical development in the college years: A scheme*. New York: Holt: Rinehart & Winston.

Perry, W. (1981). Cognitive and ethical growth. In A. Chickering & Associates (Eds.). *The modern American college: Responding to the new realities of diverse students and a changing society*. San Francisco: Jossey-Bass.

Ruiz, S., Sharkness, J., Kelly, K., DeAngelo, L., & Pryor, J. (2010). *Findings from the 2009 administration of Your First College Year (YFCY): National aggregates*. Retrieved from http://www.heri.ucla.edu/publications-brp.php.

Tinto, V. (1993). *Leaving college: Rethinking the causes and cures of student attrition* (2nd ed.). Chicago: The University of Chicago Press.

University of California, Santa Barbara. (2010). *Responding to distressed students*. Retrieved from http://www.sa.ucsb.edu/distressedstudentsguide/index.aspx.

CHAPTER 3

Skills for Academic Success at the Research University

University of Maine

This chapter will focus on the skills you will need to be successful at a research university. A large part of your education in the first year will be developing these skill sets as you take courses. It's important to note that of the 26,758 first-year students who participated in the 2009 national *Your First College Year* (YFCY) study, only 20 percent felt that it was "very easy" to adjust to the academic demands of college (Ruiz, et al., 2010), indicating that the skills you may have mastered in your previous institution might not be at the standards needed for success at a research university. If you are a freshman, you will need to develop these skills as quickly as possible, as they are very different from the skills you used in high school. If you are a transfer student, you will need to increase and further polish skills you began to develop at your previous institution, including pace, intensity, and overall quality, to be competitive in the university environment.

You can support your own success by evaluating your abilities and seeking ways to improve. Visiting faculty in office hours can be very helpful, as can utilizing any study *skills services your university offers. Remember that this is an investment not only in your college success but one that will serve you in your professional pursuits as well.*

You will generally need six types of skills for academic success. Workload skills help you, a new university student, manage your workload effectively and efficiently. Study skills help you to perform successfully in your classes at a research university. Argument and analytical skills are utilized in most of your research university assignments. Communication skills include writing and public speaking, the forms in which you deliver much of your academic work. Information and technology skills support you in learning material and completing your assignments. Finally, research skills are specific to research in your field of study or major and will help you successfully complete your degree in that discipline. The first five types of skills are common to all students; the last type will vary depending on the discipline you choose to major in. See "Point of Interest: Shifting Your Attitude."

MANAGING YOUR WORKLOAD
Workload Management

Workload management skills are very important and need to be mastered as quickly as possible, as they directly support your success from your first classes all the way through to graduation. Although you might have been very successful at managing your workload in high school or at a community college, you will find that the sheer quantity of work will increase dramatically at a research university, as will the expectations for the quality of your performance. This means that a large part of your transition depends on how quickly you adjust.

Most likely, your campus has a department or program that offers workshops and training in many of the following workload skills. You will want to locate and utilize this program as soon as possible. These trainers will provide you with valuable tips and suggestions for how to master these skills as they relate to your specific university. Many students make the mistake of thinking, "I already know how to do that." Even if you do, you will still walk away from each workshop with at least a couple of valuable new tips that you can begin using immediately. It is actually the A and B students who use these services the most, because they are seeking that extra edge to keep them at the top of their performance.

Assignment Management

For each of your classes, your faculty members will provide you with a syllabus. A **syllabus** is an official document that outlines information you need for the course, such as required textbooks, schedule of lectures, due dates of assignments, and when faculty are available to you in office hours. By looking at the syllabus, you will be able to see how much reading should be completed before each lecture and when various assignments are due.

POINT OF INTEREST

SHIFTING YOUR ATTITUDE You might be tempted to think back on your previous successes in high school or community college and think, "I'm a great student." While it is true that you *were* a great student in that previous environment, it has yet to be determined how successful you will be at a research university. The bar has been raised, and students who approach their academic work with that in mind will adjust more quickly and successfully than those who continue to approach their academics as they did before. You will receive frequent feedback, in the form of exams and assignments, on how this transition is going for you. Be open to it and learn from it. For example, if you receive a C on your first paper, you will succeed sooner if you are open to what that feedback tells you about university-level writing, rather than saying things like, "But I have always earned As on my papers." Your faculty are here to help you adjust to this new environment, and many staff will assist you as well, but you must be willing to seek out and utilize this assistance.

Assignment management skills have to do with how well you are able to identify and complete the assignments by the date they are expected of you. This will require you to: (1) accurately record your assignments, (2) assess the amount of time and effort they will take to complete, (3) schedule your time appropriately, and (4) actually do the work. At the research university, some homework may not actually need to be turned in, but is still part of preparing you for an exam or other assignment. You need to ensure that you complete your work on time and seek help if you are confused. Unfortunately, most first-year students are not good at assignment management, which contributes to lowered grades. More than three-quarters of all first-year students (77 percent) who participated in the national Your First College Year (YFCY) study had frequently or occasionally turned in assignments that did not reflect their best work and 35 percent had turned in assignments late (Ruiz, et al., 2010). These kinds of mistakes are due to poor assignment management.

To facilitate your management process, compile all the reading and assignments for your classes in one location to see the actual workload for any one week. Once you see the overall picture, allocate time for each course so that you can finish all the expected work by Monday. If you fall behind, you simply make the next week harder. All of your time management decisions, such as when to socialize with friends or visit home for the weekend, should be made with completing your workload as your first priority. See "Callie Ann's Story from the Path."

Suppose you have two chapters to read for philosophy and two more for chemistry. That might not sound like much, and you might be tempted to think, "I can do that later this week—I have plenty of time," especially when more tempting activities are presented to you. However, if you were to see all of your assignments on one list, and you accounted for the fact that most students read 15–20 pages per hour on average, you would realize that those four chapters amount to more than just a few hours. Typically students are given 200–300 pages of reading a week, which translates to 13–15 hours of reading alone. The workload grid in Table 3.1 shows the actual workload for four typical university courses. You can see that there are chapters to be read, films to be viewed, and assignments to be completed each week. Papers and exams not only have their actual due date but time set aside for the steps working up to them. Use this table to record the workload for the next four weeks.

This process of assignment management is made more challenging because you will rarely be reminded that the work needs to be done; your instructors will simply expect you to do it. If you have questions, it is your responsibility to bring them up during class discussions or visit office hours. In addition, you might find that the reading is not reviewed during class time, so no one but you will really know if you actually completed your work. Because of this you may be tempted to blow off your work because there is no obvious or immediate

CALLIE ANN'S STORY FROM THE PATH

During my first term of college, I thought that I had "the college thing" figured out. If I go to class and follow the syllabus, I'll make an "A." Boy, was I wrong! While both of these things are very important, they only make up a small portion of what it takes to be a successful student.

What I didn't realize during the fall of my first year was how much more I would learn about myself. One of the first lessons I learned was the definition of "course load"—and that my course load was too heavy for me to handle in my first semester. Many of the classes I took required a lot of reading, and I found it extremely hard to keep up. Now, I have learned to balance my classes and choose one or two that require a lot of reading per term.

I also learned the most important lesson that tied everything together: effective time management. I learned so much about myself as a freshman, but I did not organize my time in a manner that allowed me to successfully apply this knowledge. I studied at different times every day and took care of personal things without any consistency. Between school, work, clubs, organizations, and spending time with friends, it is very hard to stay on top of things! After finding the discipline to keep to a consistent schedule each week, I found that everything started coming together. It was at this point that I began to realize what college really is about: learning about yourself.

TABLE **3.1** **WORKLOAD GRID**				
CLASS	WEEK 1	WEEK 2	WEEK 3	WEEK 4
Philosophy 4 (Intro to Ethics)	Chapters 1–2	Chapters 3 and 5	Chapters 7–8	Chapters 9–10 Midterm
Chemistry 1A (General Chemistry)	Chapters 1–2	Chapters 3–4	Chapters 5–6	Chapters 7–8 Midterm
Freshman Seminar 20 (Intro to the University)	Reader pp. 1–62 View film	Reader pp. 67–140 View film	Reader pp. 141–212 View film Midterm	Reader pp. 213–280 View film
Music 50 (World Music)	Book pp. xvi–71 Listen to CD	Book pp. 72–146 Listen to CD	Book pp.147–175 Listen to CD	Book pp. 176–228 6-page paper due
Weekly total	233 pages of reading = 15.5 hours 2 hours of film 1 hour of CD Start on paper	301 pages = 20 hours 2 hours of film 1 hour of CD Study for exam First draft of paper	255 pages = 17.5 hours 2 hours of film 1 hour of CD Study for exams Second draft of paper	302 pages = 20 hours 2 hours of film 1 hour of CD Study for exams Final draft of paper
Enter your weekly total here:				

accountability. Remember, however, that anything that is said during a lecture or read for the class is fair game on an exam, so it is entirely possible that you could be asked to read a book that is never mentioned in class and yet will represent a significant portion of your grade. All this is to say that you will have a lot of work to do, and you are expected to do it all with no supervision. Assignment management is a key to academic success. See "Point of Interest: Staying on Top of Homework."

Remember, there is probably a study skills program or department on your campus that can help you develop your assignment management skills. If you are having trouble managing the workload for a particular course, talk to your instructor about it and seek his or her advice. You will most likely receive some very useful strategies.

Time Management

Given the large amount of work you will be asked to do and the relatively little structure you will be provided for doing it, **time management** skills will become crucial to your success. Interestingly, nearly half (49 percent) of first-year students in the YFCY study felt that managing their time effectively was somewhat or very difficult (Ruiz, et al., 2010). The typical university student class schedule is very deceiving because it appears that you have a lot of free time every day. You might have a class at 9:00 A.M. and then not have another one until 2:00 P.M. One of the biggest differences between high school and college is that the students' workload shifts from in-class time to out-of-class time. This is also true for transfer students in that research university classes probably meet less frequently and also expect more work to be accomplished in a shorter period of time than at their previous institutions.

It is very common for first-year students to not put enough time into studying, which is why many experience a drop in their GPA. In fact, at my campus, our freshman class enters with a collective GPA of 3.8, and by the end of the first year, it has dropped to 2.8. According

POINT OF INTEREST

STAYING ON TOP OF HOMEWORK   Many students keep the syllabus for each class in a separate notebook and look at each one individually. This does not give the student an accurate picture of the amount of overall work in a week. I strongly recommend that you create a weekly list or grid in order to see the overall workload you have per week. On the basis of your own work pace, estimate the number of hours each assignment will take. This will give you a more accurate picture of what needs to be accomplished.

Let's take a typical student schedule as an example (see Table 3.1). This student is enrolled in four classes, all with fairly common reading loads of 50–70 pages per week. Three of the classes have midterm exams, and one has a 6-page paper—all of which will require some work in order to prepare. In addition, one class requires viewing a movie each week, and another requires listening to music. If the student were to just look at the list of assignments, she or he might feel that it's fairly manageable. However, if the student calculates the number of pages to be read and estimates an average reading pace of 15 pages per hour, it becomes clear that there is 15–20 hours per week in reading alone! Add to this the time to view the movie, take notes on the movie, listen

to the CD, take notes on the CD, review lecture notes, and study the material already read, and this student has a very full schedule.

Some of your assignments require quite a bit of preparation to complete. While the due date for the assignment will be on the syllabus, your instructors will rarely provide any structure for how and when to do the work required to complete it. For example, you might have a 10-page research paper due in the fifth week of the term. To successfully complete this paper, you will need to select a topic, conduct extensive research in the library, analyze the results of your research, organize your results into a coherent argument, create an outline, write the first draft of the paper, proofread it and make corrections, proofread the second draft, make some more corrections, and, finally, submit the paper to your instructor. This could be hard to do well in just a few days, let alone starting the night before. A successful student will identify all the steps needed to complete an assignment and then create a timeline for accomplishing each step in a way that will eventually meet the deadline. It would be realistic to start this assignment three to four weeks before it was due, which means that you need to start it the second week of the term.

THE SCENIC ROUTE

Visit www.cengagebrain.com to find the companion website containing links to:

- Downloadable schedule grids and assignment management sheets
- An online calculator to determine how you spend your time
- An assignment calculator to help you plan your projects

to Ruiz, et al. (2010), of the first-year students who participated in the YFCY study, nearly two-thirds of students admitted to spending less than 10 hours per week on studying or homework, which is directly related to the drop in GPA many first-year students experience. In reality, students should be spending about 2 hours outside of class for every hour in class. This includes reading, reviewing and organizing lecture notes, working on research papers, visiting faculty during office hours, doing homework problems, and studying for exams. Clearly, first-year students have a tendency to understudy, which is ultimately reflected in their grades.

In addition, a lot of this work is not necessarily appealing or fun, so your motivation to dig into that chemistry book might not be very strong. **Motivation**, or the ability to make yourself do work even when you are not in the mood, is by far the single most important skill for your college success. You will need to assess your workload, schedule it in your day and week, and then get it done. This is what managing your time means: You need to take advantage of that time after your 9:00 A.M. class ends and before your 2:00 P.M. class begins to get as much of your homework done as possible. In addition, you will need to be sure that you eat, exercise, sleep, and even play.

To fit everything in, you will need some method of scheduling your day. Most students find that a planner (either paper or electronic) is very useful. There are several "apps" that can work with your cell phone or other device. Once you write in the weekly commitments that have a set time (classes, meals, sleep, club meetings, etc.), you can then look at the open sections of your schedule and assign the various elements of that week's workload into those time periods. It is also important to be realistic. If it really takes you 2 hours to read a chapter, then don't schedule only one hour for it or you are setting yourself up for failure. See Figure 3.1 for a sample of what a completed **schedule grid** should look like.

Time management is something that takes time and practice to master. You will definitely want to take any workshops on this topic that are available to you, and you will

FIGURE 3.1 Sample Student Schedule Grid

TIME	MON	TUES	WED	THURS	FRI	SAT	SUN
8–9	Breakfast	Breakfast	Breakfast	Breakfast	Breakfast	Sleep in	Sleep in
9–10	Phil 4	Listen CD	Phil 4	Library: Music paper	Phil 4		
10–11	Study: Phil Chapt. 7–8	FS Disc.	Chem Chapt. 6	Library: Music paper	Music office hours	Brunch	Brunch
11–12	Study: Phil Chapt. 7–8	Lunch		Lunch		Music paper	Music paper
12–1	Lunch	Chem 1A	Lunch	Chem 1A	Lunch	Music paper	Music paper
1–2	FS p. 141–175	Chem 1A	Midterm prep	Chem 1A	Phil Disc.	Music paper	Music paper
2–3	FS 20	Chem Chapt. 5	FS 20 MIDTERM!	Paper outline	FS 20	Study for Phil midterm	
3–4	FS p. 175–212	Relax	Relax	Chem Lab		Study for Phil midterm	IM Soccer
4–5	Music 50	Study for FS midterm	Music 50	Chem Lab	Music 50	Study for Chem midterm	IM Soccer
5–6	Workout	Study for FS midterm	Workout	Chem Lab	Workout	Study for Chem midterm	Shower
6–7	Dinner	Dinner	Dinner	Dinner	Dinner	Dinner	Dinner
7–8	Relax	FS Movie	Music p. 147–175	Paper outline			Study for midterms
8–9	Chem Chapt. 5	FS Movie	Music p. 147–175	Watch TV	Socialize: Party at John's	Socialize: Girls' night at the movies	Study for midterms
9–10	Study for FS Midterm	Movie notes	Chem Chapt. 6	Watch TV	Socialize: Party at John's	Socialize: Girls' night at the movies	Music paper
10–11	Study for FS Midterm	Review lectures	Review lectures	Paper outline	Socialize: Party at John's	Socialize: Girls' night at the movies	Music paper
11–12	Sleep	Sleep	Sleep	Sleep			Sleep

USING SCHEDULE GRIDS Use schedule grids to see your schedule accurately and to make the best use of your time for both academic and social purposes. You can easily create a blank master schedule on the computer and then update it each term with your current classes and commitments. This schedule should include basic activities for living (e.g., eating, sleeping, and exercising), your classes, and times for socializing and relaxing. Once you have your overall schedule set up, print out a copy of your master schedule for *each* week of the term, noting exams and important due dates. Then using the workload list you already created for your classes, schedule your homework into the blank spots on your schedule. Remember to include the various steps that lead up to the completion of an assignment. Make this schedule realistic for you; if you are not a morning person, then don't plan to use those hours because you probably won't anyway.

Figure 3.1 shows an example of a schedule grid in which the student has efficiently scheduled her time. The student began with the fixed-time items (in gray) and then used the open times to schedule that week's workload that she has realistically estimated on the basis of her reading pace and abilities. This schedule represents the third week of the assignment workload in Table 3.1. The student also has realistically scheduled her social life for the weekends and time to just hang out and relax.

probably need to do so more than once. As your classes become more intense and you add things like an internship or job and involvement in a campus club, you will need to fine-tune your skills even more. You can also find good resources in your campus bookstore and on the Internet. In general, if you are attending a research university full-time, you should expect to spend approximately 40 hours per week in class or on course work. This is the equivalent of a full-time job! If you are spending less than that, you may find it challenging to do well in your classes. See "Point of Interest: Using Schedule Grids."

Assertive Communication

Assertive communication is directly related to time management, and it is about the ability to say "no." All the best-laid plans can go awry when your roommate says, "Let's go out for a movie." You will find yourself having to choose between the fun of a movie and the dreariness of working on the English paper that's due in two days. Needless to say, most people would choose the movie, and you certainly can. But if you choose the movie or the computer game or the party every night, you will soon find your GPA far lower than you'd like it to be.

It is important to have fun in college, and balancing a fun social life with a strong academic life should be one of your goals. Good time management allows a person to create a well-rounded life, but the truth is that most students find it difficult to say "no" to friends and family who tempt them with distracting activities when their work is not yet complete. As a result, first-year students say "yes" far too often, and their GPA eventually suffers. Juniors and seniors are not necessarily smarter than freshmen, but they have usually mastered time management and the ability to say "no" in a way that supports their academic success. Some typical distractions include chatting with roommates, hanging out with friends, playing on the computer (instant messaging, Facebook, surfing the web, etc.), talking/texting on the phone, watching TV or listening to music, going to campus events, and partying.

None of these is a problem in and of itself; the problem comes when an entire block of valuable study time is suddenly gone because one or more of these distractions successfully tempted the student. Although many students think, "Well, there's tomorrow," the likelihood is that the same distractions will arise tomorrow as well. It doesn't take too many nights like this before a student is dangerously behind in course work. Of the first-year students at 457 universities surveyed for the YFCY study, 76 percent said that they socialized with friends 5 or more hours per week. However, 68 percent also stated that their social life "frequently" or "occasionally" interfered with their schoolwork (Ruiz, et al., 2010). See "Point of Interest: Planning for Yes."

On rare occasions, first-year students study too much and do only course work without letting themselves have any fun. This is equally unbalanced and also leads to negative consequences.

POINT OF INTEREST

PLANNING FOR YES At the beginning of the week, look over your schedule grid and make sure that all the assignments are covered. Determine how much free time you have in your schedule, and schedule it in as well. Allot yourself a certain number of hours when you will relax, chat, watch TV, play computer games, and so on—in other words, the number of times you will say "yes" to something tempting during that specific week. When an opportunity arises, assess whether this is the time you want to use a "yes" or whether you want to save it for a more interesting activity. By approaching it this way, you will be making an *active* choice each time, rather than inadvertently giving away your important study time.

While these students might have great GPAs, they might not be developing important social skills that are also a product of a good university education. In this case, the student might need to say "no" to studying, again keeping the estimation of 40 hours per week in mind.

Reading Skills

MANAGING THE VOLUME Part of workload management is managing the volume of reading because there is so much of it to do. You will be given an immense amount of reading to do in your classes each week. In fact, it is not uncommon to cover the same amount of material in one term that it took an entire year to cover in high school or even community college. Each faculty member makes decisions about what material you need to be familiar with to understand the topics of that particular class. Faculty are generally not given any guidelines about how much reading to assign, so you may find a wide range of workloads. And this is usually not light reading either; at the research university, you will be asked to read complex theoretical and statistical material.

Expect to have 200–300 pages of reading to do per week. You might find yourself wading through material that is confusing or hard to understand, so it will probably take longer than if you were reading 500 pages of a novel for enjoyment. Remember, however, that you don't have to read something in one sitting. In fact, since the reading you do at a research university is often complex and features higher levels of analysis, you may find it easier to break a large reading into smaller portions, which will allow you process the information before you read more.

COMPREHENSION The next important reading skill is comprehension. It does no good to have completed your weekly reading if you really didn't understand it. You will need to buy a good dictionary and thesaurus or utilize the online versions, as you will often come across words you don't know. Look them up. You will also need to devise a method of identifying which part of the reading you understood and which part you have questions about. Your faculty will be able to assist you much better if you have specific questions rather than saying, "I didn't get it."

As a result, you should *actively* monitor your understanding as you read. You need to identify when you became confused so that you can focus on regaining clarity. Some different strategies to use include creating an outline of the reading or writing a half-page summary of the text that lists the main points. From this, you can generate study questions for yourself to test your own understanding. Also, circle terms or points you did not understand—that way you can easily find them when reviewing your reading in class or meeting with your instructor in office hours. See "Point of Interest: Tips for Reading."

HIGHLIGHTS AND MARGIN NOTES Many students find themselves highlighting or underlining almost everything in the chapter because they cannot figure out what they need to focus on. The purpose of **highlighting** or underlining is to identify the *most* important concepts so that you can focus on those during your exam review instead of rereading the entire text again. As a rule, it's best to read a chapter through once before you highlight anything. This allows you to assess the overall content of the chapter and see how the concepts are related. You want to avoid highlighting paragraphs of material; instead, focus on terms, phrases, and main points.

POINT OF INTEREST

TIPS FOR READING I strongly urge my students to first skim a chapter or article just to get the overall sense of the content, and then go back and do a more thorough read of the material, creating an outline of the chapter as they do so. Here, pay attention to the natural cues the author has given the reader about how concepts are related. The placement of headings, subheadings, lists, and emphasized terms are clues to the student that usually aid in the creation of an outline and other study materials.

I also encourage students to note questions they have as they read, which they later can bring up in discussion or office hours. I recommend that they use a highlighter only *after* the second reading, and even then only to highlight the terms and concepts that are presented in the chapter.

Finally, I suggest that students read the chapter one more time to move into a deeper level of really understanding the material and relating it to their prior readings and lectures. This is also where they can review their knowledge of the material to make sure they have considered it at all levels of Bloom's Hierarchy of Knowledge. Some questions to consider are:

- What are the author's main points?
- Is his/her argument well supported? What kinds of evidence are used?
- What do I agree with? What do I disagree with?
- Where does this author's work fall in the larger academic debate of this topic?
- How does this reading relate to the topics of this course? Other readings? Lectures?
- How does this reading relate to my life or the experiences of my family, community, etc.?

In addition, make notes in the margins. These **margin notes** should help you to identify the important concepts but in your own words. Margin notes can also serve to identify questions you have about the material. More important, margin notes are where you can assert *your* own views or responses to the author. Critiquing what you are reading is an important part of critical thinking, so you should actively engage with the material in this way.

When reading math and science texts, an additional skill is required. You will need to learn *how* and *when* to use certain formulas for solving problems. Most math and science texts are organized in a way that each chapter teaches you a new set of formulas related to various topics or concepts, and each chapter will have sample problems to help you practice (i.e., learn *how* to use them). However, your exams will cover the material from several chapters, thus requiring you to identify which formulas or processes each exam question requires you to use (i.e., you must know *when* to use them). While students may have understood each chapter and successfully completed the problem sets, they may not have learned how to identify what, specifically, in the wording of the problem indicates the use of one formula or process over another. Be sure that you read your math and science texts with this focus in mind, and if it is not clear, visit with faculty in office hours.

SEEING THE BIG PICTURE You can gain some insight into your faculty's expectations by examining the readings you have been assigned. As faculty members, we each choose readings for the courses we teach, and we design our own syllabus. The choices we make tell you a lot about us—what we believe is important to know, our values, and our biases. Even for an introductory course, we have hundreds of topics from which to choose. If you examine your syllabus and reading list for these bigger clues, you will have a good idea what we are hoping to impart to you over the term and which topics we believe to be the most important. This can guide you about how best to structure your study time or which topics are certain to be on the exam. Also, each reading is part of a larger academic debate on the topic—consider where the reading is located in time and what differentiates one author's perspective from another's.

Again, all of these skills can be learned, and you would be wise to seek out the study skills program on your campus, as they often offer workshops on reading strategies and text highlighting. Your instructor can also offer you some pointers. It is fine to bring in your book or reader and show your instructor how you are reading it and the kinds of notes you are taking to see whether she or he has some suggestions for improvement.

You will probably need to adjust your reading skills to gain the level of mastery that is expected on exams and other assignments at a research university. Ultimately, your first exams and papers will provide you with feedback about your skills. Both freshmen and transfer students alike find that they could have performed better on their first assignments. While this might be disappointing, it is important to look at what this feedback tells you about your reading skills. Go over your first assignments carefully for clues about how you can adjust your reading and other academic skills, and then create strategies to do so. Use the chart below to assess your studying and performance for your midterm assignments (exams and papers). Then adjust accordingly as you prepare for the second half of the term.

	COURSE 1	COURSE 2	COURSE 3	COURSE 4
How I Studied				
Grade I Earned				
What I Need to Change				

Taking Good Lecture Notes

Taking good lecture notes is a very important skill to develop because it will be the main tool you use to capture the material your instructors are teaching. While a few faculty lecture from the book, most do not, which means that the lectures are on material you cannot get from any other source. The sheer volume of information that can be conveyed in a typical lecture might surprise you; it is common to take 8 pages of notes from a 50-minute lecture. It is simply impossible to capture it all so you have to be strategic in how you listen to and take notes of your lectures.

In addition, you will find that some faculty have very organized lectures with outlines, visual aids, and so on. You will come to greatly appreciate these instructors, as they often help you organize their comments into structured blocks of related material. They might even indicate which points are the most important. Unfortunately, you will also need to be prepared for instructors who just talk for an hour without any visual aids at all. They might be energetic and animated or speak in the quintessential monotone, boring voice, and you will need to turn their monologue into meaningful notes from which you can study. The most important thing to remember is that you will be held accountable for all the material the instructor presents, whether or not your note-taking skills are sufficient. For this reason, you will want to utilize a range of strategies for creating accurate and complete sets of lecture notes.

One aspect of note taking is simply to write fast enough to keep up with your instructor. Most of us speak faster than you can write, so you will need to quickly develop a kind of shorthand with abbreviations and symbols. You can either develop your own or find more formal methods to adopt. Some common examples are:

important	!!! or ***	confusing	???
with	w/	without	w/o
compared with	c/w	especially	esp
example	eg	that is	ie
resulting in	→	as a result of	←

against or versus	vs	equals, same as	=
less than	<	more than	>
increase	^	similar to	~
change	▲	number	#
percent	%	and	& or +
at or about	@	page	p.
people	ppl	organizations	orgs

THE LARRY PROCESS The most important thing to know about note taking is that it is an *active* process, one in which you must participate. Most students make the mistake of thinking that they just need to copy down what the instructor is saying, or every word on the slide. But the best lecture notes are those that the student actively participated in constructing. One very useful technique is the **LARRY Process.**

+ **L = Listen.** You first need to actively listen to what your instructor is saying so that you can do the next step. This means focusing not only on the visual aids but also on his or her words and the accompanying body language. All of it together conveys much more meaning than one piece alone, so you want to look at the whole picture. Obviously, this means you should not be simultaneously texting your friend or listening to music.

+ **A = Assess.** Next, assess what is important and write down only those things that *best* capture the main points or concepts the instructor is conveying in the lecture. There is not enough time to write down everything and you want to get the big picture, adding in details as you have time. You don't want to capture the example but then miss the concept that the example illustrates. First, prioritize capturing the main points, major themes, and definitions. Then add more if there is time in class or afterward in the next steps.

+ **R = Review.** After class, review your notes within 24 hours because your memory will decrease with time. While the material is still fresh in your mind, make sure you can read and understand your notes. Fix any words or phrases that are hard to read and fill in any pieces that you can recall but did not have time to write down. This might be a good time to meet with another student in the class to utilize both sets of notes to create the most complete set possible.

+ **R = Reflect.** It is important to spend a few minutes looking over what you have written and reflecting on what it means. Consider how this material relates to the bigger picture of the course. Go back to your syllabus and see whether there are any clues about the topics you were supposed to learn in that lecture or themes that related to previous lectures. Your syllabus can sometimes serve as a master outline, thus placing this one lecture in context. What connections can you draw to the readings or assignments? Where does this fall in the ongoing academic debate? Finally, identify what you might be asked on an exam.

+ **Y = You.** You will learn the material best if you personalize it to yourself. Look over the notes one more time and add your own thoughts about the material. Can you relate any of it to a personal experience you have had, something you have learned in another class, or something you've seen on TV? Note any sections where you disagree with the material or are confused about the instructor's point. These become the source of questions you can ask in your next discussion section or during the instructor's office hours. Be sure you follow up on these questions sooner rather than later. You don't want to sit down to study for an exam to discover that your notes are filled with questions you meant to ask.

Several methods exist that you can use for taking and organizing your notes. Some students use recording devices to capture the lecture and then replay it later to fill in their notes. Other students take a laptop computer to class and essentially transcribe the lecture, going back later and organizing the material a bit better. Some students work in pairs, utilizing the theory that two sets of eyes and ears (and fast writing hands!) are better than one. These tools are all fine as long as you stay active in the process and don't just copy down information.

NOTE-TAKING METHODS You can take many different types of notes and use many different methods, but always do so in conjunction with the LARRY Process, as it is a system for creating detailed, thorough, and accurate notes. Instead of relying on one type of note taking for everything, find the method that best matches the course content, your learning style, and the how the instructor presents material. This may change course by course. Consider, for example, a history course where the instructor presents information in a chronological sequence from one perspective. The type of note-taking method that works in that situation is very different from the one that would work well in a course in which the instructor describes one event in history and then discusses that event from several different perspectives. Likewise, a course that focuses on comparing and contrasting different theories of communication would require very different notes than a science course that covers the cause-and-effect relationship of a chemical on gene mutation. Among the many different methods for taking notes, the following are some common ones.

Outline Method

Most students learn this method in high school, and so it is often the first-attempted method college students utilize for lecture notes. However, it is not the best method for certain classes or teaching styles, and students would be wise to learn other methods. The outline method is for organizing material into layers of main points and supporting ideas or evidence. Each layer or level denotes a subset of the previous idea. For example, here is an outline from a lecture on the field of positive psychology (Andreatta, 2010):

POSITIVE PSYCHOLOGY
I. History
  A. New field started in 1998
  B. Idea of Dr. Martin Seligman, President of APA, University of Pennsylvania
  C. Goal was to explore humans at their best and healthiest mental states
  D. Major contributors:
    1. Dr. Edward Diener, University of Illinois
      a. studied sources of happiness
    2. Dr. Daniel Kahneman, Princeton University
      a. created assessments for happiness research
    3. Dr. Sonja Lyubomirsky, University of California
      a. studied what boosts happiness
II. Happiness
  A. 3 components
    1. Pleasure = the good feeling
    2. Engagement = depth of involvement
    3. Meaning = serving a larger purpose
  B. 4 ways to increase happiness
    1. Expressing gratitude
      a. blessings activity
      b. gratitude journal
      c. gratitude visit
    2. Acts of kindness (5 per week, all in 1 day better)
    3. Use your strengths (see reflectivehappness.com)
    4. Forgiveness (see Stanford Forgiveness Project at learningtoforgive.com)
  C. Bliss—concept coined by Joseph Campbell, encouraged people to "follow your bliss"

Visit www.cengagebrain.com to find the companion website containing links to:

- Samples of various note-taking sheets
- An overview of major note-taking systems
- An overview of different types of, and uses for, concept maps

Parallel Method

This method is suited for classes where the instructor uses handouts of the lecture material, often in the form of PowerPoint slides. Instead of copying down what is on the visual aids, students can focus on what the instructor is saying and adding notes to the handout. The goal is to focus on the verbal and nonverbal information presented in lecture, capturing important details and examples, and noting any emphasis provided, thus augmenting the meaning of the handout material.

Cornell Method

Another method for taking college notes is the **Cornell Method,** created by Dr. Walter Pauk (Pauk & Owens, 2004) who taught at Cornell University. This method divides each sheet of paper into three sections before you begin writing: notes, questions, and comments. Figure 3.2 illustrates this method applied to a lecture on the history of affirmative action in college admissions (Andreatta, 2006).

The benefit of the Cornell Method is that each section can later be covered to serve as a study tool so you do not need to rewrite lecture notes onto note cards for review. During the lecture, take notes in the notes section, and soon after class, add in the details or fix unclear handwriting. Then write some summary notes in the comments section at the bottom of the page. This is where you indicate connections to other lectures and readings and maybe even summarize the material for yourself. Finally, you generate your own exam questions for the left column or questions section. When an exam is approaching, simply cover the notes and comments sections and test yourself by reading the questions you wrote.

Concept Map Method

The concept map method is best suited to classes where several concepts are related but not necessarily in a chronological way. This method is also very good for visual learners, as it helps to denote relationships. One strategy has you start at the center of your page with the central concept and from there you move out around the center creating spokes, if you will, off the main idea. Related items are clustered together and links are noted though lines. Figure 3.3 is an example of a concept map for a lecture on holistic education (Andreatta, 2006). Another strategy starts at the top of the page and creates a pyramid-like flow chart of relationships under the main idea.

It can be challenging to create a concept map while simultaneously jotting down the instructor's ideas, so many people use concept maps as a second step, taking the lecture notes and creating a concept map from which to review and study. This also allows for other materials, such as readings and assignments, to be incorporated where they are related in a meaningful way to the topic.

NOTE-TAKING SERVICES Some campuses have note-taking services that allow you to buy a subscription to a course and receive a set of lecture notes taken by another student in the course. These services should be used only to *augment* your own notes, not as a substitute for them. Too many students are tempted to skip class or not take their own notes, and this has direct and negative consequences on their success because writing down information is one of the first steps to learning it. To combat this problem, some faculty have been known to instruct the note taker to leave out a portion of the lecture to give an advantage on the next exam to the students who attended lectures and took their own notes.

STAYING FOCUSED Sometimes, college students find it difficult to stay focused, or even awake, during lectures. This is especially true if you do not find the material to be interesting or the instructor's lecture style isn't particularly exciting. Some students respond to this challenge by reading the campus newspaper, texting their friends, or dozing. This is not only rude to your instructor and fellow classmates, but also undermines your success.

FIGURE 3.2 Cornell Method Page

Questions Section	Notes Section
●	
	History of Affirmative Action
Who created affirm action?	Pres. Kennedy mentioned affirmative action but Johnson's '65 speech when he proclaimed it: "the next and more profound stage of the battle for civil rights." Started as access to work issue.
What is goal of affirm act?	Begin to correct 200 yrs of racism and discrimination.
What is Exec Order 11246? When created/edited?	Exec Order 11246 req'd federal contractors take "affirmative action" to ensure equal employment opportunities for minorities by Census. 1967 gender added.
	Affirmative Action in Colleges
Why did colleges get involved?	Since college ed related to job prep, univ. admins. got involved to "compensate" for probs in K-12 and biased SATs. Focused on:
What are 3 goals?	1) recruitment = get minorities to apply
	2) admission = get them in
What is the problem with	3) retention = keep them, graduation
affirm act in colleges?	Since no Exec Order, colleges devised own programs for aff act.
●	**Problem!! Vast array of strategies used to eval applicant's potential & admission. Some good with min. standards of excellence. Some bad with quotas. Led to law suits.
What are 3 imp Supreme Crt cases?	Supreme Court Cases
	Each case provides new info on if affirm action constitutional in general & value of specific process used in that case. Did they violate "Equal Protection Law"?
What are findings of Bakke vs. UCD?	1) Bakke vs. UC Davis Med ('78) = quotas bad, race must be "narrowly tailored", goal of diversity "compelling"
Findings of Gratz?	2) Gratz vs. Michigan ('03) = points bad, not "narrowly tailored"
Findings of Grutter?	3) Grutter vs. Michigan Law School('03) = min standard good, compelling case for diverse student body
What are similarities/ differences in 3 cases?	Supreme Court consistently says affirm act is needed but methods must be appropriate to avoid discrimination.

Comments Section

Pro= Goal of aff act to remedy past discrimination, by socially engineering integration. Equity for all ppl to have access to all levels of jobs/$$. Focus on society as a whole.

● Con = New type of discrimination, one person denied access for sake of a group. No control over how done in college admissions. Focus on good of individual.

For now, Supreme Crt consistently says race can be used as a compelling criteria FOR PURPOSE of remedying past discrim but call for "most exacting judicial scrutiny."

FIGURE 3.3 Concept Map

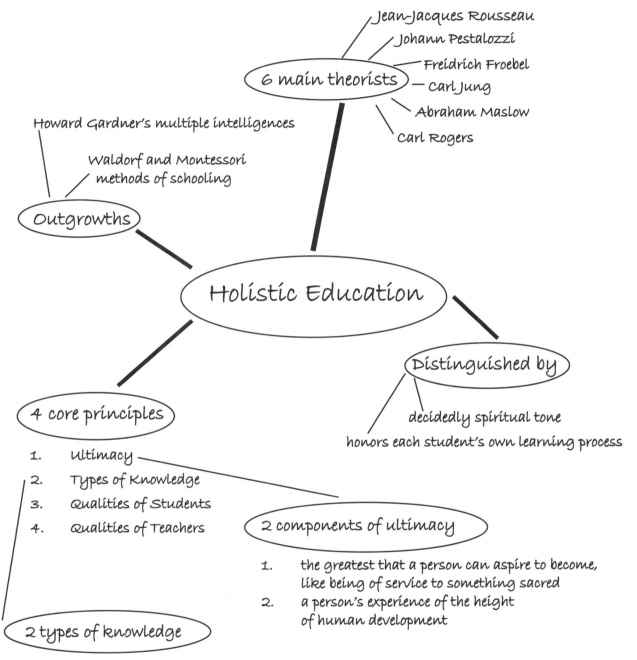

Make healthy choices that will allow you to be focused in class. Be sure you have gotten plenty of sleep the night before, sit near the front of the class, exercise before class, or drink coffee or tea. You might even divide your tuition by the number of hours you are in class to discover how much you are paying to hear that lecture—it's usually more expensive than you think. For example, a fairly modest university cost of $25,000 per year translates to $70 per lecture. It's also important to realize that many instructors do not tolerate distractions during their lectures; if you are talking, reading the paper, or sleeping, you might find yourself called out in front of the other students and perhaps even asked to leave.

IMPROVING YOUR STUDY SKILLS

The ability to study and study well is a skill. In fact, 37 percent of first-year students in the YFCY study felt that developing effective study skills was somewhat or very difficult (Ruiz, et al., 2010). Research university-level skills take time and practice, so plan to spend a good portion of your first year on this issue. Study skills are a set of processes a person uses to comprehend and master material. Often in college, studying is tied to preparing for a certain type of assignment, like an exam or a research paper. But that does not mean that studying should be "crammed" into a short period of time just prior to the exam. You will be the most successful if you use different processes and build your comprehension and mastery over the term, with additional focus occurring at exam time.

Your Study Style

Every person studies differently, and there is no one best way to study. Each person has a style of studying that works best for him or her. It is important to learn what helps you study in the most focused and efficient manner so that you can create it on demand. Take this study style assessment to learn about your study style. Write in your answers as you read the questions, focusing on what supports your best studying; complete honesty is required:

+ What time of day is your focus the best?
  Circle one: Morning   Afternoon   Evening
+ How many minutes can you go without a break and be able to consistently focus?

+ When you need a break, how many minutes or hours do you need before you can begin studying again and be focused?

+ How many times can you repeat this cycle of focused study and break until you need to stop?

+ What environment do you prefer for studying?
  Circle one: Sitting at a desk   Lounging on couch/chair   Laying on floor or bed
+ What kind of sound do you prefer?
  Circle one: Absolute silence   Some background noise   Active noise (like listening to music)
+ What materials do you need around you when you study? (Things to consider: colored markers, note cards, blank paper, food and beverages, dictionary, computer, and the like.)

All of these things make up your **study-style profile.** After you discover these things about yourself, you need to intentionally design a study environment that maximizes your style. For example, if you need silence to study effectively, then you should not study in a residence hall; the library is a better choice. If you are not sure where to find places that support your study needs, ask other students or staff like academic advisors or resident assistants.

It's also important to maximize your study habits with regard to length of time *you* can focus. If you study best in two cycles of 30 minutes with 15-minute breaks, then you need to put several of these 90-minute blocks throughout your schedule, and you should not study with a friend who can study for 3 hours. Likewise, some students study best in the morning while others are night owls. You will want to design your days accordingly. Be sure to plan your studying when it will be the most effective for you. For this reason, if you study with others, you will want to find students who share your study profile.

Finally, don't forget that the best study habits can be undermined if you don't utilize assertive communication. If you know that you focus best between 7:00 P.M. and 10:00 P.M., don't let your friends talk you into watching TV during that time. Or if you need silence and your roommate needs music, the two of you will need to find a solution that works for you both, for example, earphones and earplugs.

Another aspect of your studying that you will want to explore is your learning style. Every person has a different preferred mode for learning material. The best students know their learning styles and intentionally work with their strengths and weaknesses. See Chapter 5 for more information.

Grades at the University

Study skills are directly related to how you will demonstrate your mastery of material through exams, papers, and other assignments, and ultimately, the quality of your performance in your classes. Faculty use exams and other assignments to assess the overall quality of your work as it compares to that of the other students in the course (if the class is graded on a curve) or to a set standard of performance (if it is not graded on a curve). We also compare you to other students in your class level (e.g., freshmen or juniors). This allows us to confidently assign a letter grade to your performance as a measure of your mastery.

Remember that what is considered average or excellent at a research university is usually much higher than that which earned the same grades at a high school or community college. By the process of competitive admissions, all formerly excellent students have come together in the university classroom, so what used to earn an A is now on track for average, or a C, in this smart group of students. Don't let this simple truth dishearten you, but rather let it motivate you to study harder and differently than before. Most faculty use the following distinctions when assessing student performance:

- ✦ A = Excellent; highest quality with very little room for improvement; substantially better than what the majority of the students in the course or class level produce
- ✦ B = Good; good quality with some room for improvement; somewhat better than what the majority of the students in the course or class level produce
- ✦ C = Average/Fair; satisfactory quality with room for improvement; on par with what the majority of the students in the course or class level produce
- ✦ D = Poor; unsatisfactory quality with major room for improvement; below what the majority of the students in the course or class level produce
- ✦ F = Failing; does not meet the assignment or demonstrates little or no knowledge; far below what the majority of the students in the course or class level produce

Although you may have studied a long time for an exam or worked very hard on a paper, your performance will be measured by the product you produced, not by your effort. If you want to ensure that your performance is excellent, meet with your instructors in office hours to get advice and feedback.

Preparing for and Taking Exams

At research universities, exams are a primary way in which faculty assess the students' mastery of the material. It is our opportunity to test you to see whether you know the material well enough to have passed the subject—in other words, we can deem your performance good enough that you have satisfactorily completed a particular course.

Exams can come in many forms. There are **objective exams** that consist of questions with straightforward answers, usually demonstrating the knowledge or comprehension levels of Bloom's Hierarchy. These often include multiple-choice, true/false, matching, and term-identification questions, as well as mathematical or scientific problems that must be solved. Then there are **subjective exams** that are based on questions that involve the higher levels of Bloom's Hierarchy: application, analysis, evaluation, and synthesis. These usually require writing of some kind and so are most likely essay exams. An exam can also be a combination of these formats.

Each faculty member chooses how and when to assess students. Some faculty do not give exams at all; others give three midterms and a final. All of this will be outlined in your syllabus, including how much of your grade is accounted for by a specific exam. Find out whether the exam covers a certain set of material or whether it is **cumulative,** meaning that everything in the course up to the exam day could potentially be on the exam. Talking with your instructors and reading your syllabus carefully will give you very good clues that will aid you in your exam preparation.

TEST-TAKING STRATEGIES   There are several strategies that can be used to help improve your performance on different kinds of exams. One strategy you can utilize is to think like an instructor; in other words, imagine that you have to give an exam on the material and see what you would create for questions. Using Bloom's Hierarchy, create questions that test different levels of the hierarchy in different formats (true/false, multiple-choice, matching, term identifications, essays). Making exams is not rocket science, and you will probably identify many of the same questions your instructors do. These can serve as an excellent study guide for you. See "Point of Interest: How Faculty Make Tests."

Another test-taking strategy is to look at your textbooks to see whether they have sample problems or questions at the end of each chapter or at the end of the book. These can be good tools to use to test your knowledge and prepare yourself for the exam. Many textbooks, including this one, have online guides and resources with additional material to help students be successful. Utilize them—that will already set you apart from many students in the class. Visit www.cengagebrain.com to see the additional materials available for this text.

Guessing is a time-honored and successful strategy during an exam. Unless you are specifically instructed not to do so or will be penalized in some way, *always* guess on questions to which you don't know the answer. Never leave a question blank. There are strategies you can use to make informed guesses. First, if you don't know the answer to a question, go back through the exam and look for clues. Often, the answer for a term that you are asked to define in one question can be found in another. Second, on multiple-choice tests, eliminate any options you are confident are not the answer, thus increasing the odds of guessing the correct answer.

Third, if a question really confuses you but you know the general material, write notes of your thoughts in the margins and be sure to put your name on the exam. These notes should explain what you know and how you are interpreting the question. Later, when grading the exam, the instructor might see your notes and take them into account. In some cases, students are asked to mark their answers on a preprinted bubble form that is later scanned into an electronic grading machine. These forms usually don't have room for notes, so put your name on the exam question sheet and mark your comments there. Let your instructor know that you have done this and ask whether she or he would be willing to look at both.

On essay questions, always write something. These questions usually have several points assigned to them, and you can earn partial credit. If you remember anything at all about the topic, write down *all* that you know. If you don't remember the specific name or term, write down what you do know. For example, if you don't remember the name Bonnie Prince Charlie, you might still get points if you write "the Scottish prince who led the Jacobite uprising of

POINT OF INTEREST

HOW FACULTY MAKE TESTS   When I make an exam, I go back to my lectures and reading material, and look for material I can turn into fair questions. I look at the bigger themes, terms and definitions, broader concepts, and things that I made a point of emphasizing in my discussions with students. This list becomes the topics from which I will ask questions. Then I determine which types of questions I can make out of each topic. Things that appear in lists are perfect for multiple-choice questions, as are compare/contrast questions involving two related but very different concepts. Dates or titles are always good for matching questions, as are term identifications. Then there are the basic "describe" or "define" short-essay questions and the longer essay questions that are more complex and allow for greater analysis. It is very difficult to turn a simple term into an essay question, but it's easy to turn a description or analysis of a theory into one.

To ask a question, the creator of the exam needs to use language or phrasing that will let the test taker know what specific material is being tested. In other words, if I wanted to test you on Chickering's Seven Vectors of College Student Development, I would somehow have to identify that in the question. Whether I ask a simple true/false question or an elaborate question, I will have to give you the clue of the author and the title so you know that I am asking about Chickering's theory, and not Tinto's Model of Institutional Departure. In other words, every question on every exam you take will have some **identifying clues** (e.g., author, title, time period, scientific grouping) to let you know what material the question is about. If you studied by associating information with its identifying clues, then these clues will help you to easily recognize what the question is about. However, if you studied the material without really associating it with its identifiers, then the clues and the question might confuse you.

When you study, always focus on associating the information with its identifying clues. That way, when I ask, "Which of the following is not one of Chickering's Seven Vectors of College Student Development?" and I provide you with a list that is a mix of vectors from Chickering and concepts from Tinto's model, you know immediately which one is out of place. Otherwise, you might look at the list and recognize all the terms, and then get confused. Many students lose valuable points simply because the question clues confused them instead of helping them.

For the math, science, and engineering disciplines, you will be tested through exams that give you various problems to solve. These problems will cover all of the topics you have learned in class and can be in any order. They are designed to test your ability in three areas:

1. Whether you know what kind of problem you are being asked to solve (i.e., whether you can identify which formula or process, or combination of them, you should use to solve the question)
2. Whether you can correctly use the appropriate formula(s) or process(es)
3. Whether you arrive at the correct answer to the problem

Be sure that you learn what, specifically, indicates the type of problem it is, and what formula(s) or process(es) you need to use to solve it. If you are not sure, visit your instructor during office hours to find out before the exam date arrives.

1745." If you are drawing a complete blank, look at the question again and make up your own best answer just by taking a logical guess.

For math and science exams, where you are asked to solve problems, many of the strategies above still apply. An important strategy also occurs in the weekly studying for these courses, which is paying attention to *how* the wording of the problem gives you clues as to which formula you should use. If you do choose the wrong formula, the rest of your work on that problem doesn't matter. Another strategy that can be utilized once you are taking the exam is to look over the exam and try to identify which problems are looking for which formulas and assign them. More than likely, there is at least one problem for each major area you studied prior to that exam. Third, if you are not sure which formula to apply, but you have narrowed it down to two, do the problem both ways. That way, you might be given credit for the correct one, although this strategy only works if you have enough time to do both versions. Finally, take your time and check your work. If you rush and make a simple math error, you can cost yourself valuable points. If you have to leave a question blank, then at least be sure that all the other questions have been thoroughly checked for accuracy.

Don't forget that your instructors have weekly office hours to help you understand the material. It is better to seek assistance *before* the exam than to realize you are not really prepared once you sit down to take one.

THE SCENIC ROUTE

Visit www.cengagebrain.com to find the companion website containing links to:

- Useful study tools, including some specific to math and the sciences
- An overview of strategies for exam preparation and test taking
- An assessment and useful tips for dealing with test anxiety

Exam preparation is an essential study skill and is not just about memorizing the reading or lecture notes. One important step to take early in the term is to look over your syllabi and see how and when your performance will be assessed. How many exams will you have in one class?

How many exams do you have altogether in the term? What part of the grade does each exam represent? What format will they be (e.g., multiple choice or essay)? Take a moment to assess your exam requirements for this term and to design an appropriate study plan.

	CLASS 1	CLASS 2	CLASS 3	CLASS 4
Dates of exams				
% of grade				
Format				
Study plan				

Exams can be stressful and challenging for students because there is pressure to do your best and many points hang on one to three hours of work. Some students experience performance or **test anxiety.** If you study hard and are confident walking into the exam, but then find yourself freezing or blanking on the test, you might have test anxiety. There is usually a department on campus that can help you with this; they will help you to assess your test performance and give you very useful strategies for performing better in these situations. However, if you find that your overall performance is severely hindered by test anxiety, you might want to seek out majors that assess students by writing assignments instead of exams. You can also approach your faculty early in the term and request an alternate assessment format, but your condition would need to be well documented, and faculty are not obligated to accommodate you.

Study skills are connected to learning styles and the ability to set and achieve goals, which are covered in Chapters 5 and 9, respectively. It would be prudent to utilize the tips and strategies outlined in those chapters to help you realize your maximum potential.

Following Instructions

Surprisingly, following instructions is the skill that costs most first-year students more valuable points on assignments, both exams and papers, than anything else. Bright students who are doing A work can earn a D or F on an assignment because they simply didn't follow the instructions carefully. Your faculty will give you explicit instructions on assignments, and you can be assured that points are awarded or subtracted for each element of those instructions. It is in your best interest to read all instructions carefully and be sure you understand them. See "Michael's Story from the Path."

Errors regarding instructions occur in two ways: (1) The student either reads the question or assignment incorrectly, or (2) the student does not address a part of it, because she or he either forgot or did not think it was relevant. The first error can be addressed by simply slowing down. Especially on exams, take the time to read and reread the question and make sure that you really understand it. Many students glance at a question, see familiar terms, and say, "I know this one!" and quickly circle the answer that seems obvious, or they write down all that they remember about that topic. However, we are often asking you to take something that you learned in the class and apply it in new ways or to address the subtleties of that

MICHAEL'S STORY FROM THE PATH

Throughout my college experience, I have, for the most part, read the directions on every assignment. But when I don't I tend to fall into fatal traps. Like this one ...

One day, in my class, our professor handed out a quiz of essay questions. I looked at my so called "quiz" and read the directions. All they said was simply to put my name at the top right-hand corner of the paper and to read every question before beginning. Question number one ... I look up and see many people writing already. *These people are quick!* I go on. Question 5 ... I look up again to see a friend writing vigorously on an essay question. *I haven't even started yet!* Throughout all of this, I hear the professor laughing. I skim through the essay questions and land on the last question. It read, *"The purpose of this 'quiz' is to see how well you follow instructions. In order to pass this quiz, the only marks on this paper should be your name and date at the top of the front page. If you finish this quiz early please sit quietly in your chair."*

I looked up smiling and saw other students smiling back at me. This mutual understanding of knowing that we had just aced the quiz without any real effort gave us all a sense of pride. We giggled here and there until the other students finished writing, only to realize their mistake. Dropping their jaws in dismay, they looked up to see us smiling. "I was wondering why you guys were laughing," said one student who was slightly annoyed with his abused sense of work ethic. "Dude, not cool!" he said as he laughed with us.

The quiz didn't really count for a grade, but it was an indicator that when you don't read instructions, you can be terribly misled in the wrong direction. In this case those students who did not read the directions ended up having to think in excess and do more work. This makes me wonder, what if there was such a crucial direction on a real exam or assignment that the professor never emphasized? Imagine how many points you could lose from a simple mistake: the difference between an A and a D or F just for not following directions. But still, the activity was fun.

particular issue. Also, sometimes we add the word *not* to a question. For example, a question might ask, "Which of the following statements exemplifies the tenets of the Transformational Style of Leadership?" or it could ask, "Which of the following statements does *not* exemplify the tenets of the Transformational Style of Leadership?" The list of statements that follows either question will be very similar, so a student has to read the question accurately to be able to pick out the correct answer.

The second type of error has to do with lack of thoroughness; a student forgets to answer a part of a question or does not think it's necessary to do so, thereby automatically losing points attached to that particular piece. You would be surprised how many first-year students do this, especially in their first term or two. It seems that most students have to earn a few Cs and Ds that could easily have been As before they slow down and start getting much more careful about following instructions. However, you can avoid this by just being very careful from the beginning. See "Point of Interest: Checklist for Success."

When grading students' work, instructors can grade only what the students *actually* did on the assignment, not what they knew the students were capable of. On numerous occasions, faculty are disappointed when grading exams because we see the names of some of our best students on the exams that contain the most mistakes. Even though we know that they know the material, we absolutely have to grade what is in front of us.

Be sure to take your time and ask for guidance if you are confused. During an exam, never leave early. If you finish early, use the extra time to go back and carefully review your work. Double-check your answers and make sure that you addressed all parts of the questions. You would be surprised how many students pass over a question, plan to go back to it, and then leave without ever doing so. On written exams, you can always insert an asterisk or an arrow and then add additional information in the margins or on the back of the page. If you are not in an exam situation, you have even more assistance available to you because you can meet with your instructor ahead of time to make sure that you thoroughly understand the assignment. You can probably even show your instructor a partial and/or completed draft to make sure that you are on the right track.

CHECKLIST FOR SUCCESS The easiest way to make sure that you don't accidentally miss or forget part of an assignment is to create a checklist of things to do based on the instructions. Check them off as you do the assignment, and then review the list one last time once you are finished, just to be sure. This strategy can be used during exams as well as in writing papers, doing lab work, and creating art projects.

Here is an example of a real exam in American history, which consisted of an essay question worth 70 percent of the exam and then identification of two terms worth 30 percent of the exam. The instructions for the essay portion read as follows—I have added my own notes in parentheses where I see specific instructions for which the faculty probably assigned points:

Essay: Spend about five minutes underlining [because this is included in the instructions, there might be points assigned to it, so you should make a brief outline somewhere on the page] relevant material and arguments you will use, and then write an essay that takes a position [you will need to form a specific argument] supported by evidence [and justify your argument with specific material from class]. We will be looking for persuasive reasoning [how convincing your argument and evidence are] and accuracy [this is where the studying comes in—you'd better know your stuff] in the use of historical perspectives.

Here are two statements about eighteenth-century colonial America. Evaluate each one [you need to evaluate both historians equally], drawing on evidence from the textbook, lectures, and The Unredeemed Captive [you need to use all three, or you might lose points]. Which one do you find more persuasive and why? [This is the actual question you are answering—the rest of this information is the process your instructor wants you to use to do so.]

Historian A: "North American colonists had virtually nothing in common with each other prior to the Revolution. The only exception was their shared tendency to define themselves against outsiders, such as Indians, French Catholics, and slaves. This pattern of exclusion set the precedent of a national identity and helped them unite against Britain."

Historian B: "North American colonists had a great deal in common with each other prior to the Revolution. Religion, consumer culture, and political values united the colonies. Their exclusion of outsiders was simply a by-product of an already strong sense of American identity."

As a result of reading these instructions, you could make the following checklist (of course, accuracy would depend on whether you had done all of the reading and knew the material):

_____ Create outline

_____ Evaluate Historian A

_____ Use evidence for A from text, lecture, *The Unredeemed Captive* (use all 3)

_____ Evaluate Historian B

_____ Use evidence for B from text, lecture, *The Unredeemed Captive* (use all 3)

_____ State which historian I find more persuasive

_____ Give reasons why I find that historian more persuasive

_____ Proofread and correct errors and typos

By using this one strategy, you will significantly increase your chances of doing better in your classes because you will eliminate the little mistakes that can cost you valuable points. However, this strategy will not take the place of the reading and studying that you need to do to learn the material.

LEARNING ANALYTICAL ARGUMENT SKILLS

As the history exam example in the "Point of Interest: Checklist for Success" illustrates, students are asked to demonstrate their critical-thinking skills by engaging in assessment and analysis. Throughout your research university experience, you will be asked to learn material, and then engage the materials at various levels of Bloom's Hierarchy, with great emphasis placed on analysis and evaluation. Students are asked to demonstrate these skills on written exams, papers, and presentations. We will discuss writing skills in the next section, but first, students must learn how to form and construct an analytical argument. Each step of the process is also a place from which you can examine the validity or thoroughness of another's argument.

Forming the Argument

Related to the issue of critical thinking and Bloom's Hierarchy is the concept of forming an argument. Many of your assignments will require you to take a position of some kind on the material you learned and make a case, or argument, for that position. In fact, nearly half (48 percent) of the students in the YFCY study stated that they "frequently" had to support their opinions with a logical argument (Ruiz, et al., 2010). This is actually one of the most exciting parts of education—when you take the standard material and breathe life into it that is unique to you. Every student who took that American history midterm mentioned in the "Checklist for Success" could have had a very different answer as to which historian was more persuasive and why. And each of those answers or arguments could have been "right," as long as they were well thought out and supported with accurate evidence.

You will find argument formation to be the most common writing process you use in your experience at a research university. In fact, it is the same process that faculty utilize when writing up a research study or writing a book. They must form their own persuasive arguments and support them with accurate evidence. The ability to form and successfully support an analytical argument is a skill, and it is one that you can learn and improve with practice. In fact, it is one of the primary skills that we seek to train you in during the years of your university education, as it is so central to the process of research.

Creating an **analytical argument** requires several steps that involve analysis and assessment; hence the name. An analytical argument is essentially an argument or a position that has been arrived at through a logical and objective process; it is *not* an **opinion**. Opinions can be formed through a wide range of thoughts and experiences that do not necessarily include objective analysis. In other words, a person can hold an opinion for which he or she could not successfully create an analytical argument. The reason the process of creating an analytical argument is so crucial is because research is the search for "truth" on some level. Because humans have personal values, experiences, and worldviews, it is important that the process have logical objectivity to neutralize those subjective forces.

For students, there are many different formats in which they will be asked to create an analytical argument, from the essay exam question or the 10-page research paper to the oral presentation or lab report. Not only do faculty engage in this same process for their research publications, but so do professionals in corporations who utilize it for proposals and other business documents, as do journalists and writers. Regardless of the format, there is both a process by which an argument is created and a standard form in which it is presented.

THE FORMATION PROCESS The following steps for forming an analytical argument occur in this order, although the depth of analysis will depend on the assignment and allotted time. An exam question will require this same process but at a much quicker pace and therefore in less depth, whereas a research paper will include all of these steps in more depth. The following is tailored to academic work and utilizes critical-thinking skills at each step.

BACKGROUND RESEARCH AND ANALYSIS

1. Learning the information on that particular issue. This might require examining a wide range of sources.
2. Reviewing the information you have learned and assessing it through evaluation and analysis. The goal is to eliminate what is irrelevant or invalid while keeping the rest.

DEVELOPING THE ARGUMENT

3. Discovering what the information suggests, such as overall themes that become evident or looking for connections that exist between the material.
4. Forming several initial arguments, re-examining the information to see how well these ideas are supported by the existing data, and then eliminating arguments that cannot be supported or altering them to account for the discrepancies.

5. Narrowing the focus to the strongest argument and searching the information you have collected for the best and strongest pieces that support that argument.
6. Exploring which groupings of material and order of presentation make the most sense and are most compelling.

CREATING THE FINAL ARGUMENT

7. Writing the argument in some format, such as a report, a speech, or a paper (see the following section for more details).
8. Reviewing and editing the written argument several times to make it the most clear, persuasive, and supported argument possible. This stage might require altering and editing your original position in some way.
9. Presenting the argument to others in some format.

Presenting the Argument

The form in which an analytical argument is presented is focused primarily on walking the audience (i.e., the instructor grading the paper, the classmates hearing the presentation, the colleagues reviewing the study for publication, or the CEO reviewing the proposal) through the process by which the creator came to the conclusion that he or she did. Ideally, if you have formed a strong argument that is supported with accurate evidence, your audience will be convinced. The general form for academic work has several parts to it and a logical order.

INTRODUCTION AND THESIS (1–2 PARAGRAPHS)

1. Introduction—this introduces the reader to the general topic and why it is important.
2. **Thesis**—this is the overall argument you are trying to make; it is essentially the *endpoint* you arrived at as a result of your analysis, and it is what you hope to prove in your argument. A thesis can be more than one sentence, but in the case of university students, it should be a concise answer to the question by the assignment prompt or exam question.

BODY OF EVIDENCE (CAN BE SEVERAL PARAGRAPHS AND PAGES)

3. First assertion that supports your thesis—this is the first point you need your audience to see to get to the final argument; its placement as first is based solely on your assessment of its need to be so.
4. Evidence that supports or proves your first assertion—this is the evidence and information that supports that assertion (data, quotes, events, dates, facts, etc.), again presented in the order that is most clear and compelling.
5. Second assertion that supports your thesis—this is the second point you need your audience to see in order to get to the final argument; its placement as second is based solely on your assessment of its need to be so.
6. Evidence that supports or proves your second assertion—this is the evidence and information that supports that assertion (data, quotes, events, dates, facts, etc.), again presented in the order that is most clear and compelling.
7. Repeat this process until you have outlined all the evidence that led you to your argument—this could be several assertions and pages.

CONCLUSION (1–2 PARAGRAPHS)

8. Closing that connects all the assertions to come to the logical conclusion of the argument stated—this is where you tie all the pieces together for the audience, and it should parallel the original thesis but be in new words. The conclusion could not be written without the assertions and evidence in the body of the paper, so it very different from the introduction and thesis.

9. Resources used—this often takes the form of a bibliography or references page that lists all the sources of the information and evidence you used in your argument. You will be asked to provide these in a certain citation format (see the next section for more details).

In the case of student assignments, you are often given a specific question to answer, such as "Which historian do you find more persuasive and why?" The thesis is *the answer* to the question, for example, "This paper will show that Historian A was more persuasive because [fill in with the reasons you will be providing, in the order you will present them]." A thesis can be more than one sentence if it needs to be, but it needs to answer the question in the most clear and concise way. You'll notice that it is impossible to write a thesis before you have done all the relevant analysis steps. As a result, one strategy is to write the introduction and thesis paragraphs *after* you have written the paper.

COMMON MISTAKES   There are several common mistakes that people—students and faculty alike—make in the delivery of their final argument. Critical thinkers examine others' work for mistakes and also take measures to avoid mistakes in their own work.

1. Not allowing enough time to engage in thorough analysis or to produce a quality product. Each step takes time to complete, and the work should also be set aside and revisited to produce the best product.
2. The analysis is faulty. No matter how persuasive a writer you are, if you base an argument on inaccurate evidence or faulty logic, the argument is invalid.
3. The thesis is often not clear or specific enough to give the audience an accurate picture. The audience has to clearly see the final outcome to see how the rest of all the pieces support it.
4. The author doesn't make clear connections between the material presented and the argument or thesis being proved. You want to walk the audience through your argument and how you see the connections to be related. It is the author's words that tie the connections between the evidence and assertions back to the thesis. Students often write arguments in which the material is laid out but it's missing those important connecting sentences that tell the reader how it relates.
5. The order in which the reader is walked through the argument is confusing or unclear. There should be some sort of natural flow to the order of information presented that the reader can easily follow.
6. The conclusion is a repetition of the introduction and thesis and does not provide anything new. The old high school formula of "tell them what you are going to tell them, then tell them, then tell them what you told them" is not appropriate for college-level writing at a research university. Your conclusion should explain how your argument relates to the bigger picture of that issue or field.
7. The argument is poorly written or presented. The most wonderful argument can become completely unclear with poor sentence structure, incorrect grammar, and typographical errors—or, in the case of an oral presentation, poor delivery. A successfully presented analytical argument is 50 percent due to the analysis process the author used and 50 percent due to a clear and concise presentation.

HONING YOUR COMMUNICATION SKILLS

Over the course of your university experience, between essay exams, lab reports, papers, project proposals, and the like, you will write hundreds of pages of material and give several presentations. Faculty researchers are constantly writing journal articles, book chapters, and books, and the ability to write a lot and write well is essential to a successful research career, as is the ability to present results to others at conferences and in classes.

Writing Skills

As a result, the length and complexity of your writing assignments will grow with each year, and your skills are expected to grow as well. Because you have been admitted to a research university, it is likely that you did well in high school or at a community college, and you might be used to getting As on your papers. While you might have been a good writer compared to other students in your high school or community college classes, chances are that you are not a well-developed university writer … yet. Only 15 percent of first-year students who participated in the YFCY study indicated that their writing skills were in the "highest 10 percent" by the end of the first year (Ruiz, et al., 2010).

Writing well depends on successfully developing a series of related skills discussed in this chapter. The quality of any written project is directly connected to whether you understood what you were supposed to write, were able to break it down into the steps needed to complete the project, and then were able to devote the time and energy to complete the project by the deadline. Most students fail to master these items, thus greatly hindering their ability to produce an excellent finished product. Good writing takes a lot of careful planning, time, and revising. If you do not leave yourself enough time to write and rewrite at least a couple of drafts, you will greatly shortchange the writing process.

Remember, your faculty are engaged in this process daily, and it is not uncommon for us to work on a writing project for months before we consider it good enough to submit for publication. Faculty commonly write multiple drafts to hone and rehone their words. Because we go to these great lengths every day with our own writing, we expect you to devote a lot of time and energy to your writing as well. It's important to realize that this business of writing is vital to the field of research, and you will be expected to be as committed to good writing as we are, which means taking it seriously and devoting a lot of time to doing it well. See "Point of Interest: Starting Early Enough."

CLARITY Good writing greatly depends on your ability to say what you mean clearly and concisely. This has to do with word choice and sentence construction. Some of you might be well developed in this area, and some of you might need to really work on these skills early in your university career. This can be especially challenging if English is not your first language. You will want to construct sentences that say exactly what you are trying to convey and that are easy for the reader to understand. Remember, the reader sees only the words on the page—what you *actually* wrote—and not what you were trying to say. In addition, you will

POINT OF INTEREST

STARTING EARLY ENOUGH It is essential to leave enough time to do all the steps that are required to form an analytical argument and then to present it. First-year students are especially prone to waiting until the last minute to begin an assignment, and they simply run out of time to perform the process completely or well. Students often sit down at the computer the night before a paper is due and attempt to write the paper as they are typing it. Needless to say, this method usually produces both a weak argument and poor presentation.

If you begin the process early enough, you can utilize office hours to seek your instructor's assistance with the various stages of your analysis as well as your final product. Students can bring their faculty what is initially B or C work and, through a process of editing, reworking, and rewriting, bring that work up to an A level. Take advantage of this valuable assistance. Remember, however, that it is in your interest to bring your best effort to your instructor to review so that she or he can help you to take it to the next level of excellence.

POINT OF INTEREST →

WHAT EDITING LOOKS LIKE To give you an idea of how extensive the editing process can be, let me tell you about the chapter that you are now reading. When I originally wrote this chapter, I sketched my thoughts on the content and then wrote that material. I then read it and edited no fewer than eight drafts before I felt good about the quality of the content and the writing. Then this chapter was sent to several colleagues, who evaluated it in an anonymous review process. There were two rounds of reviewers, who provided feedback that I incorporated through three more revisions. Then it was sent to a professional copyeditor who gave me extensive feedback that I incorporated in the final draft. Next, it was laid out by a typesetter and went through another round of two drafts before it was ready to go to print. This chapter was revised approximately fifteen times and read by no fewer than ten people before it was fit to be published in the first edition. A similar process has occurred for this edition that you are reading. And after all that, I know that there are *still* typos to be found and sections that could be improved.

Now this is obviously a professional writing project, and a university student would not be expected to go to such lengths for a class paper. But I am sure you can appreciate that a faculty member might be frustrated at reading a paper that is obviously a student's first or second draft and is filled with awkward sentences, typos, and incomplete arguments. When we read that paper in a stack with thirty other papers, it's naturally going to seem of lesser quality when compared to papers written by students who edited three or four drafts before turning in their papers.

need to use correct grammar and spelling. You would be surprised how much your computer's automatic spelling and grammar check programs do *not* catch. Don't rely solely on these tools—you need to read and edit your own work several times. See "Point of Interest: What Editing Looks Like."

GENRES You may be asked to use a wide range of writing **genres** over the course of your undergraduate education. You may write scientific lab reports, fiction or poetry, film critiques, research papers, and essays about literature. It would be challenging to cover each of these genres in this text and do them justice, especially since each faculty member has personal preferences when teaching this material. Your introductory writing classes will help you learn about these genres and will provide you with opportunities to improve your mastery of them. Each course you take will provide you with guidance on how to write for that particular class or discipline.

ACADEMIC WRITING IN THE DISCIPLINES You will need to adopt an academic style of writing. **Academic writing** has a certain serious and objective tone to it—it definitely is *not* a written translation of how we talk. There is a formality to the language that is central to scholarly writing, again to create the seriousness and objectivity that are crucial in research. Academic writing is also usually, but not always, written in the third person. However, you will want to look at the specific requirements of each of your writing assignments to ascertain what that particular instructor wants from you.

Academic writing is very clear and concise. Some students attempt to make their writing seem more academic by using a lot of big words or complex phrasing. These techniques often hinder the reader's ability to follow the author's argument and actually decrease the quality of the writing instead of improving it. Avoid this temptation; instead, focus on strengthening the support of your argument and simplifying your phrasing.

Each discipline utilizes various types and styles of writing. As you take your courses, pay attention to the differences in writing you find in your assigned reading. This will give you important clues about writing for specific disciplines. As you select a major, you will become further trained in the writing traditions of that field.

IMPROVING YOUR WRITING It's good to assume that your writing is probably not yet up to the standards needed for high grades at a research university. In fact, nearly all (95 percent)

THE SCENIC ROUTE

Visit www.cengagebrain.com to find the companion website containing links to:

- An overview of each genre and excellent guides for each stage of the writing process
- Harvard University's guides for writing different kinds of papers
- University of Chicago's guide to college writing

of the 26,758 freshmen who participated in the YFCY study sought feedback on their academic work, and over half (51 percent) frequently revised their papers to improve their writing (Ruiz, et al., 2010). Here are several fairly simple ways to improve your academic writing:

1. Pay attention to the books and articles you read in your classes. Most of the articles will probably be from scholarly journals rather than popular media and will be written in the academic form. You will want to emulate this tone in your own writing.
2. Take advantage of the writing courses at your university. Many freshmen have been good writers in high school, but they have not yet learned the various forms of academic writing. Likewise, transfer students often discover that some community college writing is not in the form that is most often used at a research university. These classes will be very beneficial to your writing success in all of your courses, so approach them earnestly.
3. The academic skills department on your campus most likely has workshops or writing labs that are designed to help you develop and polish your academic writing skills. Take advantage of these as early and as often in your first year as possible.
4. There are many good books and reference guides on writing. Invest in one or two, and consult them often.
5. For a particular assignment, be sure you understand the instructions and have sufficient time to do the argument formation and writing process at a high level of quality.
6. Work with another student for the purpose of editing each other's work—this is called **peer review**. Do this only *after* you have worked out your basic argument; otherwise, you run the risk of creating similar arguments, which might appear to be cheating. To do this well, you must each put on your "editor hat," as you want to be as tough on each other as your instructor will be on you.
7. Read your writing out loud. When you read the paper silently to yourself, your brain fills in what you meant to write, not what you actually wrote. Reading out loud will help you hear those sections that are incomplete or awkward.
8. Visit your instructor in office hours to get feedback. Show your instructor a draft that is as close to final as possible. You don't want to waste your time with an instructor catching typos and awkward sentences when you could have done that yourself or with your student partner.
9. When an assignment is returned, review the comments right away. This way, you can learn how your writing was perceived, see any patterns you have (like confusing *that* with *which*, or how you use commas), and identify how you may have misunderstood parts of the assignment. This is especially important to do when you will have another assignment graded by the same instructor in the future.

CREDITING SOURCES   One of the most important features of academic writing is **citations** or references. Citations are used to give credit to any work (print, video, Internet, etc.) that was utilized in the writing of that argument and paper. Crediting another person's work is highly valued in the research environment, so it is done with utmost care and accuracy. It is quite common for researchers to read a journal article and see a reference for another book or article that they would like to utilize themselves. Citations make it easier for the reader to look up those same sources for their own purposes.

Citations or references also help to keep the research field honest, in that no one can claim another's work for his or her own. To use another's ideas or words without crediting them is **plagiarism,** which is one of the worst violations in the field of research. Academic dishonesty is taken very seriously in the world of academia, and students are held to the same standards. Be sure to cite all of your sources.

Each discipline standardizes its writing by adhering to policies and procedures that are set out in very detailed writing style manuals. These style manuals articulate everything from the size and placement of subheadings, to how many spaces should follow a colon, to the correct way to cite references. Each of the **style manuals** lays out a specific format for citing the author, year, and source where the resource was published, whether it be print, video, Internet, or lecture. The purpose for this is to standardize the writing process for researchers, since they submit work to publications from all over the world.

However, all the disciplines have not agreed on one style. For example, the American Psychological Association has created the *Publication Manual of the APA* (APA, 2009), which is the reference guide for many of the social sciences and humanities, as is *The Chicago Manual of Style* (University of Chicago Press, 2003). Many of the sciences use the Council of Biology's *Scientific Style and Format* (Huth, 1994). This text, as it is founded in the discipline of education, utilizes the *APA* style. Early in your university experience, before you select a major, you might find that each course you take requires you to utilize the style format for the discipline in which that course is found. This can be a bit confusing for students. Luckily, there are some very good reference guides that give overviews of each style's main rules you would need to use when writing papers. You will find these in your campus bookstore. A good one is *Hodges' Harbrace Handbook* by Glenn, Miller, Webb, Gray, and Hodges (2009). Once you select a major, you will want to purchase the appropriate guide as an investment in your advanced classes.

Faculty usually have clear ideas about what differentiates excellent student writing from good or poor writing. Each level exhibits certain qualities in terms of assignment completion, argument formation, and overall quality of writing. Some faculty even put these qualities into a document called a **grading rubric.** If your faculty make such a document available to you, definitely use it both in the creation and the editing of your paper. See Table 3.2 for a sample rubric from one of my classes. You can see that each major component of the paper has its own column with A–F grade distinctions. The instructor simply fills this out while reading the paper, subtracts points for certain violations, and then calculates the final score.

@myU SO HOW DOES THIS AFFECT YOU?

Your work, especially your writing, will be intensely checked for plagiarism. Your faculty know the articles and books they have assigned as well as the lectures they have given and the Internet sites on the topic. Believe me, they will know if you paraphrased or quoted something—and if it is not accompanied by a correct citation, you can and probably will be accused of plagiarism. In addition, we have access to the Internet too and most likely have seen any sites that you find. If you utilize a website in any way, it needs to be cited as well.

Finally, if you are tempted to "borrow" a paper from another student, even if he or she took the class several terms ago, don't be surprised if you get caught and accused of cheating. Some departments keep elaborate files of past work, and there are even computer programs that departments use to scan a paper and compare it to a huge database of previously submitted papers. This can also be done with papers purchased on the Internet. Remember that we are professional educators, and there is nothing you can do to "get by"

that we haven't already seen before and probably have a system for detecting.

The simple solution is to start your assignments early enough that you are not tempted to use these time- and effort-saving measures. If you find yourself behind and unprepared, it's better to earn a bad grade (which can be repeated and fixed) than to receive a bad conduct record and possibly a letter of expulsion. Visit your university's website to learn more about its rules and policies.

Penalty for cheating:

Penalty for plagiarism:

Name and location of judicial office:

TABLE 3.2 PAPER GRADING RUBRIC

ELEMENTS	QUALITY OF THESIS	QUALITY OF ANALYSIS	USE OF EXAMPLES	USE OF RELEVANT CONCEPTS	QUALITY OF CONCLUSION	QUALITY OF WRITING	SUBTRACTIONS
A 4.0	Thesis addresses academic and social integration of student and course concepts that explain them	Excellent; flows from student experience and all points are tied to relevant and provocative concepts	Excellent and in-depth descriptions; all are detailed and specific	Excellent knowledge of course materials; utilizes many (5+) of the most relevant course materials	Excellent and insightful discussion of what author learned about own academic and social integration	Excellent; no issues with flow, typos or grammatical errors, or paragraph length	−10 Per 24 hours Late
B 3.0	Thesis is either not clearly stated or not well written (still covers integrations and course concepts)	Good; flows from student experience and many points are tied to relevant and provocative concepts	Good descriptions; most are detailed and specific	Good knowledge of course materials; utilizes several (3–4) of the most relevant course materials	Good discussion of what author learned about own academic and social integration	Good; minor issues with flow, OR typos or grammatical errors, OR paragraph length	−1 Citation format −1 References −1 Interview attached −1 Cover page included −1 Over/under pages (check font & margins)
C 2.0	Thesis is neither clearly stated nor well written (may not cover integrations and course concepts)	Average; flows from student experience and some points are tied to relevant and provocative concepts	Average descriptions; some are detailed and specific	Fair knowledge of course materials; utilizes some (2) of the most relevant course materials	Discussion of what author learned about own academic or social integration	Fair; minor issues with flow, AND typos or grammatical errors, AND paragraph length	Grading _____ / 6 = ___ Subtotal _____ /100 _____ Minus
D 1.0	Thesis is not stated, but one is implied	Poor; does not flow from student experience and few points are tied to relevant and provocative concepts	Poor descriptions; few are detailed and specific	Poor knowledge of course materials; utilizes few (1) of the most relevant course materials	Discussion of what author learned about own integration (no academic or social distinction)	Poor; major issues with flow, typos or grammatical errors, and paragraph length	Total _____ /100 _____ Grade
F 0	No thesis is present	No analysis is present	No descriptions of relevant experiences provided	Minimal knowledge of course materials; none (0) of the most relevant course materials referenced	No conclusion present	Very poor; hard to read or understand; paper needs to be completely rewritten	

Grade Point Conversion * Graders will rank-order papers in this category, and assign paper grades within the range relative to performance.

4.0+ = A+ = 99–100	3.2 = B = 85	2.2 = C = 75	1.2 = D = 65
4.0 = A = 93–98*	3.1 = B = 84	2.1 = C = 74	1.1 = D = 64
3.9 = A− = 92	3.0 = B = 83	2.0 = C = 73	1.0 = D = 63
3.8 = A− = 91	2.9 = B− = 82	1.9 = C− = 72	0.9 = D− = 62
3.7 = A− = 90	2.8 = B− = 81	1.8 = C− = 71	0.8 = D− = 61
3.6 = B+ = 89	2.7 = B− = 80	1.7 = C− = 70	0.7 = D− = 60
3.5 = B+ = 88	2.6 = C+ = 79	1.6 = D+ = 69	0−0.6 = F = 0−59*
3.4 = B+ = 87	2.5 = C+ = 78	1.5 = D+ = 68	
3.3 = B+ = 86	2.4 = C+ = 77	1.4 = D+ = 67	
	2.3 = C+ = 76	1.3 = D+ = 66	

Public Speaking Skills

Public speaking is another form of communication that researchers use to disseminate to others the new knowledge they have discovered. Whether it is a presentation at a national convention, a keynote address at a government function, or a lecture to a group of students, faculty engage in public speaking all of the time. As a result, you will find yourself being asked to develop this skill as well. Many people are very nervous about speaking in front of groups, and you might even see this in your faculty. Even though public speaking can be scary, it is another skill that can be acquired and improved with time and practice. Most likely, you will engage in public speaking in the form of presentations to your class on a particular topic or assignment. Remember that you will still need to develop a strongly supported analytical argument that you essentially speak instead of write (or maybe both).

There are three main components of strong public speaking skills. The first is the presenter's knowledge of the material. No matter how polished your delivery is, if you do not know the material well, you will not be a convincing speaker. You must know and understand your material thoroughly before you can begin to hone your presentation skills.

The next aspect is the construction of your presentation, which is essentially your argument formation. What is your main premise? What is the data or evidence that supports your conclusion? What order makes the most sense for the audience to follow your argument and to be convinced by it? You will want to take the time to develop your argument and then construct it in a way that is compelling and convincing.

Third, public speaking is about the delivery of your argument. Obviously, your presentation can be enhanced through clear and illustrative visual aids. Whether you utilize posters, handouts, overheads, or a computer presentation, think about creating visual aids that will emphasize and clarify the main points of your presentation. Also, consider aspects of your verbal delivery such as the pitch and tone of your voice, the pace at which you speak, and any verbal markers you might use such as "like" or "okay." Make sure that you do not have any distracting gestures and that your body language matches the message of your presentation.

According to the national YCYF study, only 11 percent of students felt that their public speaking ability was in the "highest 10 percent" compared to their peers (Ruiz, et al., 2010). The best strategy for effective public speaking is practice. The more you practice in real time and out loud, the better and more polished your presentation becomes. Time and energy invested in developing your public speaking skills will serve not only your academic career but your professional one as well. Consider taking courses on public speaking or joining an organization like Toastmasters.

INFORMATION AND TECHNOLOGY SKILLS

Many of the academic skills that are listed in this section, as well as the research skills mentioned in the next section, rely on a solid base of information and technology skills. **Information skills** are those related to using various resources to seek information. These resources include your campus library, databases and reference guides, scholarly journals, the Internet, and a host of print, auditory, and digital media. You will find that a research **university library** is vastly different from any type you have visited before. It is dedicated to having a wide collection of the scholarly journals necessary for research as well as databases and books based on academic inquiry. You will not find any best-selling fiction novels or popular magazines. Many university libraries even boast special collections of things like music recordings, historical artifacts, or even personal libraries of famous scholars. Because the focus of so many of your assignments will require you to utilize the library, you will want to learn about its resources early in your first year. Your campus library will most likely have workshops and

THE SCENIC ROUTE

Visit www.cengagebrain.com to find the companion website containing links to:

- Toastmasters.org's overview of local chapters and useful tools
- Americanrhetoric.com's large video, audio, and print collection of famous speeches, debates, sermons, etc.
- University of Alabama's collection of resources for presentations

classes in information skills that are particular to the resources available to you. If not, utilize the library staff to guide you.

Technology skills, on the other hand, refer to your ability to use various technologies, such as computers, easily and efficiently. Most technology is computer-based and covers a range of both hardware and software options. Your campus will probably have a computing facility that offers workshops in computing skills. It would support your academic success to become competent in word processing, working with databases, using the Internet, and creating presentations. Also, many majors will require you to learn certain software packages, such as computer programming or statistical analysis, and will provide courses and labs for you to do so.

ESSENTIAL RESEARCH SKILLS

Research skills refer to the specific skills you need to conduct research within a specific discipline, and the knowledge for making the best choices for collecting and analyzing data. Each field of study has its own way of discovering and creating new knowledge. As you choose a major and take courses in that department, you will be taught the range of research methods that are most often used in your field of study. A research question can be approached in a variety of ways, and you will learn the strengths and weaknesses of each approach.

Quantitative and Qualitative Methods

One choice that researchers have is whether to explore a problem from a quantitative or qualitative perspective. **Quantitative** methods are best suited for existing data that can be numerically measured in a standardized way. This includes experiments and surveys where the data is analyzed statistically. These methods can provide information on whether the relationship between variables is causal or correlational. **Qualitative** methods are best suited for initial explorations, to get the big picture, or when the complexity of the variables needs to be kept intact. This can include participant observation and focus groups, and the data provides information on how the relationship between variables works. Both perspectives are important and can provide valuable information.

Research Methods

There are five main types of research methods:

1. **Experimental:** This involves very controlled conditions where the researcher carefully and intentionally manipulates one variable to determine the effect it has on a second variable, which is done to determine the existence and extent of cause-and-effect relationships. This method is utilized by the scientific disciplines. For example, a biologist might study how the use of one drug affects the growth of cancer cells. This method is quantitative.

2. **Correlation:** This method is also focused on determining relationships between variables, but variables are not manipulated by the researcher, so this method is nonexperimental. The focus here is looking at the direction of the relationship (i.e., which comes first) and the extent of the impact as one variable changes. For example, a sociologist might explore the incidence of hate crimes against different minority communities after significant events such as Pearl Harbor or 9/11. This method is quantitative.

3. **Observation:** This method is nonexperimental and is focused on description. The researcher observes and records a phenomenon or behavior in its natural setting, being mindful to make as little an impact as possible so as to not affect the data. This can be used for studying people and animals or physical events. For example, an anthropologist

THE SCENIC ROUTE

Visit www.cengagebrain.com to find the companion website containing links to:

- University of Washington's interactive online tutorial on research skills
- Socialresearchmethods.net's online tutorial on research skills
- Visionlearning.com's information on the scientific method

@myU   SO HOW DOES THIS AFFECT YOU?

A significant part of your university education will revolve around research skills and the scientific method. After all, that is at the core of the research mission of every research university. You will have to take several courses on these research methods and even utilize them in course projects to master them. Your courses will focus on various methods that are used to gather data (e.g., surveys, experiments, interviews, ethnography) as well as the ways to analyze data (e.g., statistical analysis or content analysis).

Although these courses might seem uninteresting or even very difficult, it is important to do as well as you can in them because much of your upper division and advanced major work will rely on these particular skills. If you have the opportunity to participate in a faculty research project or conduct your own independent research (an excellent opportunity if you hope to go on to graduate school), you will utilize these research skills on a daily basis. If you find that you enjoy the process of research, you might want to consider a career in academia.

To learn more, consult your university's catalog. Select three different majors and list the research methods classes offered and/or required.

DISCIPLINE 1	DISCIPLINE 2	DISCIPLINE 3

would live with a tribal culture and observe the members' rituals of expressing love and affection. This method is qualitative.

4. **Survey:** This is another nonexperimental study that is descriptive in nature. Behavior is studied via the self-reporting of the people answering the survey or questionnaire. For example, a psychologist might ask college students to report on their use of alcohol or their beliefs about spirituality, such as the Your First College Year survey referenced throughout this textbook. This method can be utilized both quantitatively and qualitatively.

5. **Case Study:** This is a descriptive and nonexperimental method. It utilizes existing data that was not recorded by the researcher, such as medical records, family history, or diaries (e.g., in the case of a historian studying the Holocaust). This method can also be utilized to study animals or a physical phenomenon like the impact that the 2010 earthquake had on the economy and population of Haiti or the environmental devastation caused by the BP oil spill in the Gulf of Mexico. This is a qualitative method.

RELATED MATERIALS

For Scenic Route websites, more Stories from the Path, glossary, and student activities, access the study tools for *Navigating the Research University* at www.cengagebrain.com.

REFERENCES

American Psychological Association (APA). (2009). *Publication manual of the American Psychological Association* (6th ed.). Washington, DC: Author.

Andreatta, B. (2006, February 11). *An overview of holistic education.* Lecture for Humanities 604, The nature of education. Pacifica Graduate Institute, Santa Barbara, CA.

Andreatta, B. (2007, October 19). *The history of affirmative action in college admissions.* Lecture for Sociology 102, University and society. University of California at Santa Barbara.

Andreatta, B. (2010, February 3). *Following your bliss: The science of happiness.* Lecture for Education 20, Introduction to the research university. University of California at Santa Barbara.

Glenn, C., Miller, R. K., Webb, S. S., Gray, L., & Hodges, J. C. (2009). *Hodges' Harbrace handbook* (17th ed.). Boston: Thomson Wadsworth.

Huth, E. J. (1994). *Scientific style and format: The Council of Biology manual for writers, editors, and publishers* (6th ed.). Cambridge, UK: Cambridge University Press.

Pauk, W., & Owens, R. (2004). *How to study in college* (8th ed.). Boston: Wadsworth Publishing.

Ruiz, S., Sharkness, J., Kelly, K., DeAngelo, L., & Pryor, J. (2010). *Findings from the 2009 administration of Your First College Year (YFCY): National aggregates.* Retrieved from http://www.heri.ucla.edu/publications-brp.php.

University of Chicago Press. (2003). *The Chicago manual of style: The essential guide for writers, editors, and publishers* (15th ed.). Chicago: Author.

Independence, Family, Values, and Campus Safety

© David L. Moore – Oahu / Alamy

University of Hawaii at Manoa

Going to college will have a significant impact on several aspects of your life. In addition to the academic learning one might expect, you will go through a host of other changes as well. Students have a myriad of new experiences daily that shape the way they view the world as well as how they mature physically, emotionally, and socially. These changes occur as a result of your newly gained independence combined with exposure to a wide range of people and experiences that might be different from ones you have encountered in the past. Moving away from home and the family environment in which you have lived has a significant impact on students and your transition to fully mature adults. This chapter will explore various aspects of student independence including the process of separation from the family, the student's value development as an adult, and campus safety, which is a primary concern of parents as their son or daughter moves away from home.

YOUR NEWFOUND INDEPENDENCE

Starting college brings every student new levels of freedom and independence. Part of this comes from laws and policies that treat students as adults, and part comes as students move away from their family homes to live on their own. This independence is an important part of your maturation process but also brings challenges.

In today's society, the term *family* can mean a lot of different things. Some students live with and were raised by their biological parents, while some lived in one or more families that included stepparents or other members of their biological family, such as uncles or grandparents. Some were raised by foster families or other caring people who were not related by blood. Some students might have left home at a young age and have been independent since their early teens, and some students might have children of their own. In this chapter, the term **family** refers to the person or people who physically raised you and/or had a significant impact on your development as a child.

Homesickness and Friendsickness

When you move away from home, you will experience both the excitement of newfound independence, and the loss of some of the comforts of home. New students experience many exciting adventures every day with classes, activities, parties, and just being on their own. At the same time, they often miss their family and friends as well as the comforts of home, such as their room, the family pet, home-cooked meals, and their favorite hangouts. It is the balance between the excitement of the new and the loss of the old that determines when homesickness sets in.

Homesickness occurs when the losses are more strongly felt than the excitement of the new. At some point, students begin to really miss certain elements of home and experience sadness and often tears. Homesickness is usually strongest during the first term, but the timing is unique to each student and is also tied to how far the student is away from home and how easy it is to visit. Some students find the excitement of independence quite thrilling, and the new adventures and the fun keep the thoughts of home at bay for several weeks or even months. Other students find themselves wishing for home the very first night at school.

Regardless of when it happens, almost all students deal with homesickness at some point during their first year. However, not every student experiences homesickness in the same way. Some students notice that they are missing some elements of home, but these are mostly just passing thoughts during their very busy schedules. Other students can become almost debilitated with feelings of great sadness, and find themselves feeling lost and alone and thinking more and more of leaving school and returning home. Most students experience a bit of both—fleeting thoughts one day and then great sadness another, the latter usually after a particularly bad day in which they did not feel as good about college for some reason or another.

Homesickness is generally related to how well a student feels he or she fits in at the campus, both academically and socially. Most university students came from environments in which they were quite successful; they were the smartest students and were very involved and held leadership positions. While they can be these things again, this is often not the case during their first term when they have yet to earn grades, join a club, or seek a leadership position. This can make high-achieving students feel a little lost and wish for a return to the "good old days" at home. Even if they are generally feeling successful, a bad grade on a midterm or an uncomfortable interaction with a roommate can make even the most independent students wish for some home comfort. See "Point of Interest: When Things Aren't Going Well."

Students can also experience something called **friendsickness.** When most students leave for college, they have a group of friends whom they have known for years, if not their entire lives. These are strong bonds that come from hundreds of interactions over time in which the friends have really gotten to know each other and understand each other on a deep level.

POINT OF INTEREST

WHEN THINGS AREN'T GOING WELL

All students have good and bad days. What's important to pay attention to is the ratio of these days. If the good days are in the majority, even by just a little bit, then you are doing fine. Time will increase that percentage, as each day will bring more familiarity with your campus and opportunities to make new friends and get involved. If the percentages are equal or the bad days outnumber the good ones, I recommend two things. First, assess what's not working. Take some time to write a list of all the things that don't work for you. It's important not to edit but just to vent all the things that you don't like. Write down everything—this list will become an important tool in changing your experience. Things to consider include:

◆ How are your classes?

◆ Do you feel as academically prepared as your peers?

◆ Do you like your instructors?

◆ Have you made friends?

◆ Do you like your room?

◆ Does your computer work well?

◆ Have you found a study area that works for you?

◆ Do you like the general tone and atmosphere of your campus?

◆ Do you like your fellow students?

◆ Are they people you can connect with?

◆ Do you enjoy the social scene, such as student parties and campus events?

◆ How is the weather?

◆ How are things with your family and friends back home?

◆ What activities do you miss the most?

◆ Do you like the activities the campus offers for student involvement?

◆ Are you involved in clubs or organizations?

Once you have written this list, make another. The next list will answer the question: "If I could wave a magic wand and make it all perfect, what would it look like?" Take this question seriously and really have fun with it. Let yourself fantasize; don't worry about whether what you are wishing for is feasible or not. What would you change in each of the areas that don't work? Would you need certain resources that you don't have now? Would you need specific people, or types of people, around you? Is there something comforting that would help you get through it? Keep focusing on what it would look like if it were *perfect*.

Now look at this list, and see which things you can actually accomplish. This is where you get realistic again and find out whether you can come up with some feasible solutions. You will probably see a few things right away that you can do to change your experience a bit. I recommend doing these as soon as you can. You will find that you feel more empowered because you have taken a step toward making your experience what you want it to be. Most often, these have to do with bringing home comforts to your campus environment. If you had favorite things in your room at home, have your family send them. If you used to run every day, find out where and when you can do that at your campus. If you really miss certain comfort foods, go out and buy them or ask your family to send you a care package. If you used to play with your cat every day, find out where there is a local animal shelter at which you can volunteer. There might be certain things that you cannot bring, but you will want to transplant as many of your important comforts as possible.

On your list, you will also see some areas that could be changed if you had the information or resources you needed to change them. For these items, I recommend making an appointment with an advisor or counselor who helps students with the adjustment to college. You might find these staff members affiliated with your first-year experience seminar or at the counseling center. You want someone who can help you with the bigger picture rather than just the specific area of academic advising. Show him or her your lists and share any insights you have gained from this exercise. Ask about the items you need information on; your counselor should be able to give you several recommendations or strategies that will help you.

You can use this process whenever you need to take stock of how things are going and what needs to change to make your experience better.

Friendships like this take time to forge, so most college students will not develop such deep friendships immediately at school. While you will find some interesting acquaintances, it will take time to learn enough about each other to make these friendships feel similar to the ones you left at home. As a result, many college students find themselves experiencing friendsickness— wishing for time with a certain friend who always knew just the right thing to say or wanting to hang out with the group of friends who always had fun together. This is normal, too; and again, patience will be useful in moving through friendsickness. It is also important to keep those old connections strong. Utilize e-mail, texting, snail mail, Facebook, and any other available forms of communication to reach out to those friends when you need to. Although a phone conversation is not the same as hanging out in person, it can be a good substitute when times are tough.

If you are like most students, you will have unspoken expectations about your holiday breaks that may or may not be realistic. This can be a source of frustration and even tension. One of the ways in which you can make holiday breaks more enjoyable is to encourage better communication among your family and friends about expectations. Consider discussing the following questions at the start of the break, as these are typical areas for miscommunication:

1. What expectations do you have about personal freedom and independence? You have a lot of independence at college and you'll probably expect this same level at home. But do your parents? Will there be a curfew? Are you expected to communicate about where you are going and why?

2. What expectations do you have about how house rules will be handled? Some things to consider are chores (laundry, cooking, etc.), who pays for what, and how people are to communicate about responsibilities.

3. What expectations do you have about your friends? Are you going to hang out and do the things you always did or something different? How might you talk about your university experience with your friends who are not attending college? For your friends who started college but still live at home, how might their experience be different from yours?

4. What expectations do you have about how much time the family will spend together? Are there certain days or events that are very important to either you or your family members? What freedom will there be for you to schedule time with friends, with other family members, at work, and so on?

5. Is your family planning a vacation? Are you expected to participate? What choices do you have about how you spend your time during the vacation?

By discussing each person's expectations, potential conflicts and similarities can be discovered and addressed. Some negotiation might be required, but it will increase the chances of a great holiday for everyone.

Returning home for the **holiday breaks** can be a challenging experience for students with regard to both homesickness and friendsickness. With homesickness, that visit can be just what you need to focus again at school, or it can make you miss home even more than before. Being away can make the things that used to annoy you (like your little brother) seem less annoying or even wonderful, and sometimes it can confirm that, yes, those things are annoying. And holiday breaks can be fraught with misunderstandings about whether house rules, like a curfew, still apply to you.

Some things take on such significance while students are gone that it is hard for reality to live up to their expectations, and this can lead to disappointment. Sadly, this is often true with regard to friendships. Many students find that even just one term away can change the bond between people who grew up together. This change can be even more drastic if the friends at home did not move away to go to college because then they are more likely to still be doing the "same old thing." If this happens to you, try not to be frustrated. It is actually an indication of how much you have changed while at college. You will still be able to maintain solid friendships with some of your friends, though others might not stand the test of time. Inevitably, you will find new friends that you will grow to love just as much.

The Family Educational Rights and Privacy Act (FERPA)

Another aspect of your independence that you will notice right away is that the university will expect you to be solely responsible for your actions from the first minute you get to campus.

While the university will certainly work with your family members, *you* are the primary client. The university sees you as a legal adult and will give you a lot of freedom and responsibility, which you are expected to handle maturely. While this transition may be a bit shocking, it is important for you to adapt as quickly as possible. The shift is so dramatic because all colleges and universities in the United States are held to a federal law that does not affect high schools.

This important federal law, called the **Family Educational Rights and Privacy Act (FERPA),** was passed in 1974. It states that the records of any currently enrolled student are private and cannot be discussed with, or released to, any person without the written permission of the student. The law was the result of many of the protests during the Vietnam War, when college-age students were being drafted to fight in the war. Many young adults felt that it was problematic that they were considered old enough to fight for their country, yet their grades were being sent home to their families. Many lawmakers and politicians agreed.

The passing of this law significantly changed the relationship between institutions of higher education, the students who enroll in them, and the families of those students. Before FERPA was passed, many institutions operated under a philosophy known as **in loco parentis,** which means "in place of the parent." This essentially meant that the staff and faculty at a university took on the role of parenting and watching out for the young adults, whose families had given over their care to the institution. Before passage of FERPA, institutions had many policies that facilitated *in loco parentis*, such as curfews in the residence halls, supervision in most areas of student life, and parental access to all student records, including grades, student health files, and counseling records. Essentially, the student was treated as if she or he was still a minor, and the university dealt with the family in much the same way as high schools do.

The passage of FERPA changed all this. It is important to understand FERPA because you and your family will be affected by it on a regular basis, sometimes to your liking and sometimes not. Essentially, all student records are considered private and the sole property of the student. This includes admissions files, grades, student health records, counseling notes, billing statements, attendance information, and conduct records. The institution cannot share or discuss any of these with another person, not even a parent, unless the student gives *written* permission that identifies the piece of information she or he wishes to be shared and with whom.

FERPA also protects the family's information from the student. For example, most universities require that the parents submit their tax returns and other financial records, especially if the student is applying for financial aid. The family's information is also considered private and cannot be shared with anyone, including the student, without written permission of the family members.

The positive side of this policy is that it gives you privacy and the ability to make your own choices without needing your family's approval or having to respond to their concerns. Many students find this very helpful, especially if they wish to pursue studies or activities of which their family might not approve. The negative side is that you are ultimately responsible for ensuring your own success. Because your family will not know that you are skipping class or did poorly on a midterm, they will not be able to motivate you or help you do better unless you tell them and request their assistance.

Be aware, however, that FERPA applies only to university records, not to public records, such as police records. Some universities are utilizing these public records and notifying the families of students who have been arrested for alcohol or drug offenses. The process is often called **parental notification** or something similar. You might want to find out whether your university has a similar process. Similarly, FERPA does not protect students from making their own lives public. Students can choose to share their own information with their parents, friends, or even strangers. See "Point of Interest: The Reality of Online Communities."

FERPA was created to acknowledge that a person who has gained admission to a college or university is treated as an adult (regardless of age) and capable of managing his or her university education. This new level of responsibility also brings a new level of freedom. Students can make choices and decisions about their university education and personal lives without seeking the permission or approval of their family.

THE REALITY OF ONLINE COMMUNITIES

Online communities such as Facebook and MySpace are very useful tools for networking and communicating especially among college students. As the movie *The Social Network* detailed, Facebook was created by two Harvard University students, Mark Zuckerberg and Eduardo Saverin, who changed the way we interact with each other. But it's important to remember that they are also *public* forums. The information posted on these websites is considered public information and can be seen by more than just college students including parents, faculty, potential employers, campus judicial officers, and the police.

Some universities, companies, and even law enforcement agencies are now reviewing students' online profiles to gain more information in order to ascertain personal qualities about them. Photos and postings have been used to determine a variety of things about students including:

♦ Whether a student has violated campus policies. Posted information, especially photos, has been used in conduct hearings to illustrate a student's behavior and attitude.

♦ If a graduating student should be granted an interview or even hired for a company. Posted information has been used to determine if the student exhibits the kinds of qualities the company wants in its employees.

♦ Whether a student has violated state or federal laws. Posted information has been used not only to provide evidence at court trials but also to determine sentencing based on whether the student appeared to be remorseful as illustrated by his or her postings following the incident.

Whether or not you think such practices are fair, it is important for you to know that they occur. Although privacy settings are useful and can help you protect much of your information, many departments have student employees who can be tasked with researching other students' profiles as a way around some of these privacy settings.

Consider what message you are sending about yourself with your profile, postings, and photos. What would others learn about your character and your values? The mistake that most Facebook users make is to think *only* of their friends when they are posting material. Consider that once you post something, you cannot control how it is used and by whom. In addition, be cautious about how much personal information you reveal online, such as your room number, phone number, and whereabouts at specific times of the day. There have been cases of criminals using this information to target students.

Further, online information is regularly archived, so once a piece of information or photo is deleted, it still can be accessed by others for years to come. When considering the long-term effects of your college choices on your future career goals and aspirations, also consider how important it is to be cautious in providing electronic documentation about those choices. Think about how many students post comments or photos about their drinking and drug use, or even sexual activities. Every election year, we see how a politician's past behavior can be used to discredit him or her, even when that behavior is from many years ago. With online communities, it is best to be conservative about what you share online and to consider what you would like others, who are not your friends or peers, to know about you. Learn about and use the privacy settings judiciously.

Finally, in addition to your Facebook or MySpace accounts, which can be more informal, also create a LinkedIn account. This is the professional version of social networking and you can begin building your professional image for your future career with this site.

This means that students are granted the same rights and responsibilities as any other adult in our society; in other words, they have the freedom to make choices every day about how to conduct their lives. Some choices (e.g., stealing a bicycle, drinking when underage) might be influenced by laws and various penalties that exist for breaking them, while other choices (e.g., not paying tuition or rent on time) might be influenced by other consequences that are undesirable (like fines or evictions). It is completely up to the adult to make an informed choice and to seek information or assistance if it is needed. There is no one who "forces" adults to make good choices or who tattles on them when they don't.

FERPA ensures that all college students, regardless of their wishes and ability, will be treated as adults who are capable of making appropriate choices. At most universities, this is accomplished as follows:

1. Universities give students information about relevant policies, procedures, rights, and responsibilities (usually in the form of official written guides such as college catalogs, student handbooks, and other material).

2. Universities expect students to read and understand the information they have been given, and students might be asked to sign a form stating that they have done so.

CHARLIE'S STORY FROM THE PATH
Back when I was a high school student, my mom was very involved in my life. She would often make it a point to know what was going on in both my personal and school life. She was easily able to accomplish this task due to some important circumstances. First, I saw her every day, and she and I could talk about the day's events (and sometimes she knew if I'd had a bad day or not by the expression on my face). Second, she was able to develop a close relationship with my teachers at my school, which was only a short drive from our house. My school frequently sent home information about important events that were happening, and my teachers communicated with my mom pretty openly.

In college, however, that arrangement does not exist. Due to FERPA, my university is not allowed to disclose information in my educational record (including my grades) without my consent. Even though the university has a parents' association that specifically caters to parents of its students, they do not give specific information about me or my professors to my mother. They do, however, help with general advice on being the parent of a college student.

This new arrangement changed my relationship with my mother. She still cares a lot about what's going on in my life, but she depends on me almost completely to tell her what's going on. She cannot just pick up the phone and call my professors to see how I'm doing in class. In a way, though, this has made our relationship stronger. My mom has made it a point to call me even more often to learn about what is going on with my school and private life. Although this new system has added a dimension to my relationship with my mom, I like that universities recognize that college students should be the ones responsible for keeping in touch with their parents. For me and my mom, it has helped us develop a more meaningful and trusting relationship.

3. Universities assume that students are capable of making their own choices about all aspects of their university life, such as fulfilling academic requirements, following policies and conduct codes, paying tuition, and adhering to local laws.
4. Universities provide students with many support services and people who can help them if they need assistance, such as advisors, programs, and counselors.
5. Universities assume that students will understand the consequences of their choices and take responsibility for their actions.

Each student is individually responsible for making choices that influence the success of his or her university experience, academically, socially, and personally.

This is a lot of responsibility, and many people question whether 18-year-olds are ready for it, especially those who have not been prepared in advance by their high schools and families. With the disappearance of the *in loco parentis* philosophy, universities began addressing this issue by creating a whole new range of student services designed to provide a safety net of support for new students as they gain competence with adult life skills. While universities cannot and do not force students to seek help, even if they are in trouble, students will find that they are surrounded by talented and experienced professional advisors and counselors who are there to help them succeed. However, students still need to seek out this support by going to the services and asking for help.

THE ROLE OF YOUR FAMILY It is important to remember that FERPA is a federal law that universities are mandated to follow. You would be surprised at how many times students and/or parents are rude to university personnel simply for following this law. Please remember that they have no choice but to do so. FERPA creates problems and inconveniences for staff and faculty as well. Sometimes, it would clearly be in the student's best interest to be able to work with his or her family, but the best the university can do is encourage the student to keep the family informed or to provide written permission so that the university can include them.

Many families are paying a majority of the bills for the student's education and feel that they should therefore have access to the student's information. Family members are especially interested in knowing their student's grades and whether or not the student is "in trouble." Although university staff can certainly appreciate this sentiment, it is not in accordance with federal law. The student will be informed of any relevant consequences, and it is up to him or her to share this with the family.

FERPA absolutely prohibits the release of any information about a student's academic work, including attendance, academic performance, and grades. This means that faculty are not in a position to discuss a student with his or her family. The fact that a student is attending a research university plays a role here as well. Research universities are often prestigious and hold students to a high academic standard. It is assumed that students are intelligent and able to manage the level and complexity of being an adult in a university environment. With that said, most faculty are frustrated, if not appalled, when a family member calls them to discuss their son or daughter unless it is an extreme situation. Students are expected to manage their own university experience and communicate privately with their families as they see fit. See "Charlie's Story from the Path."

In cases in which the student is incapacitated and unable to take care of business (e.g., if a student has a serious accident or illness), it is acceptable for a family member to call for the purpose of notifying the university and getting information about relevant policies and procedures for withdrawals or incomplete grades. But you would be surprised at the kinds of calls faculty members get from families. At one university, a mother called a history professor to inform him that her daughter who was enrolled in his class did not understand the paper assignment he had given and wanted him to explain it so that she could help her daughter. Needless to say, the professor told the mother that the student should come to his office hours and talk to him directly about the assignment. At another campus, a father called a math professor to say that he was worried that his son was missing his early morning math class. He wanted to know whether there was a service that could wake up the son and make sure he got to class. He also wanted the professor to call him and let him know if his son kept missing class.

Parents who struggle with letting go of their children and heeding the legal boundaries created by FERPA are called **helicopter parents** because they "hover" over their students' lives, prepared to swoop in to help their son or daughter whenever needed. Needless to say, this behavior is looked down upon by both faculty and staff at top research universities because these are institutions where the brightest minds convene to create new knowledge, and it is assumed that students are mature enough to handle their daily lives. Later in this chapter, we will discuss how you can help your family give you more independence.

Freedom and Consequences

When young adults move away from home, their level of independence increases. The implementation of FERPA increases students' independence even when they live at home because its regulations force students to take more responsibility for their education. However, students who live at home might not have as much personal independence if their family still pays their bills, wakes them up in the morning, does their laundry, cooks their meals, and reminds them to do their homework. Many research universities are designed to be venues for full-time education, and very few students attend on a part-time basis. As a result, most research universities are residential in nature, with many students living on or near the campus in housing that is separate from their family's home. This means that most university students are experiencing a new level of personal independence in addition to the responsibility and freedom provided by FERPA.

The inevitable problem arises because many college students, especially freshmen, do not have the experience or emotional maturity to handle this level of responsibility and freedom. This is especially true if they come from a home or high school environment in which parents,

Visit www.cengagebrain.com to find the companion website containing links to:
- Information on homesickness
- Information about FERPA
- Tips on dealing with your parents

teachers, and counselors took care of everything or were very involved in their student's choices. This can also be true for transfer students if they were living at home and have now moved out on their own. This new level of responsibility can represent a huge increase from what students previously experienced. Every day, students have the option to make choices with their academic, social, and personal lives. Some examples include the following:

+ Going to class ... or not
+ Seeking help on assignments ... or not
+ Being a considerate roommate ... or not
+ Drinking alcohol ... or not
+ Getting enough sleep ... or not
+ Paying bills on time ... or not

The downside to this responsibility and freedom is that some of these college responsibilities are not necessarily fun or interesting, so the temptation to avoid them might be strong, especially if more pleasant options are available.

The university sees you as an adult and trusts you to make the right choices. A university education is a choice in our society—it is not required, as is most of K–12 education—so the university does not play any role in making students complete their responsibilities. The only role the university can, and does, play is to enact **sanctions** when policies are violated. For example, students need to maintain a certain level of academic performance and adhere to certain codes of conduct in order to remain enrolled. If a student chooses to not fulfill either of these, the university doesn't force compliance but rather terminates enrollment.

This does not mean that there is no one to help you. In fact, more caring, professional staff and faculty will surround you than you have probably ever experienced before. The difference is that they will be waiting for you to initiate contact if you need it. You might never get a call from an academic advisor, but the minute you choose to walk into the advising center, help will be enthusiastically provided.

The same is true for social and personal issues. For example, students can find alcohol in most college environments, regardless of their age, and have the option to choose when to drink, how much to drink, and with whom. A student could choose to party in a way that impedes his or her academic success or even physical health. Again, no one is going to stop the student from making these choices, but someone might step in to impose sanctions for policy violations, such as a citation for a minor in possession of alcohol or an eviction from a living environment, such as a residence hall, in which alcohol is not allowed. You will find that ample information is provided on campuses about laws and policies as they relate to alcohol as well as social events and activities that do not include alcohol. You are trusted to choose and face the consequences of your choice. See "Point of Interest: Ask for Help!"

POINT OF INTEREST

ASK FOR HELP! The staff and faculty are there to help you, and there is no penalty for asking for assistance. There is nothing you are going through, no matter how dramatic it seems to you, that they have not seen before. In addition, your records are private, so no one will have to know that you asked for support. Too many students suffer unnecessary consequences because they never said anything to anyone about a problem. The whole purpose of these support services, and the people who staff them, is to provide a bridge between the level of responsibility FERPA has given students and students' ability to be successful. This is especially true for first-year students; although the law requires them to be responsible, universities know that first-year students need help with this. Utilize the help. It is in your best interest to do so.

@*myU* SO HOW DOES THIS AFFECT YOU?

Your ability to succeed or fail at the university is in your hands. You are considered an intelligent and capable adult and will be treated as such. If you choose to skip all your classes, no one is going to call you and remind you that you need to go to class. It is assumed that you know that already and are making your own informed choices. Teachers and counselors do not call students in for a meeting about missed classes—but don't think that this lack of communication means you are getting away with anything. Your absences are noted each day and will figure into your final grade. If you fail your classes, the university will notify you on your transcript, and you might get a letter from the dean reminding you that you must earn a certain GPA to maintain your enrollment. Likewise, if you choose to violate housing policies or state laws by consuming alcohol or other drugs, you might find yourself evicted in the middle of the term or needing to post bail to get out of jail.

You are absolutely 100 percent in control of what you make of your education. If you want to excel, you will be able to create an intellectually stimulating and engaging college education. This approach is much more enjoyable and rewarding in the long run and the real reason a person should attend a research university. Take a moment to look through your university's documents to find out the consequences or sanctions for:

Being a Minor in Possession (MIP) of alcohol

Being on academic probation for two or more terms

Bringing alcohol or drugs into your residence hall

Missing more than two classes in a term

CHANGES IN YOUR FAMILY

When a young adult goes off to college and leaves home for the first time, the family goes through a transition, and all members learn new ways of interacting without being in constant contact. In addition, the student's new levels of freedom and responsibility add complexity to the process. Each member of the family has different feelings about the separation process, some positive and some negative, and each person has different ways of handling it. This is especially true when the student is eager for new freedom and the family is not ready to let go. Often, parents and students have tense or uncomfortable interactions as this happens.

Bloom's Theory of Parent/Adolescent Separation

One researcher found this process of parent/adolescent separation fascinating and decided to study what happens as parents and their young adults go through it. In 1980, Michael Bloom studied several families as they went through this process, and he identified five stages. Bloom's model is very useful in helping both students and parents better understand this process. In fact, parents at some universities attend a workshop on this process as part of summer orientation, and students learn about it in first-year experience courses and seminars.

Bloom argues that there are five distinct stages of the **parent/adolescent separation** process: ambivalence, cognitive separation, emotional separation, values clarification, and new relationship. Each stage is characterized by different kinds of behaviors by both the student and the parent. The stages are linear, so a person generally moves from one stage to the next as he or she moves through the letting-go process, but each person in the family can be at a different stage, which adds to the complexity of family dynamics and interactions. It is the lack of synchronicity in these stages that creates the most challenges in family dynamics. Finally, the timing of this process is unique to each family and to each child within the same family. Some families have gone through many of these stages in junior high and high school; others are just beginning on the first day of university classes. Please note that Bloom's research focused on families consisting of biological parents and children, but the stages can apply to any family in which one or more adults raised a child for a significant amount of time.

STAGE 1: AMBIVALENCE   This stage is characterized by all members of the family transitioning from parent-child to adult-adult relational patterns. This means that the parents have to be willing to move from telling their son or daughter what to do to advising or coaching when asked. This also means that students have to take more responsibility for their life and choices and cannot ask their parents to do everything for them. On both sides, there is a lot of vacillation between authority and autonomy as parents and young adults negotiate this new relationship. Often, these are messy and tense interactions because every family member wants a different level of authority or independence in a certain situation and family members most likely do not all want the same things at the same times. In addition, people are often resistant to change at this stage, especially parents, who might not be ready to let go yet.

Parents often handle their discomfort by working with rules. They say things like "You can do this" and "You cannot do that" as a way to maintain control, especially if they are not present to enforce the student's behavior. They might also make financial or emotional support conditional on certain behaviors or choices by the student. For example, they might say, "We'll only pay for college if you major in engineering" or "We won't pay for rent if you live with your boyfriend."

Students usually vacillate between acting young and wanting to be treated like an adult. They might say things like "I'm an adult now, and I should get to make my own decisions," but later ask the parent to do their laundry. These mixed signals confuse parents. Students can help in this stage by consistently acting like an adult. If they continually demonstrate their ability to act and behave like an adult, it helps parents to see, and therefore treat, their student in new ways.

STAGE 2: COGNITIVE SEPARATION   This stage is characterized by focusing on the intellectual aspects of the separation process. In other words, the separation is talked about in very logical and unemotional terms. The student or young adult is more likely to be in this stage and exhibit the unemotional aspects of it, although some parents, especially fathers, can be in this stage too. Because the parents are most often in the next stage of emotional separation, which is characterized by lots of emotions and sadness about the separation, the student often does not relate and focuses on the "logic" of moving away from home. Students can also become annoyed by their parents' emotions and tend to view them as overreacting. The physical act of separation (i.e., moving out) helps the adolescent to define himself or herself as separate from his or her parents, so it is often met with excitement. In addition, young adults begin to define their separateness from their parents by being different in some way and accentuating those differences—for example, style of dress, music preferences, political ideology, or spiritual expression.

Parents in this stage are likely to discuss the student's leaving in very businesslike ways. The focus will be on how many bags to pack and what time the family should leave to make it to campus. There is little acknowledgment that this is more than a weekend getaway. With students, the focus is more on all the fun and exciting adventures that college will bring, with little or no acknowledgment that they are moving away from home. Students also don't see "what the big deal is," since they view their departure as temporary because they will be home for the Thanksgiving and winter breaks in just a few weeks.

STAGE 3: EMOTIONAL SEPARATION   This stage is characterized by the emotions of the separation, and often the focus is on the more negative emotions of sadness, loss, nostalgia, frustration, and uncertainty. Parents are more likely to experience this stage before their student, usually beginning a few weeks before the student leaves for college. The student typically does not reach this stage until well into the first term—this is essentially the homesickness that was described at the beginning of this chapter. It often takes students a period of time for the excitement of independence to wear off before they experience the stage of emotional separation. Parents and students are not going through these stages in sync, and that can create challenges in family dynamics.

This stage is often much more keenly experienced by the parents because they see their student's moving away as a marker that their role as a parent is ending and that their young adult has grown up. This can be disconcerting because being a parent has been a major portion of their identity for the past eighteen to twenty years. If the parents have not thought about, or have not begun planning for, the next stage of their own lives, this time can be very uncomfortable. Every letter from college and every bag that is packed is another reminder of the upcoming change. Another issue that can complicate this stage is the parents' relationship as a couple. If they have not maintained their relationship, they might not know how to relate to each other outside of their roles as parents. When the last child leaves home, this becomes even more evident. In this situation, parents might cling to their role as parents, which can infringe on the student's independence.

In addition, some parents experience some level of guilt as they reflect on their role as parents and realize that they could have done certain things differently and perhaps better. They also often question whether they have "done enough" to prepare their child for the next stage of his or her life. Some parents are tempted to cram in last-minute parenting and find themselves giving lots of advice and reminders about making good choices and being safe. They might be taking lots of pictures of the student and acting as though they might not see the student for a very long time. Both students and parents are managing the complexity of their changing roles and expectations—though not necessarily smoothly.

Parents also realize that this is the beginning of when their son or daughter becomes an adult and will not return to live at home in the same way again. This is often a result of reflecting on their own separation from their families when they were younger. They might be incredibly nostalgic and say things like "This will be our last Fourth of July together as a family." Students can help in this stage by realizing that this is a big transition for their parents that might be uncomfortable or even scary. Although parents are excited for their son or daughter, they are also experiencing emotions about their own personal transition. See "Point of Interest: Calling Home."

POINT OF INTEREST

CALLING HOME   Your family loves you and wants the best for you. They worry a lot about your happiness and safety when you are away. Some families aren't sure how to manage their student's independence, and they call too much; other families don't want to bother their student, so they call too little. You can help by giving your family some guidelines about how often, and when, you would like to hear from them. It means a lot to your family when you call them too. They want you to miss them as much as they are missing you. Consider setting up a specific weekly time to call, or better yet, use Skype. It's free and allows you to see each other on the computer screen.

One thing that students often do is call their family when they are upset about something. Being able to vent, and even cry, to someone who loves you can be the perfect thing after a bad day. However, it's important to remember that after you hang up, your family will keep thinking about the conversation and worry about you. It is a good idea to give your family a balanced view of your life at college; if you call only when you are upset, they might think that you are miserable all the time. It hurts them that you are upset, and their parental instincts kick in—it is natural for them to want to protect you, especially if you say things like "I hate it here, and I want to come home." While this might be true in the moment, they won't know that you were feeling great a few hours later unless you tell them. Be sure to call them on the days that you love school and are happy that you came.

If your family tends to be a bit more involved in your life than you would prefer, you might want to monitor how much you say to them and when. If calling when you are upset only prompts them to tell you what to do and you don't want this, you might need to find other people to vent to when you are upset. Students often unknowingly give their family the impression that they cannot handle aspects of college life (because they call home upset about various things) and then are surprised that their family treats them as though they cannot handle college.

STAGE 4: VALUES CLARIFICATION   This stage is characterized by the process the student engages in while developing new values. The student's peers exert strong influence, and parents often see their son or daughter veer away from long-held family values while testing them and exploring others. The processes of value formation in children and value clarification in young adults are described in more detail in the next section. Eventually, the student blends parental and personal values together in new ways, and the parents learn new ways to parent that allow for the student's new values.

However, Bloom's work did not address what happens when some families cannot easily embrace their child's development. If the parents are unable or unwilling to accommodate their student's values, some families can experience a split and estrangement at this stage. Parents who attempt to exert too much control in this phase (e.g., "It's my way or the highway") can cause the student and family to disengage from each other in serious and often long-term ways.

STAGE 5: NEW RELATIONSHIP   This stage is characterized by a new and positive relationship that is cocreated by the young adult and the parents. Separateness is balanced with connection and often families feel closer than ever before. The student has increased investment in relationships outside of the family (e.g., friends, coworkers, and romantic partners), and the family learns to accept that. Parents learn to provide support and guidance instead of control, and as they do so, students are more willing to seek their support and guidance. Students gain a much greater appreciation for their parents in this stage and often seek the input and wisdom that they intentionally ignored in previous stages.

Although students and parents will see these stages more distinctly the first year, the process is by no means over. Members of the family can move backward in the stages when a new issue or stressful situation arises. In fact, the stages often correlate with the values development and clarification process (described later in this chapter), so when the son or daughter makes a choice that concerns the parent, the family often responds by going back to Stage 1 and working their way back through the stages again. This process is very noticeable during the college years simply because the college environment provides ample opportunities for the separation and values clarification stages, especially when values and experimentation collide. However, all young adults go through this process with their families whether they go to college or not. Depending on the individual family and the pace at which they progress through the stages, some will be in Stage 5 during the first year, while others won't get there for years. Stage 5 will eventually become more and more common and is the hallmark of a healthy family when the young adult has become a full adult.

@myU   SO HOW DOES THIS AFFECT YOU?

You have probably already experienced some of these stages in the past few years. You and your family will have ups and downs in your relationship as you negotiate this new landscape. There will be days when you feel very close to your family and you miss them incredibly, and then there might be days when they annoy you and you want to be away from them. This is normal. The good news is that it gets better with time as each member of the family transitions through the five stages. In addition to understanding your own family's dynamics with regard to your separation and independence, this model can give you insight into the experiences of your peers. Using Bloom's model, indicate which stages you believe that you and your parents or guardians are experiencing. Write about an experience or moment that made you realize what stage each of you is in.

You:

Parent A:

Parent B:

Understanding these stages can be quite useful for both students and family members. Each person not only can understand his or her own process but also can have a greater understanding of, and therefore empathy for, the experiences of other members of the family. This model can help the family to assess which stage each member might be in and provide some insight into the separation process as a whole and some issues or behaviors that might be encountered along the way.

YOUR DEVELOPING VALUES

College will change you. In addition to providing you with a degree, it will provide you with a plethora of information and experiences that will shape who you will be, what you believe, and what you value. This is supposed to happen, as it is part of the transition from being a young adult to a full adult. While exciting, this transition can be a bit bumpy at times, especially when family members are not supportive of some of your choices. All of this freedom and responsibility allows students to make their own choices, some that yield positive results and some that yield negative ones. Each choice brings an opportunity for the student to learn and grow.

This period also begins a process that many students and families do not expect: value development and clarification. A **value** is defined as a belief upon which a person acts by choice; an enduring belief that one way of behaving (self or other) is personally or socially preferable to an opposing way of behaving. Experiences with freedom and responsibility inevitably lead to maturation and value development in young adults, which can cause changes in relationships with family and friends.

Students most often notice this process happening during their first winter break when they spend a significant amount of time with family and friends back home. All of a sudden, they realize that they have slightly different views and beliefs from those of their family and peers. In addition, families often want to influence the experiences their student has at college. Many families believe that their student still needs their guidance, and many families attempt to influence their student's choices in everything from grades and majors to careers and romantic partners. This next section discusses the ways in which young adults form new values and the ways in which their families might react to their choices.

A Theory of Value Development and Clarification

Value development and clarification make up an important part of any person's maturation process and occur throughout a person's life. However, psychologists and student development theorists have identified a period in a young adult's life known as the "coming-of-age" years, which coincide roughly with the ages of 17 to 23 years old. This is a time when young adults, who have been raised with their family's values, begin to discover new values as they interact with other people. Over time, they eventually test and clarify the values of their family and develop a set of their own values. This process can be accelerated by experiences that put a person into contact with a wide variety of people who hold different values. Many experiences provide this, such as traveling abroad or living away from home, and living near people who are different from those in the person's home community. A university campus is such a place, so value development is a process that nearly all college students experience. Ultimately, the young adult creates his or her own unique set of values that is a blend of the family's values and some new ones that are meaningful to him or her.

Every generation goes through this process, yet it can create tension between a young adult and his or her family. It probably created tension between your parents and their parents and between your grandparents and their parents. This will most likely occur between you and your family, so you will find this information useful. There are essentially two processes that occur when a student leaves home: the separation process between the young adult and the parents (mentioned earlier in this chapter) and the value development and clarification process (described next). These two processes are integrally intertwined yet really are very different. You will be affected by these processes, which will, in turn, affect your relationships with family and friends.

THE VALUES FORMATION PROCESS IN CHILDREN Every person goes through a **value formation process** during childhood. During the "formative" years (ages 8 to 13), several influential forces shape a child's values and behaviors, the most influential being immediate family members such as parents and grandparents—usually people who have regular contact with the child. Other forces of influence are teachers and others in the school environment, the home community that includes neighbors and family friends, areas of membership such as a church or athletic group, the child's peers such as friends and schoolmates, the media to the extent that the child is exposed to its messages, and of course the child's personal experiences. All of these forces teach the child a set of beliefs and values that identify what is "right" and "wrong," what is "good" and "bad," and so on.

Some of these messages may be explicit, such as a person saying, "In this family, we always clean up after our meals" or "Don't ever talk back to your elders." Explicit messages are usually conveyed verbally and are pretty clear. Some messages are implicit and are often communicated through nonverbal cues; for example, a father might look upset when a student earns anything less than an A, or an aunt might always clutch her purse more tightly when an unknown man walks past. Teachers and the media also contribute to a child's development with both explicit and implicit messages. One obvious example is how teachers treat students with regard to their intelligence. Over time, a child begins to view himself or herself as smart, average, or dumb, depending on the messages the child received in the school environment. Another example relates to how attractive a person feels. All people in developed countries pick up messages about what "attractive" means through popular media such as television and magazines. Most people in our society compare themselves to a standard of attractiveness that is narrowly defined by models and actors.

Over time, a child learns to incorporate all these messages to create a set of beliefs, behaviors, and values that guide his or her understanding of the world in both conscious and unconscious ways. This system of beliefs and values can be thought of as a **value onion** with several layers (see Figure 4.1). The innermost layers represent those values that are deeply held and therefore not easily affected or changed. These are the values that people have pretty strong feelings about, for example, abortion or the death penalty. Values on the outside of the onion are lightly held and do not elicit strong feelings; as a result, they are often easily affected and changed with new information or experiences. An example might be which fast-food chain is believed to have the best burger. Values in the middle layers generally can also be altered, but it will take more information and more experiences for these values to be affected. People usually have some feelings about these values but not to the extent that arises with deeply held values.

This value onion is built over time by influential forces in the child's life as well as by personal experiences that the child encountered throughout childhood. By the time a child becomes a young adult, the value onion is well developed, and values are situated at the various levels in the onion.

THE ROLE OF VALUES IN THE FAMILY SYSTEM Parents seek to raise their children in the best way possible with the goal of ensuring that their child outlives them. Most parents absolutely want their child to grow up to be a healthy and happy adult who lives a good life. Parents have developed their own values over time and through experiences, both positive and negative, and seek to pass these values on to their children. As parents, it is their role to help shape and protect the development of their child. Even in abusive homes where parents are physically or emotionally cruel to their children, these parents would still argue that they are "doing their best" and often can't control what they say or do because of alcohol or drug abuse, mental health problems, or their own psychological wounds.

FIGURE 4.1 Diagram of the Value Onion

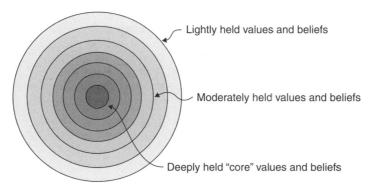

Lightly held values and beliefs

Moderately held values and beliefs

Deeply held "core" values and beliefs

Although the family generally means well, sometimes families attach their desire for their child's healthy and happy life to a certain path, such as a specific career. Somehow the desire of "I want Sabrina to have a happy life, which means being able to support herself financially" becomes "Sabrina needs to become an engineer because those are the best-paying jobs." This can happen with a variety of things: which college to attend, which major to declare, which career to pursue, and which person to date. The value is positive, but the way in which it is expressed can be limiting to the student's freedom. When the daughter calls home to announce that she wants to be an art studio major, the family is probably upset and might try to influence the choice, simply because they have associated engineering with her health and happiness. Interactions such as these occur regularly, and college students might find themselves a bit stunned at their family's reactions to their exciting news about majors, romantic partners, or school activities. This is especially problematic when the family has narrowed the "right" path to a relatively small number of options that they feel very strongly about.

In addition, the media plays a major role in shaping the values of people in the United States. The intent of the media, however, is not always positive; the media are usually involved in selling products of some kind and that requires convincing people that they need the product. One way to do this is to make people feel that their life would be better (e.g., they would be prettier, happier, more popular, or richer) if they purchased a certain product or experience. While many would argue that this is the heart of capitalism, it can't be ignored that young adults are influenced by these messages and can have their self-image and self-esteem directly affected by media influences. Your values have been shaped by the media in a variety of ways, and probably most notably around how you define attractiveness and success.

THE VALUES CLARIFICATION PROCESS IN YOUNG ADULTS When a student goes off to college, she or he already has developed a sense of values through the influential forces mentioned previously, the most important being the immediate family. For example, consider what you believe about the following and how you might act if faced with a related situation, either through your own actions or those of others:

+   Underage drinking
+   Cheating on an exam
+   Dating people of different races or religions
+   Sex outside of marriage
+   Unintended pregnancies and abortion

Leaving the family of origin and other influential forces begins the **value clarification process.** This is important because the value clarification process hinges on exposure to new values that invariably force an evaluation of those that the person previously held. This process is complex and is not necessarily completed by the time a person graduates or turns 23, but several of the stages have usually occurred by then. Over the years, I have observed students moving through seven distinct stages of the value clarification process. These are most often affiliated with individual values that are of medium to high importance—in other words, in the middle to deepest levels of the value onion. A person will go through these stages for each value separately and can be in multiple stages at the same time, each for a different value. See Figure 4.2.

1. *Separation*—This first stage is the mere act of leaving the family of origin and other influential groups in terms of constant contact and influence. For example, when a student moves into a residence hall, the family no longer sees the student on a daily basis and is not there to comment on, or influence, the student's daily choices. The student probably also left friends and teachers behind, and while contact might be maintained, it is not the primary influence in the student's life. The physical moving and living in another location is the key to this stage, whether it is 5 miles or 5,000 miles away.

FIGURE 4.2 **Diagram of the Values Clarification Process**

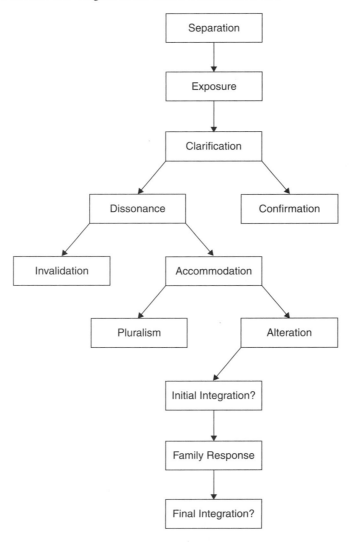

2. *Exposure*—This second stage occurs when a person is exposed to many people who hold values and beliefs, some of which may be similar and some of which may be different. This can range from little things such as how to cook spaghetti (do you put the noodles in the pot whole or break them in half?) to larger values such as political ideology or controversial issues such as abortion or the right to marry. Exposure has to do with simply seeing and hearing other people's beliefs and values. This can occur for university students in the classroom, at a club meeting, in their faculty's office hours, or while hanging out with peers. Research university campuses are especially rich with daily opportunities for exposure to different perspectives, beliefs, and values as the campus community is constantly engaging in research and critical thinking.

3. *Clarification*—Once a person is exposed to another value or belief, this stage has to do with what the person does with that exposure. There are two possibilities:
   a. *Confirmation*—If the value that is expressed is the same as or similar to the one the student holds, then the interaction likely confirms the student's original value. This can occur on the conscious or unconscious level. A student might think, "I knew I was right about that. I'm glad that she knows this too." Or the student might feel a subtle level of comfort with the other person or the experience. When values are similar, this aspect of clarification is not very noticeable or obvious because it fits with the student's original way of seeing the world. When confirmation occurs, the process for that particular experience ends here.
   b. *Dissonance*—When a student is exposed to a value that is very different, the experience is often noticeable because it is uncomfortable on some level—in essence, it conflicts with the student's original value. This is because it challenges the student's original view in some way and creates what psychologists call dissonance, or lack of agreement. The strength of the dissonance is usually correlated with the importance of the value or the depth to which is it held. When dissonance occurs, the person moves into dealing with that dissonance in some way.

4. *Response to dissonance*—This stage represents how a person deals with the dissonance of having a value not confirmed, or even directly challenged, by a person or experience. This situation has to be resolved, at least psychologically, in some way. There are two options:
   a. *Invalidation*—One response is to invalidate the source of the challenge or conflict, thereby eliminating the dissonance. This occurs when a student is judgmental and seeks to find something wrong with the source. For example, a student might invalidate the information ("He's just wrong—he doesn't know what he is talking about"), or the student might invalidate the person ("She's weird if she thinks that—no normal person would"). It is usually easier to invalidate the person if she or he is a stranger or if she or he is the first one to challenge the value. It is harder to invalidate the person if she or he is liked and/or respected. If the student chooses to invalidate, then the process stops here, and the student's original value remains intact.
   b. *Accommodation*—The other response is to accommodate the new value in some way. This usually occurs under three conditions:

      + The value is not tightly held, so it is fairly easy to alter.
      + The person who is challenging the value is respected or trusted.
      + There have been previous challenges to the value, and this one achieves some critical mass, or "tipping point," in the mind of the student.

   There are two options for accommodation:

      i. *Pluralism*—The first option requires the student to allow for more than one belief to be correct. This allows the student to hold onto his or her original value without invalidating the other. It usually sounds something like "Everyone is entitled to his or her opinion" or "That's not true for me, but I can see that it might be true for them." Essentially, the student allows for pluralistic views, which is where there can be more than one right or correct possibility.

    ii. *Alteration*—The other option is for the student to question his or her original value and assess its validity in the light of the new information. The student might seek to alter some aspect of the value by creating conditions under which it is true or not, or the student might determine that the original value is invalid.

5. *Initial choice to integrate*—This stage occurs when students alter their original value in some way. They might alter some portion of their original value to include the new value, or they might completely adopt the new value in place of the original. Again, this depends on how deeply the value is held and the source of the dissonance.

6. *Family response*—This stage involves how the family responds to the student's shifting values. The response is usually related to how tightly held the value is in the family system. Those that are tightly held will elicit a quicker and stronger response than those that are not. The family is usually the source of the original value system and has raised the student to see it as the "good/right/true" way. Generally the family will not be in agreement that the value should be shifted. The response will also depend on how much the family perceives the shift to be a threat to their child's overall health, happiness, and safety. If the threat is perceived to be strong, so will be the response.

    Families can and do utilize a wide range of responses, both verbal and nonverbal, to attempt to control the student's process. When possible, the family can attempt to invalidate the source of the new information or experience. If this is not successful, they might use more coercive tactics to influence the student as a way to exert control. When the student was living at home, the family had more options for asserting this control through sanctions, punishments, and even nonverbal disapproval that often affected a student's choices. With the student's increased freedom and independence, the family loses access to the old methods and sometimes uses more dramatic responses than ever before.

    Depending on the situation, responses can cover a wide range, including showing support, saying nothing, stating displeasure but acknowledging the student's right to choose, expressing that the student should feel guilt, reinforcing the value through religious or other culturally relevant information, yelling, threatening to discontinue support, and disowning the student from the family. The response might be brief and quickly expressed, or it might be continually reinforced until the student acquiesces. Needless to say, this can be quite upsetting to the student.

7. *Final choice to integrate*—This stage represents the choice a student still has after hearing or experiencing his or her family's response. Depending on the circumstances, the family might be able to influence the student to revert to the original value. In situations in which the student truly has returned to the previous value, everything returns to normal in the family dynamics until the next time a value is challenged. In situations in which the student does not want to return to the original value, she or he will have to find ways to keep the family either uninformed or misinformed about the choice or will have to face whatever consequences the family may be willing to administer. In this case, the student often seeks support from other people in his or her life as a way to balance the disconnection felt with the family.

Although the values clarification process occurs over and over for different values throughout a son's or daughter's lifetime, it is most pronounced in the first few years after the young adult moves away from the family. Also, each family has its own ways of going through these stages, and it won't be the same even for children within the same family. The process never really ends, as the values clarification process, and the family's response to it, lasts a lifetime. Ask any older adult, and he or she can tell you the issues that still create tension in their family and how they deal with them. The following aspects of the son's or daughter's life that tend to be the most problematic for families include:

+ Job or career choice
+ Sexual orientation or gender identity
+ Ethnic expression or identification
+ Political ideology and affiliations
+ Spiritual expression
+ Whom the son or daughter dates
+ With whom the son or daughter forms a romantic partnership
+ Risks the son or daughter takes in terms of activities, traveling, places to live, and so on (the greater the danger as perceived by the family, the bigger the concern is and the more control the family is likely to try to impose)
+ Plans for big events such as weddings or holidays
+ How the son or daughter raises his or her own children

It is important for every family to establish ways in which they will handle these issues and others that will arise as the young adult becomes a fully mature adult. See "Point of Interest: Connecting with Your Family."

POINT OF INTEREST

CONNECTING WITH YOUR FAMILY As you come up against points of disagreement with your family, you will find that you have opportunities to assert your views and make requests of your family. Remember, a relationship between adults is a two-way street, and some things will need to be negotiated. These conversations might not be easy, but it is your responsibility to guide your family in understanding what you want and how you want to interact with them. There are a few things you can do in these situations.

It's always a good idea to *really listen* to your family. Listen to what they are saying and find out whether you can hear the fears or concerns that underlie the comments they are making. If so, you can begin to address those issues directly. For example, if they want you to major in a certain field, they might be saying things like "It's important that you have a good salary and can support your family." The underlying fear is that you might end up in a low-paying job, struggling every month to make ends meet, and might not be able to have the kinds of things they wish for you, such as a home, a car, and vacations. Once you identify the fear, go do some research. Find out about the salaries in the career you wish to pursue. The more information you can give your family that addresses their specific fear, the more likely they will be to change their perspective.

Another thing you can do is ask your family to talk about their past. There is probably some aspect of their young adulthood that was important to them for which they did not find support from their family. It might have been whether, or where, they could go to college, a travel opportunity, a career path, or a romantic partner. Ask them more about it—why it was so important to them, what it meant, and how their life might have been different. Really listen to what they are saying because their words will give you clues to how best to connect with them. Then, at a separate time (do not do this next step in the same conversation), talk to them about what you want and tie it back to their own experience. This has to be very genuine and also for an issue that is very important to you; if you use this method with something of low importance, it will appear manipulative.

If your family is reacting very strongly in a negative direction, give them some time to cool off. You will not get very far if they are upset, and things could escalate. If your family is threatening actions such as not paying for college, you will have to assess whether you want to accept these consequences or not. In some situations, it will be absolutely worth it because the issue at hand is core to who you are. But sometimes, it will not be worth it. Only you can decide.

Finally, you can always give up on that one issue and accept your family's wishes. You might choose to pursue the major or career that they wish or not date the person they dislike. However, while this solution brings immediate peace, it does not help you and your family move through the rest of the stages of separation and value clarification. The process gets arrested until the next issue arises and creates conflict, which might include where you should live or with whom you should fall in love. At some point, you and your family will need to negotiate a new relationship that allows you to pursue your own path. This is an essential step in your development as an adult.

@myU   SO HOW DOES THIS AFFECT YOU?

You and your family will go through the values clarification process. You might not notice it at first, or even for a couple of years, but at some point, you will realize that your values are changing and are now somewhat different from your family's. Some of you will find that your families will be very encouraging of this process and will support your growth and development unconditionally. Others of you will have families who try very hard to shape your values or keep them from changing too much. Eventually, these families will come around and you will be able to have a peaceful relationship with them. Sadly, some of you will experience dramatic tensions and even estrangement from your family, especially if you veer drastically from deeply held family or cultural values.

Interestingly, there is a cycle to this whole process. Your adult family members went through this process with the family who raised them, and if you have children, you will go through it with yours. You will eventually find friends and a romantic partner who share your beliefs and values. If you have children, you will find yourself imparting your values to them and probably feeling that you are doing a better job than your family did. And one day, your children will leave home and begin to test and question all that you taught them. That is the beauty and irony of it all. Take a moment to list your top five values. Next, list what you think are your parents' top five values. Where might the potential conflicts and commonalities exist?

YOUR VALUES	PARENT A'S VALUES	PARENT B'S VALUES
1		
2		
3		
4		
5		

THE SAFETY OF YOUR CAMPUS

The concepts of student independence and family values merge at the issue of safety. One value that parents strongly hold is that they want their sons and daughters to live long and healthy lives. When children are minors and live at home, parents can exert a lot of control over the health and safety of their children. However, when young adults go off to college, parents no longer have the same direct influence on their student's actions. Parents, more than students, understand the fragility of life and the tragedies that can occur when young adults make inappropriate choices. Your parents want you to graduate from college and go on to a successful and long life.

While parents want their student to experience college, they also want to know what safeguards are in place at the campus to help their student make good choices and to protect their son or daughter from the choices of others. This means that issues of campus and student safety are a prime concern to parents. Every year, many parents experience their worst nightmare and receive a phone call that informs them their son or daughter is not coming home because he or she died or was killed. And many more parents receive news of injuries and accidents their student has suffered, some with lifelong implications. Although most of these situations involve alcohol or other drugs, some do not.

Aspects of campus safety that are of importance to parents and students cover a range of possible scenarios. One concern is how students will be protected and cared for during a **natural disaster** like a hurricane, tornado, or earthquake. A campus should be able to provide food, shelter, and protection to all members of its community during a disaster and have methods in place for evacuating the campus when necessary. Fire is another safety concern, especially if the student lives in university-owned housing. Campuses should have fire safety policies in place as well as plans for evacuating buildings and providing alternate shelter. A campus community includes thousands of people and controlling a crowd can make any disaster situation challenging. Be sure to ask your campus what you would need to know in these instances and how you would be notified of any actions you would need to take.

Another campus safety concern is **criminal activity** and the likelihood that a student can be a victim of a crime. Nonviolent crimes such as bicycle or computer theft may not be a serious concern for many, but violent crimes certainly are. In 1990, the **Clery Act** was signed to mandate campuses to publish their crime statistics. The law is named for Jeanne Clery, a freshman at Lehigh University who was raped and murdered in her residence hall in 1986. After the murder, her parents learned that the campus had experienced thirty-eight violent crimes in the three years prior to Jeanne's death. They partnered with other parents whose children had been victims of crimes on college campuses to bring the Clery Act to reality because they believed that all families should have access to this important information. As a result, your campus *must* notify all members of its community annually about any crimes committed on campus property. You may receive a brochure or an e-mail with a link to a website with the current information. Be sure to review this as it will give you valuable insights into the ways in which your campus may not be safe. Also, explore whether the statistics reported are for campus-owned property and how these differ from the property surrounding the campus. Remember that sexual assault is extremely underreported; it is estimated that only 5 percent of survivors report an incident, so you will want to adjust the reported number of sexual assaults accordingly.

Creating and maintaining campus safety can be quite difficult due to several challenges. First, universities are seen as open places where people come to think and share knowledge. This vision is antithetical to locked gates and security check points. In addition, public universities must provide public access as they are supported by tax dollars. Second, thousands of people—students, staff, faculty, and visitors—are on campus communities each day. As a result, most college campuses are physically open so large numbers of people can easily enter and exit throughout the day.

Third, the size of the campus community is another challenge in that communicating information immediately to all members is nearly impossible. Even with the advent of instant and mass forms of communication such as e-mail and text messages, there is no way to guarantee that all people will receive or read the notice when needed. The delay in getting a message broadcast on the radio or TV can make this mode of communication ineffective as well. And finally, privacy laws, such as FERPA, present challenges, as it is difficult for officials to have access to information that might indicate an escalating problem. Although every effort is made to keep students safe, the reality is that the size of campus communities make it nearly impossible to protect every member.

Reflections on Campus Tragedies

One type of crime scenario is when a mentally unstable person attacks and harms members of the campus community. This danger can come from an outsider or from within the community itself. A tragedy well known to the higher education community occurred on April 16, 2007, on the Virginia Tech campus in Blacksburg, Virginia. This quiet research university was shattered by the sounds of gunfire and, in a few short minutes, the lives of thirty-two students and faculty ended. This horrific act was conducted by another student, Seung-Hui

Cho, who had been plagued with mental health problems for years. In the weeks following the shooting, more and more evidence arose that there had been many red flags warning of Cho's mental instability and violent nature.

This tragedy involved the convergence of issues with privacy laws, weaknesses in mental health care in our country, and the security issues that affect any large community like a city or a college campus. FERPA played a role in this tragedy because the fact that all students' records are private prevented campus and law enforcement officials from seeing the wide range of evidence that pointed to Cho's escalating violent nature. In addition, there is another law, passed in 1996, called the **Health Insurance Portability and Accountability Act (HIPAA),** which protects the privacy of any person's medical records. This meant that Cho's hospital records were also private and not released to anyone. These laws make it extremely difficult for officials to connect vital indicators that a person is becoming more dangerous.

Privacy laws contributed to another tragedy that received national attention at the University of California, Santa Barbara. On February 23, 2001, David Attias, a 19-year-old freshmen, killed Nicholas Bourdakis, Christopher Divis, Elie Israel, and Ruth Levy. Calling himself "an angel of death," Attias drove into the four students at 60 miles per hour. Later, it became clear that Attias had a long history of mental health problems and that his troublesome behaviors had arisen in various aspects of his life, both on campus and in the community. Again, several red flags were not connected because FERPA and HIPAA prevented officials from sharing information. Attias was convicted of four counts of second-degree murder and found legally insane. He is spending up to sixty years in a mental institution.

These laws may seem problematic in light of these tragedies, and yet, they reflect a larger national value of personal privacy. As a country, we value individual freedom and privacy, which these laws are designed to protect. Campuses are trying to find ways to solve the dilemma of both protecting students while also honoring individual privacy. However, campuses are no different from any community of adults, like a town or city, in terms of the resources and processes available to address safety issues.

Further, the United States does not currently provide adequate mental health care. Mental illness is still stigmatized and facilities are not available to those in need. Even when a person is a danger to self or others, he or she can only be hospitalized for up to seventy-two hours, and can only be placed in a treatment facility if she or he gives consent. The problem with many mental illnesses is that the illness itself often prevents the person from seeing that he or she has a problem and may also make the person suspicious of those who try to help. The mental health of college students in particular has become a national concern. Recent years have shown a dramatic increase in students with severe mental illness as well as a sharp increase in the number of students who develop depression or anxiety (Benton, et al., 2003). A study of one state university system showed that students seeking counseling had risen 23 percent in the past four years with a quarter of those students already on psychotropic medication (Paddock, 2007). In 2009, 51 percent of the freshmen who participated in the Your First College Year study reported feeling depressed occasionally and another 12 percent felt depressed frequently (Ruiz, et al., 2010). While most mental illnesses can be successfully treated with a combination of medication and therapy, not all students seek help or utilize the resources available to them.

With regard to campus safety, the focus is on determining which students are *dangerous*, either to themselves or others. Determining which students might be a danger to others, or capable of **homicide,** is of utmost importance. Many campuses now have in place crisis response teams to identify and intervene with students who are troubled. Further, **suicide** rates are on the rise and protecting students who are a danger to themselves is a high priority. Nationally, approximately 1,300 college students commit suicide every year, making it the second leading cause of death for this age group. Surprisingly, another 10 percent of college students say that they have seriously contemplated suicide (Paddock, 2007). Several incidents

Visit www.cengagebrain.com to find the companion website containing links to:
- The *Responding to Distressed Students* guide
- Information on depression and suicide
- Information on controlling anger

have received national attention, such as Elizabeth Shin, 20, who killed herself while a student at the Massachusetts Institute of Technology by setting herself on fire. Shin's parents sued the university in a widely publicized case because they felt that the university was legally responsible for the mental and physical health of their daughter.

However, universities are not set up to provide the consistent and intensive mental health care that some students require. Most campuses do not have round-the-clock medical facilities and few have adequate funding to staff enough psychologists and psychiatrists. In fact, many are far below the recommended guideline of the International Association of Counseling Services that a college campus should have one psychologist for every 1,000 to 1,500 students. This places universities in an awkward position and some administrators are choosing to first prioritize the good of the community. Thus, if individual students are unwilling or unable to manage their mental health, they may be asked to leave the campus community. Although this solution can provide safety to the campus community, the individual then moves to another location and may still be a danger to him- or herself or others. The tragedy at Virginia Tech and the extent of the loss of life have brought these issues to the forefront. You will continue to see these complex concepts discussed and debated in the months and years to come.

In light of the events at Virginia Tech, UC Santa Barbara, Northern Illinois University in 2008, and University of Texas at Austin in 2010, it is important for all members of a campus community to be proactive in identifying people who might be in crisis, whether they are students, staff, faculty, or community members. It is everyone's responsibility to be aware of indicators of a problem and to communicate observations to one or more authorities. In the case of a university campus, authorities can include professional staff in housing, student health, counseling, police, and the dean of students office. Remember, someone who is in crisis may not possess the ability to identify the problem or seek help.

Students can also help identify those who are in crisis. Someone may verbalize his or her distress, show a change in performance or behavior, or otherwise cause concern. A person's distress may be due to medical, psychiatric, academic, financial, social, or personal factors. It is extremely important to encourage and help the person at the *earliest* signs of distress to seek assistance from the appropriate campus and community resources. You should contact an authority if you observe the following behaviors:

+ Excessive or inappropriate anger
+ Behavioral or emotional change
+ Withdrawal
+ Change in hygiene or appearance
+ Alcohol or drug abuse
+ Expressing unusual thoughts or exhibiting unusual behaviors
+ Decline in performance (i.e., academic or work)

Always trust your instincts, and do not second-guess your own reactions. In almost all cases, a person's sense that "something is wrong" is accurate. Contact an authority if you have the following reactions to a person:

+ Feeling uncomfortable or uneasy
+ Feeling alarmed or frightened
+ Feeling that something is not right
+ Concern about the person's ability to function
+ Worry about the person's comments or behavior

It is important to convey the strength of your concern, and it is always better to bring the issue to the attention of more than one person. However, because FERPA and HIPAA are in

@myU SO HOW DOES THIS AFFECT YOU?

Campus communities have well-trained staff in a variety of key departments, including counseling and student health as well as professionally trained security that may even include state police. Many campuses have crisis response teams in place that include key administrators from counseling, student health, security, and the dean of students. Students, staff, and faculty can bring a situation to the attention of these teams, thus creating a wide safety net for all. Free or low-cost counseling is available to students, and medical staff on college campuses specialize in issues related to this age group. Further, campuses in areas where natural disasters are likely to occur are prepared to be self-sustaining during emergencies. It is important for students and families to learn what security measures and processes are in place on the campus and to be prepared to respond when needed. Look through your campus's website to learn what you should do in the following situations:

Natural disaster

Worried about a friend

Potential or active shooting on campus

place, you probably will not receive any information with regard to what happened with the person or how the situation was handled. Ultimately, the legal issues of FERPA and HIPAA may prevent a quick resolution, so it is also important for you to take care of yourself. Consult with campus counselors or advisors to discuss the options that are available to you.

RELATED MATERIALS

For Scenic Route websites, more Stories from the Path, glossary, and student activities, access the study tools for *Navigating the Research University* at www.cengagebrain.com.

REFERENCES

Andreatta, B. (2010, January 27). *Family values, college relationships, and independence.* Lecture for Education 20, Introduction to the research university. University of California, Santa Barbara.

Benton, S. A., Robertson, J. M., Tseng, W., Newton, F. B., & Benton, S. L. (2003). Changes in counseling center client problems across 13 years. *Professional psychology: Research and practice, 34(1), 66–72.*

Bloom, M. V. (1980). *Adolescent-parental separation.* New York: Gardner Press.

Family Educational Rights and Privacy Act. (1974). Retrieved from http://www.ed.gov/policy/gen/guid/fpco/ferpa/index.html.

Paddock, R. (2007, May 23). Suicides a symptom of larger UC crisis. *Los Angeles Times.* Retrieved from http://www.latimes.com/news/local/la-me-men-tal23may23,0,6234175,print.story.

Ruiz, S., Sharkness, J., Kelly, K., DeAngelo, L., & Pryor, J. (2010). *Findings from the 2009 administration of Your First College Year (YFCY): National aggregates.* Retrieved from http://www.heri.ucla.edu/publications-brp.php.

University of California, Santa Barbara. (2010). *Responding to distressed students.* Retrieved from http://www.sa.ucsb.edu/distressedstudentsguide/index.aspx.

CHAPTER 5

Degrees, Majors, and Careers at the Research University

University of Wisconsin at Madison

As a college student, you should have as a primary goal the successful completion of all the requirements to earn your bachelor's degree. For the next two to four years, you will be taking classes, fulfilling requirements, and preparing for the next stage of your life after graduation. Whether you are a freshman or transfer student, this chapter will focus on information you need to know to make appropriate academic choices. You will learn about the building blocks of a liberal education, aspects of undergraduate courses, the connection between majors and careers, useful tools for career and major exploration, an overview of teaching and learning styles, and how the university is organized to support your student experience.

© Images-USA / Alamy

YOUR UNDERGRADUATE EDUCATION

Bachelor's Degrees

An undergraduate education is designed to culminate in a **baccalaureate or bachelor's degree** on the fulfillment of a specified set of academic requirements. There are several types of bachelor's degrees: Bachelor of Arts (B.A.), Bachelor of Science (B.S.), Bachelor of Music (B.M.), and Bachelor of Fine Arts (B.F.A.). Generally, bachelor's degrees require approximately four years of enrollment in terms of credits and requirements. This translates to twelve quarters or eight semesters, assuming a nine-month enrollment period. This general estimate was established so that a bachelor's degree would represent a certain amount of undergraduate course work regardless of the institution at which it was earned. Although there are certainly differences across degree programs in the world, they generally adhere to this level of workload.

A variety of factors can affect a student's ability to finish earning a bachelor's degree in four years, including the availability of required classes, the timing of when the student declares a major, the transferability of course work if the student transferred from one institution to another, whether the student passes the appropriate number of credits per term, and the impact of extenuating circumstances such as withdrawing for a quarter or participating in nonaffiliated programs for which credits do not transfer. In the United States, the average time it takes to earn a bachelor's degree is now five years, but many universities still maintain a four-year completion rate. You might want to ask what the **time to degree** is at your university and inquire about any programs or schedules that promote timely graduation.

All bachelor's degrees include the completion of an **academic major,** which is focused study in one discipline. Many universities offer the opportunity to **minor** in a second discipline or even to complete a double major in two disciplines. Students have even completed double majors with double minors, although this may have taken them longer than four years and they may have had very specific reasons for doing so, like preparing for a career that bridges two industries or requires knowledge of other languages and cultures. These possibilities are specific to each campus, college, and major, so you will need to consult an academic advisor to learn about the options available to you.

In addition to the major requirements, most bachelor's degrees require the completion of some additional college- or university-wide requirements, such as a minimum number of credits, courses in specified topics, a general education program, and even elective courses. You will find all graduation requirements for your university in the general catalog and other official documents. It is your responsibility to read and understand them.

Your major will introduce you to an overview of that discipline and its research traditions. You might be surprised by how many possibilities exist within one discipline. For example, the American Sociological Association has identified more than forty areas of interest within the field of sociology, including family; organizations; sex and gender; social psychology; environment; technology; aging and life course; social behavior; racial and ethnic minorities; political sociology; education; legal systems; political economy of the world system; mental health; alcohol and drugs; religion and spirituality; international migration; and history of sociology. An introductory course in sociology will touch on many of these topics, and other courses will focus on individual ones in depth.

At any one campus, students can take classes on several of the topics within sociology depending on the research specialties of the faculty at that particular campus (look at your general catalog to learn more about what is available to you). In general, introductory courses give students an overview of all that the discipline has to offer and its historical development, while more advanced classes focus in more depth on specific topics. At some universities, major courses make up the majority of a four-year education; at others, the major may represent as little as one-third of the overall degree. The difference tends to stem from whether the student is in an academic program that features a liberal arts or a professional/ technical education. Both can exist within the same university, although they are usually housed in different colleges or programs so that there is a clear distinction between students who are pursuing one versus another.

Liberal Education versus Professional Degree Program

A liberal education is based on the philosophy that it is important to gain a well-rounded education across many disciplines as well as in-depth knowledge within a specific area of study. The Association of American Colleges and Universities (2010) defines a **liberal education** as "an approach to learning that empowers individuals and prepares them to deal with complexity, diversity, and change ... it helps students develop a sense of social responsibility, as well as strong and transferable intellectual and practical skills ... and a demonstrated ability to apply knowledge and skills in real-world settings." As you can see, it is a holistic idea of developing the whole person to be able to move their intellectual knowledge into practice in the world.

One aspect of a liberal education, a broad knowledge of the wider world, is termed the **liberal arts,** which usually requires the student to complete courses from all the major discipline groupings: social science, fine arts, humanities, physical and biological sciences, and quantitative and engineering studies (see definitions in Chapter 1). This approach allows students to gain a broad understanding across a wide range of disciplines while gaining a more in-depth understanding of one discipline through their major requirements.

In a study of more than 22,500 faculty at 372 colleges and universities, the Higher Education Research Institute found that 73 percent of faculty stated that "instilling a basic appreciation for the liberal arts" was either very important or essential. Nearly all (95 percent) of faculty felt that it was very important or essential to help students master knowledge in a discipline (DeAngelo, et al., 2009).

Universities most often provide students with a liberal arts education through a structured set of requirements in which a certain number of courses must be completed in each area as part of the degree. This is often known as a general education. When a degree program has a **general education** component, the overall degree still has the same workload as those without it, but now the overall credits are split between the liberal arts and major courses. In addition, some universities allot a certain number of units for elective courses.

As a result, an undergraduate education can look quite different at each university. Even within the same university system, such as the State University of New York (SUNY), each campus might have different requirements. To illustrate, Table 5.1 lists the bachelor's degree requirements for four different research universities in the United States. You are invited to add the requirements for your university. You can see that all of these universities provide a liberal arts education and do so through general course requirements, but each program is unique in its approach.

In contrast, a **professional degree program** focuses on preparing students for specific careers that require competence in certain technology or skill sets. Some examples include engineering, nursing, accounting, law, medicine, and teaching. Some professional degrees can be earned with an undergraduate degree while others require advanced degrees. For undergraduate programs, some colleges offer intense and in-depth training in certain fields, most often in the technical and performing arts disciplines; these programs might require little or no study outside of the courses required for the major. However, there are certainly other programs that offer these same majors combined with a liberal arts education. At most research universities, even professional degrees like engineering or architecture will probably require at least a few courses from across the disciplines.

TABLE **5.1** **SAMPLE OF GRADUATION REQUIREMENTS FROM RESEARCH UNIVERSITIES**	
UNIVERSITY	**GRADUATION REQUIREMENTS (FOR 2010)**
Brigham Young University	◆ Doctrinal Foundations (Book Mormon, New Testament, Doctrine and Covenants) ◆ The Individual and Society (American Heritage, Global and Cultural Awareness) ◆ Skills (First-Year Writing, Advanced Written and Oral Communication, Quantitative Reasoning, Languages of Learning) ◆ Arts, Letters and Sciences (Civilization 1–2, Arts, Letters, Biological Science, Physical Science, Social Science) ◆ Electives ◆ Major of 20 minimum semester units ◆ Total of 120 semester units to graduate
Colorado State University	◆ All-University Core Curriculum that consists of the following four areas: 　— Basic Competencies (Intermediate Writing, Mathematics) 　— Communication (Advanced Writing or Oral Communication) 　— Foundations and Perspectives (general education in eight different discipline areas) 　— Depth and Integration (elements of the major that connect with the Core Curriculum and end with capstone course) ◆ Major of 27 minimum semester units ◆ Total of 120 semester units to graduate
University of Illinois at Chicago	◆ General Education Core (Analyzing the Natural World, Understanding the Individual and Society, Understanding the Past, Understanding the Creative Arts, Exploring World Cultures, Understanding U.S. Society) ◆ University Writing Requirement ◆ Major of 27 minimum semester units ◆ Total of 120 semester units to graduate
Massachusetts Institute of Technology	◆ General Institute Requirements (total of 17 subjects in the following areas): 　— Science requirement (chemistry, physics, calculus, biology) 　— Restricted electives in science and technology 　— Laboratory requirement (scientific methods) 　— Humanities, arts and social sciences requirement 　— Communication requirement (writing, public speaking) ◆ Major of required and elective courses (wide range of units) ◆ Unrestricted electives of 48 or more units ◆ Total of 180–198 units to graduate (beyond GIRs)

ACADEMIC CLASSES

Course Workload

The primary way that an undergraduate education is attained is through the successful completion of academic classes. Successful means that the student received the minimum grade required to earn the credits associated with that class. The criteria for **passing** depend on many things. At some universities, any grade above an F is passing; that is, a grade of D-minus would grant the student the credits for the course. In other programs, passing is only achieved at the C level, and sometimes higher. Check your undergraduate general catalog to find out the policies for your university. In addition, you might find that your major has different criteria for specific courses or for your overall grade point average (GPA) in your major. For example, you might be expected to earn no less than a B average in premajor courses to be admitted to the full major.

Each course is assigned a certain number of **credits,** sometimes called **units**, which is determined by the overall workload affiliated with the course. In general, a four-credit course will be more work than a two-credit course. However, it's not necessarily twice as much work. At most universities, the general estimate is that one credit involves about two hours of work per week outside of class time. In other words, a typical four-credit class requires eight hours of work per week that students can expect to do in the form of reading, reviewing notes, working on assignments, studying, and so on. In addition, students have in-class time (e.g., lecture, discussion section, or lab time) for about another four hours per week, making the one course worth about twelve total hours of work per week for the student. For universities that are on the ten-week quarter system, classes are generally four credits, whereas fifteen-week semester courses are often three credits. Classes can come in a wide range of forms, ranging from as little as half a credit to as many as six, depending on the course, the department, and the university.

Over time, a given course will be taught by various faculty members in the department, each of whom can offer a completely different syllabus as long as the course still follows the general catalog description. This allows each faculty member to make the course his or her own; it also means that students might find a wide range of workloads, content, and teaching styles associated with the very same course. This is why any course's credit load is just a rough estimate of the course's actual workload. To get a true estimate, students would need to see the actual syllabus of the course compiled by the faculty member who is teaching the course the term it will be taken.

For all first-year students, some adjustment is necessary to get accustomed to the pace of the workload at your university. It usually takes students one to two terms to get a feel for the pace, workload, exam scheduling, and other differences from the previous institution. Transfer students can often be caught off guard by the higher level of intensity or the increased pace, especially if the university is on the quarter system. In addition, it takes time to get used to the feel of a twelve-credit schedule or a sixteen-credit schedule.

The purpose of each individual class is to teach a specific set of critical concepts and learning outcomes to students. The faculty member who initially creates a course determines what the set of information will be, and the description that you find in the general catalog will give you a general overview of the topics in the course. However, the content of these topics and the way in which they are taught will be unique to each faculty member who teaches the course. In certain disciplines, such as math and the sciences, there is more consistency in the material, as it is fact-based, but each faculty member can still bring a very different teaching style and method to the material. However, in most of the other disciplines, there is much less consistency, as there can be different perspectives and interpretations of the topics. In the social sciences and humanities, it is not uncommon to have two offerings of the same course that bear little resemblance to each other. In addition, some disciplines seek to teach a range of theories or perspectives on the material. This can often be disconcerting to students who are used to being taught, and later tested on, the "right" answer.

Course Levels

Another aspect of academic classes is the **course level,** that is, the level of student toward whom they are geared. Most introductory courses are geared toward first- and second-year students (i.e., freshmen and sophomores). Each campus denotes these differently. At the University of California at Santa Barbara (UCSB), introductory courses are called **lower-division** courses and are numbered 1 to 99, for example, Anthropology 5, Art History 87, or Education 20. Read your general catalog to learn how these distinctions are indicated at your university. Generally, these introductory courses provide an overview of the course topics. For example, a history course might cover a long range of time, or a communications class might

TABLE **5.2** SAMPLE OF COURSE NUMBERING SYSTEMS FROM RESEARCH UNIVERSITIES			
UNIVERSITY	**INTRODUCTORY COURSES**	**ADVANCED COURSES**	**GRADUATE COURSES**
University of Idaho	100–299	300–499	500–699
University of Hawaii, Manoa	100–299	300–499	500–800
University of Illinois, Urbana-Champaign	100–299	300–499	500–799
Yale University	course numbers have no connection to level and vary by department		
University of California, Santa Barbara	00–99	100–199	200–599

cover all of the major areas of communication theory, such as interpersonal, mass media, and organizational.

More advanced courses are geared toward third- and fourth-year students and often have **prerequisites**, which are courses you must complete before you can enroll. These are called **upper-division** courses at UCSB and are numbered 100 to 199, for example, Sociology 102 and Education 173. More advanced classes tend to go into a narrower range of topics in more depth. For example, a history class might cover a very narrow specified period of time in more depth, such as the civil rights movement, or a communications class might focus on one specific form of communication, such as intergenerational communication.

Graduate-level courses are offered at a more advanced level for students who are pursuing master's or doctoral degrees in that particular discipline. At UCSB, these are numbered 200 to 599. Generally, undergraduate students do not enroll in graduate courses except under very special circumstances by faculty request.

Table 5.2 illustrates how these differences in course level are indicated at a few research universities. Again, check your general catalog to learn about yours.

Introductory courses in each discipline are usually open to all interested students, whether or not they are pursuing the major. In contrast, the research methods classes are usually taken only by those students who are earnestly pursuing the major and are often required before students can begin taking the major's more advanced classes. These classes prepare you for the more in-depth material that is found in the advanced classes. You will also find that research is still the primary focus of the upper-division classes, but the focus is more on what research tells us about that particular topic. For example, a course on the effects of television viewing on children will most likely involve reading and learning about various studies that have been done on this topic. Students are expected to engage in critical thinking to assess the validity of these studies and their relevance to understanding of the issue. In addition, more advanced classes may have students conduct a mini–research project of their own or participate in a university-sponsored research project.

This seeming lack of consistency in course content can be a frustrating thing for many first-year students. The K–12 system often teaches students to look for the "right" answer so that they can do well on the exam. At a research university, we are much more focused on thinking critically about the concepts and looking at multiple perspectives rather than one view or one answer. One skill that you will want to develop is to adjust quickly each term to each faculty member's way of teaching and his/her expectations, and then produce your work accordingly. This might mean that you have to utilize different strategies for each of your classes each term.

It is important that you understand related academic policies and structures at your university. Look in your college catalog and other documents to determine the following:

Circle the degrees offered at your university:

B.A.   B.S.   B.M.   B.F.A.

Which type of education are you enrolled in?

Liberal Arts   Professional Degree

Which course numbers denote lower-division or introductory?

Which course numbers denote upper-division or advanced?

Which course numbers denote graduate-level?

What constitutes your general education requirements?

ENROLLING IN YOUR COURSES

Selecting Your Courses

To ensure that you end up in classes that you enjoy, you will need to do some investigating. Students often wait until the class schedule is available and then scramble to pick classes when it's time to register. Often, students' choices are based on things like the time of day the class is offered, whether it meets on Fridays, or whether it is considered easy. While you will certainly find some enjoyable classes this way, you are essentially making a gamble, and you will probably end up with more classes that you do not enjoy than those that you do. In addition, you will find that there are not many "easy" classes at a top-rated research university. To learn more, you will need to be proactive and seek out information about classes. Read university publications, look at online resources, talk to and meet with advisors, and talk to other students. See "Point of Interest: Picking Good Classes."

The Importance of Academic Advising

Given all of the information above, it is important for students to be prepared and informed when selecting classes each term. The university community holds students responsible for their choices, so you are expected to take the actions necessary to make informed decisions. This includes reading official university documents and websites as well as seeking help when needed. It is your responsibility to read about the various **degree requirements** you need to fulfill, both for your major and for your overall degree. If you have questions or concerns, you will find that many **academic advisors** are available to help you. You will usually find them in your college's main office as well as your major department and they are trained to provide you with accurate information tailored to your specific undergraduate experience.

You are also responsible for making sure that you are fulfilling your requirements in a timely manner with the appropriate grades. Most campuses have a deadline for when all students must select a major. Don't let this sneak up on you without intentionally exploring your options. Many students find that it is helpful to keep an ongoing record of the courses they have taken and the requirements that they have satisfied with those courses. Some colleges and majors will give you prepared checklists that you can use to keep track of your progress. At other campuses, you might be on your own for doing so. You might wish to create a chart or

POINT OF INTEREST

PICKING GOOD CLASSES   You have many, many classes to take during your undergraduate experience, and investing a little time and energy can greatly improve the chances that you will enjoy your classes. By following the steps below, you can greatly increase your chances of having the educational experience you desire:

1. Go through your university's general catalog and highlight any class that sounds interesting to you. Don't worry that it might not be in your major or that it is for more advanced students. If the class sounds like something you would like to take, highlight it. If you have a general education program at your campus, I strongly recommend going through the same process for each requirement: Review the list of classes that fulfill each requirement and highlight *only* the classes that seem interesting to you. If there is only one required course, find out whether different faculty teach that course and what the differences are between their offerings. Choose the one that best suits you.

2. When the class schedule becomes available for a term, look at what is being offered and compare it to your list of classes that interest you. If a class that you would really like is not offered, wait until it is. In the meantime, choose another requirement for which something that interests you is available.

3. Check out the faculty member who is teaching the class. Ask friends whether they have had class with him or her. Find out more about what that student liked and disliked and compare those things to your own preferences. Remember to inquire about learning and teaching styles. If the class schedule does not indicate who will be teaching the class, call the sponsoring department and ask; they should be able to tell you who will be teaching it. Some even publish teaching evaluations of courses and make them available for students to review.

4. If you would like more information about a faculty member's teaching style, I recommend watching him or her in the classroom for a few minutes. You can tell a lot in a short period of time. To do this, you would need the class schedules for both next term and the current term. Find the name of the person who is teaching next term and then look that person up in the current schedule to see when she or he is currently teaching. It doesn't have to be for the same class; you're focusing only on the instructor's teaching abilities. Then visit the class for a few minutes and see for yourself whether that instructor's style meets your needs. Just be sure to stand or sit quietly in the back so as to not disturb the class.

5. If you want to know more about a specific course, you can contact the faculty member who will be teaching it and ask whether he or she has a copy of the syllabus you can look at. If not (some of us wait until the last minute to pull the syllabus together), you can see whether there is an old syllabus that might be available or even just ask a few questions about the content and workload. Just be sure that you phrase your request in an appropriate manner; for example, you might say, "I'm thinking of enrolling in your course, and I'd like to know more about the content, the assignments, and your teaching style." That will be received much better than "I'm checking out your course—I don't want anything too hard, so I'm wondering how much work your class will be."

6. Finally, make a list of several courses, placing some as your top choices and some as your alternates. That way, you can maximize your registration opportunities, even as classes fill up.

table that has an area for each term for all four years. Then pencil in various requirements at the time when you plan to take them. Once you take a course, write it in the correct place in pen and indicate the requirement(s) it fulfilled and the grade you earned. Periodically review your progress with an academic advisor and make adjustments as necessary.

In addition to degree requirements, your university will provide you with ample information about the process for **registering** for your classes. Most registration systems are set up according to seniority by credits, the most advanced students registering first and the students with the fewest credits registering last. Some groups might get priority registration no matter what their credit standing, such as honors students or athletes in their competitive season.

Once you have registered, keep a record and check it to make sure that it is accurate. If you need to make adjustments to your schedule, such as addressing a time conflict when one class overlaps another or adding or dropping a class, it is your responsibility to do so. Most

DEALING WITH DEADLINES Many first-year students have experienced serious problems because they missed important deadlines. To avoid this problem, I recommend that you transfer all important deadlines to your weekly planner or monthly calendar so that you decrease your chances of missing them. Write them in big, red letters on your planner or calendar. Also, be sure to note times as well as dates. For example, at my campus, the deadline for many items is at 4:00 P.M., when the office of the registrar closes. Although this time is adequately stated in all materials, many students write down only the date and are often very frustrated when they attempt to drop a class or pay their fees online after 4:00 P.M. only to find that the online system has shut down or the office has closed. Also, there is often a flood of student activity at 3:00 P.M., and many students find that they cannot get online or call in to the phone system because of the heavy traffic. Avoid these hassles by planning ahead.

Do not think that because you have stopped going to a class, you have been dropped from it. Many universities have a policy that only the student can drop a course from his or her schedule. At the end of the quarter, faculty find that there are a few students on their grade sheet who never came to class. Because these students have not completed any work, the instructor has no choice but to give them an F. Although the students can usually fix this situation through an appeal, it would have been so much easier if they had officially dropped the course by the deadline. Always be sure to drop any class you do not plan on attending.

registration systems include opportunities to make changes to your schedule, but again, these may have certain time frames or deadlines in which you need to function.

There are usually specified times and **deadlines** with regard to registration, some of which might have serious consequences if they are missed. These consequences can include missing out on available classes because you did not utilize the time in which you were supposed to register, late fees or fines, and even being dropped from classes or blocked from registering in the future for failing to heed important deadlines. Your university might have an appeal process for certain deadlines, but this will probably require a written petition and documentation of an extreme circumstance that prevented you from adhering to the process or deadline. See "Point of Interest: Dealing with Deadlines."

If you are unsuccessful in enrolling in a class that you need through the regular registration process, see if you are automatically put on a waiting list for that course. If not, you will need to try more creative ways to get the course. First, continue to try to add the class through regular registration methods during the window of time assigned to you to add and drop courses. Over that time, students are continually adding and dropping classes, which means that spots are often opening up in full classes just to be snatched up again a few minutes later. The student who repeatedly tries to add the class will likely gain one of these open spots. Also, there might be certain deadlines that precipitate classes opening up. For example, your campus might drop students from their classes if they fail to meet the fee payment deadline. That means that on that day or the next, spaces open up in quite a few classes; again, the observant student will be able to utilize this opportunity.

If these methods fail you, then the next step is to contact the faculty member who is teaching the course and request to be added. Most faculty have the ability to add or drop students, although they might or might not have reserved spaces to do so. If the instructor adds you or puts you on the waiting list, write back to say "thank you" and then be on time for the first class, because you could lose the spot you have gained if you are late.

Your final option is to "crash" the class. **Crashing classes** is a long-standing tradition on many university campuses, and it is the process by which students gain a spot in a class that is full. You essentially show up the first day and try to gain a spot, along with other people who are trying to do the same. If you were successful in being added to the waiting list, then you should be one of the first people the instructor adds. If not, the instructor will most likely have a process by which he or she handles crashers, such as taking people in the order of their class standing (seniors first, juniors second, etc.) or on a first-come, first-served basis.

Some faculty deal with crashers right away; others wait until the end of class. Be prepared either way. Also, persistence pays off in crashing. The more class periods you attend, the better your chances. If you really need or want a class, come to the first three or four sessions before giving up. You would be surprised how many students who are enrolled drop the class during the first week or fail to show up. If a spot does open up, you will be in line to get it. And if one doesn't, the instructor might just add you anyway because of your perseverance. Of course, if you are attempting to crash a course, demonstrate that you would make a positive contribution to the class by arriving on time, paying attention, and participating in class discussions when appropriate.

Selecting Majors and Minors

One of the many good things about attending a research university is that a degree from one is usually highly regarded by employers and graduate schools. In general, research universities tend to be more selective in their admissions process, which means that they can attract the best and brightest students in addition to world-renowned faculty. Together, these things create a prestigious institution of higher education. This positively affects students' postgraduate options because the students will possess a nationally respected degree. Because the final degree is prestigious, this increases the students' ability to pursue a wide range of majors.

Each university, and sometimes even each college within the same university, has its own process for **declaring majors,** which is the formal way a student indicates the major she or he plans to complete upon graduation. Usually, the process involves some kind of formal paperwork so that the appropriate departments are notified and the student's choice of major can be tracked. Some majors are open to anyone, so any interested student can declare them. Other majors require a certain level of competency, so there may be auditions or certain minimum criteria that must be met in order to pursue them. You will want to read about these policies in your university's catalog or speak to an academic advisor to learn more. The timing of when to declare a major usually depends on three things: the university's policies, a student's ability to find something that she or he wants to major in, and the need to graduate within four years. Needless to say, these things will not always be in perfect alignment.

The best way to select a major is based on two criteria: **interest and aptitude.** First and foremost, the student should pick a major on the basis of his or her interests. It is very difficult for a student to pursue four years of study and excel in classes that he or she does not find interesting. Lack of interest directly and negatively affects a student's focus and enthusiasm for a class, both of which are necessary to perform strongly. Aptitude is also a strong factor in determining an appropriate major. Unfortunately for first-year students, lack of university experience, appropriate workload management, and academic skills can influence their ability to perform well. Aptitude can be accurately assessed only when these other issues are handled—usually by the end of the first year. Only when these adjustments to university-level work have been made can a student truly know whether she or he is good in a subject.

Generally, if a student is working very hard, using all of the university resources that are available, and is still doing poorly, then it is safe to assume that the student will probably not be strong in that particular discipline. Although students may still choose to pursue the discipline, they might find that they have to work far harder than their peers and still might not do quite as well. When students find the perfect blend of interest and aptitude, they look forward to attending their classes and doing their homework, and they generally feel that it is easy to excel. See "Sarah's Story from the Path."

Needless to say, students who choose their major on the basis of interest and aptitude tend to do well in their major classes, and this opens many doors in the worlds of both graduate school and employment. They will often have a high GPA and can get strong letters of recommendation, both of which are important for postgraduate opportunities. See "Point of Interest: Choosing a Major."

SARAH'S STORY FROM THE PATH

I came to school this year without any idea about what I wanted to major in. I just started taking classes to fulfill the general educational requirements, hoping that I would get some ideas. My first quarter, I took classes in a variety of topics: history, classics, and philosophy. I enjoyed them all, but I really liked my classics class, so I took another one my second quarter, along with biology, art history, and geology. Again, my classics class stood out as the most interesting and enjoyable. That quarter, I was also enrolled in the freshman experience course. One of our lectures was on finding a major, and the speaker talked about how important it is to find a passion, something you love to study. It hit me right there in class. I love to study classics! The reading is totally interesting to me, and I looked forward to every lecture. So I have declared the classics major and am really happy. It's a very small department so I already know most of the faculty, and I am doing a directed reading with one of my professors. Luckily, my parents have been really supportive of my choice. I am not sure yet what I will do for a career, but I have time to figure that out. There are actually lots of career possibilities for classics majors, and I can always expand my options with some internships, which I will be looking into next quarter.

Early in a student's college experience, the urgency to declare a major depends on the complexity of major requirements. Students in the sciences usually need to get started early on their major course work because it involves so many year-long series of science courses. If they want to graduate within four years, students in the sciences need to begin their major requirements the first term. While second-year students can certainly begin a science major, they will usually not be able to complete it within four years. However, this might be a fine trade-off if they truly want to pursue the sciences as a lifelong career.

In addition, students in certain technical and arts majors may have been admitted to a particular college or program. Changing majors out of that general discipline might require a change of colleges or academic programs, and this may even involve an application process.

POINT OF INTEREST

CHOOSING A MAJOR Remember, choosing a major is about discovering what you would like to study. Here are three simple ways to see if a major might be for you. One is to read about the major in your general catalog. There is usually a description of the discipline and the specific subfields that are offered at your campus. Read the course descriptions, both introductory and more advanced. If you find a lot of classes that sound interesting to you, then you might enjoy this major.

Second, visit the campus bookstore and peruse the shelves associated with that particular major. Look at the books that are assigned for different classes. Glance over the table of contents and skim a few pages. If they sound interesting to you and like something you would like to read, then that is another clue that it might be worth exploring.

Finally, talk to more advanced students in the major. Find juniors and seniors and ask them about the classes and the overall major. Remember to account for personal differences like interests, aptitudes, and learning styles. If you like what you hear, that is another good sign that you should check out this major by taking a course or two and then deciding for yourself.

How do you know whether a class or discipline interests you enough to consider it as a major? A discipline is a good bet for a major when the following are true for you on a regular basis:

- You find yourself looking forward to a class.
- You don't want to miss class.
- You find the reading enjoyable and intriguing.
- You enjoy doing the assignments.
- You highly recommend the class or discipline to others.

If you are not sure about what career opportunities might be available, meet with a career or major advisor. You might just be surprised at how many opportunities there are even for majors that seem somewhat limited in terms of career potential. For example, many students and families assume that sociology majors are limited to careers in social work. This is simply not true. The American Sociological Society identifies a wide range of career opportunities for people with a degree in sociology, including jobs in business, social service, government, journalism, politics, public relations, public administration, law, education, medicine, criminal justice, social work, counseling, advertising, real estate, public health, environment, finance, investing, and writing.

While some majors and colleges have strict policies like those previously outlined in this section, many do not. Many majors can be finished within two years and so can be declared by the end of the sophomore year and the student still will be able to finish the degree within four years. This type of timeline can allow a student to explore a wide range of options through general education and elective courses that lead to the selection of a major. You will want to find out about these policies and options at your university by consulting the catalog or an academic advisor.

Some majors, usually the most popular or crowded ones, might have some type of screening process to handle the demand. There might be a set of courses that all students who are interested in that major must complete, and there might even be a minimum GPA that must be met. In such cases, the introductory classes are often difficult and very competitive, as the intention is to weed out the less serious or apt students. If you are interested in one of these majors, be sure you really focus on doing well by utilizing your resources (office hours, study groups, tutors, etc.). If you fail to meet the GPA requirement, you will not be allowed to pursue the major, and you will have to find another one.

Changing a major depends on the complexity of the majors and the timing in which the change occurs. Changing a major is usually accomplished through filling out a form or an online process. Changing from one major to another will be affected by all of the issues stated in this section, and this can limit some possibilities. If done quite late, it certainly can affect whether the student will be able to graduate within four years. In fact, some campuses do not allow students to begin a more complex major if they seek to do so after the second year. This is because many research universities are committed to graduating their students in a timely manner in order to accommodate future incoming classes. Visit an academic advisor to learn more about your options. See "Point of Interest: When to Drop a Major."

Many universities offer students the option of pursuing double majors and/or minors. A **double major** usually means that the student completes the work for two complete majors, with little or no overlap. To do this, some programs require students to use their elective courses for the second major. **Minors** are less work than a full major but still provide a significant amount of contact with the discipline. Not all academic departments that offer majors offer a minor, so explore the options at your campus. In addition, speak with an academic advisor to ensure that

POINT OF INTEREST

WHEN TO DROP A MAJOR When a student selects a major, it is often for reasons that have little to do with the actual major. The student might believe that a certain major will lead to a certain career or will ensure a certain future earning level. As already stated, it is very important to explore these beliefs and expectations with career and academic advisors at your campus so that you can make accurate and informed choices. However, it will still be important that you actually enjoy the major that you finally choose. Some majors sound great when you read the catalog but are disappointing in reality. Or they might be great majors, but a student cannot seem to perform at a level that is competitive with his or her peers.

This is the bottom line: If you have tried the suggestions I have previously offered (in terms of choosing classes wisely and finding faculty you enjoy) and you are still not enjoying or doing well in the major, do not pursue it! The major is clearly not a good match based on the criteria of interest and aptitude, and you would

be better served by finding another major. I have seen students stick with majors that they either did not enjoy or were not good at, and it was painful to watch. These students spent four years in drudgery, unmotivated to attend class, unenthusiastic about learning, and, inevitably, unimpressive to future graduate programs and employers because of their grades.

I truly believe that every person has a passion, something that makes your heart sing and that you find interesting and exciting. It is important for you to find that for yourself. There are many great assessment tools (see next section) that can point you in the right direction, but ultimately, you have to listen to yourself and what you find compelling. This might be very different from what your parents wish for you or from what is supported by others. Ultimately, it is you who sits in the desk every day and must spend this precious time of your life focusing your energy on your studies. It is imperative that you make selections on the basis of your preferences and passions.

You will be held responsible for knowing relevant academic policies and adhering to relevant deadlines. You will also be expected to seek help if and when you are confused. In addition, in order to maximize your university experience, you will want to know the options available to you in terms of majors and minors. Take a moment to look in your university's documents or its website to determine the following information:

Academic advising in your college—

Location:

Phone:

Website:

Academic advising in your major—

Location:

Phone:

Website:

Deadlines for this term—

To pay fees:

To drop a course: ...

To add a course: ...

To change grading options: ...

To withdraw: ...

To file an incomplete: ...

To declare a major: ...

Can students double major?   Y   N
Can students major and minor?   Y   N

Three majors or minors that interest you:

1.

2.

3.

you clearly understand the process for pursuing these options and how to do so without taking too long to graduate.

The options of double majors and minors are usually considered when a student is genuinely interested in more than one field of study. In addition, these options allow the student to put two fields of study together in preparation for a unique career. A double major of any field paired with a foreign language opens up opportunities for international work as well as domestic careers in areas in which there are multilingual communities or clients. Be sure to explore these options with a career advisor on your campus so that you choose wisely and are not following out-of-date or inaccurate information. It is through these options that students can maximize their education at a research university with savvy career preparation that will poise them for successful careers.

THE CONNECTION BETWEEN MAJORS AND CAREERS

Most students and their families rightfully believe that a person who earns a bachelor's degree has more employment opportunities than a person who does not. In addition, the salary earnings over a person's lifetime can be far greater for a college graduate, with even more earnings possible with postgraduate degrees. Data from the College Board indicates that a person with a bachelor's degree earns nearly $22,000 more per year than a person whose education ended with high school (Baum, Ma, & Payea, 2010). That is more than a million dollars over a career lifetime.

With this in mind, many students and parents believe that the path to high-paying jobs begins with the selection of the major. However, this is not true for most careers. Most careers, including the "popular" ones, such as medicine or law, can be pursued with a variety of undergraduate majors. The careers that do require a certain major are the professional or technical careers, such as engineering or nursing, in which a specific course of study is required to have the qualifications needed for most entry-level jobs. Students who wish to pursue these careers spend their undergraduate years in a focused and intense program of study.

Most students and their families have expectations that an undergraduate education serves as a form of vocational preparation—in other words, training for a specific job. This is true at some colleges, especially those that offer specific job-training courses such as hotel management or journalism, but it is generally *not* true at research universities. However, degrees from research universities are considered prestigious because employers usually seek the critical-thinking, analytical, and writing skills that are taught at a research university. Employers know that students will have learned the latest theories and information for a field and, better yet, will have the skills to stay abreast of future developments.

Because classes at a research university do not teach other specific career or job skills, many students choose to augment their degree with job-preparation activities. All students can gain this applied knowledge and job-skill training by utilizing research opportunities, holding several internships, and taking advantage of university workshops on important job skills such as public speaking, leadership, and computing. Consult with the career services office at your university for more information about what is offered on or near your campus. Regardless of the major, most students can build an impressive resume while in college by designing their own vocational preparation program.

Common Career Myths

Several career myths are widely held by students and parents alike.

+ **Myth #1:** There is a strong relationship between a college major and a specific career. This is simply not true. In almost every career field, you will find successful people who have a wide range of college majors, with the exception of careers that require a strong background in technical training, such as engineering. This means that most undergraduate students can choose from a whole host of majors and still pursue almost any career that interests them. With this said, it is important that students and their parents not let these myths dictate the students' choices for a major. It is truly a shame when students limit their focus to one or two majors without even trying a wide range of classes. High school students have never been exposed to most of the disciplines they will find at a research university, so how can they select a focused field of study without exploring their options? And how good can a choice be if it is based on misinformation or myths? The best way to seek advice about career planning is to visit the career services office at your university. The staff there can give you concrete information on the various paths that lead to certain careers, the salaries and opportunities that various careers offer, and other important information.

+ **Myth #2:** A student needs to major in biology if she or he wants to get into medical school. This is simply not true. While medical schools require the completion of a certain set of courses during the undergraduate education (known as premed courses), students can complete these while pursuing a whole range of nonscience majors. In fact, there are so many biology majors who apply to medical school that a student actually *improves* his or her chances of admission by being anything but a biology major! What medical schools look at most is the grades in the premed courses and the MCAT scores. If a student has done well in these two areas and has pursued a major other than biology, his or her chances are actually greater because of the unique educational background that the student would bring to the medical school. Of course, the student would need to have excelled in the chosen major and have a strong GPA.

CAREER PLANNING   It is never too early to visit your campus career services office to gain information about the available opportunities as well as to learn more about careers that interest you. While your use of the career center will increase during your university years, it is important to start early, even if you have no idea what career you wish to pursue. Most career centers even have assessment tools that can help you learn more about your preferences and talents, which can guide you in the selection of your future career. The career center can probably even connect you with alumni who are currently in the career you wish to pursue so that you can learn more about what it is really like and how to best prepare to enter that field. As you get closer to graduation, the career center can help you prepare your professional résumé, assist you with interview skills, and may even bring employers to campus to conduct real job interviews.

As with any office, a career center has a range of people who can assist you. Once you find a person with whom you connect, be sure to schedule future appointments with him or her. Over time, this person can guide your undergraduate experience and career development in ways that are best suited to you. Don't forget that your faculty can also assist you with career exploration and planning.

+ **Myth #3:** A student needs to major in political science or government to be admitted to law school. Again, this is simply not true, and in fact, students with non–political science majors and strong LSAT scores will again be more competitive against the hundreds of applicants with political science degrees.
+ **Myth #4:** A student needs to have an undergraduate degree in the same field in which he or she wishes to pursue a master's or doctorate degree. Although this is true for some fields, namely, the sciences, most graduate programs accept students from a wide range of majors with very few requiring any undergraduate course work in the field. Check the admissions criteria for that graduate program for more specific information.

It is important to distinguish choosing a major from choosing a career. **Choosing a major** is about discovering what you love to study. This means finding out what you would enjoy reading and writing about for four years. Separately, **choosing a career** is about discovering the type of work you love to do. This involves learning what you would enjoy doing or engaging in for forty or more hours per week. Both decisions are very important but require different considerations for different times of your life; therefore, they should be approached separately.

According to the 2009 Your First College Year (YFCY) study, 68 percent of the 26,758 freshmen surveyed said they were satisfied or very satisfied with the relevance of course work to their future career plans, and 62 percent felt the same about the relevance of course work to everyday life (Ruiz, et al., 2010). Interestingly, in a study done on faculty in 2004–2005, nearly three-quarters (73 percent) of faculty felt that preparing students for employment after college was very important or essential, while 61 percent felt the same about graduate or advanced education. However, only 30 percent felt that increased earning potential is the chief benefit of a college education (Lindholm, et al., 2005). See "Point of Interest: Career Planning."

Tools for Major Selection and Career Planning

Selecting a major and planning for a career can seem daunting, especially to first-year students at research universities, because there is so little focus on vocations. However, you can use several tools to learn more about yourself, which will aid you in finding a good match for your personality. Again, academic and career advisors can assist you, so be sure to visit yours early and often.

HOLLAND CAREER TYPOLOGY   One frequently used tool for major and career exploration is the Holland Career Typology, created by John Holland in 1959. Holland believed that people are most happy in jobs that match their personality type. Based on his research, he argued that there are six main personality types: Realistic, Investigative, Artistic, Social, Enterprising, and Conventional (Holland, 2007). We each have all six types within us but express one the most often in our lives. Descriptions of these six types follow:

1. **Realistic:** This type is very physical, and is affiliated with people who are strong, athletic, and coordinated. People of this type prefer to work with things like machines, plants, animals, and tools, preferably outdoors but still in a structured work environment. This type is not very interested in being social so also values work that has significant time alone. Some preferred careers are carpenter, pilot, engineer, animal trainer, and naturalist.

2. **Investigative:** This type values concepts or theories and utilizes logical analysis to solve problems. People of this type enjoy working with data and information and are often good at math and science. They preferred unstructured environments and are drawn to careers like scientist, researcher, computer programmer, and doctor.

3. **Artistic:** Imagination is the hallmark of this type along with creative expression of all kinds. This type dislikes rules and regulations so prefers unstructured environments and independence. People of this type are intuitive and emotionally expressive. Potential careers include the performing arts (dancing, singing), design (fashion, graphic), writing (books, screenplays), and the business aspect of creative works like galleries or museums.

4. **Social:** This group enjoys connecting with others so likes to work in group environments. These people have good "people skills" and are drawn to helping others. Relationships are important to them, and harmony in the workplace is key. Good career matches include education, counseling, child care, training, and all health-related fields.

5. **Enterprising:** Like the previous group, this type enjoys working with other people but in a leadership role rather than a helping one. These people are good leaders and tend to be assertive and confident. They like harmonious work environments but are driven by results. Potential careers include entrepreneurs, lawyers, politicians, sales reps, managers, and leaders of organizations like chancellors and CEOs.

6. **Conventional:** This group actually enjoys rules and regulations because their strengths are organization, precision, and attention to detail. People of this type thrive in orderly work environments and enjoy working with things that are concrete, like money or computer programming. This group would enjoy careers in accounting, information technology, finance, and administration.

Students can take an assessment to determine their top three types, which gives them a three-letter code like RAS or ISC. This can help students to explore related majors and careers in those areas. Some university career centers are even organized around these six types, making it easy for students to find relevant material.

MYERS-BRIGGS TYPE INDICATOR® Another wonderful tool is the **Myers-Briggs Type Indicator®** (MBTI®), which is a personality test that is used by thousands of people around the world. It is often used for assisting students to select majors and careers, and is also really helpful in understanding the nature of conflict in relationships (e.g., roommates, romantic partners, parents, coworkers, etc.), as different types approach the world in different ways.

The MBTI® is based on the work of Carl Jung, a psychologist who studied psychological types. Isabel Myers and Katharine Briggs, a mother-daughter team, created the test to measure Jung's theory. It has four scales that are continuums and a person can place on either side of the midpoint, with the distance from the midpoint indicating strength of preference or how set that aspect is for them. The higher the score, the more set it is, with close to the midpoint indicating transition. The MBTI® is also developmental, as people change over time as different life experiences shape their personalities.

It is useful to take the MBTI® in college, as it can give some clues about potential majors and careers. But this is also a time of great emotional and intellectual change, so another score in the late 20s is advised. The official MBTI® costs money, but many campus learning and career centers offer it for students at a reduced rate (e.g., Career Services at UCSB charges only $15). You can also find the MBTI® online for a fee of $55 at www.discoveryourpersonality.com. However, as with most things, you can find free online adaptations—just search for free Myers-Briggs or Jung Personality tests. These are close approximations and will give you a sense of your score, but they lack the reliability and validity of the official MBTI® that now has the data of thousands of people from all countries and cultures around the world. You should take time to get your own score before reading about the scales. You will receive one of sixteen possible four-letter codes, like ENFJ or ISTP, and a number associated with each letter. The number represents the strength of that preference.

According to Molly Steen (2010), a professional career advisor, the first scale is the Extraversion/Introversion (E/I) scale. This is a measure of how people get energy, not of social skills or "outgoingness." Extraverts get their energy from being around others whereas Introverts get their energy from being alone or in the company of a couple of trusted friends. After a party, an Extravert will be energized while an Introvert will be drained. Other distinctions include:

(E) EXTRAVERSION	INTROVERSION (I)
✦ Get energy from being around others	✦ Get energy from being alone
✦ Prefer busy environments	✦ Prefer quiet environments
✦ When working, can jump from thing to thing easily, and work from the top	✦ When working, like to focus and go deep into the project
✦ Process information externally and achieve clarity by talking it through	✦ Process information internally and achieve clarity by thinking it through
✦ Value making connections with others	✦ Value internal thoughts, feelings, and emotions

The next scale is the Sensing/Intuition (S/N) scale and measures how people get information. Sensors prefer information that is factual or concrete, while Intuitives prefer information that is theoretical or conceptual. In other words, Ns like the bigger picture, while Ss like the details. Other distinctions include:

(S) SENSING	INTUITIVE (N)
✦ Prefer information is that factual or concrete	✦ Prefer information that is theoretical or conceptual
✦ Like detailed data that is practical and can be utilized as is	✦ Like understanding concepts but not real interested in the proofs
✦ Good at taking ideas and putting them into real-world applications	✦ Good at creating ideas through brainstorming and innovation
✦ When working, value thoroughness over speed	✦ When working, value speed over thoroughness
✦ Work from data to concepts	✦ Work from concepts to data
✦ Like to learn something and then do it over and over again to gain mastery	✦ Like to learn something, get the hang of it, and then move on to another

The third scale measures how people make decisions and is called the Thinking/Feeling (T/F) scale. Thinkers use a linear and analytical process while Feelers utilize an internal and emotional process. This scale has no correlation to the previous S/N scale in that both Thinkers and Feelers can prefer either sensing or intuitive data. Other distinctions include:

(T) THINKING	FEELING (F)
• Use a linear and analytical process • Use a step-wise process to look at data and consider the pros and cons • Concerned with doing the "smart" thing • Value an impersonal and objective process • Focus on the "head"	• Use an internal and emotional process • Use a process that involves imagining the outcome to consider how it feels • Concerned with doing the "right" thing • Value a personal and subjective process • Focus on the "heart" or "gut"

Western society tends to value the Thinking style and you will certainly see a heavy bias to the Thinking style at research universities. But research has actually shown that both types of decision making are equally effective, that is, decisions made with Thinking or Feeling strategies are equally likely to be successful.

The final scale is the Judging/Perceiving (J/P) scale that measures people's response to decisions they have made. Judgers prefer to make a decision and feel better once it is done, while Perceivers like to keep their options open and feel trapped after a decision is made. In other words, Js like to plan ahead and Ps like to be spontaneous. For example, Js will travel by having reservations and itineraries made well in advance, while Ps like to get to their destination and then choose where they want to stay and what they want to do. Other distinctions include:

(J) JUDGING	PERCEIVING (P)
• Prefer to have decisions made (feel secure knowing what's going on) • More time-oriented and value punctuality—will prioritize being on time for the next thing, even leaving the current thing in the middle • Manage life by using organization systems like calendars, lists, etc. • Like to have lots of control; sometimes perceived as "control freaks"	• Prefer to keep their options open (feel trapped if decision is made) • More process-oriented and value being in the moment—will prioritize finishing what's started even if that makes them late for the next thing • Manage life by using their sense of what is needed in the present moment • Like to have lots of options; sometimes perceived as "flakes"

Judgers can be spontaneous but often plan a time for it (e.g., "I'll take Saturday afternoon to go with the flow)" and Perceivers can be planners when needed (e.g., for a work project or a special event), but the difference is mainly due to the emotional reaction that Js and Ps have to making decisions. Since this scale is tied to strong personal feelings (i.e., in control versus trapped), the inherent tension between these opposing preferences can create conflict in relationships.

The MBTI® produces sixteen different personality types based on the various combinations of the four scales. Each personality type not only has the distinctions charted above but also has preferences for communication style, work environment, and leadership. The value of taking the official test is that you get a complete report with information on all of these aspects of your score.

The MBTI® can help students choose majors and careers because there is a lot of data correlating what types of careers the different personality types prefer. For example, 95 percent of university professors are INTJs, and if you think about what a career of research is about, that makes sense—they get energy from being alone or in small groups, they prefer theoretical or conceptual data, they make decisions in an analytical process, and they prefer to plan ahead.

HEATHER'S STORY FROM THE PATH

I came to college already having chosen my major, and I knew exactly how long it would take me to earn my degree. I had planned for this moment in my life since the beginning of high school, and there was no way that I was going to stray from my perfectly laid plan. No matter what it took, I was going to graduate from my university with an undergraduate degree in biomedical sciences.

My first semester went pretty smoothly, except for a few bumps here and there. I noticed that I didn't enjoy my science classes as much as I had in high school, and I became bored quickly while trying to study or pay attention in class. At the time, I figured that I was just going to have to train myself to stay more focused on my work. The next semester, my major required me to take chemistry, biology, and calculus; I knew this combination was going to be hard, but I was an experienced college student, and I thought that I could handle it. Boy, was I wrong! I quickly became bored with biology and calculus, and I absolutely hated chemistry. While some students around me loved them, these classes were just not a good fit for me! I remember thinking

to myself that if I could just make it to the end of the spring semester, I could go home and take a break and hit the ground running again in the fall.

Fall semester arrived quickly, and I found that it was no different from my last. Three of my classes were biology- and chemistry-based, but I was stubbornly determined to conquer them no matter what it required of me. Three weeks into the semester, I realized that once again, I did not like going to my science classes. I realized that I didn't want to do medicine because I loved it—I wanted to do it because it was what my parents do, and what I had always planned on doing myself.

After coming to this conclusion, I decided to talk to a counselor at the career center. She had me take a few assessments that helped to match my interests with careers and majors that supported them, and she eventually helped me decide on a major better suited to my interests and abilities. The best advice I can give you is that if you are having trouble in your classes, go seek help! You could be in the wrong major (for you), and if you don't have any idea of what you want to do, the counselors at the career center can help you find the perfect major for you!

THE SCENIC ROUTE

Visit www.cengagebrain.com to find the companion website containing links to:

- Potential careers affiliated with MBTI® scales
- Activities affiliated with the *Major in Success* book for college students
- Bureau of Labor Statistics *Occupational Outlook Handbook* information on careers including salaries, prospects, daily duties, and so on

But the reality is that any type can do any occupation. Many universities use the MBTI® to help students choose classes, majors, and careers.

STRONG INTEREST INVENTORY® Another popular tool for major and career exploration is the Strong Interest Inventory®. It is based on work done by E. K. Strong, Jr., and measures occupational themes, interest, and personality style. It is grounded in the premise that if a group of people enjoy their jobs, and you share similar interests with them, you might find those same jobs enjoyable. The assessment measures a wide range of interests and the corresponding report generates a series of occupations to explore. It utilizes some aspects of the Holland Career Theory by measuring the same six areas plus many others. The one tool that combines it all is the Strong Interest Inventory® and Myers-Briggs Type Indicator® Career Report that you can find at www.discoveryourpersonality.com. It costs $80 and is well worth the price because it will give you very useful and concrete information for major selection and career planning. Again, your campus might offer it at a much lower rate—visit your career center for options. See "Heather's Story from the Path."

Career Skills

One of the things to consider during your first year is how you can develop the skills you need to be competitive in the current job market. While your degree will definitely teach you critical-thinking and analytical writing skills, and you will graduate with knowledge of the most current research in your discipline, you also need to work on your career-related skills so that you can market yourself appropriately. According to the National Association of Colleges and Employers (NACE, 2009), the top five personal qualities or skills that employers are seeking in applicants are:

- ✦ Communication skills
- ✦ Strong work ethic
- ✦ Teamwork skills

- ✦   Initiative skills
- ✦   Analytical skills

Dr. Alan Farber, author of *How to Prepare for a Career and Get a Great Job* (2009), states that today's employers are also looking for:

- ✦   Evidence of relevant work experience
- ✦   Leadership skills
- ✦   Community service
- ✦   Communication skills
- ✦   Computer skills
- ✦   Cultural competence

Consider how you can utilize all the opportunities at your campus, both curricular and cocurricular, to develop in these areas (see Chapter 8 for more information).

You will want to be able to create a résumé that illustrates your skills and experience. Some students even create portfolios of their academic work and work experience to present at interviews.

THEORIES OF TEACHING AND LEARNING

Some factors that greatly influence the experience a student has in an academic class are the instructor's personality, attitude, and teaching style. Some faculty members are lively lecturers who are energetic and passionate about the topic. Others are incredibly shy and are very uncomfortable when speaking to a large audience. Sadly, a few might even feel that teaching is a waste of valuable time that could be better spent on research. Students tend to most enjoy classes that are taught by faculty who enjoy teaching and are comfortable speaking to an audience. In addition to their personality and general enthusiasm about undergraduate education, each of your faculty members will also engage in different teaching styles.

Teaching Styles

Dr. Anthony Grasha (1996, 2007) determined that instructors generally use one of five **teaching styles.** He argued that instructors can use these styles in different combinations based on the needs of the classroom environment, including the students' learning styles and ability to handle the material, students' needs regarding instructors' control of tasks, and the instructors' willingness to build relationships with their students. Each student tends to have a teaching style preference, which makes some instructors a good match for that student while other students would not enjoy those instructors' classes as much. The five teaching styles are as follows:

1. **Expert:** Instructors focus on providing specific content to their students and helping their students become proficient with that material. The instructor perceives him/herself

as an expert on the material and wishes to maintain that status among the students by demonstrating his/her knowledge. For example, the instructor would teach the history of the civil rights movement through lectures and readings, probably of his/her own writing.

2. **Formal Authority:** Instructors focus on specific learning outcomes in terms of content and Bloom's Hierarchy. The instructor also is concerned with teaching the correct or appropriate process for doing things and provides students with a strong structure within which to learn. This instructor would teach the content through lectures and other class activities but would also build in modules about how to write a good research paper or how to analyze historical documents.

3. **Personal Model:** Instructors focus on students performing or demonstrating mastery of the content through a procedure. The instructor believes in role modeling and uses demonstrations and student participation to teach students how to do the particular process. This is followed by observation, feedback, and encouragement. For example, the instructor would teach students how to write an analytical argument, and then students would be asked to research and write an argument on some aspect of the civil rights movement. Students would be provided with feedback and allowed to rework aspects of the assignment to build competence.

4. **Facilitator:** Instructors focus on the learning process of the students. The development of learning skills is as important as the content, if not more so. Instructors utilize student-centered activities to teach students how to use the content to problem-solve in that discipline. There is a lot of focus on helping students develop their own independent and critical-thinking skills. For example, the instructor could ask students to research and design a model for bringing about change on a current social justice issue of relevance to the student. Students might be required to use the civil rights movement in their learning and preparation.

5. **Delegator:** Instructors focus on the personal growth of the students and use content to help students enhance their human potential. Often, delegators focus on social skills such as communication, value-based decision making, or effective citizenship. This style is the most dynamic and requires the instructor to know the students' capabilities intimately and adjust the learning environment accordingly. Strong emphasis is placed on student autonomy. For example, an instructor might design an interactive weekend retreat to explore issues of racism and other oppression.

Interestingly, 80 percent of freshmen who participated in the 2009 Your First College Year survey indicated that they were "satisfied" or "very satisfied" with the overall quality of instruction they received, and 67 percent felt the same about the amount of contact they had with faculty. Thirty-six percent of freshmen indicated that they interacted with faculty in office hours one to two times per term while 28 percent did so one to two times per month. Another 27 percent visited faculty office hours once a week or more (Ruiz, et al., 2010).

Another study conducted in 2007–2008 of more than 22,000 college faculty found that faculty used a wide range of teaching and evaluation methods in their classes (DeAngelo, et al., 2009). The top five methods used in "most" or "all" classes by faculty were as follows:

1. Cooperative learning/small groups (59 percent)
2. Group projects (36 percent)
3. Multiple drafts of written work (25 percent)
4. Student evaluations of each other's work (24 percent)
5. Reflective writing/journaling (22 percent)

Grading on a curve was used by only 17 percent of the faculty, and short-answer exams were utilized by 46 percent.

THE SCENIC ROUTE

Visit www.cengagebrain.com to find the companion website containing links to:

- Indiana State University's Center for Teaching and Learning
- Specific strategies for students to utilize based on their learning style
- An online learning styles questionnaire

FIGURE 5.1 Learning Styles Continuaa

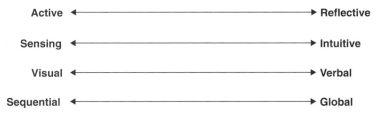

Learning Styles

Preference for teaching style is related to the student's **learning style,** which is the person's preferred or best mode for processing information. Students learn best when the information that is presented matches their preferred mode. Originally, research in this area indicated that students fell into one of three categories: visual learners (who learn best by reading or seeing information), auditory learners (who learn best by hearing information), and tactile or kinesthetic learners (who learn best by doing). Felder and Silverman (1988) more recently discovered that there are actually four continuums of learning preferences (for a total of eight different learning styles), and students can utilize a combination of them as well (see Figure 5.1).

Dr. Felder currently teaches at North Carolina State University. Following is a brief description of the eight styles and learning strategies that are useful to each particular style.

1. **Active:** These students prefer to learn by doing and also prefer working with others. Some learning strategies that work well for active learners are to work in groups, explain material to others, take notes while reading or listening to lectures, brainstorm potential exam questions, apply the material to their personal experience, and have hands-on experiences with the material.
2. **Reflective:** These students prefer to learn by thinking about things and also prefer working alone. Some learning strategies that work well for reflective learners are to review the material, listen and read about material, think about possible exam questions, and build memory skills.
3. **Sensing:** Students who prefer this style tend to be good at memorizing and want to learn concrete information such as facts and rules. Learning strategies include asking instructors for concrete examples, thinking about practical applications of the material, and seeking out hands-on experiences.
4. **Intuitive:** Intuitive learners like to ponder concepts and innovate new possibilities. Useful learning strategies for this style are to have instructors help connect the material to the bigger picture, link material to broader theories and concepts, and find meaning in facts, statistics, and the like.
5. **Visual:** These students prefer information to be presented visually, through pictures, demonstrations, and models. Learning strategies include using color to organize material, highlighting information, drawing or diagramming concepts to see relationships, finding visual representations of the material, and using films and other visual media for learning.
6. **Verbal:** Students who are verbal learners like to have material presented in words, either written or spoken. Some learning strategies that work well for verbal learners are outlining notes of what they have heard or read, writing summaries of material, discussing material with others, and asking questions of instructors.
7. **Sequential:** Sequential learners like to learn information in a step-by-step process. Learning strategies include defining the steps to learn a task, organizing material in a sequential order, and outlining notes of lectures and readings in a systematic fashion.

8. **Global:** These students prefer to see the big picture in order to learn the details of the material. These students are best served by reviewing their syllabus and skimming reading before going back to learn the details, relating what they learn to their personal experience and knowledge, and studying one topic in depth rather than many topics over a short period of time.

Students often utilize more than one learning style, and they can also develop other styles over time as they gain new skills and abilities. You might find that specific disciplines are more likely to align with certain learning styles, which is why some students feel an immediate connection with a certain course or discipline. For example, sequential learners often enjoy the field of history.

Students learn best when their preferred learning style matches the instructor's teaching style because the instructor's methods automatically line up with the student's best mode of learning. Table 5.3 shows how these two models of teaching and learning styles intersect to form matches between the instructor and the student.

Although learning styles indicate the mode in which a student learns best, students cannot always control the form and method by which they are taught. As a result, they might need to translate the information they have been taught into the form that works best for them. For example, if you are a visual learner in a class that is taught by an instructor who uses the formal authority style, you might have to take your lecture notes and create visual representations of the material. Although this will take additional time and effort on your part, it will assist you in mastering the material and equalize your learning with that of students in the class who are auditory learners.

Many great books and resources on learning styles are available. Your campus might even offer workshops on these topics, which would be very useful to a first-year student. It's a good idea to assess your learning style as early in your college career as possible so that it can guide your learning and studying strategies.

TABLE 5.3   MATRIX SHOWING THE INTERSECTION OF TEACHING AND LEARNING STYLES

| | TEACHING STYLE | | | | |
LEARNING STYLE	EXPERT APPROACH	FORMAL AUTHORITY APPROACH	PERSONAL MODEL APPROACH	FACILITATOR APPROACH	DELEGATOR APPROACH
Active			X	X	X
Reflective	X	X			X
Sensing	X	X	X		
Intuitive			X	X	X
Visual			X	X	
Verbal	X	X			
Sequential		X	X	X	
Global			X		X

Getting recommendations for courses from other students can be helpful in your own search for classes. However, remember that the accuracy of a recommendation depends on several things:

♦ *Who is teaching the course?* A course can be wonderful or horrible depending on the instructor's personality and teaching style. Find out whether your friend liked the instructor and what, specifically, your friend enjoyed. Find out whether that same instructor will be teaching that course again. If not, then your friend's recommendation will not give you much help.

♦ *What are your preferred learning and teaching styles?* It is often the alignment of the instructor's teaching style and the student's learning style that makes a course enjoyable for a student. You might find that you do not enjoy the exact same class that a friend

does because of your preferences for teaching styles and differences in your own individual learning styles. You will want to find students who are similar to you to know that their recommendations would be relevant to you.

♦ *What does the syllabus include?* The course your friend took had a certain content and workload that affected the lectures, the readings, and the assignments. If your friend loves objective exams while you prefer papers, you might not assess the class in the same way. Also, unless you enroll with the exact same instructor, you might have an entirely different syllabus from your friend's. Be sure to ask about these details to ensure that you will get the same experience. See "Point of Interest: When You Don't Like a Class."

Enhancing Your Learning

In addition to your learning style and how it interfaces with the teaching styles of your instructors, several aspects of your own learning process affect your ability to learn in college and perform well at the research university level. These include motivation, praise, the imposter phenomenon, stress, and sleep. Understanding how these aspects impact you personally and how you can adjust your own habits can maximize your ability to succeed.

MOTIVATION TO LEARN Some new and interesting research has shed light on what we know about intelligence and students' motivation to learn. One compelling finding is that the human brain is actually still developing well into a person's 20s and that working at learning something literally *grows* the brain by building more neural connections or synapses (National Institute of Mental Health, 2010). In other words, a college student who works hard at studying calculus can actually build the math part of his or her brain, much like working a muscle. Intelligence is not as fixed or innate as once thought, which means that the college years have a profound impact on a person's brain development and intellectual skills.

Another interesting development is new findings on motivation and learning. Dr. Carol Dweck, of both Columbia and Stanford universities, has done some fascinating research on

POINT OF INTEREST

WHEN YOU DON'T LIKE A CLASS If you don't like a class, ascertain what, specifically, you don't like about it. But move quickly because you have a limited amount of time at the beginning of the term to drop or change courses. If it is the content, then explore other courses that satisfy that same requirement. There are probably more options than you realize, and other classes in that same subject area might interest you. However, if you don't like a class because of the instructor, then you don't want to give up on an entire discipline simply because of one person. Give the field another try, but do more research about the faculty member who is teaching a particular course. Also, once you find an instructor you like, take more of his or her classes. Most faculty know what they will be teaching for the next two or three terms—ask and you will be able to plan your schedule accordingly. In addition, if you like a particular teaching assistant, ask which courses and sections he or she will be assigned to next term and be sure to enroll in them. Finally, realize that you may not be able to work around some courses or instructors. In that case, you will need to "suck it up" and make the most of the situation.

the effect of praise on a person's motivation to learn. She found that students who were praised for being smart or intelligent were actually less motivated to work hard than those who were praised for their effort (Dweck, 1999, 2007). This effect was true across gender and economic classes and even for younger children in preschool.

When students believe that their intelligence is fixed, which Dweck called "the fixed mind-set," they are less likely to work hard because they don't believe it makes a difference. These students spend their energy trying to maintain the image of being smart, and so they avoid challenging tasks and actually can be deeply affected by even mild criticism or feedback. When they do perform poorly, they are more likely to lie about their scores than their peers.

Children who are praised for their effort, on the other hand, learn that effort makes a difference and they are more likely to work hard in the future. This creates a "growth mind-set," and they are also more likely to attempt challenging tasks, since they don't worry about their image. More importantly, they are more resilient when they do struggle, responding to setbacks with increased effort.

This is relevant to students at research universities because they are likely to have been praised all their lives for their intelligence. They are also going to be experiencing big academic challenges as they transition to university-level work. Dweck's research indicates that they are more likely to hold the "fixed mind-set" and not turn to increased effort when they face a challenge. In other words, they may not change their study habits and writing skills as needed or even seek help from professors and staff. In addition, they could be more likely to avoid challenge by searching for "easy" classes, fall into depression or anxiety when they do struggle, and even lie to others about their grades.

Know that your academic experience will be filled with all kinds of challenges as you attend a research university. You are part of a community of scholars who engage in higher order thinking skills on a daily basis. You are not expected to be good at these skills yet, but you will be given many opportunities to develop them. Embrace the challenge and seek out classes and opportunities that will push you. Utilize this opportunity to develop and grow your brain by working hard at new skills and learning new material. If you have often been praised for your intelligence, focus on your effort instead, and ask those around you to do the same.

THE IMPOSTER PHENOMENON The findings on the relationship between praise and motivation relate to another important concept called **the imposter phenomenon.** This term describes the feeling experienced by highly accomplished people who believe that their accomplishments are not really due to their effort or talent but rather by luck or accident (Langford & Clance, 1993). Although these people may appear to be very confident to others, internally they do not hold a strong sense of their skills and abilities. As a result, they experience fear that they will be found out and people will discover that they don't really know what they are doing.

The imposter phenomenon can be seen in college students who have perceived themselves as being smart, often due to the praise given to them by parents, teachers, and school counselors. As long as their grades validate this notion, things are fine because the grades match their internal idea of being intelligent. But when they struggle and maybe even experience a dip in grades, as is common with first-year students, they can experience anxiety and even depression from worrying that others will find out that they are an "imposter." These students see a poor grade as proof that the university made a mistake in admitting them. The perceived failure can cause shame and a sense of unworthiness, and in turn, these students are reluctant to share with others and seek the help they might need. This, of course, can lead to more poor grades and a vicious cycle of a self-fulfilling prophecy.

It is important for you to know that it is common, and even expected, that first-year students experience some lower grades as they transition to university-level work. Top research universities are quite thorough in their assessment of student applicants and only admit students who show a high probability of success for completing the degree, not necessarily acing the first term. If you suspect that you might be affected by either the "fixed mind-set" or the imposter phenomenon, speak with a counselor to get appropriate support and guidance.

THE EFFECTS OF STRESS AND SLEEP ON STUDENT SUCCESS   Another important issue that can affect how you learn and ultimately perform in college is how you respond to stress. **Stress** is defined in the Merriam-Webster OnLine Dictionary (2010) as "a physical, chemical, or emotional factor that causes bodily or mental tension." It can be caused by something positive, like winning an award, or something negative like failing an exam.

According to health educator Joanna Hill (2010), stress is a common factor in college students' lives, especially for students at research universities where the academic demands are even tougher. In fact, according to the American College Health Association (2009), college students reported that stress is the number-one health impediment to academic success, followed in order by sleep difficulties, anxiety, and cold/flu (all of which are related to stress as well). Additionally, 51 percent of college students reported experiencing more than average or a tremendous overall level of stress in the twelve months prior to the survey. While many students think of stress as the hurried feeling when trying to accomplish a task in limited time, the signs of stress actually include:

+ Feeling anxious without knowing why
+ Lack of focus
+ Feelings of sadness
+ Feeling overwhelmed
+ Headaches, neck or back pain
+ Gastrointestinal issues
+ Inability to sleep, fatigue
+ Getting sick frequently (compromised immune system)
+ Losing the pattern of your normal routine

One important aspect of stress is how students react to change and difficulty, two hallmarks of the university experience that contribute to stress. Fred Newton, the director of Counseling Services at Kansas State University, identified three general groups of students and what they do when faced with change and difficulty (Newton, 1998). The first are **adaptors,** who respond to change by embracing uncertainty. They still experience stress but are not flustered by it, and they ask for help when facing difficulties by using campus services. Another group, the **avoiders,** don't like to face change so they try to pretend it's not happening. They seek to minimize change and difficulty by not taking risks and seeking the easiest route, and they also take a little pride in their ability to survive or get by. This group only seeks help or uses resources when already in crisis and only to get out of it. Finally, there are the **casualties,** who are deeply and negatively impacted by their inability to respond to change and difficulty. This group often develops more serious issues like depression, eating disorders, and alcohol or drug misuse or addiction. They are much more likely than the other groups to not survive their college experience, either due to flunking out, dropping out, being kicked out, or being injured or killed.

You can help yourself succeed by paying attention to your stress levels and taking the issue of stress management seriously. In college, you will develop habits and practices for coping with stress that either support your success or detract from it. Some proven strategies for managing stress include (Hill, 2010):

+ Try to identify your stressors and eliminate those you can.
+ Make a plan to manage your commitments.
+ Set realistic expectations (don't overbook yourself).

Visit www.cengagebrain.com to find the companion website containing links to:

■ Excellent resources, assessments, and exercises on stress and relaxation

■ Utah State University's assessment on sleep hygiene

■ Range of information on sleep

+ Say NO to things (or give yourself 24 hours before you respond).
+ Schedule in some down time.
+ Meditate or use some other calming practice.
+ Eat well and exercise regularly.
+ Ask for help (see a counselor or talk with a friend).
+ Get enough sleep.

As the previous list shows, getting enough sleep is an important part of how university students can manage their stress. However, the reality is that students rarely get enough sleep to function at their best, and this has serious ramifications for their academic performance and overall health. According to the national survey by the American College Health Association (2009), only 12 percent of college students reported getting enough sleep to feel rested in the morning.

@myU SO HOW DOES THIS AFFECT YOU?

Stress (too much) and sleep (not enough) will be part of your daily experience at a research university. Yet, both are directly tied to your ability to succeed academically. Just as you consider going to office hours, or doing another draft of a research paper, as essential to earning good grades, so should you consider managing your stress and protecting your sleep as necessary for learning.

Utilize the strategies listed in this section, but if you find that you need more support, seek out stress management counselors on your campus. Talk with your roommate about the importance of good sleep and find ways to support each other in making your room as sleep-conducive as possible. This may include using earplugs or using a white-noise machine to block out sounds from others, darkening your windows, and not using electronic devices like cell phones or laptops in bed.

Take a minute to rate your stress, on a scale of 1 (not at all stressed) to 10 (very stressed) for the past week.

MON	TUES	WED	THURS	FRI	SAT	SUN

Is there any noticeable pattern? On which days were you most stressed, and why? List your top 3 stressors, and something you can do to reduce each one:

1.   2.   3.

Now do the same for sleep. List how many hours of sleep you got each night during the past week, and rate the level of restorativeness from 1 (not at all) to 5 (very).

MON	TUES	WED	THURS	FRI	SAT	SUN

Is there any noticeable pattern? On which days did you get the least sleep, and why? List 3 things you can do to improve the amount and quality of your sleep:

1.   2.   3.

Though scientists are still learning about the concept of sleep, one thing sleep research certainly has shown is that sleeping too little not only inhibits your productivity and ability to remember and consolidate information, but also leads to serious health consequences and jeopardizes your safety and the safety of individuals around you (Hill, 2010). For example, short sleep duration is linked with:

+ Decreased ability to pay attention or remember new information (due to inability to store and maintain long-term memories)
+ Increased risk for psychiatric conditions including depression and substance abuse
+ Increased obesity (decreased production of leptin, which increases appetite)
+ Increased risk of motor vehicle accidents (due to depressed ability to react quickly as well as falling asleep at the wheel)
+ Increased risk of diabetes (from disrupted insulin production)
+ Decreased immune system (altered white blood cell production)

The positive effect of good sleep on academic performance has been documented by scholars around the world (Bronson & Merryman, 2009). Dr. Kyla Wahlstrom, at the University of Minnesota, found a direct correlation with amount of sleep and grades. Students who got the most sleep were the ones earning As, while the next best sleepers earned Bs, followed by the group who earned Cs, and so on. This is due to the biological process of storing memory. Dr. Matt Walker, at the University of California at Berkeley, discovered that each stage of sleep plays a vital role in storing the experiences and memories from the day (including attending college lectures) into various regions of the brain. The more you study, the more restorative sleep you need to turn that hard work into memories you can recall.

While students may agree that getting enough sleep in college is important, it can be challenging to accomplish because of the group living environments, starchy food, and prevalence of caffeine and alcohol. Students need to be mindful of their sleep, paying attention to their **sleep hygiene,** which refers to the daily habits that support quality restorative sleep (Hill, 2010). Some strategies for improving your sleep hygiene include:

+ Establish consistent sleep and wake schedules, even on weekends.
+ Create a regular, relaxing bedtime routine, starting an hour or more before the time you expect to fall asleep.
+ Create a sleep-conducive environment that is dark, quiet, comfortable, and cool.
+ Sleep on a comfortable mattress and pillows.
+ Use your bedroom only for sleep and sex (keep "sleep stealers" out of the bedroom—avoid watching TV, using a computer, or reading in bed).
+ Finish eating at least 2–3 hours before your regular bedtime.
+ Exercise regularly during the day or at least a few hours before bedtime.
+ Avoid caffeine and alcohol products close to bedtime, and give up smoking.

RELATED MATERIALS

For Scenic Route websites, more Stories from the Path, glossary, and student activities, access the study tools for *Navigating the Research University* at www.cengagebrain.com.

REFERENCES

American College Health Association. (2009, Spring). *ACHA National College Health Assessment II: Reference group executive summary.* Linthicum, MD: Author.

American Sociological Association. (2004). *Careers in sociology* (5th ed.). Washington, DC: Author.

Association of American Colleges and Universities. (2010). *What is liberal education?* Retrieved from http://www.aacu.org/leap/What_is_liberal_education.cfm.

Bronson, P., & Merryman, A. (2009). *NurtureShock: New thinking about children.* New York: Hatchette Book Group.

Baum, S., Ma, J., & Payea, K. (2010). Education Pays 2010: The benefits of higher education for individuals and society. New York: College Board Advocacy & Policy Center.

DeAngelo, L., Hurtado, S. H., Pryor, J. H., Kelly, K. R., Santos, J. L., & Korn, W. S. (2009). *The American college teacher: National norms for the 2007–2008 HERI faculty survey.* Retrieved from http://www.heri.ucla.edu/publications-brp.php.

Dweck, C. (1999). Caution—Praise can be dangerous. *American Educator, 23*(1), 4–9.

Dweck, C. (2007). The perils and promise of praise. *Educational Leadership, 65*(2), 34–39.

Farber, A. (2009). *How to prepare for a career and get a great job.* Dayton, OH: Woodburn Press.

Felder, R. M., & Silverman, L. K. (1988). Learning and teaching styles in engineering education. *Engineering Education, 78*(7), 674–681.

Felder, R. M., & Soloman, B. A. (2004). *Index of learning styles questionnaire.* Retrieved from North Carolina State University website at http://www4.ncsu.edu/unity/lockers/users/f/felder/public/ILSdir/styles.htm.

Grasha, A. (1996). *Teaching with style* (p. 154). Pittsburgh, PA: Alliance.

Grasha, A. (2007). *Teaching styles.* Retrieved from http://www.indstate.edu/cirt/id/pedagogies/styles/5styles.html.

Hill, J. (2010, February 10). *College students and wellness.* Lecture for Education 20, Introduction to the research university. University of California, Santa Barbara.

Holland, J. (2007). *Making vocational choices: A theory of vocational personalities and work environments.* Lutz, FL: Psychological Assessment Resources, Inc.

Langford, J., & Clance, P. (1993). The imposter phenomenon: Recent research findings regarding dynamics, personality and family patterns and their implications for treatment. *Psychotherapy, 3*(3), 495–501.

Lindholm, A. J., Szelenyi, K., Hurtado, S., & Korn, W. S. (2005). *The American college teacher: National norms for the 2004–05 HERI Faculty Survey.* Los Angeles: Higher Education Research Institute, UCLA. Retrieved on October 29, 2007, from http://www.gseis.ucla.edu/heri/PDFs/ACT_Research%20Brief.PDF.

Merriam-Webster OnLine Dictionary. (2010). Retrieved from http://www.merriam-webster.com.

National Association of Colleges and Employers (NACE). (2009). *Job outlook 2009.* Retrieved from http://www.naceweb.org/WorkArea/linkit.aspx?LinkIdentifier=id&ItemID=3856.

National Institute of Mental Health. (2010). *Teenage brain: A work in progress (fact sheet).* Retrieved from http://www.nimh.nih.gov/health/publications/teenage-brain-a-work-in-progress-fact-sheet/index.shtml.

Newton, F. (1998, May/June). The stressed student. *About Campus,* 4–10.

Ruiz, S., Sharkness, J., Kelly, K., DeAngelo, L., & Pryor, J. (2010). *Findings from the 2009 administration of Your First College Year (YFCY): National aggregates.* Retrieved from http://www.heri.ucla.edu/publications-brp.php.

Steen, M. (2010, February 16). *Myers-Briggs Type Indicator results interpretation.* Lecture for Education 118, The transfer student experience at the research university. University of California, Santa Barbara.

CHAPTER 6

Alcohol, Drug Use, and Sexual Activity among University Students

© Andre Jenny /Alamy

New Mexico State University

University students are given a lot of freedom and responsibility, which allows them to make their own choices about many things. This freedom includes choices about alcohol, drugs, and sexual activity. It is common for young adults to experiment in all three of these areas, even though this experimentation might put their health or safety at risk, or be against the law. This experimentation seems to expand when young adults move away from home, as they no longer have some of the limitations that were placed on them by their family. As a result, most college campuses are greatly affected by their students' choices with regard to alcohol, drugs, and sex because of the potentially dangerous legal and health consequences of making poor choices. Although individuals make these choices, the impact of these choices often spills over beyond the one person to affect others around him or her as well as the local environment. This chapter will focus on student freedom, alcohol and other drug use among college students and some of its consequences, and sexual activity among college students. It offers many useful tips and suggestions regarding these topics.

FREEDOM VERSUS SAFETY

An inherent tension exists on college campuses between allowing young adults the freedom and responsibility guaranteed by the Family Educational Rights and Privacy Act (FERPA), managing student behavior and conduct as it relates to laws and campus policies, and, finally, keeping students safe and healthy. These three things might not be in alignment, as the student might want to engage in behaviors that break the law and/or are potentially dangerous—for example, underage drinking or having unprotected sex. Students' families often have expectations that the university will guide and protect their student from making inappropriate choices, much as they tried to do when he or she was living at home. Although parents did have the choice of calling the police if they found their child smoking pot, most did not and instead attempted to manage their child's behavior through other methods such as curfews and various punishments.

While a child's behavior can be guided, it is virtually impossible to force adults to make good and/or lawful choices. Even our society acknowledges this through its legal system. All adults in our society have the freedom to choose whether or not to abide by the law. Sure, there are consequences for not doing so, but first the person must be caught in violation of the law and then sent through a legal process that determines the person's guilt and any relevant penalties.

Obviously, parents do not want their young adults engaging in behaviors that might endanger their health and safety, even if they are technically adults. Parents spend eighteen years keeping their child alive and safe, and it can be very difficult to let that go. When parents send their son or daughter off to college, they want him or her to be alive in four years. Unfortunately, this doesn't always happen. Every year, parents get calls from police or campus officials with sad news. A few get calls that their son or daughter is in jail for a serious crime. Many more get calls that their son or daughter is seriously injured and might not ever be the same. And some receive the devastating news that their son or daughter has died. The tragic part is that *almost all* of these situations involve alcohol and/or drugs and could have been prevented. These stories are in the media all over the country, and they heighten parents' concerns about their own child's safety. Parents tend to put a lot of pressure on the university to keep their student safe and healthy.

Separate from the pressure of parents, there is a general national concern for the health and well-being of young people. Many national studies are done each year that explore various elements that endanger youth. For example, the Centers for Disease Control (CDC, 2004) conducted a large study in 1995 called the National College Health Risk Behavior Survey (NCHRBS). This survey involved 4,609 undergraduate college students from public and private colleges and universities (both two- and four-year) across the United States. The results are considered representative of undergraduate college students nationwide aged 18 years or older. The questionnaire focused on "health risk behaviors that contribute to the leading causes of death, illness, and social problems among young adults in the United States," including:

+ Tobacco use
+ Unhealthy dietary behaviors
+ Inadequate physical activity
+ Alcohol and other drug use
+ Sexual behaviors that may result in HIV infection, other sexually transmitted diseases, and unintended pregnancies
+ Behaviors that may result in unintentional injuries (e.g., motor vehicle crashes) and violence, including suicide

The results of this study and many others like it have been sent to college administrators and faculty and featured in many higher education publications, which has increased awareness of these issues and prompted a more focused commitment on the part of administrators and faculty to address them.

As a result of all these pressures, most university administrators and faculty find themselves managing rather complex situations. They cannot force young adults to make good and/or lawful choices, but they can and do create policies and rules and enforce penalties for breaking those rules. The kinds of penalties that universities can apply are limited to what they control: enrollment, education, and access to university property. University penalties are likely to be fines, mandatory educational programs, eviction from university property, and expulsion from the university. The local, state, and federal legal systems also have jurisdiction in any university environment and may be involved in prosecuting a young adult for his or her choices in addition to, or separate from, any process in which the university engages.

Finally, students have expectations too. While students want to be alive and healthy at the end of their college experience, they also want to have fun, and according to many young adults, fun often involves alcohol, drugs, and sex. Students have a different impression of what is dangerous and when it is dangerous, and this impression might not match those of their parents, the university, and the legal system.

In high school, young adults find creative ways around their curfews and their family's rules, and they are just as creative in college. Students who *want* to drink and/or take drugs will find a way to do so, despite policies and laws. And the students who do *not* want to do these things will still find themselves affected by the students who do. This is also true for sexual activity. Sexuality is a healthy part of any adult's life, and although sex is not illegal between consenting adults, a student should make smart choices involving this issue. These choices affect other students around him or her and may also be of concern to the student's family, who might have different expectations about sexual behavior. Even in the best circumstance of a loving and committed relationship, students still need to worry about sexually transmitted infections and pregnancy.

PARTYING: ALCOHOL AND STUDENTS

Colleges and universities put much emphasis on the alcohol consumption and drug use of students for many reasons, always with the goal of decreasing these behaviors and increasing student safety. The primary reason is that the health and safety of its students are every campus administration's goal. Many campus presidents, chancellors, and deans have suffered the pain and anguish of talking to a parent whose son or daughter will never come home again. This is always much more tragic when the incident could have been prevented. No dean wants to make that call, and yet almost every dean has had to make many of these calls during his or her career.

Another reason campus administrators are concerned is that the institution's reputation is important because it influences the overall value of the degree and reflects on both the faculty and administration. A reputation as a party school can harm an institution's abilities to recruit the top, most serious student and faculty scholars. This in turn can negatively affect funding and other financial support, such as donors' monetary gifts and grants. Finally, a poor reputation can decrease the value of the degrees the institution confers, which harms every student who graduates from that campus.

With that said, there is probably no campus in North America where the discussion of alcohol and other drug use is not prevalent. Even a simple search on the Internet will yield hundreds of sites dedicated to the issue of decreasing college students' consumption of alcohol and other drugs. Most campuses have policies that attempt to control the availability and consumption of alcohol and drugs, as well as methods of enforcement for these policies. In addition, many attempts are made to compete with the lure of alcohol and drugs, so campuses dedicate a lot of money and energy to offering other tempting events, such as concerts, dances, and movies, to compete with weekend parties.

Why all this hoopla? When you talk to average college students, many perceive their campus's efforts as an attempt to crack down on fun and believe that the administration over-reacts to typical student partying. The difference lies in what the two groups see on a daily basis. A student might drink every weekend and attend many parties and not see, or recognize, any negative consequences of his or her behavior. The student might have good grades and suffer only the occasional hangover. In fact, this is especially true at research universities, where the top students are admitted. Students often *can* party frequently and still maintain excellent grades, a combination that many students use as the primary indicator that they are "doing fine."

On the other hand, the administration sees the bigger picture. They hear the reports every weekend of how many students went to the local emergency room for alcohol poisoning, how many students were victims of an alcohol-related crime, how many students had to drop out of school because of alcohol and drug problems, and how many students were victims of sexual assault in which alcohol or drugs were involved. What follows are national statistics about college students and consumption of alcohol and other drugs. These, as well as the local statistics for your campus, are always in the minds of administrators and faculty.

Current Data on Alcohol Use

Alcohol is the most commonly used and prevalent drug on college campuses. Although the legal drinking age in the United States is 21, many college and high school students gain access to alcohol and drink while underage. The problem is not low or moderate use of alcohol—having a beer with pizza after a big exam would not yield any negative health effects (although there might be some for violating underage drinking laws or campus policies).

The most problematic type of drinking is called **high-risk or binge drinking,** which is defined by the National Institute on Alcohol Abuse and Alcoholism (NIAAA, 2010) as "a pattern of drinking alcohol that brings blood alcohol concentration to 0.08 gram percent or above ... . [T]his pattern corresponds to consuming 5 or more drinks (male), or 4 or more drinks (female), in about 2 hours." High-risk or binge drinking—in other words, drinking a large amount of alcohol in a short amount of time—is what is most closely correlated with the negative effects of alcohol use, where use becomes abuse. According to the NIAAA, out of every five college students, two (or 40 percent) have engaged in binge drinking in the past two weeks, two more (another 40 percent) drank but not to excess, and one (20 percent) did not drink alcohol at all. The concern is that when students drink, they tend to do so in excess, the kind of drinking that is the most potentially dangerous or lethal to self and others (i.e., high-risk). In 2006, the Harvard University's national College Alcohol Study found that binge drinking students consumed 72 percent, nearly three-quarters, of all the alcohol consumed by college students.

Nationally, 84 percent of college students have indicated that they consumed alcohol in the previous year, and of those students, 72 percent drank in the previous thirty days. On average, undergraduate students drink 5.4 drinks per week. Fifty-five percent identify themselves as heavy drinkers and 24 percent consider themselves both heavy and frequent drinkers. These statistics come from the Southern Illinois University's CORE Survey done in 2006 with 71,189 undergraduate students at 134 colleges in the United States.

The CORE Survey also identified why students drink and found that students *perceive* that alcohol will bring a variety of positive social and sexual effects. Three-quarters (77 percent) believe that alcohol helps break the ice, 62 percent believe that it allows people to have more fun, 54 percent think that it facilitates sexual opportunities, and 18 percent believe that it makes them sexier.

Negative Consequences of Alcohol Use

The problem is not the use of alcohol and drugs per se. If students drank and were able to be healthy, happy, and safe, there would not be such a focus on alcohol and other drug use. The fact is that use of alcohol and other drugs consistently leads to negative consequences for the student and for the college student population as a whole. Although an individual college student might not see evidence of all of these problems, every campus administrator and faculty member does, as do many families of college students. The students in the 2006 CORE Survey reported problematic experiences from their alcohol and other drug use as shown in Table 6.1. Mark on the table which experiences you have had by marking Yes or No.

TABLE **6.1** PERCENTAGES OF STUDENTS WHO EXPERIENCED NEGATIVE CONSEQUENCES OF ALCOHOL USE		
%	EXPERIENCE	YOU? Y / N
63%	Had a hangover	
54%	Got nauseated or vomited	
37%	Did something I later regretted	
34%	Had a memory loss (i.e., blacked out)	
32%	Got into an argument or fight	
31%	Was criticized by someone I know	
30%	Missed a class	
27%	Drove a car while under the influence	
22%	Performed poorly on a test or important project	
16%	Was hurt or injured	
14%	Got into trouble with police or college authorities	
11%	Thought I might have a drinking or other drug problem	
10%	Was taken advantage of sexually	
7%	Damaged property (e.g., pulled fire alarms, vandalized)	
5%	Tried unsuccessfully to stop using	
5%	Seriously thought about suicide	
3%	Took advantage of another person sexually	
2%	Was arrested for DWI/DUI	
1%	Tried to commit suicide	

Most college students *do* see these negative consequences over time—if not for themselves, then for their friends, roommates, or romantic partners. Each term, I ask the students in my class whether they know someone who has a problem with alcohol or drugs. Almost all of the hands are raised. That's because, over time, the negative effects of alcohol and other drug use catch up to the students who use these substances frequently. While the students might get by for a few weekends without seeing or experiencing any problems, they will inevitably experience many of the problems listed in Table 6.1.

The CORE Survey discovered a direct link between excessive drinking and academic performance. The following relationship exists between the number of drinks per week and grade point average:

+ As = 3.6 drinks per week
+ Bs = 5.5 drinks per week
+ Cs = 7.6 drinks per week
+ Ds = 10.6 drinks per week

In fact, the NIAAA (2010) states that "Excessive drinking among college students is associated with a variety of negative consequences that include fatal and nonfatal injuries; alcohol poisoning; blackouts; academic failure; violence including rape and assault; unintended pregnancy; sexually transmitted diseases including HIV/AIDS; property damage; and vocational and criminal consequences that could jeopardize future job prospects."

Here are some other disturbing statistics from the Task Force of the National Advisory Council on Alcohol Abuse and Alcoholism (2010) which studied students aged 18 to 24:

+ 1,700 college students between the ages of 18 and 24 die each year from alcohol-related unintentional injuries, including motor vehicle crashes.
+ Each year, more than 696,000 students are assaulted by another student who has been drinking.
+ Each year, alcohol is involved in 600,000 unintentional injuries of college students.
+ Annually, alcohol is involved in 97,000 cases of sexual assault and acquaintance rape of college students.
+ Alcohol use is associated with high-risk sexual behavior; 400,000 students had unprotected sex and 100,000 were too intoxicated to know if they gave consent or not.
+ More than 150,000 students developed an alcohol-related health problem.
+ Last year, 2.1 million students drove under the influence of alcohol.
+ Based on self-reports of their drinking, 31 percent of college students met criteria for a diagnosis of alcohol abuse and 6 percent for a diagnosis of alcohol dependence.

Connected to these statistics is a new concept known as **secondhand effects,** which refers to how drinkers, especially binge drinkers, can negatively affect others around them who are not drinking to excess, in much the way that secondhand smoke can be damaging to a nonsmoker's health. The Harvard School of Public Health College Alcohol Study (2006) found that 61 percent of non–binge drinking students who live on campus have had their study or sleep disturbed by someone else's drinking. In addition, 50 percent of these students have had to "babysit" another student who had drunk too much at least once during the past year.

Secondhand effects from drinking can range from the annoying (e.g., noise, vomit, and litter), to the damaging (e.g., vandalism and property damage), to the truly dangerous (e.g., physically or sexually assaulting other students or causing accidents that kill people). Alcohol is involved in approximately 50 percent of all fatal traffic crashes among 18- to 24-year-olds—crashes in which someone, not necessarily the driver, dies. Many college students have been killed in fatal crashes involving alcohol; sometimes they were the intoxicated drivers, and sometimes they were the sober passengers, other drivers, or pedestrians.

Separate from all these serious consequences of alcohol use, alcohol also contributes to people just doing dumb things—things that hurt their friends and their community. It is no secret that alcohol impairs judgment; people become more likely to say and do things they would not normally do when sober. This includes making hurtful comments to friends, roommates, and romantic partners, things that often cannot be fixed the next day with a simple apology. Students who are under the influence also can say and do racist, sexist, and homophobic things that harm the overall campus community. This can change the whole feeling of safety that students of color, women, and the gay community have on a college campus, one that lasts long past the weekend.

Your college experience *will* be affected by drug and alcohol use. Either you will experience the direct effects of your own drinking or you will experience the secondhand effects of others'. You can mitigate the negative effects of alcohol and other drug use by your own choices of behavior, including selecting the people you hang out and live with and the activities in which you participate. Although your university will do its best to address these issues, it is ultimately your responsibility to take care of yourself and protect your own health and safety.

In addition to the other effects, students may develop **alcoholism.** Even students who are from families with no known alcoholism can become alcoholics. Students often don't identify alcoholism because they "only drink on the weekends," but alcoholism is focused on what happens to the person *when* she or he drinks, not how often or on what days. An alcoholic is a person who is dependent on or addicted to alcohol. This dependence can be psychological, physical, or both. This is differentiated from **problem drinking,** in which there is no dependence. However, the problem drinker is any person whose drinking causes a problem, whether academically, medically, legally, psychologically, or in relationships with people such as family or friends.

The following are indications that someone is experiencing problem drinking:

+ *High tolerance*: The ability to consume large quantities of alcohol or other drugs and not show the effects
+ *Blackouts*: A temporary loss of memory in which the individual was awake and functioning but later cannot remember anything about a given period of time
+ *Negative consequences*: The person experiences them as a result of alcohol or other drug use (e.g., DUI) and continues to use in the same way
+ *Denial*: The person does not believe or admit that use is causing problems
+ *Avoidance*: The person does not like to talk about his or her use

If you or another person has any of these indicators, you might want to speak with a professional at your campus student health service, preferably someone who is trained in counseling on alcohol and other drug issues. This person can work with you, either to help you prepare to talk to your friend or to help you make changes in your own behavior. See "Point of Interest: How to Help a Friend."

Drinking Responsibly

The point is not to avoid partying but rather to party safely and responsibly. Partying is an important part of the social scene on college campuses, and the most successful students find a way to enjoy the scene with low to moderate alcohol use. To do this, it helps to understand exactly how alcohol works in the system and what causes the good and bad feelings associated with drinking. See "Carol-Hannah's Story from the Path."

Most people understand the concept of **blood alcohol content (BAC)**—a measure of how much alcohol is in the bloodstream; it is what is measured in determining whether a person is legally intoxicated. Police officers can measure BAC through devices such as the Breathalyzer, but the most accurate measure is made by taking a sample of a person's blood and having it tested. In addition to its usefulness for law enforcement officers, the BAC is a great

POINT OF INTEREST

HOW TO HELP A FRIEND Here are some useful tips for helping someone with a substance abuse problem (adapted from the University of Miami's PIER 21 Program, 2004):

- Realize the negative effect that alcohol or other drug use is having on the person and that he or she needs to change some behavior. Be confident that your involvement is the right and caring thing to do.

- Don't do it alone. Talk with someone else, preferably a counselor, about the best way to approach the situation.

- Talk with your friend when he or she is sober. Make sure your friend sees what you see and knows how you have been affected as well.

- Be prepared for negative responses, excuses, and even criticisms of your own behavior. Stay calm and don't take anything personally. Keep the conversation centered on your friend and how substances are affecting him or her.

- If your friend responds negatively, try again after the next instance of abusive behavior. Repeat after each incident, and be consistent with your message.

- If your friend responds positively, work with him or her to develop a plan for change. Suggest an appointment with the advisors at the student health center and offer to come with your friend.

- If your friend's drinking habits do not change, set some limits for yourself and remove yourself from situations that upset or potentially harm you. Ultimately, your friend needs to make his or her own decisions—only that person can be responsible for his or her actions.

- Find support for yourself and get attention for your needs. This is a tough thing to go through, but you do not need to do it alone. Many resources are available to help you through this. Take advantage of them.

CAROL-HANNAH'S STORY FROM THE PATH

As a freshman, I made the decision not to drink. Not only was it illegal (since I was under 21), but it was also against my personal set of values. I knew that other students would have value systems different from me, and some would choose to drink, whether or not they were of legal age. I worried that if I attended parties, I would be made fun of for choosing not to drink and possibly find myself in dangerous situations that could have a profoundly negative impact on me later in life. I also had a preconceived notion that every party was like those I saw in the movie *Animal House*—I imagined people getting in fights, windows being broken, and people doing things they wouldn't normally do when sober.

As school started, my roommate and I began getting invitations to parties from some of the people we had met in our classes. At first, I refused to attend, believing that the environment would prove to be more trouble than fun. After the first few months, however, I got tired of saying no; I felt like I was missing out on meeting new people and experiencing new things—not to mention that football season had arrived and it seemed like everything centered around the tailgate parties before the games.

One night, my roommate and I decided to go to our first college party. I was nervous, and worried that one of my *Animal House* nightmares would be realized. When we got to the party, the music was loud and so were the people. At that point, I had serious second thoughts about being there. When we finally met up with the students who had invited us, I was immediately offered a drink. When I said that I did not care for anything, I was surprised that I was not made fun of at all. They did not push me, but rather respected my decision and I was able to enjoy the party.

As the semester continued, classes increased in difficulty and demanded much more study time. I decided to cut down a bit on my cocurricular activities and focus more on school. That's not to say that I didn't go to parties, I just chose to put my studies first. As for some of my classmates ... they continued to party as if it were their number one priority. When final exams approached, the students who chose partying over classes saw the consequences of their poor decisions in the form of low grades. This resulted in problems with financial aid, scholarships, and their relationships with their parents.

Now that I have turned 21, I look back and I am glad about the decisions that I made. I avoided many stressors and negative consequences like bad grades and being in trouble with the law because of underage drinking. I know that everyone will not make the same decisions I made as a freshman, and some will choose to drink at parties. If you do, however, remember your priorities, mind the law, and make sure you are safe.

tool for college students. Understanding how your body is responding at different levels of intoxication can help you to make good choices about how much and how fast to drink. Blood alcohol content (BAC) is also known as **blood alcohol level (BAL)**.

First, let's look at some quick facts about alcohol. Katie Budke (2004), a health educator at the University of Iowa, has the following to say:

Alcohol (ethanol) is a powerful, mind-altering chemical, no matter what form it is in—beer, wine, or liquor. Because alcohol consumption is so common in our culture, we often forget that it is a drug that the body treats as a toxin—a poison. It is a depressant that is absorbed into the bloodstream through your stomach and intestinal lining (remember, it is not digested like food) and is transmitted to all parts of the body. When alcohol reaches the brain, it affects the control centers resulting in poor judgment, slower reflexes, blurred vision, and problems with coordination. Your liver processes alcohol out of your system at an average rate of about 1.5 ounces of 80 proof alcohol an hour. Nothing you can do will speed this process up ... not exercising, vomiting, or drinking 3 shots of espresso. Drinking faster than your body can process alcohol causes intoxication (literally alcohol poisoning).

So how do you figure out your BAC? Obviously, students would probably not take a break from a party to calculate their BAC, but using this information *before* going to a party can help students determine how fast they will reach certain levels and plan their consumption pace accordingly—it's how you engage in responsible drinking. Having your blood drawn and tested is the most accurate way to know your BAC, but this is not a feasible option for most students. The Breathalyzers that the police use aren't usually readily available either. However, there are handy strips you can purchase that you put on your tongue to get a quick reading of your BAC. While not totally accurate, they can be a good guide and are easy to carry with you, so you can use them during parties.

Another useful tool is a BAC calculator, many of which are available on the Internet. You enter your gender, weight, number of drinks, and time in which they were consumed, and it gives you an estimate of your BAC (type "BAC" into any Internet search engine, and it will return links to hundreds of sites). Some of these calculators even allow you to input the exact type of drink you had (e.g., light beer, margarita) and the type of glass you drank out of to give you the most accurate results. These online calculators are based on weight charts that have been created to estimate BAC. Table 6.2 shows alcohol impairment charts for both men and women (modified from MedicineNet.com, 2010).

Charts like those shown in Table 6.2 are also useful for calculating BAC. For example, a woman who weighs 120 pounds can see that having two drinks in an hour will give her an estimated BAC of .08 percent. She would most likely be breaking the law if she drove at this level, but she might even be violating public intoxication laws if she went out in public (these laws vary by state, so check with your local police). You'll also notice that the chart is slightly different for men; a man who weighs 120 pounds could drink three drinks in an hour before reaching the legal intoxication level. This is because men have an enzyme in their stomachs that causes them to metabolize alcohol differently than women (Frezza, et al., 1990). Pound for pound, men have less fat and more muscle than women so they can metabolize more alcohol per hour. This gives men a natural advantage in the unsafe practice of drinking competitions.

It's important to remember that charts like these are just a general guideline based on the assumption that a person metabolizes one drink per hour. The truth is that every person metabolizes alcohol differently, which is why you can have two people who weigh the same and drink the same number of drinks, but one person is much more affected by the alcohol. Every person has a different **tolerance** to alcohol, and there is no chart that can factor that in, so use these charts only as a rough guideline.

THE SCENIC ROUTE

Visit www.cengagebrain.com to find the companion website containing links to:

- FactsonTap.org's great tools for college students
- Collegedrinkingprevention. gov's useful information for college students
- Alcohol use quiz at George Washington University

TABLE 6.2 ALCOHOL IMPAIRMENT CHARTS

FOR <u>WOMEN</u>

APPROXIMATE BLOOD ALCOHOL PERCENTAGE

	Drinks	90	100	120	140	160	180	200	220	240	
N E V E R	0	.00	.00	.00	.00	.00	.00	.00	.00	.00	Only Safe Driving Limit
	1	.05	.05	.04	.03	.03	.03	.02	.02	.02	Impairment Begins
D R I N K	2	.10	.09	.08	.07	.06	.05	.05	.04	.04	Driving Skills Affected
	3	.15	.14	.11	.10	.09	.08	.07	.06	.06	
	4	.20	.18	.15	.13	.11	.10	.09	.08	.08	Possible Criminal Penalties
	5	.25	.23	.19	.16	.14	.13	.11	.10	.09	
&	6	.30	.27	.23	.19	.17	.15	.14	.12	.11	Legally Intoxicated
D R I V E	7	.35	.32	.27	.23	.20	.18	.16	.14	.13	Criminal Penalties
	8	.40	.36	.30	.26	.23	.20	.18	.17	.15	
	9	.45	.41	.34	.29	.26	.23	.20	.19	.17	DEATH ZONE
	10	.51	.45	.38	.32	.28	.25	.23	.21	.19	

Subtract .01% for each 40 minutes of drinking.

One drink = 1.25 oz. of 80 proof liquor, 12 oz. of beer, or 5 oz. of table wine.

Deaths documented at BAC levels of .30 and higher.

FOR <u>MEN</u>

APPROXIMATE BLOOD ALCOHOL PERCENTAGE

	Drinks	100	120	140	160	180	200	220	240	
N E V E R	0	.00	.00	.00	.00	.00	.00	.00	.00	Only Safe Driving Limit
	1	.04	.03	.03	.02	.02	.02	.02	.02	Impairment Begins
D R I N K	2	.08	.06	.05	.05	.04	.04	.03	.03	Driving Skills Affected
	3	.11	.09	.08	.07	.06	.06	.05	.05	
	4	.15	.12	.11	.09	.08	.08	.07	.06	Possible Criminal Penalties
	5	.19	.16	.13	.12	.11	.09	.09	.08	
&	6	.23	.19	.16	.14	.13	.11	.10	.09	Legally Intoxicated
D R I V E	7	.26	.22	.19	.16	.15	.13	.12	.11	Criminal Penalties
	8	.30	.25	.21	.19	.17	.15	.14	.13	
	9	.34	.28	.24	.21	.19	.17	.15	.14	DEATH ZONE
	10	.38	.31	.27	.23	.21	.19	.17	.16	

Subtract .01% for each 40 minutes of drinking.

One drink = 1.25 oz. of 80 proof liquor, 12 oz. of beer, or 5 oz. of table wine.

Deaths documented at BAC levels of .30 and higher.

What happens to your body at the different BAC levels? A useful resource is available at www.factsontap.org (Facts on Tap, 2010) along with a lot of really great information about alcohol and students. Compare these descriptions taken from that website to the previous BAC charts to get a sense of how many drinks per hour each level represents (reprinted with permission):

+ *.02–.03 percent:* You feel mildly relaxed and maybe a little lightheaded. Your inhibitions are slightly loosened, and whatever mood you were in before you started drinking may be mildly intensified.

+ *.05–.06 percent:* You feel warm and relaxed. If you're the shy type when you're sober, you lose your feelings of shyness. Your behavior may become exaggerated, making you talk louder or faster or act bolder than usual. Emotions are intensified, so your good moods are better and your bad moods are worse. You may also feel a mild sense of euphoria.

+ *.08–.09 percent:* You believe you're functioning better than you actually are. At this level, you may start to slur your speech. Your sense of balance is probably off, and your motor skills are starting to become impaired. Your ability to see and hear clearly is diminished. Your judgment is being affected, so it's difficult for you to decide whether or not to continue drinking. Your ability to evaluate sexual situations is impaired. Students may jokingly refer to this state of mind as beer goggles, but this BAC can have serious repercussions.

+ *.10–.12 percent:* At this level, you feel euphoric, but you lack coordination and balance. Your motor skills are markedly impaired, as are your judgment and memory. You probably don't remember how many drinks you've had. Your emotions are exaggerated, and some people become loud, aggressive, or belligerent. If you're a guy, you may have trouble getting an erection when your BAC is this high.

+ *.14–.17 percent:* Your euphoric feelings may give way to unpleasant feelings. You have difficulty talking, walking, or even standing. Your judgment and perception are severely impaired. You may become more aggressive, and there is an increased risk of accidentally injuring yourself or others. This is the point when you may experience a blackout.

+ *.20 percent:* You feel confused, dazed, or otherwise disoriented. You need help to stand up or walk. If you hurt yourself at this point, you probably won't realize it because you won't feel pain. If you are aware you've injured yourself, chances are you won't do anything about it. At this point you may experience nausea and/or start vomiting (keep in mind that for some people, a lower blood alcohol level than .20 percent may cause vomiting). Your gag reflex is impaired, so you could choke if you do throw up. Because blackouts are likely at this level, you may not remember any of this.

+ *.25 percent:* All mental, physical, and sensory functions are severely impaired. You're emotionally numb. There's an increased risk of asphyxiation from choking on vomit and of seriously injuring yourself by falling or other accidents.

+ *.30 percent:* You're in a stupor. You have little comprehension of where you are. You may suddenly pass out (that is, lose consciousness) at this point and be difficult to awaken, but don't kid yourself; passing out can also occur at lower BACs. With an alarming BAC like .30 percent, your body will be deciding to pass out for you. Students have died at this level of BAC and higher.

+ *.35 percent:* This blood alcohol level also happens to be the level of surgical anesthesia. You may stop breathing at this point.

+ *.40 percent:* You are probably in a coma. The nerve centers controlling your heartbeat and respiration are slowing down. It's a miracle if you're not dead.

If people drank slowly and achieved each of these BAC levels one by one, they most likely would not keep elevating their BAC once they got to some of the pretty yucky feelings. However, when people drink a lot of alcohol in a short period of time, they can shoot up through several of these levels very quickly and may arrive at a higher level before they realize how drunk they are. Unfortunately, once alcohol is in the bloodstream, it cannot be quickly dispersed. Most college students end up with dangerously high BACs through activities such as beer bongs, shot competitions, and slides, and are in physical danger before they realize it. Unfortunately, by that time, judgment is impaired, and students sometimes continue to drink, increasing their risk of alcohol poisoning and death. Approximately fifty college students per year die from alcohol poisoning or almost one per weekend. An Internet search will yield the names and circumstances of your peers who suffered this tragedy in the past few years.

What Is a Drink?

One thing that is important for college students to know is what one drink really is. Most students have heard the information that one drink is 1.25 ounces of 80 proof liquor, 12 ounces of beer, or 5 ounces of table wine. But what does that really mean? Most students don't carry accurate measuring cups with them, and most university logo shot glasses are far larger than 1.25 ounces. It obviously will depend on the size of cup you use to serve alcohol— a 24-ounce cup filled to the brim with beer is two drinks, not one. Yet most students will call that one beer.

To give you an idea of how much difference cup size can make, look at the comparison in Figure 6.1. All measurements were made using the typical red plastic cup (shown actual size)

FIGURE 6.1 Number of Drinks in a 16- to 18-ounce Plastic Cup

Fill line

If filled with beer,
it would equal 1.3 drinks.

If filled with wine,
it would equal 3.2 drinks.

If filled with margaritas,
it would equal 8.5 drinks.*

If filled with Long Island ice tea,
it would equal over 10.25 drinks.*
* Traditional recipes (no ice) from
www.webtender.com.

Dixie 16/18 oz.
red plastic cup

TABLE **6.3 SYMPTOMS OF ALCOHOL POISONING**	
SYMPTOMS	WHAT TO DO
◆ Person cannot be awakened ◆ Cold, clammy, or bluish skin ◆ Slow or irregular breathing ◆ Vomiting while unconscious ◆ Shortness of breath, unconsciousness	◆ Call 911 immediately! Do not wait—these symptoms indicate that the person is in trouble. ◆ Turn the victim on his or her side to prevent choking on his or her own vomit. ◆ Continuously check on the victim until medical personnel arrive. If breathing stops, administer CPR.

found at most grocery and warehouse stores. The cup reads "16/18 oz.," which means 18 ounces if filled to the rim or 16 ounces if filled to just 1/4 inch below the rim. I used the 16-ounce level, or 1/4 inch below the rim—you can see that this cup can hold up to 10 drinks depending on the beverage.

Symptoms of Alcohol Poisoning

Every year, many college students die from **alcohol poisoning.** Often, their friends didn't want to get them into trouble and believed that they would just "sleep it off." Alcohol poisoning is just like any other type of poisoning in that the body is saturated with chemicals that can slow down or stop its basic survival functions. However, alcohol poisoning can usually be treated successfully if the person is given medical care soon enough. Don't take any chances with your friends. If you notice the symptoms listed in Table 6.3, call 911 immediately because the person is exhibiting indicators that he or she is poisoned and needs medical help to survive.

The Biphasic Response to Alcohol

If you go back and look at the list of what happens to your body at different BAC levels, you'll notice that the first two levels have more of the "positive" feelings—the ones that feel good and the reason most people choose to drink. The rest of the levels have more and more negative feelings, ending with dangerous and lethal consequences. This illustrates what is known as the **biphasic response to alcohol** (Marlatt, 1999). Researchers have found that the enjoyable part of alcohol consumption comes in the first couple of drinks as your BAC rises to .055—this seems to be the peak at which a person most enjoys the stimulant effects of alcohol that create the "good" feeling or the "buzz" (the first phase). After that point of .055, people start to experience the negative effects of alcohol as it begins to act as a depressant on the system (the second phase). As the BAC climbs beyond .055, the feelings get more and more "bad," and the dangers increase as well. We all know this, but we also live in a culture that believes that if a little of something is good, then more will be better. This is just not true for alcohol. While you might think that if you feel good after drinking three beers, you will feel even better after ten, in fact you won't. The truth is that once you reach the BAC level of .055, it's all downhill from there. Furthermore, if someone develops a high tolerance for alcohol, the euphoric feeling, or "buzz," is not as intense. The person often drinks more, not realizing that he or she is just moving more quickly into the depressant or dysphoric phase. Figure 6.2 illustrates this model.

In addition to intentionally using the biphasic response to alcohol to your advantage, there are some other good tips for drinking responsibly, which can make a big difference in decreasing the chances that you will experience negative consequences of alcohol consumption. The most important is to choose to drink for positive reasons, not to escape from problems—

FIGURE 6.2 Biphasic Response to Alcohol Consumption

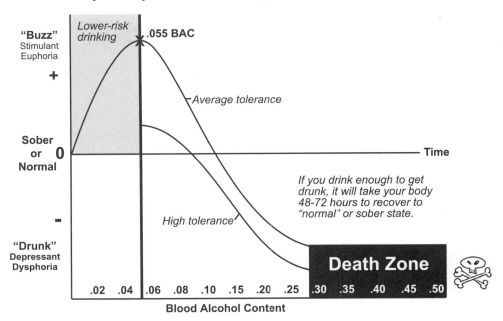

when you do that, you still wake up to your problems, but now you have new ones too. If you are drinking to reduce stress or to try to forget, it is best to tackle this problem straight on; there are many positive ways to decrease your problems without adding new ones associated with alcohol. Make an appointment with a counselor at your campus to start working on the heart of the problem. Another important tip is to believe that alcohol is a complement to an activity, not the primary focus. See "Stephanie's Story from the Path."

Here are some other useful tips from the University of Miami's PIER (Prevention-Intervention-Education-Referral) 21 Program:

- ✦ DO set a limit for yourself before going out and having drinks. You should know, according to your body type and tolerance, how much alcohol you can safely have.
- ✦ DON'T go out with people who make you feel uncomfortable about not drinking. The people worth hanging out with are the ones who will respect you and your choices.
- ✦ DO be careful at bars, clubs, or parties where "Ladies Drink Free"—women are generally affected more quickly by alcohol than men, and an intoxicated person may be targeted for sexual assault.
- ✦ DON'T guzzle, play drinking games, or use devices to consume more quickly (e.g., beer bongs, funnels, shot slides, tubes, double shot glasses, etc.). Your body can only safely process 0.5 ounce of alcohol (about half the amount in an average drink) an hour. So, have one drink/hour and alternate with nonalcoholic drinks.
- ✦ DO take a break from drinking. Show yourself and your friends that you don't need alcohol to go out and have a good time. If you can't do that, then that is an indication that you may have a problem with alcohol.
- ✦ DO eat before and while drinking alcohol—it will slow down the absorption rate of the alcohol into your bloodstream. However, eating after you drink will not

STEPHANIE'S STORY FROM THE PATH

Like many students, I choose to drink at parties. One of the best things I learned to do was "ride the buzz." Although I didn't particularly care about its scientific explanation (the biphasic response), I definitely knew that after I drank some alcohol, I would get that giddy, giggly feeling that was pretty enjoyable. We called that the "buzz," and it was the feeling you were going for. What became clear was that, if you didn't pay attention, you could kill the buzz by either drinking too little or drinking too much once you were feeling it. If you drank too little and the buzz started to fade, it was easy to increase it again, but if you drank too much, you soon found yourself not caring and drinking more and more until you got sick, blacked out, or both. Needless to say, those nights developed into horrible and messy mornings, which were dangerous too.

My friends and I started to learn that it required some practice and skill to "ride the buzz"—the phrase we coined for finding that perfect balance of drinking at just the right pace to keep the buzz going before going over the top—it almost felt like surfing! Riding the buzz is an important skill that students who choose to drink should master. It's not about ingesting large amounts of alcohol quickly—beer bongs and shots are the fastest way to shoot past the buzz because your body goes through the "good zone" too quickly and into the zone of poor judgment and negative effects. It's about finding a way to stay near .055 BAC over a long period of time. Here are some other pointers for learning how to "ride the buzz":

♦ Keep your tolerance low! It is possible to increase your tolerance by regularly drinking large amounts of alcohol ... but why? You just make it harder and more expensive to reach the buzz. The buzz feels the same whether you get there on two beers or twelve, so you might as well be cost-effective about it.

♦ Once you start to feel the buzz, ride it! This is where you want to start monitoring your feelings and drink at the pace to stay in the good zone. It usually means slowing down a little. You want to get all of the good feelings out of the current buzz before you drink more; otherwise, you are wasting the good feelings that your first drinks brought you. When you start to feel it fade a little, drink a bit more but not as much as it took to get to the buzz in the first place (because your BAC is already elevated, you'll probably just need a little). If you want to have a drink in your hand, alternate between alcoholic and nonalcoholic beverages. Besides, people won't bug you if you have a drink in your hand—a plain cola looks just like rum and cola, and water looks like vodka.

♦ Don't compare your buzz to others'. Everyone has a different reaction to alcohol, so it's important to focus on when *your* buzz begins. It might only take you half a beer to feel it, while your friend might need four. If you try to match your friend beer for beer, you are going to fly past the buzz zone and end up having a much yuckier morning than your friend will be having.

♦ Toward the end of the evening, let your buzz start to fade. If you get good at riding the buzz, you will know exactly when to stop drinking to be in good shape the next morning.

My friends and I found riding the buzz to be the perfect solution—all of the fun of partying without any of the mess!

change anything—once alcohol is in your bloodstream, nothing can reduce the rate of absorption.

♦ DON'T go to places where you will be bored if you're not drinking or where you will be uneasy without a drink in your hand.

♦ DO talk to your friends before going out to discuss what to do if: (1) someone is drinking too much, (2) someone gets drunk and starts hooking up with someone they probably wouldn't want to, (3) someone wants to leave but the others want to stay out. Prepare yourself and your friends to take care of each other and to support each other in making responsible choices.

♦ DON'T leave your drinks unattended, let someone else get your drink for you, or drink from a punch bowl—predatory drugs are out there!! They are colorless, odorless, and will leave you completely vulnerable to be taken advantage of. You are not always in a "safe place" with "safe people." Get your own drink, watch it being made, and keep it with you where you can see it at all times.

+ DO get involved when you see someone else putting him/herself in danger. Alcohol poisoning, accidents, sexual assaults, drug overdoses, and drunk driving deaths are all real! Better to have someone ask you why you tried to keep them from having a good time than to have his/her parents or the police ask you why you let them leave the party drunk. Care enough to get involved and do the right thing. Wouldn't you want someone to do that for you?

Date Rape Drugs

There are several drugs that rapists can use to facilitate their crime, including Rohypnol and GHB. Called **date rape drugs,** these chemicals are odorless and colorless so they can be easily slipped into the intended victim's drink without him or her knowing. According to Takahara and Signa (2010), there are three phases to how these drugs work that facilitate sexual assault. The first phase is that the drug makes the person feel ill to the point that she or he would want to leave the party. The person usually heads for home not realizing that that they have been drugged. The next phase happens very quickly, usually before the person can get home. The drug affects the person's ability to move and speak so that they appear extremely drunk and unable to take care of themselves. The rapist has usually followed the victim and is waiting for this phase to step in and "assist" the victim. Onlookers usually do not perceive that anything is wrong as it appears that a sober person is helping his or her drunk friend. The drug continues to affect the person's motor skills and leaves the victim essentially unable to move or speak for several hours but conscious of what is happening to them. It is during this stage that the rapist harms the victim. The last stage of the drug affects memory so that the next day, the victim has no real clear memories of the perpetrator or incident, and therefore cannot help police apprehend the suspect.

Students can do several things to prevent being a victim of this crime. The first is to assume that rapists come in all forms, including young adults who look like students. Some rapists intentionally focus on college towns because of the open parties that occur where alcohol is served and is easy to drug. Just because someone is at your friend's party does not mean that your friend knows this person or that she or he is not a potential threat. As a result, *always* pour your own drinks and keep them with you at all times. If you have to set your drink down, get a new one. Also, crowded parties can make it easy for someone to reach over and pour drugs in a drink—even while you are holding it—so be attentive to your surroundings. If you feel ill, immediately suspect that you may have been drugged. Do not leave the party but instead find people whom you know and trust to help you. You want to find a safe space before the next stage of the drug sets in, where you appear very drunk and become unable to communicate. Students can help each other by never letting a friend leave a party alone or leaving them behind. If you witness a scenario where a very drunk person appears to be being helped by an individual, don't assume that everything is okay. The best way to thwart this crime is to go up and insist on helping as well, or to call the police—that way you can ensure that the person is really escorted home and left in the care of friends.

Finally, realize that police officers in college towns are looking out for this exact scenario. If they see a very drunk person being helped by another (especially a drunk woman being helped by a man), they will most likely approach and ask the drunk person some questions. They are trying to ascertain if this a potential assault in progress. If the drunk person is not able to communicate clearly or does not seem to really know the person with them, the police may take the drunk person into custody in order to protect him or her. Unfortunately, they cannot really take the drunk person home because then she or he would still be vulnerable to others and the police could be held liable for anything that happened. As a result, it's really best to go out as a group of friends who look out for each other and keep each other from harm.

See "Point of Interest: For Students Who Do Not Drink."

POINT OF INTEREST

FOR STUDENTS WHO DO NOT DRINK If you are one of the 20 percent of college students who do not drink at all, regardless of your age, then you might find the following information helpful. If your campus is known for its social scene, you might find it a bit challenging at first because it is most likely that many of your peers chose your campus because of its reputation. There might be a big emphasis on partying, and it might seem that there is nothing to do outside of the party scene. That is not true, but it can look that way, especially as most of your first-year peers will be eager to participate in the scene at the beginning of the term. (It's important to note that this generally wears off over the term as people get tired of the party scene, especially its negative effects.) Going out with your friends is certainly an option, but you might find yourself "babysitting" the others who drink too much or always being the designated driver.

♦ Bring good dance music to the party. That way you can be sure to have something fun to do and others will likely join in.

♦ Remember that it is becoming more and more acceptable for students to not drink.

♦ Choosing not to drink doesn't mean that you have to sit home alone on a weekend. You can still party and have a good time while sober.

♦ Choose an understanding group of friends—friends who either don't drink themselves or will support your choice to not drink even though they might choose to.

♦ Some universities have residence halls or apartments for students who choose not to drink. See what options exist at your campus.

♦ Participate in campus activities and social events that don't focus on alcohol. While the student party scene might revolve around drinking, there are many other fun activities and events to participate in that don't. Check your campus newspaper and fliers posted around campus to find out more.

♦ Attend parties with nondrinking friends as a support system.

♦ Drink water, soda, and the like at events where alcohol is served. If you are not sure whether nonalcoholic options will be provided, bring your own. Remember, it's still important to watch your drink even if it is nonalcoholic. Predatory drugs work in sodas too.

Campus Policies and Local Laws

As was stated earlier in this chapter, universities have felt compelled to respond to these issues for the health of the students. In fact, the U.S. Surgeon General (2004) has said, "Binge drinking is the most serious public health problem on American college campuses today." The U.S. Senate and House of Representatives have already passed resolutions calling for national action to address college binge drinking. Many universities are doing so and utilizing a wide range of methods to combat the problem of excessive alcohol and drug use among students. According to the Higher Education Center for Alcohol and Other Drug Prevention (2010), these efforts focus on five primary prevention strategies:

1. *Education:* Through academic classes, workshops, and programs in university-owned living environments
2. *Early intervention:* By providing counseling support and treatment to students who are experiencing problems with alcohol and other drug use
3. *Environmental change:* Addressing the campus and community climate around alcohol and other drug use as well as availability
4. *Enforcement:* Through campus policies, and local and state law enforcement
5. *Evaluation:* Frequently assessing the alcohol and other drug use of college students as well as the effectiveness of these prevention strategies, making adjustments as needed

Campus policies and local and state laws are a primary way in which student behavior is controlled. If you are living in a university-owned building, there will be policies regarding whether or not alcohol may be on the premises (regardless of the residents' ages) as well as policies that discourage large parties—policies about the number of people that can be in a room, noise regulations, and the like. Even if a living environment consists of students who are over 21 years of age, you will still find policies that govern the presence of alcohol in the

@myU SO HOW DOES THIS AFFECT YOU?

You will find many resources available at your university related to alcohol and other drugs. Regardless of the climate of your campus and the choices of your peers, you will be able to find the types of experiences you desire and make the social scene work for you. Use the tips provided on previous pages to increase your chances of fun and decrease your chances of negative consequences. The most important tip to remember is to go with friends and make a pact to look out for each other. Don't leave friends unattended no matter what. Also, take advantage of the various programs and activities your campus offers. There are some really fun things to do on the weekends that don't revolve around alcohol and drugs. This might require

you to break away from the group mentality of always going to the party scene. But just because your friends might not be interested in going to that concert or attending the Wii competition doesn't mean that there will not be lots of people there. If you can't find anyone to go with you, call the campus escort service and go anyway. You will probably meet lots of new people, including students who share some of your interests and who have also chosen to forgo the party scene for the night.

If you do decide to drink alcohol, make sure you know the consequences for doing so. Look through your university's publications to find the rules and sanctions for the following:

LOCAL OR STATE LAWS	HOUSING ENVIRONMENT	
	RULES FOR ALCOHOL & DRUGS	SANCTIONS
MIP		
DUI		
BUI		

Look for upcoming campus or local events that you can attend instead of going to a party, and list them here:

1.

2.

3.

public areas. Housing staff often have the job of enforcing the policies in living environments, and these may be connected to campus judicial processes.

Local and state laws also play a role and go through the state legal system; laws against a **minor in possession (MIP)** of alcohol, public intoxication, and **driving under the influence (DUI)** are frequently used to attempt to keep students safe. Law enforcement agencies also utilize other, related laws to control alcohol and other drug use, such as laws against open alcohol containers in public, urination in public, noise ordinances, and regulations against large gatherings of people. Students can even be cited for **biking under the influence (BUI),** which carries the same penalties as a DUI. Many students don't know that they can be held liable for purchasing alcohol for others or serving alcohol to others, especially minors. Many college students over the age of 21 have found themselves in jail and held accountable for the injuries or deaths of partygoers who got the alcohol or drugs at their party.

In a new trend across North America, called parental notification, universities use public police records (to avoid violating FERPA) to discover which enrolled students have been cited for an alcohol- or drug-related issue. These records are then shared with the parents of those students. Many campuses that have adopted this process have experienced a decrease in alcohol-related behavior among their students.

TABLE 6.4 PREVALENCE OF USAGE FOR VARIOUS DRUGS IN 2006		
SUBSTANCE	PREVALANCE FOR LAST YEAR	PREVALANCE FOR LAST 30 DAYS
Marijuana	30%	17%
Cocaine	5%	2%
Amphetamines	6%	3%
Designer drugs	3%	1%
Hallucinogens	4%	1%
Sedatives	4%	2%
Opiates	1%	1%
Inhalants	1%	1%
Steroids	1%	0.5%
Other drugs	2%	1%
Tobacco	39%	26%
Alcohol	84%	72%

GETTING HIGH: DRUGS ON CAMPUS

While alcohol is by far the most prominent drug on college campuses, students also use a whole host of other illegal drugs. The second most common drug is marijuana, but every drug can be found if students wish to do so. Campuses are struggling with a rise in the inappropriate use of prescription drugs. Students often see these as "safer" because they are made by pharmaceutical companies and prescribed by medical doctors. However, prescription drugs can be dangerous and cause negative consequences, especially when not appropriately monitored by a physician. In addition, they can still qualify as illegal, depending on how they were acquired.

Current Data on Drug Use

Table 6.4 shows the current national statistics for other drug use on a monthly and annual basis, from the CORE Survey done in 2006 with 71,189 undergraduate students at 134 colleges and universities in the United States.

The National Institute on Drug Abuse (NIDA) has a very informative website that gives the latest statistics on use, forms, and effects of the most prominent drugs; check it out at www.nida.nih.gov. Although there is not the same wealth of information on the drug use of college students, there is still much to be learned by looking at national trends and common effects.

Effects of Commonly Used Drugs

The following information is from NIDA and www.erowid.org on the five kinds of drugs (after alcohol) most used by college students (according to the 2006 CORE Survey). See also "Point of Interest: The Rising Risk of Prescription Drugs."

POINT OF INTEREST

THE RISING RISK OF PRESCRIPTION DRUGS

A new and dangerous trend has been happening on college campuses. Students are taking prescription medicines that are not theirs. In fact, according to the 2009 National College Health Assessment survey, 12 percent of college students have used prescription drugs without a prescription. Nearly 75 percent of them have used prescription painkillers such as Vicodin and OxyContin and more than 40 percent have used a stimulant like Ritalin and Adderall. Medical practitioners are very concerned because these medicines are still drugs and can be very addictive. Students make the mistake of thinking that the drugs are safe or clean because they are from a pharmaceutical company, but the truth is that they can be very dangerous. For one, students who rely on stimulants such as Ritalin and Adderall will find that they can quickly become addicted and no longer be able to study without them. Painkillers are opioids, just like heroine, and are very habit forming in a short amount of time; students can experience withdrawal symptoms even after only a few uses.

In addition, because these medicines are so powerful, prescriptions are screened by both doctors and pharmacists for each individual patient to make sure that there are no possible dangers. Some medications become lethal when combined with other prescriptions for common health conditions like diabetes or high blood pressure. When students use another person's prescription, they are bypassing this important safety net. Many students are drinking alcohol or taking other medicines because they do not have the labels that warn against dangerous combinations. This creates a huge health risk with serious life-threatening consequences as evidenced by the tragic deaths of Heath Ledger, Brittany Murphy, and Cory Haim.

Finally, there are legal consequences as well for students who buy or sell prescribed medications. Both state and federal laws carry heavy fines and prison sentences. Being found guilty of a drug charge can certainly have a serious impact on both a student's ability to complete college and his or her career opportunities later in life.

MARIJUANA

+ People use marijuana to get the following effects: increased relaxation, mood lift, increased awareness of senses, pleasant muscle sensations, relief for medical symptoms of pain and nausea, and increased appetite.
+ Students who smoke marijuana get lower grades, are less likely to graduate, score significantly lower on standardized tests, and have reduced intellectual skills (e.g., registering, organizing, and using information) compared to their nonusing peers.
+ Marijuana quadruples a user's risk of heart attack in the first hour after use because of its effects on blood pressure, heart rate, and reduced ability of the blood to carry oxygen.
+ Marijuana smoke contains 50–70 percent more carcinogenic hydrocarbons than tobacco smoke, leading to cancers of the lung, respiratory tract, and mouth.
+ Marijuana is known to contribute to depression, anxiety, and personality disturbances in users.

HALLUCINOGENS

+ People use hallucinogens, like LSD and mushrooms, to experience the following effects: increase in energy, creative thinking, awareness and appreciation of music, awareness of senses, mood lift, closed- and open-eye visuals, and "profound life-changing spiritual experiences."
+ The effects of LSD and mushrooms are unpredictable and are usually first felt about thirty to ninety minutes after ingestion and can last up to twelve hours. Users may experience extreme and/or simultaneous mood swings as well as delusions and visual hallucinations.
+ Some users experience severe, terrifying thoughts and feelings; fear of losing control; fear of insanity and death; and despair. Fatal accidents have occurred during states of hallucinogen intoxication.
+ LSD users may manifest relatively long-lasting psychoses, such as schizophrenia and severe depression.

AMPHETAMINES AND METHAMPHETAMINES

✦ People use amphetamines and methamphetamines to experience the following effects: increased energy and alertness, decreased need for sleep, feelings of euphoria, increased sexuality, decreased appetite, and weight loss.

✦ Methamphetamine causes increased heart rate and blood pressure and can cause irreversible damage to blood vessels in the brain, producing strokes. It also causes respiratory problems, irregular heartbeat, brain damage, paranoia, and extreme anorexia.

✦ Over time, methamphetamine appears to cause reduced levels of dopamine (a neurotransmitter), resulting in symptoms like those of Parkinson's disease, a severe neurological disorder.

DESIGNER DRUGS SUCH AS MDMA OR ECSTASY, ROHYPNOL OR ROOFIES, AND GHB

✦ People use Ecstasy to experience the following effects: extreme mood lift; increased willingness to communicate; feelings of comfort, belonging, and closeness to others; the urge to hug and kiss people; increased awareness of senses (sensations are bright and intense); and dissolution of neurotically based fears.

@myU SO HOW DOES THIS AFFECT YOU?

If you choose to use drugs, it is important that you understand the effects they have on your body. While the sensations might feel enjoyable, they can actually be affiliated with short- and long-term damage. Many useful and informative websites offer accurate information about drugs and their effects. It is also important to control, to the extent that you can, the quality and quantity of any substances you use, as these can greatly affect your body's response. Drug dealers often cut drugs with other substances such as baby powder or even rat poison to make a bigger profit. People have gotten very sick and even died from other substances that were in the drugs they were taking.

You will also want to assess how much, and in what ways, your drug use is affecting your ability to be successful academically, socially, and personally. Ultimately, only you can weigh the pros and cons of your use and make choices to stop or continue use. If you have questions about drugs or your own use or are concerned about your health, remember that the services of the student health office may be very valuable to you. Because of FERPA, if you seek confidential medical advice and personal counseling for alcohol and drug issues, your family will not be informed.

If you do not use drugs, you might still witness others' use or be affected by their use. You can always choose to find other nonusing students to socialize with, but if you are living with someone, the chances are greater that his or her drug use will affect you. You might need to talk to your friend and/or roommate to request certain limitations on drug use in your presence or your shared space. You have a right to enjoy your space just as much as another person. If these negotiations do not go well, you might seek the assistance of housing staff or a campus mediator, or you might wish to find other housing arrangements. Look up the following resources for your campus:

DRUGS USED MOST OFTEN BY STUDENTS	POLICIES/CONSEQUENCES FOR POSSESSION OF THESE DRUGS	COUNSELING AVAILABLE

- Ecstasy is a psychoactive drug with amphetamine and hallucinogen qualities. In high doses, it interferes with the body's ability to regulate temperature, leading to dehydration and hyperthermia, which have caused liver, kidney, and heart failure in users.
- Ecstasy changes brain function, affecting cognitive tasks and memory. It can do long-term damage to serotonin neurons (a study using primates showed that only four days of exposure to Ecstasy created damage that was still evident six to seven years later). Ecstasy users often experience symptoms of depression for several days after its use.
- People use GHB and Rohypnol ("roofies") to experience the following effects: effects similar to those of alcohol but longer-lasting, mild relaxation, increased sociability, and decreased motor skills.
- While often used as "date rape drugs," they are also taken recreationally because they create feelings of euphoria. Both can become lethal when mixed with alcohol and/or other depressants.

COCAINE AND CRACK

- People use cocaine to experience the following effects: increased alertness and energy, elevation of mood, a mild to high degree of euphoria, increased athletic performance, decreased fatigue, clearer thinking, and increased concentration.
- Cocaine and crack are the same drug in different forms (crack is the cheaper, more potent version most often used by lower-income people, although the legal penalties for its use are nearly ten times higher). Cocaine is a very addictive drug that stimulates the central nervous system. One use of crack can be habit forming.
- Rates of cocaine use by college students have varied between 2 percent of all students in 1994 to 4.8 percent in 2000. Adults 18 to 25 years of age currently have the highest percentage of cocaine use of any age group.
- High doses or prolonged use can trigger paranoia as well as depression. Users can develop ulcerations of the mucous membranes in the nose. Users can die suddenly and unpredictably from cardiac arrest, seizures, and respiratory arrest. Consuming alcohol during use increases the risk of sudden death.

HOOKING UP: STUDENTS AND SEX

After all this discussion of alcohol and other drug use, it might seem odd to move on to the discussion of sexual activity. After all, sex is not an illegal activity and is part of most healthy adult relationships. While that is certainly true, the inclusion of sex in this chapter on health and safety focuses more on the fact that while sexual activity should be fun, healthy, and consensual, it often isn't, especially when students are consuming alcohol and other drugs. **Consensual** sexual activity can pose a health risk when people do not take precautions against sexually transmitted infections and diseases. Additionally, many college students want to avoid pregnancy. Finally, sex that is not consensual, meaning that someone was **assaulted or raped,** is definitely of great concern, as the survivors of these crimes often suffer emotional damage in addition to the physical damage that can affect their entire life and certainly their college experience.

Administrators on university campuses have long been concerned about the sexual activity and health of their students. Several decades ago, before the passage of FERPA, the concern arose out of a desire to enforce the societal moral codes about sexual activity—more accurately, that there should be no sex until marriage. Many of the *in loco parentis* policies and procedures focused on keeping men and women separated and monitoring their evening activities.

All of this changed with FERPA and the nearly simultaneous shift in societal values about sexual behavior. FERPA allowed a student's room to become his or her private living space, and it removed responsibility from the university to monitor its students' sexual behaviors. Although many living environments still maintained single-sex status, the removal of curfews and other policies allowed students to do what they wanted with whomever they wanted as long as they were not disturbing their peers.

Many sectarian schools still have policies in place to regulate social, and potentially sexual, interactions between students. **Sectarian schools** are private and can maintain policies and procedures that would not be legally viable in public institutions. In addition, sectarian schools focus on religious teachings and trainings and attempt to make the campus environment conducive to the spiritual teachings of the particular religion on which the school is based. There are several sectarian research universities in the United States, including Brigham Young University and Pepperdine University.

Although universities have moved away from trying to prevent sexual encounters between students, there is still a strong concern about students' sexual practices. This concern stems from the health risks that have been identified since the sexual revolution of the 1970s, such as more dangerous and incurable **sexually transmitted infections and diseases (STIs and STDs)** including HIV and AIDS. In addition, the awareness of sexual assault, especially acquaintance sexual assault, has increased dramatically in the past three decades and is a major concern on campuses nationwide. Given that many social and therefore sexual encounters between students now involve alcohol, the connection between excessive drinking and negative sexual experiences is also a serious concern.

Current Data on Sexual Activity and Its Negative Consequences

The American College Health Association (2010) did a national study in 2008 that involved 34,208 undergraduate college students across the United States. Results from the National College Health Assessment survey that are relevant to this topic include the following:

+ 34 percent had not had sexual intercourse (oral, vaginal, or anal) in the previous 12 months
+ on average, students had 2 sexual partners in the previous 12 months

Of students who reported having vaginal sex in the previous 12 months:

+ only 52 percent of students had used a method of contraception
+ 13 percent of students who reported having vaginal sex in the previous year had used emergency contraception or the "morning-after pill"
+ 4 percent of students had been pregnant or had gotten someone pregnant

Students who used a condom or other protective barrier method (which would protect against sexually transmitted infections) were reported as follows:

+ 6 percent of students engaging in oral sex
+ 52 percent of students engaging in vaginal sex
+ 30 percent of students engaging in anal sex

Clearly, many of these statistics indicate that college students are not practicing the most basic of **safer sex** practices. Obviously abstinence is the only true "safe" method, but using a barrier method, such as a condom, during sexual intercourse can greatly reduce your risk, thus making it safer than no method at all. This lack of protection increases the risk of developing sexually transmitted infections and diseases, including HIV/AIDS (Handler, 1990). Some other alarming statistics include the following:

+ It is estimated that 8 million young adults under the age of 25 are infected with STDs.

+ According to the National Clearing House for Alcohol and Drug Information, 60 percent of college women who acquire an STI, such as HIV or genital herpes, were under the influence of alcohol at the time they had intercourse.
+ In 2010, HIV was the sixth leading cause of death for Americans between the ages of 25 and 29.
+ It is estimated that people under 25 years of age represent at least half of all new HIV infections in the United States, most of whom are infected sexually.
+ One-third of people living with HIV are aware of their status and in treatment, one-third are aware but not in treatment, and one-third are not aware and have not been treated.

Combine this with the data in this section about the number of college students who are engaging in unprotected sex and the previous information about alcohol's effect on safer sex practices, and you have a dangerous situation on college campuses.

This information is scary enough when it relates to adults who are having consensual sex, but it becomes even more terrifying for students who are raped or sexually assaulted. According to the CDC's National College Health Risk Behavior Survey (2004), 13.1 percent of college students reported having been forced to have sexual intercourse against their will during their lifetime. It is estimated that 22 percent of all women (almost one out of four) and 2 percent of all men will be the victims of a forced sexual act sometime during their life. Some of these sexual assaults may occur prior to college and some may occur later in life, but data indicate that the years of 16 to 24 are the most "rape-endangered" years in a person's life—and these are ages when college attendance is likely.

On most university campuses, the problem is not strangers attacking and sexually assaulting students, although this certainly does happen. In college communities, the problem is **acquaintance assault, or "date rape,"** which occurs when a person is assaulted by someone he or she has had prior contact with, such as a friend, a hallmate, or someone the person had previously met at a party. Nearly 90 percent of acquaintance sexual assaults involve alcohol, which indicates that one or both parties had their judgment and physical abilities impaired in some way. More often than not, these cases begin with consensual kissing and making out. At some point, one person decides that the situation has gone as far as she or he is comfortable with. What ensues after that might range from subtle pressure from the other person to unending harassment to physical force. When the situation ends in a sexual encounter that one person did not want to happen, this is the legal definition of sexual assault; if physical penetration occurred, it is rape. It doesn't matter what the person who was assaulted was wearing, how many sexual partners she or he had previously, or how much she or he had to drink—if the person said "no" and it was not listened to, then it was sexual assault or rape.

Both men and women can be victims of sexual assault and rape. The assailant can be someone of the same sex or the opposite sex. Although the majority of reported sexual assaults occur with a man assaulting a woman, other scenarios can and do occur on college campuses each year. See "Point of Interest: When a Friend Has Been Sexually Assaulted."

It is important to distinguish sexual assault from **regretted sex.** Most adults experience regretted sex sometime in their life. Regretted sex occurs when, after you chose to engage in a sexual encounter, you later wish that you hadn't. "Later" can be the next hour, the next day, the next week, or even months or years later. Although a person might later wish that she or he had not done something, the fact that the person chose this action earlier means that it was not sexual assault or rape because it was consensual at the time it occurred. Obviously, regretted sex is not a pleasant experience either, and it is also often influenced by alcohol and other drugs. Students who are under the influence of some substance frequently make choices that they would not normally make when fully sober.

WHEN A FRIEND HAS BEEN SEXUALLY ASSAULTED If someone you care about has been raped or sexually assaulted, you might be upset and confused about how to best support her or him. Here are some suggestions that you might find helpful, adapted from the University of Colorado at Boulder and Pennsylvania State University:

• *Be clear that the rape or assault is not the survivor's fault:* Regardless of the circumstances, nobody deserves to be sexually assaulted, and the survivor is not to blame.

• *Listen without judgment:* Feeling able to tell her or his own story without pressure or fear of condemnation will help the survivor process the experience of the sexual assault.

• *Believe the survivor:* Feeling that she or he is believed by family and friends is essential for a rape survivor's recovery. This person has to overcome many obstacles to be able to speak out about what has happened.

• *Encourage the survivor to get support:* In addition to offering your own support, encourage the survivor to reach out to sexual assault/rape counselors. They have expertise in the survival and recovery process and can greatly assist a survivor in her or his recovery.

• *Respect the survivor's individual process and decisions:* Remember that a survivor needs to make her or his own decisions as a step in regaining control and overcoming feelings of helplessness. If you feel frustrated that the survivor is taking "too long" to recover emotionally, remind yourself that everyone needs to process a traumatic experience at her or his own pace and in his or her own way.

• *Take care of yourself:* As a cosurvivor, you might also need support in coping with a loved one's sexual assault. Taking advantage of counseling and victim advocacy services not only will help you personally, but also will help you support the survivor more effectively.

What to Do If You Are Sexually Assaulted

The following information on what to do if you are sexually assaulted was adapted from Cornell University's CARE (Cornell Advocates for Rape Education) Program (2010):

• *Take care of yourself:* Remember that what has happened to you is not your fault. You are not to blame for what took place before or during the incident. No matter what you did or how you behaved, you did not deserve to have your rights or body violated. The assailant is completely responsible for what happened. And you have a right to get the care and attention you need to heal from the experience.

• *Tell someone what happened:* Talk to a friend or trusted confidant or call your local rape crisis center; there is usually a free and confidential 24-hour hotline staffed by counselors who are knowledgeable about the needs of rape survivors, who can lend support, and who will offer to accompany you to get the help you may need. Many university campuses also have counselors who help students who have experienced sexual assault.

• *Get medical care:* As soon as you can, get medical care from the student health center, the hospital, or a private physician. You will benefit from being examined for physical injury and disease. You might need to discuss options for pregnancy prevention. A medical report can also be useful if you decide to press charges against the person who assaulted you. Do not bathe, shower, douche, or change clothes before the medical exam.

• *You might want to report the incident:* It is your decision whether to report the attack. You can notify the campus police or the local or state police. Filing an informational report does not obligate you to press charges. Should you choose to press charges later, a report will significantly increase the possibility of successful prosecution. You might want to talk to a rape counselor or a law enforcement officer about reporting procedures and options. Your campus office of judicial affairs or dean of students office can consult with you about violations that occur on campus property or between enrolled students. If the perpetrator is a member of the campus community, there might be campus judicial actions that can be taken.

✦   *Get support:* After the initial process of talking to advisors and getting medical care, you will want to get some more long-term support. Survivors often need the support of a counselor who is trained in working with sexual assault issues to recover both physically and emotionally from the attack. It is not uncommon for sexual assault survivors to experience any or all of the following symptoms: emotional shock, denial, nightmares, sleeplessness, intrusive memories or thoughts about the assault, inability to work or make decisions, impaired relationships, guilt, despair, depression, fear, anxiety, self-blame, and anger. You will also want to surround yourself with friends and family who are supportive in your healing process.

Campus Policies

Unlike the situation with alcohol and other drugs, there are very few campus policies that govern consensual sex between adults, with the exception of sectarian schools. There might be policies in university-owned living environments about overnight guests and noise or actions that disturb roommates, but even those do not directly address sexual contact. Students are largely on their own to make good choices about when, with whom, and in what ways they engage in sexual encounters with others.

Some campuses, like Brown University, have sought to decrease the incidents of acquaintance sexual assault by instituting recommendations for **clear consent**, meaning that people must give clear and verbal consent to each act of intimacy before it is initiated. For example, a student would need to ask, "May I kiss you?" and receive a clear "yes" before moving ahead. Some argue that if a person is drunk, then consent cannot really be given because she or he is under the influence; the partner should not move ahead even if a "yes" has been given. Although cumbersome, clear consent is useful in raising awareness about the importance of consent, especially when alcohol is involved, but its value has been strongly debated on college campuses across the country.

Pay attention to any campus policies or discussions of these topics as they might influence your choices and experiences.

Resources for Healthy Relationships

Because of health education in K–12 schools in North America, most students are fairly informed about the basics of sexual intercourse, safer sex practices, and pregnancy. But this is not true of all students—you would be surprised by how many students don't know a lot of very important information.

With that said, it is each student's responsibility to ensure his or her own sexual safety and pleasure. Unlike high schools, where the topic of sexuality often requires parental permission to discuss, university environments can and do have many open and confidential forums and resources to help students have safe and healthy sexual lives if they so choose. Obviously, some students will have personal or religious values that guide their choices around premarital sex, birth control, and the like, so their college years may be about practicing abstinence. Others will engage in sexual activity throughout their college experience and beyond. Universities want to support the range of students' needs so you will find information and resources available for both sexually active and abstinent student populations. In addition, universities are aware that students have a wide range of sexual orientations and can provide information that is relevant to heterosexual, bisexual, lesbian/gay, and transgender students. Your campus health center is a good place to look for information about sexual health, sexuality, and relationships.

Regardless of when and how you choose to become sexually active—as part of a long-term committed relationship or as a casual "hookup" one weekend—you will find that your relationships will be enhanced by three factors. The first is **self-awareness,** which is the extent

THE SCENIC ROUTE

Visit www.cengagebrain.com to find the companion website containing links to:

▪ Columbia University's "Go Ask Alice!" service for health questions

▪ Studenthealth101.com's free online newsletter

▪ SUNY Buffalo's sexual assertiveness survey

to which you know yourself, both emotionally and physically. Emotionally, you will want to know your values around sex, intimacy, and relationships. What assumptions do you have about each one? How are they related to each other, if at all? What kinds of experiences have you had in the past? Both positive and negative experiences shape our beliefs about sex, intimacy, and relationships. Understanding your values will allow you to communicate them clearly to a partner, which will increase the likelihood that your values will be honored.

Physically, you will want to learn about your body and its sexual response. The sexual response is a human function, just like digestion or sleep. Knowing how your body functions sexually is just as important as understanding what foods are nutritious and promote healthy digestion. This information is very useful in helping you know how to protect yourself from unwanted pregnancies and sexually transmitted infections. In addition, it can help you have a more enjoyable and satisfying sexual life, whether it be within a marriage or a casual encounter. Learning what you find pleasurable and what enhances your excitement is a personal exploration that is really no different from learning about what foods you like and which ones you are allergic to. Knowing your preferences will allow you to communicate them clearly to another person, thus increasing your chances they will be honored.

This exploration leads to the second important factor: **communication.** All relationships, whether they involve intimacy or not, require communication. When a relationship includes emotional intimacy, sexual intimacy, or both, the need for good communications skills is increased. You will need to be able to tell your partner what you value, what you need, and what you want. Likewise, you will need to listen to your partner share his or her values, needs, and wants. With regard to sexual intimacy, communication can become far more challenging because of the difficulty people have discussing this topic. People may have discomfort with their own sexuality; even if they are comfortable, they may not feel comfortable with sexual terms and vocabulary, and this can hinder good communication. Finally, sexual intimacy is an intensely personal topic and, because the fear of rejection can be strong, it requires each person to be vulnerable. This makes sexual communication one of the most challenging areas in relationships.

As couples communicate their individual values, needs, and wants, it is rare that they have complete alignment in all areas. Most likely, they have some differences that need to be addressed. This brings us to the third factor: **negotiation.** This requires the couple to find ways to negotiate a solution that both can be happy with. Some couples move into a competitive mode, where one person will get his or her way and the other person loses. This exacerbates their differences and eventually causes resentment over time and can breed mistrust and dislike. Others find ways to support and encourage their partner while still speaking up for what they want. If they work together to find a solution that works for both parties, their differences can actually strengthen the relationship. This is especially true for sexual intimacy. Most likely, each person enjoys different things and is excited or bothered by different aspects of sexual activity. Finding a common ground is the basis for a healthy sexual relationship. See "Chelsea's Story from the Path."

Self-awareness, communication, and negotiation are skills that you will want to learn and enhance for the betterment of all your relationships. Many campus resources can help you develop these skills. Simply attending university courses and living in a diverse campus community will build them, and you will find workshops on these topics offered by your campus counseling center and leadership program. When you choose to become emotionally and/or sexually intimate with another person, you will want to strengthen these skills even more. Some of the campus resources that are likely to be available to you include the following:

+ Academic courses on human sexuality, relationships, communication, and other related topics
+ Sexual health education programs that offer workshops and other educational presentations

CHELSEA'S STORY FROM THE PATH

When I entered college as an 18-year-old freshman, I was excited for the newfound freedom and possible dating situations I could encounter. I had attended both Catholic middle- and high schools and was arguably very ignorant to the possible consequences of sexual activity, and I had not bothered worrying about them since I had stayed sexually abstinent up until college. Suddenly I was at a public university living in a hall with both men and women, attending parties where guys were hitting on me, and most of my friends were sexually active.

During my first quarter of college, I found that a lot of people thought nothing of casual sex and "hooking up" with a different partner every weekend. Becoming sexually active excited me, yet I had many worries too. I decided to take a human sexuality course my first year; if I was going to have sex, I was going to know more about the consequences—and pleasures—of sex. Taking that course was one of the smartest things I've ever done. Even if you're planning on staying abstinent right now, chances are you might want to have sex at some point in your life—so the best thing you can do is be educated about it!

College classes can provide much more information than most high schools allow. I learned all about human sexual anatomy and response; birth control; the transmission routes, symptoms, treatments, and possible complications of sexually transmitted infections (STIs); the correct way to put on a condom (most condom failure is due to user error!); and how to communicate with a potential partner about my wants, desires, and sexual values.

College students have different values about sex and sexuality—some of your friends may be saving sexual activity with a partner until marriage or a lifelong commitment, while others may pursue many sexual relationships at this point in their lives. I have learned to uphold my values and to not judge others for their decisions. I chose to become sexually active and have realized what I value in a relationship, both nonsexually and sexually.

As a college student I also unfortunately realized that adding alcohol to a sexual experience can really complicate it—from a lack of physical arousal and pleasure to regretting an experience later on. And even worse, the majority of sexual assaults occur under the influence of alcohol.

One thing that has really helped me with communicating more clearly with a partner about sexual activity is the CORE model from AIDS Project Los Angeles:

C: Clarify intentions—know what you want; decide your own sexual limits and share these with your partner; use "I" statements to communicate your needs, wants, and desires.
O: Options—look for common ground with your partner; determine what sexual activities you are both comfortable with.
R: Reach for agreement—come to an agreement on what will or will not happen.
E: Enjoy or exit—if an agreement is reached, then enjoy! If an agreement is not reached, this is a good time to say no to the sexual activity or maybe even no to being with that partner. In other words, this might be the time to exit. If someone is not willing to respect your decision, this person is not respecting the boundaries that were set, and this can set the stage for sexual assault, which occurs when one person's boundaries are not honored.

The CORE model has really helped me communicate to partners what I am and am not comfortable with. Recently, it helped me realize that a potential partner was not ready to uphold and respect my sexual limits, so I exited. College can be a really exciting time of life, and the last things you want to deal with are STIs, unintended pregnancies, sexual assault, or even just getting your feelings hurt. Educate yourself and communicate with your partner!

+ Doctors and nurses who work at the student health center and can address sexual health questions
+ Health educators who can meet with you and provide counseling/advising on a variety of topics including relationships, communication, and intimacy
+ Counselors and advisors who work with the lesbian/gay/bisexual/transgender populations
+ Rape prevention education and sexual assault counselors
+ Books and Internet sites that address these topics

RELATED MATERIALS

For Scenic Route websites, more Stories from the Path, glossary, and student activities, access the study tools for *Navigating the Research University* at www.cengagebrain.com.

@myU SO HOW DOES THIS AFFECT YOU?

Knowing yourself and your values is important in all relationships, but especially in ones that are sexually intimate. Before you find yourself in a sexual situation, take the time to reflect on the following issues and how you might communicate your feelings and values to your partner.

+ Sex before marriage

+ Oral sex, anal sex, and vaginal sex

+ Protection from sexually transmitted infections

+ Protection from pregnancy

+ Monogamy

+ Casual sex

+ Sex under the influence

+ Privacy

REFERENCES

American College Health Association. (2010). *Reference group executive summary*. Retrieved from http://www.achancha.org/reports_ACHA-NCHAoriginal.html.

Budke, K. (2004). *The effects of alcohol*. Retrieved from http://www.uiowa.edu/~shs/substance.htm.

Centers for Disease Control (CDC). (2004). *National college health risk behavior survey*. Retrieved from http://www.cdc.gov/mmwr/preview/mmwrhtml/00049859.htm.

CORE Institute. (2006). *CORE alcohol and drug survey*. Southern Illinois University. Retrieved from http://www.core.siuc.edu/.

Cornell Advocates for Rape Education. (2010). *What to do if you are sexually assaulted*. Retrieved from Cornell University, Cornell Advocates for Rape Education website at http://www.care.cornell.edu/help.html.

Facts on Tap. (2010). *Blood alcohol and you: Behavior by numbers*. Retrieved from http://www.factsontap.org/factsontap/naked_truth/by_the_numbers.htm.

Frezza, M., di Padova, C., Pozzato, G., Terpin, M., Baraona, E., & Lieber, C. S., et al. (1990). High blood alcohol levels in women: The role of decreased gastric alcohol dehydrogenase activity and first-pass metabolism. *New England Journal of Medicine, 322,* 95–99.

Handler, A. (1990, June 20–23). The role of negotiation skills in safer sex practice when educating at-risk youth. *International Conference on AIDS*. AIDS Project Los Angeles, California. Retrieved from http://gateway.nlm.nih.gov/MeetingAbstracts/ma?f=102196561.html.

Harvard School of Public Health. (2006). *About CAS*. Retrieved from Harvard School of Public Health, College Alcohol Study website at http://www.hsph.harvard.edu/cas/About.

Higher Education Center for Alcohol and Other Drug Prevention. (2010). *What campuses and communities are doing*. Retrieved from http://www.edc.org/hec/framework/.

Hingson, R. H., Zakocs, R., Kopstein, A., & Wechsler, H. (2002). Magnitude of alcohol-related morbidity, mortality, and alcohol dependence among U.S. college students age 18–24. *Journal of Studies on Alcohol, 63*(2), 136–144.

Marlatt, A. (1999). *Brief alcohol screening and intervention for college students*. New York: Guilford Press.

MedicineNet. (2010). Alcohol impairment charts for men and women. Retrieved from http://www.medicinenet.com/script/main/art.asp?articlekey=52905.

Narcanon. (2010). *Cocaine and cocaine addiction information*. Retrieved from http://www.stopaddiction.com/index.php/Addiction/.

National Institute on Alcohol Abuse and Alcoholism (NIAAA). (2010). *High-risk drinking in college: What we know and what we need to learn*. Retrieved from http://www.collegedrinkingprevention.gov/.

National Institute on Drug Abuse (NIDA). (2010). *InfoFacts*. Retrieved from http://www.drugabuse.gov/infofacts/infofaxindex.html.

Pennsylvania State University. (2010). *Helping victims of violence*. Retrieved from http://studentaffairs.psu.edu/womenscenter/awareness/rapeandassault.shtml.

Takahara, M., & Signa, M. (2010, February 17). Alcohol and drug use among college students. Lecture for Education 20. University of California, Santa Barbara.

Task Force of the National Advisory Council on Alcohol Abuse and Alcoholism. (2010). *A snapshot of annual high-risk college drinking consequences*. Retrieved from http://www.collegedrinkingprevention.gov/StatsSummaries/snapshot.aspx.

U.S. Surgeon General. (2004). *HIV/AIDS and adolescents*. Retrieved from http://www.surgeongeneral.gov/AIDS/factsheets/adolescents.html.

University of Colorado at Boulder. (2010). *Support for sexual assault victims*. Retrieved from http://www.colorado.edu/studentaffairs/victimassistance/quickassist/sexual_assault.html.

University of Miami PIER 21. (2004). *Helping family or friends with substance abuse problems*. Retrieved from http://www.miami.edu/index.php/student_life/student_services/student_health/pier21/peer_education/tips_on_staying_safe_and_healthy/#HTHF.

The Vaults of Erowid. (2010). *Plants and drugs*. Retrieved from http://www.erowid.org.

CHAPTER **7**

The Diverse University Community

JOE SKIPPER/Reuters /Landov

University of Miami

Most universities and colleges value diversity in all its forms, but research universities see it as central to their mission. There is an inherent assumption at research universities that in order to discover new knowledge, you need to embrace diverse ways of thinking about a topic because multiple views and perspectives aid in the process of discovery. In addition, most university administrators and faculty believe that the educational process is enriched for all when a wide range of diversity is found in the students, faculty, and staff. A diverse community brings the strengths of all of its members, and each person can learn from interacting with the others. However, diversity also brings challenges. When people do not share an experience, belief, or value, they might not communicate effectively, or they might even experience conflict or tension. Also, people and institutions can value diversity in theory, but their daily actions might not actually achieve that. In this chapter, we are going to specifically look at issues of diversity on university campuses and how they affect the community of scholars. Using current statistics and theoretical models of identity development, we will explore many aspects of human identity that shape the university experience.

YOUR DIVERSE UNIVERSITY

In this chapter, you will find many references to two national studies done by UCLA's Higher Education Research Institute (HERI). Each year, HERI conducts a nationwide study of incoming college freshmen; in 2009, the study included 219,864 first-year students at 297 colleges and universities across the United States (Pryor, et al., 2009). This study has been done annually for 45 years and has become a central source of data on current freshmen as well as trends over time. In addition, HERI now conducts an annual study of college freshmen at the end of their first year of college, called Your First College Year (YFCY). In 2009, this study sampled 26,758 college freshmen at 457 four-year institutions in the United States (Ruiz, et al., 2010). Although not all of the participating institutions are research universities, the data provide an overall picture of the current freshman experience in the United States.

Because research universities bring together so many unique populations (e.g., faculty, staff, administrators, undergraduate students, graduate students, alumni, parents, donors, surrounding community members) from around the world, the term **diversity** takes on a far greater meaning than just ethnic or racial diversity. The university community is unique in that it actually creates a microcosm of society that is not replicated in any other type of institution—people of all ages and backgrounds are living and working together year-round, and this creates opportunities for both wonderful and problematic interactions. Each group within the university community, and each member within each group, has their own needs and preferences, some of which might be at odds or in conflict with the needs of others. This chapter will explore some of these issues in more depth.

Understanding diversity should be important to every college student. It is through the college experience that you can gain valuable experiences and information that will prepare you to work in a global economy and live in a multicultural society. Many college students seem to understand the importance of this opportunity and embrace it. According to the 2009 YFCY survey, many students indicate an interest in social awareness issues and say that this interest grew over their first year in college. Students indicated the following as being either "essential" or "very important" in their life goals at college entry compared to the end of their first year:

Entry

39%	Helping to promote racial understanding
51%	Influencing social values
39%	Becoming a community leader
80%	Helping others who are in difficulty

In addition, students indicated that they had grown (that is, felt stronger or much stronger) in the following areas compared to when they entered college (Ruiz, et al., 2010):

61%	Knowledge of people from different races/cultures
61%	Understanding of social problems facing our nation
60%	Understanding of global issues
60%	Understanding of problems facing their community

These discussions are an important part of your education and career preparation. Many employers now are acutely aware of the multicultural society and global community in which they must compete. Many are seeking to hire students who have developed what is called **cultural competence,** which is an awareness of various ideas of diversity and how they might shape a person's experience and interactions within a community. Becoming culturally competent is an important skill for college students to master, and the ideas discussed in this chapter can serve as the groundwork for that development.

Many students find the information presented in this chapter to be a bit eye-opening. This is normal—as people, we have only our own personal experience in the world, and it is often not easy to think about how someone else's experience might differ from ours, especially in a place like a university community where people are sharing the same daily experiences in ways that most communities do not. College can create a unique sense of community among students simply because of the commonality of sharing large classes, late-night study sessions, boisterous sporting events, engaging instructors, and fun parties. Many students find a sense of camaraderie with others in sharing and surviving the trials of university life.

However, this camaraderie can often mask important differences that students feel affect their college experience. For example, a male student might feel perfectly safe on campus and never consider that his female friend does not. Likewise, a White student might always feel comfortable in the dining commons, not ever considering that her Latina roommate might feel suddenly self-conscious about being a "minority," especially if the campus is not ethnically diverse. Generally, being in the minority of a campus's population creates additional challenges and experiences in comparison to those experienced by the students in the majority. Regardless of which aspect you experience for the different parts of your identity, you will want to listen to, and learn about, the experiences and views of others. See "Point of Interest: Keep an Open Mind."

Dimensions of Identity

In discussing "diversity," it is important to look at all the different aspects of a person's identity. There are **primary dimensions** of our identity, which are the things that we are born with or cannot easily change about our physical being. These are gender, race, ethnicity, sexual orientation, age, and physical abilities/qualities. Then there are **secondary dimensions** of our identity—elements that still significantly shape who we are but that there is some degree of choice or ability to change. These include geographic location, education, economic status, religious beliefs/spirituality, political ideology, work experience/style, physical appearance, learning style, marital status, parental status, military experience, language/dialect, and personality. All of these factors interact in unique ways to create the identity of any one individual. Even a group of people who share a primary identity will find a huge range of differences based on their other primary and secondary dimensions. As you grow and develop, you will learn about yourself and your own self-concept, including issues related to these primary and secondary dimensions of diversity. In addition, you will interact with a wide range of people and develop your interpersonal skills and acceptance of diverse ideas and ways of being.

POINT OF INTEREST

KEEP AN OPEN MIND Before we get started, I want to address the importance of this chapter. By far the biggest obstacle to college success for many students is how they are treated by their peers regarding aspects of their identity. Students of color, low-income students, lesbian/gay/bisexual/transgender students, and students with disabilities not only experience additional challenges, but also often experience verbal and physical harassment. This issue is of great importance to institutions of higher education, and you will find that conversations about diversity issues are common at your university.

In my experience, some first-year students, especially freshmen, are resistant to talking about diversity. They say things like, "But I already attended several diversity workshops. I don't want to talk about it anymore." While they might have talked about diversity in some ways before, the truth is that dynamics on university campuses are far different from those in high school; the ways in which these issues can be discussed and addressed are very different as well. I encourage you to read this chapter with an open mind and to see how diversity issues might be different from what you already know or have experienced.

As students go through these developmental processes, in relation to both their own personal identity and their abilities to interact with others, both positive and negative interactions can occur. Many common themes of the first-year student experience revolve around these issues. This chapter will focus on the dimensions that seem to be most closely connected with the university experience: age, gender, sexual orientation, race and ethnicity, economic class, spiritual identity, and political ideology. While other aspects of identity are certainly important, space prevents us from exploring more than just a few.

AGE AND GENERATIONAL ISSUES

One aspect of the university community that makes it unique is that it contains members of all ages ranging from 0 (newborn babies of students, staff, and faculty) all the way up to the 90s (emeritus faculty who are still involved in campus business and even students who have chosen to attend college late in life). According to the 2009 HERI study (Pryor, et al., 2009), the majority of freshmen are either 18 (68 percent) or 19 (29 percent) years old. Faculty age was assessed by HERI in its 2008 study on the American College Teacher, sampling 22,562 faculty at 372 four-year colleges and universities (DeAngelo, et al., 2009). These researchers found that faculty had ages ranging from the late-20s to more than 65 years old. This means that the university community facilitates interactions among all of the living generations in ways that are not seen in most neighborhood and work environments. Each generation is unique, and understanding the different needs and styles of each generation is useful for successfully interacting with members of the university community.

Many researchers look at the various generations of people within a society. A **generation** is defined as a societywide peer group that collectively has common values and attitudes. A generation is determined by birthrates, which tend to rise and fall in a classic bell-shaped curve; the lowest point of the curve approximates the end of one generation and the beginning of the next. According to Neil Howe and William Strauss, authors of *Millennials Rising: The Next Great Generation* (2000), the current living generations are as follows:

G.I. generation	Born 1901–1924
Silent generation	Born 1925–1942
Baby boomers	Born 1943–1960
Generation X	Born 1961–1981
Millennials	Born 1982–2002
Homeland	Born 2002 or later

Every generation is shaped by history and events, technology, economy, society, and culture. These events have the most impact during the so-called formative years (ages 8 to 13 years) and the coming-of-age years (ages 17 to 23), when they can significantly shape a person's attitudes and behaviors. Although not all people in a given generation are affected in the same way, researchers have been able to identify widely held shared values and attitudes. Table 7.1 is a chart of the events that have significantly shaped each generation and the common values and attitudes that members of that generation share (this information is adapted from *Millennials Rising* by Howe and Strauss, 2000, and *When Generations Collide: How to Solve the Generational Puzzle at Work* by Lancaster and Stillman, 2002).

It is clear from reading the descriptions in Table 7.1 that there are likely to be conflicts and tensions between the different generations because some of their primary values are in opposition. Lancaster and Stillman (2002) argue that generational differences are at the forefront of current personnel issues across the country. The effects can be seen in matters ranging from poor communication and not understanding each group's lingo to serious issues such as

TABLE 7.1 COMPARISON OF THE LIVING GENERATIONS AT THE UNIVERSITY

Traditionalists (Combination of the G.I. and Silent Generations), Birth Years: 1901–1942

In university communities, they are in the higher leadership roles (e.g., presidents, deans, directors), senior faculty (emeriti and full professors), and occasionally older/re-entry students.

Shaped by	Values and Attitudes
• World War I • Roaring 20s • Great Depression • New Deal • Pearl Harbor and World War II • Korean War • "American Dream"	This group is characterized as hardworking and patriotic. They are the epitome of loyalty and truly believe that the best way to accomplish something is to put aside individual needs and work together as a group for common goals. The Depression shaped their financial views, making them careful and thrifty—they have the highest saving rate of any generation. They are likely to look to institutions for help because of the role the government played in recovering from the Great Depression. They tend to be very hierarchical in their approach to management and expect the respect due their position.

Baby Boomers, Birth Years: 1943–1960

They are the middle- to upper-level administrators, faculty (all levels), and some re-entry students and graduate students.

Shaped by	Values and Attitudes
• Kennedy assassination • Beatles, Rolling Stones • First moon landing • Civil rights movement and Martin Luther King, Jr. • Woodstock and counterculture • Women's liberation • Vietnam War • Watergate • Television and credit cards	Television greatly shaped this generation, through both the ability to see world events live and the power of TV shows and advertising as a way to define pop culture. Boomers are considered optimistic and competitive, and this has led to more focus on individual and personal accomplishment—they are deeply defined by their work. They experienced economic growth that allowed them to have affluence in a way the traditionalists never saw. Credit cards debuted during their lifetime, and as a result, boomers have the lowest saving rate of any generation. This generation was more educated and idealistic than the traditionalists were, which led to questioning the status quo and bringing about change in the United States. They are more likely to challenge authority and focus on change. They are the generation that fought for equality and justice for many marginalized groups. They tend to be more liberal in terms of political ideology.

Generation X, Birth Years: 1961–1981

They are low- to middle-level administrators, entry- to middle-level faculty, and some re-entry students and graduate students.

Shaped by	Values and Attitudes
• John Lennon's murder • *Challenger* explosion • Chernobyl • Fall of Berlin Wall • Operation Desert Storm • Latchkey children • Massive corporate layoffs	The Internet and other media inventions (e.g., computers, cell phones) greatly shaped this generation and made them information-focused multitaskers with not much patience. They grew up at a time when more mothers worked outside the home and divorce rates tripled, making them the generation with the most latchkey children. This forced them to become independent and highly self-sufficient. During their lifetime, every major American institution was called into question, causing them to distrust institutions and relationships—skepticism and cynicism are the terms that are most used to define Generation X. This has led Xers to become very independent, resourceful, and pragmatic.

(Continued)

TABLE **7.1** CONTINUED	
Millennials, Birth Years: 1982–2002	
They are undergraduate students, some graduate students, and future college students who are still in the K–12 system.	
Shaped by	**Values and Attitudes**
✦ War in Kosovo ✦ Oklahoma City bombing ✦ Princess Diana's death ✦ Clinton impeachment ✦ Columbine shootings ✦ September 11, 2001, attacks and the war on terrorism ✦ Most "wanted" generation in history (planned pregnancies) ✦ Children in danger (Baby Jessica, Polly Klaus, etc.), which increased parent concern for safety ✦ Greatest economic boom (until 2001)	Millennials were also greatly influenced by technological inventions but are much more comfortable with them than any previous generation. The Internet has made the world accessible from their homes. The apparent rise in school shootings and other threats to child safety has made this generation (and their parents) very safety conscious. This has caused the parents of millennials (boomers who do not trust authority) to become actively engaged in almost all aspects of their children's lives in an effort to protect them. Their optimistic, idealist boomer parents also raised them to believe in their personal power to take action to fix things. As a result, millennials are often more confident than their abilities justify. Millennials have maintained optimism as one of their key traits, but it is paired with realism. Another key trait is their appreciation of diversity, and their acceptance of others. However, as a result, they often do not see or recognize the injustices that other generations identify. Millennials have been included in most of the major family decisions, so traditional lines of authority are not particularly relevant to them—they are more likely to focus on collaboration and believe in their right to participate. This generation has also been very pressured to achieve, and performing poorly is often quite upsetting to a millennial. Politically, this tends to be a more conservative generation.

resentment and poor teamwork. As a result, many companies now work to address generational issues in the workforce.

Each generation is known for different traits, and these differences often create challenging interactions. For example, the tech-savvy millennials are often frustrated by their traditionalist faculty who lecture without using even the most basic of multimedia tools. Faculty who are boomers and value civil rights and challenging authority are shocked by what they perceive to be apathy on the part of the millennials regarding social justice issues. Gen X administrators who could not wait to move away from their parents cannot relate to the closeness the millennials have with their parents and their parents' insistence on being involved with their student's life.

This affects how students are treated by older generations. Often, the traditionalist, boomer, and X generations see the optimism of the millennials as insincere and annoying; they grew up in times of stress and are likely to view the world with some skepticism or even cynicism. They also do not relate to being close with one's parents so are likely to see it as a sign of dependence and immaturity.

Another way this issue will affect you is the fact that you have the opportunity to gain valuable insights and skills from these interactions. There are entire businesses devoted to helping the various generations work together in the work environment—for example, the books *When Generations Collide* (Lancaster & Stillman, 2002) and *Managing by Defining Moments* (Meredith & Schewe, 2002) are both dedicated to helping businesses and managers understand these issues. If you are able to become savvy about the various generations, how they work, and what they value, you will be well positioned for future career opportunities, especially those that require people skills or management expertise. This is just one aspect of developing your cultural competence.

RACE AND ETHNICITY

Both race and ethnicity play important roles on college campuses because of how they influence the experiences that students have, as well as how people interact with each other. Race and ethnicity are often thought of as interchangeable, but they are actually quite different. According to the United Nations (2010), **race** "refers to a group of people who share the same physical characteristics such as skin tone, hair texture, and facial features. The transmission of traits from one generation to another is a complex process that is examined in a field of study called genetics." Because people can be grouped by any number of physical differences (height, foot size, resistance to certain diseases), race is an artificial way to categorize people. Nonetheless, race remains an important concept because of the social and political issues that arise from the history of colonization. By contrast, **ethnicity** "refers to membership in a particular cultural group. It is defined by shared cultural practices, including but not limited to holidays, food, language, and customs" (UN, 2010). Examples include Italian, Kurdish, and Bantu. People of the same race can be of different ethnicities, for example, Asians can be Japanese, Thai, Venezuelan, or many other ethnicities.

While the United States is fairly diverse, college campuses are less so. Table 7.2 shows a comparison of 2000 national census data and data collected by the National Center for Education Statistics (NCES, 2010) for four-year institutions in 2006–2007. (Note: Some categories were merged to create equivalent comparisons, but exact matches were not possible.) Look up the demographics for your campus and enter the information.

Some racial groups are overrepresented on college campuses, while others are underrepresented. In general, however, White students represent almost three-quarters of college students in the United States, while students of color represent about one-quarter. In addition, nearly two-thirds of college freshmen reported that their high school was all or mostly White (60 percent) and 70 percent stated that the neighborhood in which they grew up was all or mostly White as well. In contrast, only 16 percent said that their high school was all or mostly non-White with 17 percent stating that about their neighborhood (Pryor, et al., 2009). Of the freshmen who participated in the national Your First College Year study in 2005, 11 percent agreed or strongly agreed with the statement "There is a lot of racial tension on this campus," and another 20 percent felt the same about the statement "I have heard faculty express stereotypes about racial/ethnic groups in class" (Ruiz, et al., 2010).

TABLE **7.2 COMPARISON OF RACE AND ETHNICITY FOR U.S. POPULATION AND COLLEGE STUDENTS**			
RACE/ETHNICITY	**U.S. POPULATION**	**BACHELOR'S DEGREES CONFERRED**	**YOUR CAMPUS**
White/Caucasian	75%	72%	
Black/African American	12%	10%	
American Indian/ Native Alaskan	1%	1%	
Asian/Asian American/ Pacific Islander	4%	5%	
Hispanic/Chican@/Latin@/ Puerto Rican	13%	12%	
Other	1%	N/A	
Two or more races	24%	N/A*	

*NCES data did not include multiracial or biracial selections.

Interactions between different races and ethnicities have an important influence on the experiences of first-year students. This is because of the types of interactions, both positive and negative, that each student has with others. In the United States, this process is different for each of the racial and ethnic groups because each group has a unique experience within the larger society, especially because White culture is the dominant culture, both statistically and in terms of representation in the major institutions of the country, such as politics, media, medicine, and law.

Unfortunately, people of color still experience discrimination and prejudice based on their racial and ethnic identities. Some of these experiences stem from a lack of information or knowledge about race and ethnicity or a certain group of people. And some are definitely intentional, with a goal of causing physical or emotional hurt, such as vandalizing someone's property or physically assaulting them. According to the National Institute Against Prejudice and Violence (2004), 20 to 25 percent of minority students on college campuses are victimized annually by acts of hate and ethnoviolence, with lesbian, gay, bisexual, and transgender students experiencing the highest rates. **Ethnoviolence** is an act or an attempted act that is motivated by group prejudice and intended to cause physical or psychological injury, including intimidation, harassment, group insults, property defacement or destruction, and physical attacks. Ethnoviolence becomes a hate crime when a legally defined crime is committed. A **hate crime** is defined as any criminal act, or attempted criminal act, motivated by hatred based on race, ethnicity, religion, sexual orientation, disability, or gender.

Given this context, it is no surprise that minority groups would go through a different process than those in the majority. Two models are useful for understanding how people gain a sense of their racial or ethnic identity over the course of their lifetimes; one for minorities and one for the majority. These models can easily be applied to university students because all students will be at some stage of the process during their college experience.

Theories of Racial Identity Development

RACIAL MINORITY IDENTITY DEVELOPMENT MODEL In 1998, Atkinson, Morton, and Sue created a model that describes the stages of identity development for ethnic minority groups and their relationship to the dominant culture, that is, White culture in the United States. Their model was based on previous research and models that were focused on one particular ethnicity, such as Black or Latino. They argue that ethnic minorities develop their identity amid negative stereotypes and oppression of all kinds and that this affects their sense of identity. People move through these stages in order and over time. See "Sabrina's Story from the Path."

Conformity

In this stage, the person reflects the values of larger society; the dominant culture's values are preferred, and the dominant culture is idealized. The person's own ethnic group and other ethnic groups that are nondominant are devalued. The person assimilates many aspects of White culture and demonstrates few aspects of his or her own culture. This is not a conscious choice but rather a naïve acceptance of, and preference for, the dominant culture's values.

Dissonance

A person in this stage is starting to notice and question negative stereotypes about non-dominant cultures, especially his or her own. Personal experiences provide a catalyst for realizing that not all things about White culture are positive and not all things about their culture are negative. A person often experiences mixed feelings of appreciation and devaluation for both dominant and nondominant cultures, including self and others. This stage often initiates feelings of anger and conflict about race and society.

Resistance

In this stage, a person is self-reflective about having bought into White values and having devalued his or her own culture, family, community, or self. This can cause feelings of guilt, shame, and/or anger. A strong focus is placed on valuing all things about the nondominant culture and devaluing everything about White culture. A person can often feel empathy for other nondominant cultures in this stage, but the primary focus is on the person's own culture. This stage is almost a complete swing to the opposite of the first stage of conformity.

Introspection

A person in this stage is beginning to question the extreme and dichotomous views of the previous stage (i.e., "everything about my culture is good, and everything about White culture is bad"). Instead of reacting against negative stereotypes, a more authentic and positive self-identity is developed. In addition, a person is able to see and criticize aspects of his or her

SABRINA'S STORY FROM THE PATH

As a first-generation student, I entered college with great excitement. I believed that the university would be a place of acceptance and higher thinking and I wanted nothing more than to fit in, excel in my classes, and make my parents and my community proud. But as a multiracial person, I soon found that my racial identity—both how I understood my own identity and how others perceived me—would be a crucial factor of my college journey.

I began college very much in the stage of conformity. I idealized my faculty, and I imagined myself building on the legacy of the founders of my discipline and achieving greatness in my field. It did not cross my mind that the founders, faculty, and leaders were mostly White and *I was not*.

After a few subtle racial instances in my classes and residence hall, it became harder to pretend that race didn't matter at college. It was the little things, "harmless jokes," assumptions about my hometown or the music I liked, conversations we had about policies impacting people of color, and classroom dynamics. When a professor questioned my ability to understand the material because I used slang when framing my analysis, I realized that I would even have to change the way I communicated. My "linguistic capital" was not valued in academia and I wondered how I could embrace my heritage and learn the dialect and practices to succeed at the university.

At the same time, my classes taught about the inequality experienced by communities on the margins, and they looked like mine. In the dissonance stage, I struggled to make sense of the economic, racial, and other barriers like stereotypes that groups like mine experienced. I found myself frustrated and confused. I soon became one of those students who had a quick rebuttal for any statement that seemed unjust. I was angry and tired.

Although I am multiracial, my physical features cause me to be solely read as a person of color, of some "exotic" blend. During college I felt ethnic pride for my mixed heritage, but imagined myself solely as a woman of color because of how I looked and was treated. Additionally I sought to find a place where I belonged.

Because of my mixed heritage I didn't fit in just one racially affiliated organization like the Black Student Union or the Asian Alliance, but I also didn't feel like the predominately White clubs, such as the Community Service Board, were my home either.

My racial and ethnic ambiguity posed a different challenge for me as a student leader. I became a Resident Assistant and my job was to create community. However, through a resistance lens, all I wanted to do was assert my community pride and affirm my cultural background. That was complicated when I had to shut down my residents' parties and they would respond with racial slurs. Other times my residents would be genuinely interested in who I was, including my heritage, so it was hard to know when to let my guard down.

As a junior, I became much more comfortable with my racial identity and found myself in introspection. My classes had taught me to think critically and question institutions, including the university, as well as dynamics in my home community. All institutions have histories of inclusion and exclusion. It is our job as students to help our universities change in positive ways to meet the needs of all students. I decided that I would use my love for community and my multiple heritages to serve as a bridge among students. I joined student government, hosted dialogues and conferences, and advocated for many social justice issues.

By my senior year I understood that all people are at different places with their own racial identity and understanding of social justice, so I didn't depend on them as much to validate my own experiences. As I became much more comfortable with my own racial identity, I found myself giving other people a lot more grace in learning about their own. I also had a group of friends who were self-identified as allies.

My journey with identity was not linear, and the models cannot encompass all of the challenges and joys of the journey. At the end of the day, my journey as a multiracial woman of color on a predominately White campus was not easy. However, I reflect on Plato's words, "Be kind, for everyone you meet is fighting a hard battle." The battle became a lot easier when I realized I was not alone.

own culture without feeling bad. The person also is having positive experiences with some Whites and is no longer comfortable uniformly devaluing White culture.

Integrative Awareness

This final stage allows the person to experience a "true appreciation for one's own culture and selective appreciation of White culture." The person recognizes and believes that all cultures exhibit both positive and negative elements. There is true pride in one's own culture as well as critical acceptance of the dominant group. This stage is very different from the first stage because the person is committed to maintaining his or her own cultural identity and not assimilating into White culture.

WHITE RACIAL CONSCIOUSNESS DEVELOPMENT MODEL

Unlike racial minorities who develop their cultural identity in response to negative stereotypes, White people in the United States do not experience this process. Because they are members of the dominant culture, Whites grow up with either lots of positive messages about their cultural heritage or an absence of negative messages. Some theorists believe that Whites engage in a different process that is more about their awareness of race consciousness, rather than their own racial identity. Rowe, Bennett, and Atkinson (1994) propose a model that explores this process. They state that there are essentially two main statuses of White racial consciousness, and there are several types within each status. This model is less linear in nature (that is, it does not outline a series of stages that a person passes through), but people do switch types on the basis of their experiences. The two primary stages are unachieved racial consciousness and achieved racial consciousness, each resulting in different types of beliefs and attitudes about people of color and the issues of race and ethnicity. The statuses and types are as follows.

Unachieved Racial Consciousness

The types in this status reflect either a lack of exploration of, or commitment to, racial issues and concerns.

+ *Avoidant type:* White people of this type do not consider racial issues relevant and usually avoid, deny, or minimize racial issues or concerns. They are likely to think that people of color are "too sensitive" or misinterpret what they consider to be racial experiences.
+ *Dependent type:* White people of this type adopt some beliefs and attitudes about people of color without any personal exploration. In essence, a person of this type adopts someone else's views (e.g., those of parents or the media), and regardless of whether the beliefs are negative or positive, the person does not explore *why* she or he holds those views.
+ *Dissonant type:* White people of this type are in some kind of transition. Usually, personal experiences have conflicted with beliefs they have held, so they have been moved into a more active exploration of racial issues. Because they are not yet sure of what they believe, people of this type often experience confusion.

Achieved Racial Consciousness

The types in this status reflect an exploration of, and commitment to, racial issues and concerns.

+ *Dominant type:* White people of this type have strong views of White supremacy. They see minorities as truly inferior and therefore believe that any problems people of color experience are due to their own qualities and not any societal disadvantage.
+ *Conflictive type:* White people of this type believe in equality among all races. Although they might support certain antidiscrimination legislation, they might not support other programs that appear to promote people of color at the expense of

THE SCENIC ROUTE

Visit www.cengagebrain.com to find the companion website containing links to:

- Diversityweb.org's info on diversity on college campuses
- Diversity awareness quizzes
- Online class about race, racism, and Whiteness

White people, such as affirmative action. White people of this type still find themselves more comfortable around their own race, although they are careful to not be racist in their own language and actions.

+ *Reactive type:* White people of this type have explored racial concerns and are committed to addressing them. In comparison to the dominant type, they see all issues as involving oppression and minorities as innocent victims, no matter what the circumstances. They dismiss any personal responsibility on the part of people of color and are upset with White culture and those who are not committed to ending the status quo. They have often romanticized or overidentified with one particular minority group to which they are especially committed. The concept of **White guilt**, which is feeling guilty or bad for receiving privileges that people of color are denied, is often affiliated with this type.

+ *Integrative type:* White people of this type have explored their own "Whiteness" and have achieved comfort with it while also being committed to social change. They acknowledge and work to change societal forces that oppress people of color through contributing to or participating in organizations that work against oppression. Their commitment does not arise from emotional needs, such as anger at or guilt about Whiteness or from a need to oppress or idealize people of color, but rather from caring about creating a society that is equal and just for all.

BIRACIAL AND MULTIRACIAL IDENTITY DEVELOPMENT MODEL In our society, many people are of two or more races. They may be children of parents from two different races, and are **biracial,** or their ancestry may include several races, and are **multiracial.** Research on the experiences of biracial and multiracial people is fairly new, so models in this area are still under development and there are several different models from which to choose. One model, by Kerwin, Ponterotto, Jackson, and Harris (1993), is useful in exploring the identity development of bi- or multiracial college students because it focuses on identity formation over time, especially as it relates to experiences in the school system. They argue that six phases shape a person's identity and that a person goes through them chronologically.

Preschool

In this stage, up to the age of 5 years, a child is becoming aware of race. This process is accelerated for bi- or multiracial children because they notice differences between their parents in terms of physical characteristics like skin tone and hair texture.

Entry to School

In this stage, children begin to interact with other children and bi- or multiracial children are frequently faced with the question "What are you?" In an attempt to answer this question, children begin to use terms and labels to classify themselves and/or their group. The recognition of different social categories begins to emerge.

Preadolescence

The categorization of differences expands beyond skin tone to include other factors such as other physical traits or languages spoken. Students begin to explore who they fit in with among their peers and are drawn to those with whom they fit in most. This stage may also include the child's first experiences of racism or segregation.

Adolescence

The theorists argue that this stage is the most difficult for bi- or multiracial youth because of the social pressures that teens of all backgrounds seem to experience. All students are trying to find their place among their peers and may change their behaviors to fit in with a particular group. Bi- or multiracial students often feel forced to choose between the different aspects of their identity—in other words, they choose one part of their racial identity with which to align and minimize or avoid the other. This can cause problems in their family relationships as one parent might feel rejected. The choice is influenced by the makeup of the school and/or neighborhood community.

College/Young Adulthood

This phase is characterized by the deepening immersion in one of their racial identities resulting in the rejection of the other. The choice may be the same as was made in middle or high school or it might be a shift from that period to the other racial identity. Students in this group still do not feel comfortable embracing all aspects of their racial identity. In addition, the student's personal appearance might put him or her in situations where others do not realize his or her racial identity. In these cases, the student may hear derogatory remarks about an aspect of his or her heritage and, as a result, become more aware of the advantages and disadvantages of being bi- or multiracial.

Adulthood

This final stage lasts the rest of the person's adult life and is the continued exploration and integration of his or her racial identities. Many adults find a way to embrace all aspects of their racial heritage at some point. Certain events can create catalysts for further exploration such as entering into a romantic relationship or having children.

Every day, students interact with each other in both formal and informal settings. These interactions are affected by each student's own process of identity development. How they see themselves and others of their own racial and ethnic groups and how they see people from different backgrounds are influenced by the stages of their developmental process. This can create awkward and even tense interactions between students of different ethnicities. This is especially true when students of color are in the stages of dissonance or resistance and they

---

@myU SO HOW DOES THIS AFFECT YOU?

Use these models to aid your empathy for yourself and others. You will experience your own development and the development of others in this arena throughout your college career. Spend a few moments assessing your own racial identity development.

Your race/s:

Your ethnicity/ies:

What have you learned from your family about your race and ethnicity? From the media?

Which model is related to you?

What stage are you in?

It's important to take a look at the messages we have received and to examine how these might shape our beliefs, attitudes, behaviors, and actions. This is true for examining your views about others as well. When others talk about their race or ethnicity, listen. Listen not only to what they are saying but also to what stage they might currently be in. Ask questions, such as the ones listed here. Also, be willing to educate others. There might be times when someone you interact with does not understand your experience or even says something insensitive. Most likely, this person is doing it from a place of ignorance, not malice. If you feel able to, turn the experience into a "teachable moment." Say something like "I'm sure you didn't mean to but what you just said was hurtful to me because _____." Most people will be quite sorry that they did something harmful and will appreciate the opportunity to fix it. If not, then at least you got to speak up for yourself, and that can be an empowering experience.

interact with White students who are in stages of unachieved racial consciousness, or when bi- or multiracial students interact with others who do not recognize their multiple identities. Learning about the impact that race and ethnicity have on both individuals and diverse communities is a very important part of your education. It's one aspect of developing your cultural competence.

GENDER AND SEXUAL ORIENTATION

Gender and Biological Sex

In discussing the biological sex, gender, and sexual orientation of any person, including a college student, it is important to understand the complexity of this topic. Although the general public believes these issues to be simple, they are not. Sociologists and biologists have discovered that enormous complexity exists and that the categories are not as neat or exclusive as was previously thought.

Gender is often confused with biological sex. **Biological sex** is the scientific or biological determination that makes a person male or female. Medical doctors use several indicators to assign a person's biological sex; these include chromosomes, hormones, internal reproductive organs, external genitals, and secondary sex characteristics such as breasts and facial hair (since these become prominent during puberty, they are not used in identifying the sex of a newborn). When all of these indicators align, it is easy for a doctor to declare a baby to be male or female.

However, many people (1 in 2,000 births) have one or more of these characteristics that don't line up with the others; in other words, they share biological indicators of both the male and female sexes. This group of people is called **intersex,** and their parents and doctors face a lot of societal pressure to choose a sex early on. When intersex people reach maturity, some discover that they don't "feel" like the gender they were assigned at birth. One to 4 percent of the U.S. population is intersex; however, most don't even know that they are, because of surgery done when they were infants. Most discover it in adulthood when loss of feeling during sex prompts them to discover that they are/were intersex.

The term *gender* is often used to refer to someone's biological sex, but that is incorrect. **Gender** is the socially defined character traits that are prescribed for a particular sex within a given culture. These traits are what we typically think of when we think of *masculine* or *feminine*. Within every culture, young people are socialized to act in "appropriate" ways for their sex— also known as traditional *gender roles*. For example, in the United States, young boys are taught that it is not okay to play with dolls, and young girls are taught that they should want to be mothers someday. Because these are actions done by choice, sociologists and biologists often refer to this as *gender expression*, and while children's gender expression is often highly controlled and monitored by adults in their lives, there is more freedom for young adults and adults to make their own choices about adhering to or stepping out from these prescribed gender roles.

This is different from **gender identity,** which is someone's psychological sense of being male or female. Most people's gender identity matches their biological sex, and they do not experience any conflict between the two. However, for many people who are intersex or whose biological sex does not match their gender identity, this can create problems because of society's strong need for clear gender expression. The term **transgender** is used as an umbrella term to classify people who do not have a gender identity that is either clearly male or clearly female. This includes people whose biological sex assignment does not match their gender identity, people who feel that they don't neatly fit into one gender category, people who intentionally resist gender categories and gender roles, people who perform as the other gender (i.e., drag queens and kings), and people who are sexually aroused or emotionally gratified by

TABLE **7.3** MATRIX OF VARIOUS IDENTITY MARKERS AND POSSIBLE OPTIONS			
IDENTITY MARKER	POSSIBILITIES		
Biological sex	Male	Intersex (aspects of both)	Female
Gender expression	Masculine	Androgynous (equally both)	Feminine
Gender identity	Man	Transgender	Woman
Sexual orientation	Attracted to women	Bisexual (attracted to both)	Attracted to men

THE SCENIC ROUTE

Visit www.cengagebrain.com to find the companion website containing links to:

- Info on sexism and violence toward women
- Info on men, masculinities, and gender politics
- Info on starting a safe zone

wearing clothing associated with the other gender (i.e., transvestites). Table 7.3 provides a chart that illustrates the interplay between these various concepts.

According to the National Center for Education Statistics (2010), male students make up 43 percent of all students attending a four-year degree-granting institution, and females make up 57 percent. This ratio is true for college freshmen as well. However, this measure of biological sex does not convey data about students' gender identity, expression, or sexual orientation.

Sexual Orientation

Completely separate from one's biological sex, as well as one's gender identity and expression, is the concept of **sexual orientation,** which refers to whom a person is attracted to physically and emotionally. A person can be attracted to men, women, or both; it is pairing sexual attraction with a person's sex and gender that then determines whether one is attracted to the "same" or the "opposite" sex or both. Some people think of sexual orientation as a dichotomy, that someone is either heterosexual or homosexual. However, researchers have found that this is not the case. Alfred Kinsey discovered in his survey of thousands of people that sexual behavior exists on a continuum (see Table 7.4), the ends representing sexual encounters exclusively with the same or opposite sex and the middle of the continuum representing rare, occasional, or frequent encounters with the different sexes (Kinsey, et al., 1948).

In this model, **bisexuality** is harder to define; some argue that it is represented by those in the middle of the continuum (number 3) because they have sex equally with both sexes. However, others would argue that any encounter with a member of the opposite sex is bisexuality (numbers 1–5).

Another researcher, Fritz Klein, found that sexual orientation is more complex than that. He believed that one's true sexual orientation is based not just on actual sexual encounters but on other things as well. He argued that a person's sexual orientation could change over time and was actually a reflection of seven factors (Klein, et al., 1985). He created the model shown in Table 7.5 to articulate the complexity of sexual orientation. In addition, he said that one should examine not only a person's present experiences, but also the person's past ones as well as those that would be "ideal." Klein argued that this gives a more authentic and complete picture of a person's sexuality.

TABLE **7.4** KINSEY'S CONTINUUM OF SEXUALITY						
0	1	2	3	4	5	6
Sex exclusively with other sex			Sex equally with both sexes			Sex exclusively with same sex

TABLE **7.5** KLEIN'S MATRIX OF SEXUAL ORIENTATION

	PAST	PRESENT	IDEAL
1. Sexual behavior (with whom you actually have sex)			
2. Sexual attraction (to whom you are sexually attracted)			
3. Sexual fantasy (about whom you have sexual fantasies)			
4. Emotional preference (for whom you feel love)			
5. Social preference (with whom you prefer to socialize)			
6. Lifestyle (in what "culture"—gay or straight—you spend the most time)			
7. Self-identification (how you see yourself)			

Again, not much data focus on the sexual orientation of college students, but various national studies indicate that anywhere from 2 percent to 15 percent of any population identify themselves as lesbian, gay, bisexual, and/or transgender. This is certainly true for university communities as well.

Theories of Sexual Orientation Identity Development

LESBIAN/GAY IDENTITY DEVELOPMENT MODEL Theorists McCarn and Fassinger (1996) created a model that looks at how lesbian women form a sense of their identity. Although they did not do research on gay males specifically, this model is still useful for understanding how sexual identity development occurs among nonheterosexuals. McCarn and Fassinger discovered that this process occurs with reference to two areas: the individual herself and her relationship to group membership. Four main stages occur within both of these contexts: awareness, exploration, deepening commitment, and internalization or synthesis.

- *Awareness:* The individual is aware of feeling different from his or her peers toward opposite and same sexes, and is also becoming aware of the existence of different sexual orientations.
- *Exploration:* The individual is exploring erotic feelings for the same sex (either with one particular person or in general), and is also exploring his/her position to others as a group (i.e., gay men or lesbians).
- *Deepening commitment:* The individual deepens his/her self-identity, becoming more fulfilled in committing to his/her inherent sexuality, and is also deepening personal involvement with the reference group, being aware of oppression and other consequences.
- *Internalization/synthesis:* The individual internalizes his/her love for same-sex people, and overall identity as being lesbian/gay, and is also internalizing identity as a member of a minority group across contexts.

This process usually leads to a person **coming out,** which means that the person tells others of his or her identity as a lesbian, gay, bisexual, or transgender person. The coming-out process is truly that—a process—and not a single event. A person has to come out continually over the course of his or her life in different situations and with different people. Some people are "out" to a select few people in their life; others come out to everyone they meet. Coming out is necessitated by the assumption made by most heterosexual people that everyone is heterosexual, in other words, everyone is "straight until proven gay." Because of

ARE YOU A SAFE ZONE? Many students believe that they do not know anyone who is LGBT, or at least not any close friends or family. This is just not true. There are definitely LGBT people in every community of the university campus, from the students to the faculty to the staff and administrators. You probably actually know several people, but they just might not be "out" to you yet. Remember, coming out is a risky thing to do. Most LGBT people have been hurt, emotionally and physically, because of their identity; nearly all have experienced verbal harassment, and quite a few have been physically assaulted. As a result, most LGBT people look for clear clues that a person is accepting of their sexuality and will not pose a threat to them. If you want more people to feel comfortable enough to come out to you, you need to make sure you are sending clear signals that you are safe.

The first and most obvious is your language. Using more inclusive language that does not assume that someone is heterosexual is a great start. Saying things like "Are you dating someone?" or "Let me introduce you to my partner" (as opposed to boyfriend/girlfriend) sends a message that you are aware how heterosexist society is. Certainly, not saying derogatory things like "fag" or "That's so gay" can make people feel safer as well.

You can choose to display LGBT-supportive images in your space, such as a rainbow flag or "safe zone" sticker. Many university campuses have Safe Zone projects that allow people to indicate with a symbol that they are supportive and accepting of all sexualities; search your campus website for more information. You can show your support of the LGBT community by attending programs, workshops, rallies, and events that address LGBT themes or support the rights of LGBT people. Of course, how you vote in campus, local, and national elections also makes a difference. All of these things show that you are an ally of the LGBT community—someone who is committed to fairness for all people and does not support discrimination of any kind.

this assumption of heterosexuality, lesbian, gay, bisexual, and transgender (LGBT) people are put into uncomfortable or awkward situations regularly that force them to either come out or misrepresent their identity. For example, asking a woman whether she has a boyfriend or whether she has met any cute guys recently assumes heterosexuality and can put her in an awkward position if she is not heterosexual. The reason this is awkward is because she has to make a choice to either conceal her identity or come out, which is not always physically safe to do. See "Point of Interest: Are You a Safe Zone?"

The murder of Matthew Sheppard, a college student in Wyoming, as well as the thousands of other hate crimes that are committed annually constantly remind LGBT students that it can be risky to come out to others. The Policy Institute of the National Gay and Lesbian Task Force issued a report entitled *Campus Climate* (Rankin, 2003). It was a national perspective on the experiences of LGBT people at U.S. colleges and universities, and it featured a national survey of students, faculty, and staff/administrators from across the United States. Results indicated that 36 percent of LGBT undergraduates had experienced harassment within the past year, and 79 percent said that the harassment came from fellow students. Of all respondents (students, faculty, and staff), 20 percent feared for their physical safety because of their sexual orientation or gender identity, and 51 percent concealed their sexual orientation or gender identity to avoid intimidation. Nearly half (43 percent) rated the campus climate to be homophobic. On a positive note, 72 percent felt that their institution provided visible resources on LGBT issues and concerns.

HETEROSEXUALITY IDENTITY DEVELOPMENT MODEL Another theorist, Jonathan Mohr (2002), explored how heterosexuals situate their identity in relation to others. Similar to the White identity model, Mohr believed that heterosexuals engage in a different process that is more about their awareness of sexuality consciousness rather than their own sexual orientation. He argued that there are essentially four types of heterosexuality identity and a person can switch from one to another on the basis of knowledge and experiences.

Democratic Heterosexuality

This type of person sees all people as the same and equal and does not consider sexual orientation an important factor—he or she sees sexual orientation as an inherent trait, similar to eye color. People of this type essentially believe that "people are people" and, as a result, do not consider that someone's sexual orientation might have an impact on his or her experience. Their own sexuality has not been examined.

Compulsory Heterosexuality

People of this type feel that heterosexuality is the only acceptable model, often for cultural or religious reasons. They believe that sexuality is a form of behavior, and therefore a choice. They idealize their own heterosexuality and denigrate the sexuality of others who may be different, viewing it as wrong or a sin.

Politicized Heterosexuality

A person of this type focuses on the sociopolitical ramifications of sexual orientation and is conscious of the oppression that lesbian, gay, bisexual, and transgender people experience. These people often are angry at the privileges that heterosexuals receive in society, like the right to marry, and experience some guilt about this. They see others as either LGBT affirmative or as homophobic; they have little patience for those who do not accept LGBT people.

Integrative Heterosexuality

This person views sexual orientation as a complex construct with multiple variables and levels. These people do not see any significant difference between heterosexuality and homosexuality (it's only one aspect of a person's identity) but acknowledge that privilege and oppression exist. They see that society is an oppressive system in which all people participate and that there are no good and bad people with regard to their stance on sexual orientation.

Interestingly, neither McCarn and Fassinger's model nor Mohr's model is inclusive of bisexuality, and neither addresses the variations in development that bisexuals experience. For example, the coming-out process is even more challenging for bisexuals because so many people see sexuality as a dichotomy—a person is either gay or straight—so bisexuals often face

---

@myU SO HOW DOES THIS AFFECT YOU?

University campuses tend to be a focal point for discussions around issues of sex, gender, and sexual orientation. You will most likely find that there are many forums, workshops, and other educational programs about these topics and that your campus values tolerance and nondiscrimination around a wide range of identities, including sex, gender, and sexual orientation. Your campus might boast a center and staff that focus on these issues, and there certainly will be student groups that do. Look through your university's resources to find campus programs, events, and classes that address sex, gender, and sexual orientation.

CLASSES	EVENTS	DEPARTMENTS/PROGRAMS

If you are questioning your own sexuality or identify as LGBT, you will most likely find many caring people and safe places to support your identity. If none exist on your campus, look to another campus in your area or on the Internet. Learning about the impact that sex, gender, and sexual orientation have on both individuals and diverse communities is a very important part of your education. It's one aspect of developing your cultural competence.

even more frustration when coming out because both gay and straight communities erroneously believe that these people just "haven't made up their mind yet."

College is a time when young adults are establishing their identity separate from that of their family of origin and home communities. This freedom allows students to explore aspects of their identity that they might not have previously considered or seriously explored. This is especially true for issues of gender, sex, and sexual orientation. University campuses nationwide are at the center of discussions of these issues because college students are at the forefront of this exploration.

THE IMPACT OF ECONOMIC CLASS ON COLLEGE SUCCESS

Across North America, high school students find that their educational future is greatly affected by their parents' income and their socioeconomic status. **Income** is the amount of money their parents make each year, and **socioeconomic status** "refers to individual differences in wealth, income, economic power, or social position," according to the definition used by the United Nations (2010). People often use terms such as *upper class*, *middle class*, and *working class*, which have sociopolitical ramifications. For the purpose of this chapter, we will focus primarily on parental income and its impact on a student's success.

According to the recent HERI study, the estimated **parental income** for 2009 freshmen ranges from less than $20,000 a year (10 percent) to more than $250,000 a year (7 percent). Twenty percent of parents make $21,000 to $49,999 a year, another 23 percent make $50,000 to $99,999 a year, and 30 percent make $100,000 to $249,999 a year (Pryor, et al., 2009).

Although students at a particular campus come from homes where their parents make from a little to a lot of money, they end up at the same university, taking the same classes, and competing with each other to do well. Long before many students set foot on a university campus, their future is shaped by their parents' income, and this affects their ability to apply for, be admitted to, and eventually attend and graduate from college. Students from middle- and higher-income families have far more resources and opportunities than do poorer students, and therefore have distinct advantages in college preparation and success. These advantages are separate from students' intellectual abilities and performance both in high school and on standardized tests.

For example, students from low-income households or communities find that they do not have access to the same educational opportunities as do students from higher-income communities. A primary difference has to do with the quality of the K–12 schools. Not all junior high and high schools are equal in quality, nor do they receive the same resources. It is not uncommon for poorer public schools to lack current textbooks, honors and AP classes, computer labs, and adequately trained teachers and counselors, as well as other resources that help prepare students to be competitive when applying to colleges.

In addition to the school's resources, each student's family resources play a role in college preparation. Low-income families tend to have one or both parents holding multiple jobs, which means that they might not be available to help the student with homework, drive him or her to practice, or attend college fairs. The family might even need the student to work and contribute income to the household and this limits the student's opportunities to participate in cocurricular activities and to study adequately. The home might not have a computer or access to the Internet, a range of books, newspaper subscriptions, and other useful resources for academic work. Low-income students rarely can afford SAT preparation courses or private tutors, nor can they afford the costs of some extracurricular activities.

Even basics such as medical and dental care might be scarce or nonexistent. Furthermore, poor communities tend to have higher crime rates, which can add stress and safety concerns to the equation. All of these things affect students' abilities to perform well and have the well-rounded experiences that make them competitive with their peers from higher-income families.

Even applying to college can be more challenging for the lower-income student. College choice often depends more on the cost of tuition and the availability of financial aid than on whether the campus is a good fit for the student. In addition, attending a residential campus is far more expensive than living at home and commuting, so location may be a primary factor, especially if the student will need to continue working and sending money home while in college. According to the HERI study, 80 percent of freshmen will live in a residence hall, and 14 percent will live with family or other relatives. The HERI study also found that more college freshmen have concerns about financing their college education and are not sure they will have enough funds to complete college, with 55 percent having "some" concerns and 11 percent having "major" concerns. Only 33 percent have no concerns at all because they have sufficient funds (Pryor, et al., 2009). In addition, 42 percent of students stated that "the cost of attending this college" was a very important factor in determining their attendance, the highest rating this question has ever received in the 45 years this annual study. Not surprisingly, this was matched by 45 percent of freshmen indicating that an offer of financial aid was also very important.

Once the student is admitted to a university, the journey can become more challenging. For students who are able to attend a residential campus, economic disparity becomes very clear during the move-in process when some students are unpacking computers, stereos, lots of clothes, and mini-fridges. Even things like splitting utility bills can become an issue if one person wants lots of add-on features and the other can't afford them. Low-income students often begin to feel "different" at this stage and might feel somewhat disconnected socially from their wealthier peers. This can be aggravated if many social activities involve additional money, such as eating out, going to the movies, or dancing at nightclubs.

Higher-income students usually do not have to work to support themselves in school, so they have more time to focus on studying, getting involved in cocurricular activities, and utilizing campus services such as advising, student health services, and educational workshops if they so choose. If low-income students are working a lot (more than twenty hours per week), they often find that their academics suffer. If the working student faces difficulties in making ends meet, she or he might have to make hard choices about buying required textbooks or even eating three meals a day.

In 2002, the Higher Education Project of the States Public Interest Research Group (PIRG) published a report entitled *At What Cost? The Price That Working Students Pay for a College Education* (King & Bannon). This national report found that 74 percent of all full-time college students also work while attending college. Of this group, 46 percent work twenty-five or more hours per week. The students who work the most, more than twenty-five hours per week, experience some difficulties: 42 percent of these students said that it negatively affected their grades, and 53 percent said that working limited their class schedule. Almost two-thirds (63 percent) said that they could not afford college if they did not work full time.

All of these issues add a layer of stress on the low-income student. Interestingly, research indicates that despite all these disadvantages, low-income students are more likely than their wealthier peers to make the most of their educational opportunities (Flacks & Thomas, 1998). Students from disadvantaged backgrounds are more likely to value their education more, utilize services more, interact with faculty more, volunteer more, and party/binge drink less than their privileged peers.

@myU SO HOW DOES THIS AFFECT YOU?

It is very rare to find a college campus that has a homogeneous population in terms of income levels. Even the most expensive and elite private colleges admit low-income students and provide financial support for their attendance. No matter what your own economic background is, you will find students who are both richer and poorer than you on your campus. As stated, economic disparity can create challenging interactions between students. Learning about the impact that parental income and socioeconomic status have on both individuals and diverse communities is a very important part of your education. It's one aspect of developing your cultural competence. See "Point of Interest: Class Differences among Your Peers."

Take a moment to research the economic status of your peers and also campus services that are available to support low-income students.

Percentage earning:

$ 21,000 or less (poverty level in U.S.):

$ 22,000–50,000:

$ 51,000–99,000:

$ 100,000–250,000:

$ 251,000 or more:

Where students go to find out about:

Financial aid

Emergency loans

Campus jobs

POINT OF INTEREST

CLASS DIFFERENCES AMONG YOUR PEERS *If you are a low-income student ...* you might want to prepare for interacting with other students who have more financial and material resources than you do. It can be frustrating at times to see others with more resources, especially if they take those resources for granted. You might have to work harder, and with less, than some of the students with whom you are competing in classes. This might feel unfair, and at times it is. These are normal feelings, but it is important not to let them get in the way of your success. When things get challenging, seek out support. There is likely a department on your campus that serves low-income students (e.g., the educational opportunity program or dean of students office). The advisors in these programs are especially knowledgeable about campus resources that might be valuable to you. They can also advocate for you with financial aid and other campus departments.

Most universities provide access to important resources such as computer labs, transportation, and medical and dental care. If they are not open at the hours you need, speak to the director and make a request. Sometimes it takes a student speaking up for administrators to realize that they need to make some shifts to make students' lives easier. Finally, form a network of friends who share your experiences. They can be a great support to you on difficult days, and you might even be able to pool your resources to assist in each other's success. It will also help you deal with

frustration you might feel with your wealthier peers who are most likely not aware of your financial situation.

If you are a middle- or high-income student ... you might also face some challenges attending a campus that is economically diverse. First, you might experience some frustration if people assume that because you have financial resources, you have an easy college experience. This is absolutely not true—even high-income students struggle in college and have personal challenges that can interfere with their success. If you find that you are not accurately understood, speak up for yourself. Also, don't feel guilty about what you have. It's a wonderful thing to have support and resources available to you, so enjoy them and appreciate them.

Second, you will probably be attending classes and perhaps living with low-income students. It is certainly not your responsibility to make their lives easier, but it can be helpful to be aware of, and sensitive to, some of the challenges that they face. Being sensitive to others' financial limitations and not putting them in awkward situations can be very helpful. This spares low-income students the embarrassment of having to say that they cannot afford something or not being able to participate. It's also supportive to honor other peoples' pride and not try to "help" them when they have not requested it. Most important, remember that good listening and communication skills can guide you in most interactions with students, regardless of the issue.

SPIRITUAL IDENTITY

As students go off to college each year, they also take with them their spiritual or religious identities. Some students have deeply held spiritual values based on religions that they have practiced their entire lives, while others only celebrate their religions on one or two holidays per year, and even others do not believe in any kind of religion or spiritual practice.

Religion and spirituality are different, although there certainly is overlap between them. The Merriam-Webster OnLine Dictionary (2010) defines **religion** as "the service and worship of God or the supernatural; commitment or devotion to religious faith or observance; a personal set or institutionalized system of religious attitudes, beliefs, and practices," whereas **spiritual** is defined as "of, relating to, consisting of, or affecting the spirit; of or relating to sacred matters." These definitions are useful when we explore data on college freshmen, as students may differentiate between their spirituality and their identified religion.

The 2009 HERI study asked students to indicate their "religious preferences" and found that 22 percent did not identify a religious preference, while 88 percent did, as shown in Table 7.6 (Pryor, et al., 2009). In recent years, more and more students have indicated that their spirituality is an important factor in their lives. In 2000, HERI began a longitudinal study of the spiritual development of college students. The most recent sample in 2003 included 112,232 freshmen students from across the United States who attended 236 colleges and universities (HERI, 2006a):

+ Eighty percent had an interest in spirituality and 64 percent stated that their spirituality was a source of joy.
+ Three-quarters said that they were "searching for meaning/purpose in life" and 83 percent believed in the sacredness of life.
+ Seventy-nine percent said that they believed in God and 69 percent said they prayed (61 percent at least weekly).
+ Four out of five attended religious services occasionally or frequently and 69 percent agreed strongly or somewhat that their religious beliefs provided strength, support, and guidance.
+ In addition, students showed high levels of tolerance and acceptance with 83 percent agreeing that "non-religious people can lead lives that are just as moral as those of religious believers" and 64 percent agreeing that "most people can grow spiritually without being religious."

Almost two-thirds of students in the HERI study, 62 percent, indicated that their professors never encouraged classroom discussions of religion or spirituality. This might be why enrollment in the nation's 104 "Christ-centered" colleges has risen 27 percent since 1997. However, another HERI study (2006b) on faculty and spirituality found that 81 percent of faculty consider themselves to be spiritual people. Seventy percent have a goal to develop a meaningful philosophy of life and 69 percent seek out opportunities for spiritual growth. This study was done in 2004–2005 with 65,124 people at 511 colleges and universities.

One issue that became evident was that students experience challenges and struggles in the development of their religious/spiritual identities. The HERI study (2006a) states:

Well over half of the freshmen report that they have at least occasionally "felt distant from God" (65 percent) and questioned their religious beliefs (57 percent), and about half have at least occasionally "felt angry with God" (48 percent) and disagreed with their families about religious matters (52 percent). In response to the question "How would you describe your current views about spiritual/religious matters?" fewer than half indicate that they feel "secure" in their views (42 percent). Twenty-three percent indicated that they were "seeking" and 15 percent were

THE SCENIC ROUTE

Visit www.cengagebrain.com to find the companion website containing links to:

+ UCLA's study on spirituality among college students
+ Religioustolerance.org's info on a variety of issues
+ Anti-Defamation League's range of info on tolerance

TABLE 7.6	RELIGIOUS PREFERENCES OF COLLEGE STUDENTS IN THE UNITED STATES		
RELIGION	**PERCENT**	**RELIGION**	**PERCENT**
Roman Catholic	27%	Muslim	1%
Baptist	11%	Hindu	1%
Methodist	5%	Eastern Orthodox	0.6%
Lutheran	4%	Mormon (LDS)	0.3%
Presbyterian	3%	Seventh-Day Adventist	0.3%
Jewish	3%	Quaker	0.2%
Episcopal	1%	Other Christian	13.1%
United Church of Christ	1%	Other religion	3%
Buddhist	1%	None	22.7%

"conflicted." Another 10 percent were "doubting" and 15 percent were "not interested."

These last statistics reflect a common process for many students in college: questioning some of their values and beliefs. See "Point of Interest: Exploring Your Spirituality."

Theory of Faith Development

Different researchers and theorists have explored spiritual development to ascertain the various processes that occur as a person develops and maintains a set of spiritual beliefs. One model that is useful is Fowler's faith development theory. Fowler (1981) created the following six-stage model to articulate faith development from infancy to full adulthood. It's important to note that many of these stages correlate with typical child-development patterns, and Fowler has articulated how faith development is interwoven into the traditional developmental process.

POINT OF INTEREST

EXPLORING YOUR SPIRITUALITY University communities are often wonderful places to explore spirituality because many of the campus and local congregations are more focused on young adults. Churches, synagogues, mosques, temples, and other places of worship that are near college communities might have an almost entirely student-aged congregation as well as leaders who are close in age to college students. Many students find that there are avenues for their spiritual practice and expression that are age-appropriate and address the kinds of issues that college students often struggle with.

With this in mind, I recommend seeking out and exploring religious/spiritual opportunities near your campus. Explore them all until you find a good match between your own needs and interests and the services provided by the various organizations. In addition, intentionally learn about and explore a wide variety of faiths. Even if you are very committed to your own, this will make you more knowledgeable about, and sensitive to, the experiences and values of different communities, which will serve you in the future. You will also gain a better understanding of many global issues and conflicts that are rooted in religious beliefs—another aspect of cultural competence.

Prestage: Primal

This phase sets up the six stages and occurs when a child is zero to 2 years old. No faith development, per se, occurs in this prestage; rather, this is a time when the infant's environment teaches the infant about trust, hope, courage, and love, and about abandonment, inconsistencies, and deprivation. These experiences serve to establish the relationship the child has with his or her parents and caregivers. Whether a child has a healthy and happy environment or a threatening and scary one, these issues will eventually underlie or undermine later faith development.

Stage 1: Intuitive-Projective Faith

This occurs when a child is 2 to 5 years old. In this stage, a child is often permanently and strongly affected by the visible faith of primary caregivers (e.g., parents). Developmentally, children at this age have powerful imaginations and fantasies that are not inhibited by logical thought. This makes religious/spiritual stories and images quite impactful and long-lasting if they are introduced at this time.

Stage 2: Mythic-Literal Faith

Children are around 7 to 9 years old in this stage. Developmentally, children at these ages are beginning to integrate the stories, beliefs, and observances of their family and community into their own sense of self, and their interpretations are often quite literal. The processes become more concrete, and there is a decrease in the use of imagination and fantasy. Stories become quite impactful and often become a primary way to give meaning to experiences, but the child is not able to step back and reflect or form conceptual meanings. In terms of spirituality and religion, symbolic and dramatic materials can affect a child powerfully and deeply; children can often describe or repeat religious stories with endless detail but not be able to reflect on their meanings.

Stage 3: Synthetic-Conventional Faith

This often occurs during the teenage years when conformity is a primary focus. While teenagers might hold strong beliefs, these are largely unexamined. The person's identity has not been developed to a stage at which independent reflection is common. As a result, religious/spiritual values are often held simply because the family and/or community holds them. While the teenager's values might be deeply felt, these values have not been independently or critically examined at a thorough level. This stage can extend into college and young adult years.

Stage 4: Individuative-Reflective Faith

This stage is less associated with a specific age but most likely occurs in young adulthood, and is highly correlated with ages of college attendance. Developmentally, the person begins to develop a sense of identity that is separate from family and community. The person begins to develop his or her own worldview, which may be different from, or in conflict with, those of important close friends and family. During this process, long-held beliefs and values are often tossed out en masse while the person sorts through what she or he believes versus what she or he was taught to believe. This obviously can include religious and spiritual beliefs, which can be a bit more difficult to reinforce and maintain owing to busy schedules and other challenges in the college environment. In addition, people in this stage often begin to notice contradictions in their faith or issues that their faith does not adequately address, and this can lead to increased questioning of faith.

Stage 5: Conjunctive Faith

This stage represents moving through some of the questions that were generated in the previous stage. A person is able to create a new sense of faith or spirituality that reflects his or her worldview and also accounts for paradoxes. This person might return to or again embrace the faith in which she or he was raised or might find or create a new sense of faith through a different religion or spiritual practice or a combination of many. This person is also able to acknowledge and support the values of others and the various faiths they choose to embrace.

Stage 6: Universalizing Faith

Few people achieve this last stage, as it requires the person to take his or her faith and move it to a central role in his or her life. Often, this includes serving others in a faith-based way, and there are strong and deep ties to their faith that guide the actions of people in this stage. Most religious leaders, such as rabbis, priests, imams, and nuns, are at this stage. Mother Teresa is the perfect example of a person who achieved the epitome of all that this stage represents.

POLITICAL IDEOLOGY

Another aspect of a student's identity is his or her political ideology. College students often arrive at campus having been socialized by the values of their family, neighborhood, school, community, spiritual center, and media. The degree to which college students are informed of, or care about, political matters has often been a function of their parents' views and activities as well as these other socializing entities. Political ideology is also influenced by a person's experiences. For example, membership in a marginalized group, such as an economic, ethnic, or sexual minority, brings about awareness of sociopolitical issues that members of the dominant group often cannot or do not see. In addition, a particular experience, such as being sexually assaulted or becoming physically disabled, brings a painful awareness of the rights and experiences of people who have had a similar experience. Such experiences can lead to a greater awareness of, and commitment to, engaging in the political process on some level.

Some students are not particularly interested in or informed about political matters, while other students are actively engaged in them. For some students who are actively engaged, this interest is focused on the local campus community, where they participate in school government, while other students are more focused on state, national, or global matters and participate in activities that seek to bring about systemic change. Either way, students will find most universities to be hotbeds of political discussion, as there are frequent forums, lectures, and informal conversations about all kinds of national and international matters. See "Point of Interest: Becoming an Informed Citizen."

Don Daves-Rougeaux (2004) has been involved in campus politics since his own student days in the 1980s. In his role as the executive director of student government, he mentored and advised the student government, including the elected student officers. He classifies students' political development on the following continuum:

BECOMING AN INFORMED CITIZEN

College is a wonderful time to gain more information about current events and political issues locally, nationally, and abroad. You will find that most universities host internationally renowned speakers and authors, and students can attend these events for very low cost or even free. After graduation, you will not have the same kind of access to these forums and debates, so it's an excellent idea to take advantage of them. Campuses usually bring many famous speakers to campus, from biologists to historians to politicians. Usually, the speakers who are doing a speaking tour are in the news and represent some of the current views on a wide range of topics. Again, this is an excellent opportunity to open your mind to other thoughts, ideas, and views and to increase your cultural competence.

In addition, you will be able to actively participate in the political process through campus, local, state, and federal elections. You will be able to make decisions that affect your daily experiences as a student on your campus, as a member of your local town or county, as a resident of your state, and as a citizen of this country. Your voice really does matter, and your vote really does count—so vote! But before you do, get informed. Whether you are voting on a campus referendum to build a new stadium or for the president of the United States, find and read information about the issue or candidate, go to public debates, and use the critical-thinking skills you have developed.

* *Apathetic:* These students just don't care about politics of any sort and do not bother to become informed.
* *Actively uninformed:* These students actively choose to stay out of politics, often because they are too busy.
* *Aware but uninvolved:* These students are fairly aware of issues but choose to participate minimally, sometimes only through voting.
* *Conscious but minimally active:* These students are aware of issues and participate on simple levels such as attending forums and rallies. They would probably get involved if approached but might not actively seek out involvement.
* *Disillusioned:* These students are aware but don't believe they can make a difference so they have given up on participating. They may have been involved and had a negative experience with trying to bring about change.
* *Active:* These students are keenly aware of issues and actively participate in a range of activities to bring about change; these are often the activists and are at the forefront of social change.

Any number of experiences can affect where someone is on the continuum, and movement on the continuum often coincides with college attendance for a number of reasons. Because citizens in the United States cannot vote until the age of 18, the college years coincide with the student's first foray into participating in this country's political process. College students are an important voting entity and will find themselves subjected to many efforts to get them registered to vote and recruited to support certain issues, parties, or candidates.

In addition, each campus has a different kind of political climate. Research universities have historically been places of political movements, especially movements that are counter to the status quo. University students have access to new ideas, cutting-edge knowledge, and vast resources (computers, libraries, and free Internet access), as well as the time and energy (compared to working adults with families) to become informed and get involved. Students have often been the first to speak out and seem to be the most in tune with the changing moods of society. The protests against the Vietnam War began on college campuses, as did concern about apartheid in South Africa and the recent activities of the World Trade Organization.

This is not just limited to campuses in the United States; the uprising in Tiananmen Square in China was the work of university students, including the brave soul who stood in front of the tanks while the world looked on. Students often see universities for what they are—institutions that are part of the bigger sociopolitical structure of the country—and change brought about at universities can have a ripple effect through the rest of society. If a campus is rife with political activism, the students who attend will be more likely to be exposed to, and possibly inspired by, their active peers.

A student's political ideology is also often influenced by his or her personal commitment to being involved. Many students find that they do not have the time to be politically involved simply because of their academic and cocurricular commitments; other students prioritize their political involvement above their studies and participation in other campus activities. Activism inherently comes from dissatisfaction, so student activists are more likely affiliated with people who are marginalized in some way or who are aware of the marginalization of others. According to the Merriam-Webster OnLine Dictionary (2010), **activism** is "a doctrine or practice that emphasizes direct vigorous action especially in support of or opposition to one side of a controversial issue." Student activists are committed to bringing about change, especially around dismantling social and institutional structures that oppress certain groups.

Finally, university students are exposed to new aspects of political dialogue in the classroom. Most students will be required to take a course that focuses on some aspect of political issues, either domestic or foreign, which exposes them to new ideas, historical information, and multiple perspectives. Some of these may come from the content of the course, and

TABLE 7.7 POLITICAL VIEWS OF STUDENTS AND FACULTY

	STUDENTS		FACULTY
VIEWS	1970	2009	2008
Far left	2.9%	2.8%	7.9%
Liberal	35.7%	29%	43.4%
Middle of the road	43.4%	44.4%	29.2%
Conservative	17.3%	21.8%	18.8%
Far right	0.8%	2.0%	0.7%

some may come from the personal views and life experiences of their faculty, who often have lived through some aspect of the history the course discusses.

A recent issue on many college campuses has stemmed from the perceived differences of political views between faculty and students. Students today, the millennials, are more conservative politically than the previous generations who make up the faculty. According to the HERI study (Pryor, et al., 2009), college freshmen have become much more politically aware in the past thirty years, but their political views and affiliations have also changed; many students have moved more to the center or right (from 1970 to 2009). This can be compared to the political views of faculty, as shown in Table 7.7 (DeAngelo, et al., 2009).

Students today are less liberal than their faculty, and this is creating a tension in classrooms across the United States. In 2003, when President Bush declared war on Iraq, many faculty expressed their displeasure in the classroom and even staged "teach-ins" and "sit-ins"—the tactics that many of them used during their student days during the Vietnam War. Many students who did not share their faculty's views were frustrated by this activity and felt that it not only negatively affected their academic experience but also was an inappropriate use of the faculty's and institution's resources. Some students also have had faculty who made disparaging remarks about certain political leaders, ones for whom the students might have voted. This has led some students to feel uncomfortable in the classroom—afraid that if they disagree with the faculty member or put forth a different view, they might be treated differently. Others feel that their education is being shortchanged because they perceive a lack of **intellectual diversity** in which several different and opposing viewpoints can be explored.

This relates to **academic freedom,** a cornerstone of the tenure system and the research university. Some faculty feel that academic freedom gives them the right to believe, say, and teach anything they desire in their classrooms as long as it does not cross any legal or ethical boundaries—an aspect of **freedom of speech.** Others feel that political and personal views belong in the classroom only if they are specifically relevant to the content of the course being taught. There has been a surge of activity nationwide around this issue. In addition, conservative speaker David Horowitz has created an **Academic Bill of Rights** that he claims is aimed at creating more balanced intellectual diversity in college classrooms (www.studentsforacademicfreedom.org). Others feel that this bill is a hindrance to academic freedom and is an attempt to silence more liberal views. Regardless of where you stand on this issue, you will most likely hear it debated on your university campus and in the national media.

There are many more aspects of identity that clearly affect the student experience, and each is worthy of a chapter, if not an entire book. For the sake of space, this chapter focuses on the elements of identity that are most often mentioned in research on the first-year experience. However, it is important to know that the experiences of the following populations, and many others, are worthy of exploration and reflection: immigrant status, physical ability, language or dialect, marital and parental status, physical appearance and size, and military involvement. Your campus has courses, programs, and services that address these aspects, and it is important that you seek them out.

BUILDING COMMUNITY

Research universities in particular have an impetus for being committed to building a diverse community because the creation of new knowledge is based on the premise that all views and perspectives should be explored. Ideas and thoughts need to be able to be voiced, critiqued, and evaluated within a context of honest and respectful exploration.

In addition, because prejudice and discrimination (e.g., racism, classism, religious oppression, sexism, homophobia) still exist in society and in its institutions, including higher education, university communities are actively engaged in dialogue about these issues. You will find that many groups and individuals at your campus spend time and energy discussing matters of race, class, sexual orientation, political ideology, and the whole range of primary and secondary identities.

Together, these conditions form a strong motivation for universities to create true community among a diverse group of members, where all people are valued and respected. Diversity, without respectful relationships, would not be enough to build community because diversity, in and of itself, often breeds conflict as people have opposing views, beliefs, and experiences. In addition, individuals always bring their personal biases and prejudices, both conscious and unconscious, to their interactions. As members of the diverse community of scholars, you will be in a place to participate in community building on many levels. It's important for you to know that this is a large part of your university experience, and, more important, your education.

The goal of this chapter is to give you information about the experiences that are affecting you and your peers, even if you do not see or experience them directly yourself. The concept of building community requires people not only to embrace that which they do share, but also to become informed about, and sensitive to, those things that are not shared. The primary focus of getting an education is about learning those things that you did not previously know—in other words, becoming open-minded in the fullest sense of the word. This is true not only in terms of courses such as physics and anthropology, but also in terms of the human experience and the diversity that it represents. Building community is an active process that requires everyone to be open to learning in order to better the experience for all.

Actively engage in this process, not only for the sake of your campus community but also for your own future. As was stated at the beginning of this chapter, many employers are now acutely aware of the multicultural country and global community in which they must prosper. Many are seeking to hire students who have developed *cultural competence*, which is an awareness of these various ideas of identity and how they might shape a person's experience. In addition, your education will be enhanced if you actively seek to gain this cultural competence by exploring various aspects of identity and how they shape the human experience. Your campus probably has many services and programs that will expose you to these concepts, such as academic courses (e.g., history, ethnic studies, and sociology), discussions, films, lectures, readings, informational fairs, and performances. Take advantage of them.

One of the best sources to help you expand your cultural competence is the other members of your university. They will have many different views, ideas, and experiences with these issues, and it's important to listen. By listening, you will gain something very precious: knowledge that is denied to you because of your own individual identities. If you are a male, you will never be able to have the experience of being female in this society—but you can learn about it by listening, asking questions, and, most importantly, believing what someone tells you. A White person can never know what it is like to experience racial discrimination and oppression on a regular basis, and a straight person cannot appreciate the fear that homophobic remarks generate. The same is true for every single one of the primary and secondary identities mentioned at the beginning of this chapter. Seek out experiences that will help you grow in all areas of cultural competence.

However, it's important to gain many different views as well. It is generally not a good idea to ask one woman about an issue and think that you know how all women feel. Nor does it make sense to conclude that one person of color speaks for his or her entire group or for all minorities. Every identity has a vast range of diversity within it because of the complex interplay between the primary and secondary identities. Seek out many, many experiences to successfully gain a richer and therefore more accurate understanding.

Students, especially those in the minority, often find themselves cast in the role of spokesperson for their group and spend much of their time educating others. Although many of these students want to help others learn, it can also be very tiring because it is an ongoing process. Within one week, a student might be asked several times to explain something about his or her culture, group, or experience. Even though many of these inquiries are genuine requests for education, they are still an additional responsibility on top of those of being a university student. For that reason, look at the many different ways in which you can *educate yourself* about the issues. This is especially useful because it empowers you to work on your own learning and not always need other people to teach you. Another great way to learn about the experiences of others is to read books and watch movies that focus on issues of identity. It is another way to actively increase your cultural competence. Visit www.britt andreatta.com for a comprehensive list.

The Dynamics of Oppression

Not everyone on a university campus is informed about, and sensitive to, the experiences of others, nor is everyone actively working to build community. Oppression exists on university campuses, just as it exists in all elements of our society. In addition to its presence on campuses, oppression has already affected many of the lives and experiences of its members, as seen in the various identity development models. This directly affects relationships and interactions on campuses because past painful experiences have shaped how people view themselves and others. This ultimately affects communication, respect, and trust between individuals and groups.

Although you might be an open-minded and aware individual, it doesn't mean that your roommates and friends are. The truth is that students regularly experience ignorant comments and attitudes from their peers, which deny their real experiences, feelings, or both. In addition, some people (students, staff, and faculty) hold stereotypes of, or engage in prejudicial or discriminatory behavior against, other members of the campus community. Negative slurs, jokes, and comments are heard at parties and in classes, living environments, and neighborhoods. Some students even experience physical harassment, vandalism, and assault because of their identities. These words and actions can greatly harm the overall feelings of acceptance and even safety that a student has in the university environment, thus destroying a sense of community.

Some of these phrases or words are recognized as offensive by everyone, so their use is usually intentional, with the purpose of degrading a person or group. Other words and phrases, such as "That's so gay," have become popular among young adults without people really understanding the negative impact they have on people. This concept of **intent versus impact** is useful to consider. In many cases, tension between individuals or groups around issues of identity often stem from confusion about the intent versus the impact of words and actions. One student might feel offended or hurt by the words or actions of another (the impact) while the other student "didn't mean it that way" (the intent). These two people can end up arguing unless they are able to listen to each other. The first person would need to believe that the intent was not negative, and the other person would need to acknowledge that the impact was indeed negative. If both parties can explore intent versus impact, many possibilities for understanding and reconciliation are created.

As a student, you might receive feedback that some of your own words or actions have impacts other than those you intended. You might learn that you said or did something that offended or hurt another member of the community. While it can be difficult to hear this feedback, the fact that the other person shared it with you is a sign that they see the possibility for more positive interactions with you and wish to build community. If you wish to build positive relationships with other individuals or groups, take this feedback and examine how you might incorporate it in your life. Everyone is learning how to navigate diversity and build community, so mistakes are to be expected as part of this process. If the intent is positive, then words and actions can be adjusted to create the desired impact.

While many students are able to create tolerance and respect in their own words and actions, they are not always sure what to do when they see or hear others violating these standards. It can be difficult to overhear a racist joke or witness a homophobic act and not be sure how to respond. Many people wrongly assume that the person who was the target of the joke or act should speak up about it, but often that person is too stunned, hurt, or fearful to respond. Another situation that often occurs is that people say and do offensive things only when members of the target group are not around to see it or hear it—implying that there is some kind of unspoken agreement among the rest of the people that it's okay to do this. You will probably find yourself in situations in which you see and hear things that offend your belief in tolerance and respect and are a threat to the sense of community. Prepare now for how you will respond.

Theories of Privilege and Oppression

To understand some of the concepts underlying these kinds of campus interactions, it is useful to explore some theories about societal groups and the dynamics of oppression. Adams, Bell, and Griffin (1997) argue that for every major identity in our society, there is a group that is in the majority and another that is in the minority, in terms of numbers and/or representation in power structures such as the government, legal system, education, and media. Because the minority group is not represented in the power structures, its members tend to be misunderstood by the rest of society. In addition, various events in U.S. history have contributed to negative connotations about the minority group for every primary identity. For example, Native Americans were feared as ruthless murderers during the westward expansion, Asian Americans were feared as enemies after Japan bombed Pearl Harbor during World War II, and many people have assumed all Muslims are terrorists since 9/11. As a result, the minority group is likely to suffer various forms of oppression by the majority group.

Stereotypes, prejudice, discrimination, and "isms," such as sexism or racism, are all part of oppression. Some occur at the individual level and then build to become systemic or societal. Jarrod Schwartz (2000), who expanded on the work of Kate Kirkham, created a model to explain the dynamics of oppression (see Table 7.8). According to Schwartz, **stereotypes** are fixed ideas about a group or person that are based on information gained from societal systems such as media, education, and interactions. Stereotypes live in individuals' thoughts and can be positive or negative, but they do not tend to match reality. For example, Black men are often stereotyped as criminals, and Asian students are often seen as good at math.

Prejudice is "prejudging" a person or a group, and the judgment is usually based on stereotypes. This leads to feelings of like or dislike, of fear or comfort, and also occurs on

TABLE 7.8	DYNAMICS OF OPPRESSION		
	INTRAPERSONAL (WITHIN INDIVIDUALS)	INTERPERSONAL (BETWEEN INDIVIDUALS OR GROUPS)	SYSTEMIC/ INSTITUTIONAL
Thoughts	Stereotype		
Feelings	Prejudice		
Behaviors		Discrimination	
Policies, procedures, practices, structures, etc.			Systemic oppression ("isms")

THE SCENIC ROUTE

Visit www.cengagebrain.com to find the companion website containing links to:

- Peggy McIntosh's article *White Privilege: Unpacking the Invisible Knapsack*
- List of books and films on a variety of diversity topics
- Variety of speeches, songs, quotes, and teaching tools on social justice

the individual level, as it is housed in feelings—for example, a White person feeling fear or distrust around Black men, or a Black student feeling jealous of an Asian student. **Discrimination** occurs when stereotypes and prejudice become expressed as actions or behaviors toward another person or group. This is when it leaves the internal world of an individual's thoughts or feelings and becomes expressed as visible words or actions—for example, not giving a Black man an application for a job or apartment or asking an Asian student for help with homework simply because he or she is Asian.

Finally, systemic **oppression** occurs when enough people share stereotypes, prejudice, and discrimination that get woven into the policies, procedures, laws, and systems of the larger society and culture. One example is racial profiling, a law used to target minorities like African-Americans or Middle-Easterners. Another example is the difference between crack and cocaine laws and their penalties. The reality is that the substance is the same but the populations who use the two forms (the rich and the poor) are different, thus oppressing the poor. These systems of oppression then feed or confirm the stereotypes, thus creating a cycle of socialization that affects the next generation in society.

Although this describes a broad pattern, the history of oppression for each minority group is unique. To learn more about a specific group, enroll in ethnic studies and history courses that explore these concepts in detail and can illuminate the specific historical events and societal factors that contributed to the oppression of that group.

Hardiman and Jackson (1997) argue that in most societies, the minority group experiences oppression of some kind while the majority group does not. The group that does not experience oppression is often referred to as the dominant or **nontarget group,** or the group with **privilege,** as they have the privilege of not experiencing the negative actions and words that make up the various forms of oppression. The minority group is often called the oppressed or the **target group** because they are the targets of various forms of oppression. Hardiman and Jackson have explored the privilege and target groups in the United States for many of the primary identities discussed earlier, and they are illustrated in Table 7.9. Dr. Peggy McIntosh, from Wellesley College, was the first person to coin the concept of privilege in her groundbreaking article *White Privilege: Unpacking the Invisible Knapsack* (find it online at Case Western Reserve University). McIntosh (1988) says that privileges are given in the form of unearned entitlements (things that everyone should have) and conferred dominance (things no one should have).

It is clear that any individual can be in both privileged groups and target groups for various aspects of his or her identity. For example, a disabled man would have privilege around gender but could experience oppression around ability. A heterosexual would have privilege around sexual orientation but could be targeted if he or she is Jewish. And a White person would have race privilege but might be targeted for gender or economic class. This makes

TABLE 7.9 PARTIAL LIST OF PRIVILEGED AND TARGET GROUPS IN THE UNITED STATES

IDENTITY	PRIVILEGED GROUP	TARGET GROUP
Race and ethnicity	Whites	People of color
Gender	Men	Women
Age	Adult	Young, elderly
Religion	Christians	Jews, Muslims, Buddhists, etc.
Sexual orientation	Heterosexuals	Lesbian, gay, bisexual, transgender people
Economic class	Middle and upper class	Poor and working class
Disability (psychological, physical, developmental)	Able people	Disabled people

understanding these concepts incredibly complex because there is a multitude of layers, and people have a range of experiences. See "Garrett's Story from the Path."

This also means that there are no "bad guys" or "good guys" because everyone experiences both sides of the privilege/oppression coin, and many of the identity development models demonstrate the process by which individuals discover, react to, and adjust their perceptions of their own group and other groups. The fact that every person in the United States shares the experience of privilege and oppression allows for diverse groups of people to connect because they probably can identify with others around these experiences.

However, just because all people share the dynamics of oppression doesn't mean that they have no responsibility for changing these dynamics. Some theorists who study the dynamics of oppression believe that there are several players in any oppressive situation. There is the person or people who are engaging in the oppressive acts toward others, there are those who are experiencing the oppression, and then there are the bystanders. According to Griffin and Harro (1982), people's reactions to oppression fall along a continuum, with one end representing actions that support oppression (i.e., collude with it), and the other end representing actions that confront oppression. Their model is illustrated in Figure 7.1.

Griffin and Harro argue that actively participating involves actions against people or groups (e.g., telling offensive jokes, insulting, avoiding, verbally or physically harassing) based

FIGURE 7.1 Action Continuum for Oppression

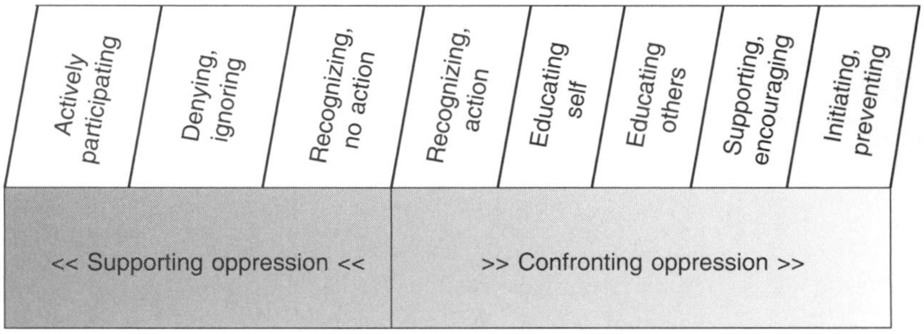

GARRETT'S STORY FROM THE PATH The day I moved away to college, I unknowingly embarked on a journey of awareness that I remain on today. I had always considered myself a good person, who wasn't prejudiced and who didn't engage in acts of bigotry. What I didn't realize was that while this self-assessment was true to a point, it didn't take into account the larger system of oppression and social injustice of which I was a part. What I didn't know about my own unearned power and privilege (which came from being a White, upper–middle-class, heterosexual, able-bodied man) was contributing to me not being the "safe space" that I thought I was.

I often equate the process of beginning to understand racism or other systems of oppression with a scene from the film *The Matrix*. In the film, the main character, Neo, is given a choice by Morpheus. Morpheus explains that the world is not what it seems, and that people have been programmed by machines to live in a world of illusion. Morpheus holds his palm out to Neo and inside it rests two pills, a red pill and a blue pill. If Neo takes the blue pill, he will forget what he has learned from Morpheus and wake up in his bed, unaware of the system of control that he unconsciously participates in every day. If he takes the red pill, he will never again see the world the same. He will see that people have been programmed by a complex system that is violent and oppressive, but is designed to keep them from seeing the harm that is propagated against themselves and others.

In a sense, my time in college was like taking the red pill. Being a student at a research university provided me with multiple opportunities to begin an education of awareness and become an aspiring ally—someone who recognizes and works to disrupt the very systems of oppression that afford individuals the unearned privilege that comes with being a member of a dominant group.

This newfound awareness did not occur overnight. It has been, and still is, a gradual and sometimes difficult journey.

For me, this awareness began in the residence halls. The best education I received my first year was not in the classroom, but rather during late night conversations in the hall lounge. These conversations ranged from casual topics like sports to other, more politically charged and provocative topics like war. Whatever the topic, each of us was learning from others who were from different parts of the state, country, and in some cases, the world, and were thus being challenged by different cultural beliefs and values.

The university classroom was another important part of my awareness education. Taking courses that focused on race and ethnicity, world religions, and gender and sexuality exposed me to ideas to which I had not been previously exposed. I actively sought out these courses because the more I learned about diversity and social justice, the more I realized how much I didn't know. I was eager to learn more. Ethnic studies, sociology, and religious studies courses were a major part of my awareness education.

The most valuable part of my awareness education in college came from my involvement in student leadership when I was hired to be a student advisor for Orientation Programs. During our required training, I was exposed to information about different cultural identities, but more importantly, I was challenged to look inward and examine what it meant for me to be part of a system that endowed me with unearned power and privilege. The goal was not to make me feel guilty, but to incite in me a commitment to actively work against social injustice.

My awareness education that began at my university stays with me. I carry those lessons as I continue on my journey in my life after college.

on their identity. Some of these people truly believe that another group is bad or inferior, but young adults sometimes participate in these activities just to be cool without really thinking about the true meaning of their actions or words. The next group is people who deny or ignore that oppression exists. When they hear someone describe an incident in which she or he felt discriminated against, they are likely to say things such as "You're being too sensitive" or "You took that the wrong way." This still supports oppression, even though they might not be actively oppressing others themselves. Similarly, people who recognize that oppression is occurring but still take no action are also supporting oppression. Often, this lack of action stems from confusion about what is happening, uncertainty about what actions to take, and fear.

Confronting oppression has various levels as well, and each level makes an effort to end oppression. The first level of confronting oppression involves recognizing oppression and taking action, i.e., changing one's own language and actions if these words or actions are oppressive in some way—in other words, honoring impact regardless of intent. At this stage, a person might interrupt a racist joke that is being told. The stage of educating self is about

@myU SO HOW DOES THIS AFFECT YOU?

Regardless of how you view issues of oppression or your personal experiences with them, you will find that they are frequently discussed and hotly debated at research universities. The concepts of privilege, oppression, and stereotypes are mentioned in many social science and humanities courses, as these disciplines seek to explore various aspects of society. You will also find them discussed in residence halls, student activities, public performances, and casual conversations. You will find that members of all levels of the campus community will be engaged in this discussion from students to deans, and from professors to presidents. There are many opportunities to learn more about these issues and to engage in both analytical and passionate discussions about them. In addition, you will witness many of these concepts at play in interactions among the members of your campus community.

You will have many opportunities to explore your own relationship to these issues and to take responsibility for your words and actions as well as opportunities to interact with others about these topics. More importantly, you have the opportunity to hone your cultural competence skills and prepare for your role in the next generation of national and global leadership. Society invests in its bright young adults to solve problems, and leadership is needed around issues of diversity, oppression, and privilege. As you step into leadership roles, professionally and personally, what impact will you have? Take a moment to identify some groups or communities that are targeted or oppressed on your campus, and list ways you can take action as an ally.

GROUP OR COMMUNITY	WAYS I CAN BE AN ALLY

taking actions to learn more about oppression and groups through the many ways already discussed in this chapter. Educating others moves beyond the self to engaging with others and discussing the issues. With regard to a racist joke, in addition to just stopping it, a person in this stage might initiate a discussion about why the joke is offensive.

Supporting and encouraging is about connecting with others who are committed to confronting oppression by joining groups and organizations and supporting others who are speaking out against it. Finally, the step of initiating and preventing is about working on dismantling oppression in the larger context of systems, policies, and institutions. This might involve planning educational programs, working for passing relevant legislation, and ensuring the full inclusion of oppressed groups in organizations. Many student activists are working at this stage of the continuum, although they might be doing it for only one or two groups.

This concept of confronting oppression is known by another phrase—it is called **being an ally,** and you will hear this phrase on many campuses across the country. An ally is a person of the privileged group (e.g., men, Whites, heterosexuals) who takes a stand against social injustice directed at people in the target groups. For example, an ally would be a White person who confronts a racist joke, a man who fights for equal wages for women, a wealthy person who votes for laws that benefit poor people, or a Christian who speaks out against vandalism of Muslim sanctuaries. An ally works to be an agent of social change rather than supporting oppression. An ally is someone who is not experiencing oppression of a certain type but who takes a stand against the oppression of another. Allies work toward social justice.

POINT OF INTEREST

STRATEGIES FOR ALLIES

1. Assume that you have the perfect right to be concerned about other people's oppression and that it is in your best interest to do so and to be an ally.
2. Think about the privileged and target groups you belong to—recognize privilege where you have it and oppression where you experience it.
3. Believe that people from oppressed groups are the experts on their own experience and that, as an ally, you have much to learn from them.
4. Recognize that membership in one or more oppressed groups does not absolve you of the responsibility of being an ally to members of an oppressed group to which you do not belong.
5. Take responsibility for learning about oppressed groups' history of struggle and resistance, as well as the history of how allies have engaged in struggles involving the rights of oppressed groups. Learn as much as you can about issues affecting oppressed groups. Seek out information sources (e.g., books, magazines, films, courses, other media) that are authored by people from that group. Create opportunities for learning about these issues and histories for members of your own group through invited speakers, films, forums, book clubs, and the like.
6. Begin to act as an ally now, as best you know how, but be open to feedback, criticism, and learning. Do not let the fact that you "do not know enough" be an excuse. Everyone always has more to learn, and everyone is learning.
7. Start where you are. Being an ally can take many different forms, and all contribute to ending oppression. There is no ranking of "fair-good-excellent" allies, so focus on making a difference in your own sphere and honor your comfort zone. Also, you might find that certain identities are easier for you to connect with. Maybe it's easier to start with race or class. That's fine. Focus on learning in those areas and using some of the strategies listed here. Down the road, review the list of identities and choose the next identity issue to explore and take action on.
8. Recognize that as a member of a privileged group, you know best how to use your privilege to interrupt oppressive attitudes and behaviors among members of your own group. Recognize that as an ally, you have the responsibility to work to improve your ability to do this and develop other allies by sharing strategies that have worked for you. You can certainly learn more about being an ally through the Internet, various books, and workshops on campus.
9. Assume that other people in your group also want to be allies. You are not the exception to the rule. Assume that you will always have something to learn about how to be a more effective ally, but have confidence in your ability to be an effective ally and to help others be more effective as well.
10. Realize that members of the oppressed group can spot oppressor socialization (behavior that perpetuates privilege and oppression). Realize that as a member of a privileged group, you often do not. Do not try to convince them that this conditioning did not happen to you—it happened to everyone who was raised in the United States.
11. Unlearning oppressive behavior is one step toward building a stronger, more inclusive movement for ending oppression; it allows us to communicate and work together better so that we may collectively fight oppression better. It is not so that you can learn to be less personally or overtly prejudiced or to assuage the guilt you might feel as a member of a privileged group.
12. Assume that people in the oppressed group want you and members of your group as allies but that their experience of oppression and previous experiences with members of your group might make them reluctant to accept you as such. Recognize that considering the history of mistreatment and mistrust between some groups, actions often speak louder than words.
13. Do not expect gratitude from members of the oppressed group. Remember, being an ally is a matter of choice for you, while being oppressed is not. If you are committed to social justice, being an ally is a responsibility.
14. Be an ally with no strings attached. For example, do not allow yourself to think, "I'll oppose your oppression if you oppose mine." Everyone's oppression needs to be opposed unconditionally. Nobody wins a competition of oppressions, so resist thinking of oppression in a hierarchical way.
15. Being an ally is an action, not a status. You must be *doing* something to be an ally.
16. Remember that we are never done. Fighting oppression is a lifelong process. Pace yourself and don't expect ever to "arrive." You will certainly see your own growth, and you will participate in changes that are visible on your campus or in our society, but as long as there are majority and minority groups, there will be a need for allies.

Adapted from a handout entitled "Strategies for Allies," author unknown.

Any person can be an ally to another, but this concept is most often applied when talking about the primary identities that were mentioned at the beginning of this chapter. In essence, being an ally is often about using the privileges you have to fight oppression and bring about social change for others. As noted, there are several primary and secondary identities, and each has a privileged and target group. Members of the target groups can also be allies to other communities, for example, an African American who confronts homophobia or a young person who protests budget cuts to Medicare for the elderly. This means that people can be allies to several communities simultaneously. See "Point of Interest: Strategies for Allies."

Students have very different reactions to this information on oppression and privilege. For students who are part of marginalized groups, they often can see their own experience and the experience of their group mirrored in the content. But for the dominant group, it can be more challenging because they may not have seen or experienced, or may have difficulty believing in, the levels of injustice that oppression creates. They certainly can struggle with their own personal reactions to the idea that a system has given them "unearned privileges that are granted not as a result of merit, hard work, talent, or accomplishment, but rather as a result of the inequitable systems that award these privileges to some and not others based solely on social group membership" (Edwards, 2006).

A person's choice to become an ally is affected by many things. Reason, Millar, and Scales (2005) did a study on White students who became allies on racial issues. They found that students were affected by factors both before and during college attendance. Prior to college, students were impacted by their own sense of Whiteness and attitudes about racial justice, the diversity of their high school, parental influence, and positive interactions with minorities. During college, they were affected by intentionally diverse living arrangements and race-related course work, which led to diverse friendships and an understanding of their Whiteness. Also, if they had an experience to be "in the minority," in an ethnic studies class for example, they had more sensitivity to the experience of their peers. Ultimately, to take racial justice actions, students had to have the invitation and opportunity to participate in ally work as well as support to do so, and White ally role models to emulate.

Your university education will provide many opportunities to explore all of the issues discussed in this chapter. Your cultural competence will develop and grow as you explore issues of race, ethnicity, gender, sexual orientation, age, spirituality, economic class, disability, political identity and many more that could not be addressed in this text. Embrace every opportunity you have to learn more about these issues, to challenge your beliefs about groups, and to ultimately change your actions.

RELATED MATERIALS

For Scenic Route websites, more Stories from the Path, glossary, and student activities, access the study tools for *Navigating the Research University* at www.cengagebrain.com.

REFERENCES

Adams, M., Bell, L. A., & Griffin, P. (1997). *Teaching for diversity and social justice: A sourcebook*. New York: Routledge.

Andreatta, B. (2010, February 24). Cultural competence for leaders. Lecture presented at Education 173, Introduction to leadership development. University of California, Santa Barbara.

Associated Press. (2007, April 23). *Pay gap begins 1 year after college: Study finds women make only 80 percent of salaries of male peers*. Retrieved from http://www.msnbc.msn.com/id/18262058/.

Atkinson, D. R., Morton, G., & Sue, D. W. (1998). *Counseling American minorities*. Boston: McGraw-Hill.

Daves-Rougeaux, D. (2004, January 29). The political development of college students. Lecture presented at Interdisciplinary 20, University of California, Santa Barbara.

DeAngelo, L., Hurtado, S. H., Pryor, J. H., Kelly, K. R., Santos, J. L., & Korn, W. S. (2009). *The American college teacher: National norms for the 2007–2008 HERI faculty survey.* Retrieved from http://www.heri.ucla.edu/publications-brp.php.

Edwards, K. E. (2006). Aspiring social justice ally identity development: A conceptual model. *NASPA Journal, 43*(4), 39–60.

Flacks, R., & Thomas, S. (1998, November 27). Among affluent students, a culture of disengagement. *Chronicle of Higher Education, 45*(14), A48.

Fowler, J. (1981). *Stages of faith: The psychology of human development and the quest for meaning.* New York: Harper & Row.

Griffin, P., & Harro, B. (1982). Action continuum. In M. Adams, L. Bell, & P. Griffin (Eds.). *Teaching for diversity and social justice: A sourcebook (Appendix 6C).* New York: Routledge.

Hardiman, R., & Jackson, B. W. (1997). Conceptual foundations for social justice courses. In M. Adams, L. Bell, & P. Griffin (Eds.). *Teaching for diversity and social justice: A sourcebook* (pp. 20–23). New York: Routledge.

Higher Education Research Institute. (2006a). *The spiritual life of college students: A national study of college students' search for meaning and purpose.* Los Angeles: UCLA. Retrieved from http://spirituality.ucla.edu/publications/research-reports/.

Higher Education Research Institute. (2006b). *Spirituality and the professoriate: A national study of faculty beliefs, attitudes, and behaviors.* Los Angeles: UCLA. Retrieved from http://spirituality.ucla.edu/publications/research-reports/.

Horowitz, D. (n.d.). *Academic bill of rights.* Retrieved from http://www.studentsforacademicfreedom.org/.

Howe, N., & Strauss, W. (2000). *Millennials rising: The next great generation.* New York: Random House.

Kerwin, C., Ponterotto, J. G., Jackson, B. L., & Harris, A. (1993). Racial identity in biracial children: A qualitative investigation. *Journal of Counseling Psychology, 40,* 221–231.

King, T., & Bannon, E. (2002). *At what cost? The price that working students pay for a college education.* Washington, DC: Higher Education Project of the States Public Interest Research Group.

Kinsey, A. C., Pomery, W. B., & Martin C. E. (1948). *Sexual behavior in the human male.* Philadelphia: Saunders.

Klein, F., Sepekoff, B., & Wolf, T. J. (1985). Sexual orientation: A multi-variable dynamic process. *Journal of Homosexuality, 11,* 1–2.

Lancaster, L., & Stillman, D. (2002). *When generations collide: How to solve the generational puzzle at work.* New York: Harper Collins.

McCarn, S., & Fassinger, R. (1996). Revisioning sexual minority identity formation: A new model of lesbian identity and its implications for counseling and research. *Counseling Psychologist, 24*(3), 508–534.

McIntosh, P. (1988). *White privilege and male privilege: A personal account of coming to see correspondences through work in women's studies.* Wellesley, MA: Wellesley College Center for Research on Women.

McIntosh, P. (1990). *White privilege: Unpacking the invisible knapsack.* Retrieved from http://www.case.edu/president/aaction/UnpackingTheKnapsack.pdf.

Meredith, G. E., & Schewe, C. D. (2002). *Managing by defining moments: America's seven generational cohorts, their workplace values, and why managers should care.* Indianapolis, IN: Hungry Minds.

Merriam-Webster OnLine Dictionary. (2010). Retrieved from http://www.merriam-webster.com/.

Mohr, J. (2002). An identity perspective on sexual orientation dynamics in psychotherapy. *Counseling Psychologist, 30*(4), 532–566.

National Center for Education Statistics (NCES). (2010). Degrees conferred by sex and race. Retrieved from http://nces.ed.gov/fastfacts/display.asp?id=72.

National Institute Against Prejudice and Violence. (2004). *The Prejudice Institute factsheets*. Retrieved from http://www.prejudiceinstitute.org/factsheets.html.

Nellie Mae. (2001). *2001 credit card usage analysis*. Retrieved from http://www.nelliemae.com/library/research_9.html.

Painter, K. (2004, March 2). Colleges throw a lifeline to students. *USA Today* [Electronic version]. Retrieved from http://www.usatoday.com/news/ health/2004-03-02-college-mental-health_xhtm.

Pryor, J., Hurtado, S., DeAngelo, L., Blake, L., & Tran, S. (2009). *The American freshman: National norms for Fall 2009*. Retrieved from http://www.heri.ucla.edu/research-publications.php.

Rankin, S. (2003). *Campus climate for gay, lesbian, bisexual, and transgender people: A national perspective*. New York: Policy Institute of the National Gay and Lesbian Task Force.

Reason, R., Millar, E., & Scales, T. (2005). Toward a model of racial justice ally development. *Journal of College Student Development, 46*(5), 530–546.

Rowe, W., Bennett, S. K., & Atkinson, D. R. (1994). White racial identity models: A critique and alternative proposal. *Counseling Psychologist, 22*(1), 129–146.

Ruiz, S., Sharkness, J., Kelly, K., DeAngelo, L., & Pryor, J. (2010). *Findings from the 2009 administration of Your First College Year (YFCY): National aggregates*. Retrieved from http://www.heri.ucla.edu/publications-brp.php.

Schwartz, J., & Kirkham, K. (2000). *Dynamics of oppression [Handout]*. Santa Barbara, CA: Just Communities.

United Nations (UN). (2010). *Cyberschoolbus*. Retrieved from http://cyberschoolbus.un.org/discrim/ethnicity1.asp.

U.S. Census. (2002). *U.S. population: The basics*. Retrieved from http://www.census.gov/popest/estimates.php.

Worthington, R., Savoy, H., Dillon, F., & Vernaglia, E. (2002). Heterosexual identity development: A multidimensional model of individual and social identity. *Counseling Psychologist, 30*(4), 496–531.

CHAPTER 8

Leadership Development at the Research University

Western Michigan University

photo by Neil Rankin

In addition to completing degree requirements, many university students wish to gain leadership experience in order to make a difference on their campus and to prepare themselves for future careers. In fact, following a college degree, leadership training is the first thing employers look for in a candidate. Even the most focused student scholars find that their education is enriched by engaging in cocurricular activities. Whether you are interested in getting involved just to have a little break from your studies, you wish to bring about change in your community, or you want to seriously develop your leadership skills, you will find a host of options available to you. This chapter will cover the importance of leadership development, provide an overview of opportunities for getting involved on research university campuses, and review two theoretical models of leadership.

YOUR RESPONSIBILITY AS A LEADER

A successful university education is not measured just by completed requirements and exemplary grades. It is also about how a student matures and develops as a person and a future leader. It is a widely held assumption that the next generation of local, national, and world leaders are cultivated at research university campuses where the brightest minds gather to be educated. As a result, universities tend to offer a plethora of opportunities for leadership development. These opportunities reflect a wide range of options from the curricular to cocurricular and even many that are off-campus. These different kinds of involvement can provide significant experiential training for both graduate school and future careers. While thousands of students graduate each year with a degree from a research university, far fewer also have a well-developed résumé built on involvement and leadership. The students who do are highly sought after by graduate programs and employers alike because they have already demonstrated advanced levels of maturity and leadership.

Another consideration is that getting involved in some aspect of campus life directly contributes to a student's university success. Getting involved can positively affect your transition by helping you feel more integrated in the academic and social aspects of campus. Curricular and cocurricular opportunities allow students to develop their scholarship and leadership skills while also connecting with other members of the campus community.

Furthermore, getting involved and holding leadership positions are ways in which undergraduate students can play an active role in affecting their campus community, an aspect of citizenship. Faculty, administrators, and staff come to campus each day for their jobs and might not always accurately see the current state of the student experience. As a result, it is the leadership and commitment of the students that bring about important changes to campus. How else can we ensure that our universities change and grow in ways that are appropriate for the education of future generations?

Separate from affecting the university community, many people argue that leadership roles in college prepare young adults for leadership roles within the larger state, national, and global community. In fact, many feel that the real purpose of a college education is to create leaders who make a difference in the world. See "Point of Interest: Scholarship, Leadership, and Citizenship."

POINT OF INTEREST

SCHOLARSHIP, LEADERSHIP, AND CITIZENSHIP One way to think of your development is to look at three areas: scholarship, leadership, and citizenship. This phrase has become the motto of my campus and was coined by Dr. Michael Young, the Vice Chancellor for Student Affairs. These three important areas contribute to a rich and engaging college experience and also position you for wonderful opportunities after graduation. You are at an amazing place, where the best and brightest minds in the country come together to discover new knowledge. You are now part of this community of scholars, and it is a true privilege to be so. You owe it to yourself and to the millions of people who cannot be in your place to take your education seriously. Don't just passively go through the motions of checking off your requirements and getting that piece of paper at graduation. Engage! Squeeze everything you can out of your education. Meet those world-renowned professors and find out what you can learn from them. Build your repertoire of skills—not only those for academic success, but also those for your success as a future leader. Get computer savvy, learn to be a strong public speaker, and become culturally competent.

Reflect on your first year and set goals for the remainder of your college experience. How can you use the resources that are available to you to not only earn your degree, but also to prepare you to be an important and effective leader in the future? How can you get involved on your campus in ways that support your development as a scholar, leader, and citizen? What leadership positions are available to you and how might you step into them? Are there ways to begin using your education now, while you are still in college, to be the voice of others or to improve the experience of others?

Remember, education at a research university is not a right, but a privilege. How will you make the most of yours?

Students seem to agree that making a difference is important. According to the nearly 27,000 freshmen students who participated in the national 2009 Your First College Year survey (Ruiz, et al., 2010), students indicated that the following goals were either "very important" or "essential":

- Helping to promote racial understanding (39 percent)
- Influencing social values (44 percent)
- Adopting "green" practices to protect the environment (51 percent)
- Participating in a community action program (39 percent)
- Becoming a community leader (39 percent)
- Influencing the political structure (22 percent)
- Improving understanding of other countries/cultures (58 percent)

The Purpose and Power of a College Education

Dr. Claudine Michel (2004) has some wonderful thoughts about the purpose and power of a college education. She has a Ph.D. in international education and has been on the faculty of the University of California at Santa Barbara for more than 25 years. She is adored by students—her classes are always filled to overflowing, and students line up at her office hours, more often just to talk with her than to review an assignment. She talks about education as not a tangible thing that you can buy, but a process, a lifelong process that opens our minds and opens doors for us. She often recounts the life of the famous slave, Frederick Douglass, to make her point. Douglass was being taught to read by his master's wife, and one day, his master discovered them and was very angry. Douglass recounts hearing the master say, "Do you realize that if you educate him, you will forever make him unfit to be a slave?" It was at that moment that Douglass realized that education was the pathway to freedom. He eventually escaped and became a famous orator, abolitionist, and published author. Much of his work was the cornerstone for debunking the myth that Blacks were inferior to Whites, and leading to the end of slavery.

Dr. Michel goes on to say that when you really educate someone, you open all kinds of doors and opportunities for that person, and you literally change his or her life forever. The change is not limited to just this one person—you also affect the lives of those in his or her family, workplace, and community. Education is a process that develops important abilities, plays a role in socializing people to be part of society, is the key to many important opportunities, and develops not only a person's mind, but also his or her heart and character. To deny someone an education is to deny him or her the opportunity to learn and develop critical faculties that are necessary to take charge of one's life and to make contributions to the world.

The importance of education in the global context is underscored by examining how it is utilized in countries around the world. Many governments have used the importance of education—or more accurately, denying people access to education—to stay in power and control the people. For example, China, which does not acknowledge Tibet as a free country, has done many things to control the people of Tibet including destroying Buddhist monasteries, murdering dissidents, and closing down all the schools so that Tibetan children can no longer get an education. Tibetan parents send their children, as young as 3 years old, on dangerous treks across the Himalayan Mountains to escape in order to reach a school outside of Tibet (Florio, et al., 2002). Many children die on these trips, and even if they do survive, most never see their families again. This clearly illustrates the power of education; people will risk even death to have access to it. Education creates freedom, and it gives people the power to change the world.

This is the same philosophy that drives Greg Mortenson to travel each year to Afghanistan and Pakistan, to build schools in some of the remotest villages in the world. He knows that education is the key to transforming the lives of individuals and the health of a community and country. His inspiring work is chronicled in the bestselling books *Three Cups of Tea: One Man's Mission to Promote Peace ... One School at a Time* (2007) and *Stones into Schools:*

Promoting Peace with Books, Not Bombs, in Afghanistan and Pakistan (2009). Mortenson found himself the unlikely champion of this cause when he was in a climbing accident on the infamous K2 Mountain. Barely alive, he stumbled into a small village in Pakistan where the local community saved him. He wanted to repay their kindness and the village chief asked for help in building a school. This began Mortenson's quest, and after several years, much fundraising, and many trips later, the school was finished.

By then, he had seen the power of education—that by giving children, and even adults, access to learning, they were far less likely to be drawn into the Taliban or al-Qaeda groups that still dominate the area. With education, people's health improved, families grew closer, and villages thrived because the students applied their knowledge to improve their community. Word of Mortenson's work spread and he was soon besieged with requests from other chiefs to build schools in their towns, because they also know the power of education—it is the single greatest force in promoting individual and community well-being. According to the *Three Cups of Tea* website (2010), Mortenson, through his organizations of the Central Asia Institute and Pennies for Peace, has built more than 131 schools, which have educated more than 58,000 students to date. In 2009, Greg received Pakistan's highest civil award, the "Star of Pakistan," and he was nominated for the Nobel Peace Prize in both 2009 and 2010.

Education is this powerful because it does much more than simply teach a student a basic concept. Dr. Michel argues that education does three things: it informs, it forms, and most importantly, it transforms. **Informing,** of course, is the process of taking people from one level of knowledge to another level by providing them with facts, information, perspectives, and interpretations. This process is closely linked with Bloom's Hierarchy of Knowledge. This informing process is certainly present when you take a course in chemistry, for example, and learn about acid and alkaline balance. But as the work of Greg Mortenson illustrates, it also occurs when you teach people about principles of crop and livestock management, and basic health concepts like decontaminating water or ensuring that a wound stays clean.

Forming is the process by which people take this new knowledge they have learned and form new values and beliefs. At this point, people take ownership for what they think, what they are about, and how they will live their lives on the basis of what they have learned. You might see this in yourself as you learn more about climate change and how it relates to your carbon use. As a result, you might commit to changing your everyday behaviors like recycling and driving. In the villages that Mortenson worked with, students taught their families about basic health care, and as a result, the death rate of children dramatically declined.

The final process, **transforming,** is using your education to transform—to better yourself, your family, your community, your country, and your planet. Again, you might use knowledge you have gained at the university to confront racism in your community or to tackle a local or national problem like children living in poverty. An example from Mortenson's work is that as students went through the levels of their schooling, many became more and more committed to continuing their education. Mortenson has funded the college tuition of several students—one woman in particular went on to medical school and now not only provides treatment in her own village but also travels widely in the surrounding area to help others. As she does this, she continues to educate her community about health care practices, thus saving the lives of many.

In that context, Dr. Michel strongly urges university students to consider the idea that education without responsible use is of no use. The power of education should be taken seriously and honored for the privileges it provides. It should not be used for frivolous goals but to bring about change in the world. Dr. Michel argues that this is especially true for students at a research university. Research universities are the top educational institutions in the world, with a cadre of brilliant minds brought together in the community of scholars. The best and brightest are admitted to research universities, giving these students even more responsibility for using their education for the common good, especially if those institutions are publicly funded because taxpayers are funding the students' education in order to develop future leaders. Only 28 percent of adults in the United States, less than one-third, ever earn a college degree, so a college education is not what the majority, or even half, of U.S. residents experience.

Of that 28 percent, far fewer attend research universities. Many research universities admit a limited top percentage of the state's high school graduates, such as 12 to 15 percent, and this model is echoed at campuses across the country. Dr. Michel argues that this 12 percent of students have a responsibility to the other 88 percent to use their education to be leaders and make the state, country, and world a better place in which to live. She believes that you have a responsibility to use this amazing privilege (attending a research university) to better not only your own life, but also the lives of others. Every student should ask himself or herself, "How can I use my education to be the voice of others who are not here? How can I improve their experience?"

In addition, the world has serious problems that need to be solved. Consider what role you could play in curing diabetes, ending racial discrimination, uniting the Middle East, or reversing global warming. A scan of the world news will show you the areas or issues in which your leadership is needed.

Examples of Outstanding Student Leaders

To give you an idea of the kind of leadership that students demonstrate during their years at a research university, here are two stories of students who believed in the power of education and who exemplify Dr. Michel's ideas.

INVISIBLE CHILDREN AND THE WORK OF JASON RUSSELL, BOBBY BAILEY, AND LAREN POOLE In 2003, three university students from Southern California decided to take a trip to Africa to create a documentary film. Jason Russell and Bobby Bailey were students in the film program at the University of Southern California, and Laren Poole was attending the University of California at San Diego where he was pursuing an engineering degree. While they had intended to have an interesting adventure, mishaps led them to Northern Uganda where they became stranded. What they found in Uganda was horrifying. Young children were being kidnapped and trained as soldiers by the rebel Lord's Resistance Army (LRA), and used as weapons in a violent and bloody war. These children are robbed of their childhood and forced to commit murder and other heinous acts or else be killed themselves.

The students started documenting what they found and returned to California to release the film *Invisible Children: Rough Cut* (2004). This film was shown to friends, family, and fellow university students who quickly passed the word to their peers. The film was so moving in its ability to capture the tragedy that a grassroots movement soon began, traveling from student to student, across colleges and universities. Students would schedule film screenings on their campuses and hold fundraising events. As the word spread, people wrote their legislators and demanded action, and the media took notice with coverage on CNN and the National Geographic Channel. And as a result of this one short film and the work of these three university students, the tragedy in Uganda received national and international attention. Today, Jason, Bobby, and Laren work with a team of people to run their nonprofit organization, Invisible Children, Inc. (2010), to continue to bring change to the lives of innocent children in Africa. If you wish to learn more, visit www.invisiblechildren.com.

WENDY KOPP AND TEACH FOR AMERICA Wendy Kopp is the Princeton University student who is responsible for creating Teach For America and leading it to its current status as one of the most powerful change-agent organizations in the United States. During her senior year at Princeton, Wendy was working on her undergraduate thesis project and used

THE SCENIC ROUTE

Visit www.cengagebrain.com to find the companion website containing links to:

- Information on Greg Mortenson's work
- Information on Invisible Children, Inc.
- Information on how you can apply or donate to Teach For America

it as an opportunity to create a proposal for a new nonprofit organization designed to bring quality teaching to some of the poorest communities in our country (Kopp, 2003). She was very concerned that about the inequity that existed in K–12 schools and how this affected students' abilities to attend and graduate from college and become upwardly mobile. About half of all high school students in low-income schools do not graduate.

She also believed that her generation was misnamed the "me generation" and that opposed to the belief that they were only seeking self-serving experiences, many of her peers were eager to make a difference in the world. She saw this as an opportunity to create a teaching corps where students, upon graduating from college, would volunteer to teach for two years. Instead of just letting her idea live in a file drawer at Princeton, Kopp was determined to make it a reality. She met with corporations, private donors, legislators, and the media to create Teach For America. You can read about her journey in the book *One Day, All Children … The Unlikely Triumph of Teach For America and What I Learned Along the Way* (Kopp, 2003) or her new book *A Chance to Make History: What Works and What Doesn't in Providing an Excellent Education for All* due out in 2011.

Currently, Teach For America serves 35 urban and rural regions around the United States and impacts 450,000 students annually, using more than 7,300 corps members. Since its inception, nearly 17,000 college students have proven Wendy right by choosing to teach after graduation, and their service has reached 3 million children (Teach For America, 2010). Wendy Kopp and all of the students who join the corps demonstrate again and again the power and privilege of an education. Consider being part of this amazing organization and apply in your senior year. Learn more at www.teachforamerica.org.

Clearly, all of these students took the opportunities and experiences offered to them as part of their research university education and utilized them to bring about significant change in the world. They continue to lead a legacy of change and transformation long after graduation, and they epitomize the power and privilege of an education. While their stories are impressive, it's important to remember that they started off in college as first-year students as well—like you, they also had to deal with learning how to study, managing their time, and meeting new friends. Leadership like this is a process, and it takes time to develop the skills needed to be successful. Use your time in college to try new things and get involved in a variety of ways. Make a point to challenge yourself and try serving in various types of leadership roles. It can begin with simply joining a club or applying to be a peer advisor.

@myU SO HOW DOES THIS AFFECT YOU?

You are surrounded daily by students who have the potential to be the next great leaders of the world, including you. It's important that you be mindful about your identity as a leader and intentional in your development. Each year, your university will honor both its graduating seniors and alumni with various awards for leadership and service. For example, Brown University has the Alfred Joslin Award, while Montana State University has the Torlief Aasheim Community Involvement Award, and the University of California at Santa Barbara's highest honor is the Thomas Storke Award. Search the Internet for recent winners of these three awards and note some of their achievements below.

As you read about these students, consider how you might make use of your years at your university to be eligible for similar accolades.

1.

2.

3.

GETTING INVOLVED ON YOUR CAMPUS

The best way to begin this process of developing yourself as scholar, leader, and citizen is to get involved in a few areas. Don't take on too much at first; devote some of your energy to mastering other transition issues mentioned in this book. However, it is fine to pick one or two involvements your first year and then build from there. Many students want to get involved in some way but are not sure how to begin. The most important thing you need is simply to have the desire. There are literally hundreds of opportunities on campus, and they are there for those who want the experience. Next, you'll want to become familiar with the options available to you. Your university probably has an office of campus activities or student life, and this is a great place to start; the staff there will be able to provide you with more specific information about how and where to go to pursue your interests.

In this section you will find an overview of both academic and cocurricular options that are commonly found on research university campuses. Read through them and mark all the ones that interest you. It is fine to pursue many options—you have two to four years to do so, and you can either pursue a wide range of involvements, or pick one or two and become more deeply involved over a long period of time. If you are still figuring out what interests you, start by exploring several interests and narrow them down as you get clearer about what you enjoy and what you are good at. See "Point of Interest: Ways to Get Involved."

Some opportunities will be open to all students all year-round, so it will be easy to participate; for example, most clubs and organizations take new students throughout the year. Others may have specific times for getting involved, such as Greek life, which has a formal period of recruitment, or athletic opportunities that begin and end around competition seasons. In addition, some opportunities have an application and selection process. It's always a good idea to call about options that might interest you and write down their typical cycle so that you can plan out

POINT OF INTEREST

WAYS TO GET INVOLVED Many universities have some kind of club day or activities fair early in the fall term. This event usually brings together many, if not all, of the campus clubs and organizations and other involvement opportunities. This makes it very easy for a student to peruse all the options, meet folks, and learn about the different possibilities. It's usually possible to join or sign up right on the spot. If your campus has a day like this, be sure to write the date on your planner and attend.

Another great way to find out about opportunities is to become an avid reader of all the fliers and posters you see around campus. You would be surprised just how many things are going on at a university at any one time. Some of them might be events, such as lectures or movies, and some might be meetings. Attending events and meetings will help you find out what you enjoy and put you in contact with the students and groups that are hosting them. Your campus may have a centralized location for learning about campus events, such as an online event calendar or a central place where fliers are posted. Get in the habit of checking it out every couple of days. If you find something you like,

write it in your planner. Students often fail to attend something and miss out simply because they forgot. The best way to ensure that you don't miss something is to write it in your planner, and be sure to also note the time and location so that you won't end up wandering around trying to find it.

Finally, don't be shy. If you see something happening on campus that interests you, stop in and check it out. Most campus events and activities are open to everyone or are clearly marked if they are not. So if you see or hear something that intrigues you, just walk up and check it out. You might stumble across the perfect opportunity for you.

Once you find a few (or twenty!) possibilities that interest you, make contact. Find the phone number or e-mail address of a person who is responsible for, or affiliated with, your interest and contact that person. Simply introduce yourself, express your interest, and request the information you need or the response you would like. This method works for all kinds of opportunities. If you don't get a response, don't give up—just send the note again. Sometimes people are very busy and lose track of things to which they are supposed to respond.

your future involvement. For example, applications for the highly coveted summer orientation staff positions can be due as early as January. There might be a lengthy selection process that takes weeks or months. Those who are selected most likely train during spring term so they are ready to help new students and their families in the summer. Resident assistant jobs are similar, often beginning the hiring process in winter for the following fall.

Academic and Curricular Opportunities

Within the academic, or curricular, aspect of a university education, there are many ways to get involved, and research universities offer a range that is not seen at other campuses. These are especially important to explore for the students who are considering graduate school or a career in higher education. The options that are purely academic and involve additional course work and assignments or projects will be excellent preparation for further studies beyond the bachelor's degree. In fact, they may provide the base for a student's research or teaching career and usually culminate in some kind of final project that could be presented or published in a variety of venues.

Each university is organized differently, so it is difficult to give concrete information on where you would find information about these options. However, most academic advisors in major departments and college offices should be able to point you in the right direction. In addition, you might want to look at your general catalog or campus website for information. The following descriptions provide an overview of the academic and curricular opportunities available to students at research universities. As you read the following options, mark those that interest you on Table 8.1.

TABLE **8.1** OVERVIEW OF CURRICULAR OPPORTUNITIES		
OPPORTUNITY	**POSSIBLE REQUIREMENTS**	**INTERESTS YOU**
Independent study and directed readings	Major, GPA, faculty sponsor, credits	
Academic conferences	Fee	
Colloquiums and seminars	—	
Faculty research projects	Major, GPA, credits	
Senior thesis projects	Major, GPA, senior standing	
Graduate-level courses	Major, faculty sponsor, credits	
Studying abroad	GPA, language, credits, application	
Academic peer advisors	Major, GPA, selection	
Curricular and career clubs	—	
Professional organizations	Fee	
Honors societies	Major, GPA	
Honors programs	Major or college, GPA	
Honors at graduation	GPA, credits	

INDEPENDENT STUDY AND DIRECTED READINGS Students who wish to gain exposure to a discipline that is not available through current course offerings can approach faculty members to sponsor them in independent study projects or directed readings. These are usually arranged between a student and a faculty member on a case-by-case basis, and the student initiates the process. Directed readings allow the student to earn credit for doing more in-depth reading or exploration of a topic. The sponsoring faculty member assigns readings and books that are customized to the student's needs. Independent study projects can take a wide variety of forms and are often codesigned by the student and faculty member. Both of these options are often most utilized by juniors and seniors.

ACADEMIC CONFERENCES Each year, national and international academic conferences are held at university campuses. These conferences tend to bring together the top minds in that particular discipline from around the world to share ideas and findings. Students often can attend free of charge or might be able to volunteer for certain portions of the conference. This is an excellent way to learn more about a discipline and to network with faculty (especially useful if you are thinking about graduate school). Faculty ultimately decide graduate admissions for their department, so make a point to meet faculty who work at universities where you want to apply.

COLLOQUIUMS AND SEMINARS Every term, individual academic departments organize a series of seminars or presentations, called colloquiums, on a variety of topics related to that discipline. Sometimes the speakers are the resident faculty, who share their recent findings or ideas on a particular topic, and sometimes guest speakers are invited who are doing interesting or groundbreaking work in the field. These events are usually open to the campus community and are free.

FACULTY RESEARCH PROJECTS The primary mission of a research university is to conduct research. Faculty often use undergraduate assistants in their research projects, doing tasks that can range from simple duties to high levels of responsibility and involvement. While these opportunities may have qualities similar to those of jobs or internships (that is, a set number of hours per week, established compensation), they also provide students with a unique opportunity to participate firsthand in research. This experience is quite impressive to graduate programs because it indicates that a student has familiarity with the research process and desires to pursue it further. See "Point of Interest: The Grad School Edge."

POINT OF INTEREST

THE GRAD SCHOOL EDGE You can significantly improve your chance of graduate school admission by participating in a research project as an undergraduate, for either a faculty member's project or your own. This involvement sets you apart from the thousands of students who apply to graduate programs because they believe that an advanced degree will get them higher-paying jobs. While this might be true, faculty at research universities are interested in training future researchers who are serious about careers in academia. The majority of the degree will be designed to train a future researcher, and this might not be the experience a naïve applicant was seeking.

If you participate in a research project as an undergraduate, your application will be taken more seriously because it is assumed that you understand the general process of research as well as what a research career entails, and therefore will make the most of your advanced degree education. This does not mean that you have to pursue a career in research, but it means that you will be perceived as less likely to experience disappointment or to drop out of a research-focused program compared to the other applicants.

In addition, you will most likely be able to include a letter of recommendation from a faculty member who can attest to your research skills and potential as a graduate student. This will also set you apart from the majority of your peers. If you choose to not pursue graduate school, your faculty supervisor can still write an excellent letter of recommendation about your skills and abilities that will make you a strong candidate for a variety of professional jobs.

SENIOR THESIS PROJECTS   These are usually sponsored by an academic major for its advanced students. A senior thesis or research project has the student serving as the primary investigator, as opposed to the faculty member. These research projects are often smaller in scale than a faculty member's project and are designed to be finished within an academic year. The topic and research methods would be aligned with the student's major or discipline and so would be unique to each individual student. For example, a student in the social or hard sciences might identify a problem, conduct a study or experiment, and write up the final results in a senior thesis, while a student in the arts might create an original piece such as a dance or music composition. Some universities recognize completion of a senior thesis by awarding some type of special distinction in the major upon graduation.

GRADUATE-LEVEL COURSES   In some circumstances, faculty members can approve an undergraduate student's request to take a graduate seminar in the department. Usually, the student is a senior with an interest in graduate school, and the seminar matches his or her scholarly interests. Graduate seminars are usually very small (two to ten students), and the undergraduate is expected to participate fully in readings, discussions, and assignments.

STUDYING ABROAD   Most universities offer some type of study abroad program in which a student can live and study in a foreign country for one term or up to one year. This is an amazing, life-changing experience, and one that is not to be missed if you can do it. The best types of programs are officially connected to, or sponsored by, your university, because they can guarantee that the credits and course work you complete abroad will transfer and count toward your degree and/or major. Often you continue to pay the same tuition and to receive financial aid as you otherwise would, as the program is administered through your campus. In addition, there will most likely be a formal model of mentorship and assistance in place in the foreign location, such as a faculty member who lives in that country and oversees the program.

You would be amazed by the range of opportunities that is available in study abroad programs, including programs that are specific to certain majors. For example, my campus offers a six-week summer program for biology majors working in the rain forests of Costa Rica, one of the most biologically diverse places on the planet. Many of these programs have language requirements; find out about them early in your college career so you can plan accordingly. Most students travel abroad as juniors or seniors, but there are some sophomore programs too, and transfer students can also participate during their senior year.

There are also many opportunities to study abroad that may not be officially affiliated with your university. These are also worth exploring, although they might require more work on your part, and the credit may or may not transfer. Check out the Internet for these opportunities.

ACADEMIC PEER ADVISING   These are usually paid positions in which a student holds a job with academic advising duties for either the major department or college. These students are trained in the relevant requirements and policies and can provide general advising to their peers. Usually, these positions require the student to be in good academic standing and to be a member of that department or program.

CURRICULAR AND CAREER CLUBS   These are usually student-run clubs or organizations that are composed of students pursuing a certain major or career. For example, there may be an economics club or a premed association. The student members determine the focus of the club and work together to create meetings, events, and opportunities that are beneficial to the current members. Often, these clubs are designed to help prepare students for future opportunities, such as graduate schools and professional careers, so activities might include guest speakers, workshops, field trips, and the like.

STUDENT CHAPTERS OF PROFESSIONAL ORGANIZATIONS   Most academic disciplines have professional organizations of which the faculty are members. For example, many faculty who research or teach in higher education or related fields are members of the College Student Educators International (ACPA), and most mechanical engineers are members of Pi Tau Sigma. National and international associations like these provide a series of benefits for members (in exchange for annual dues) such as national and regional conferences, monthly publications like newsletters or journals, and networking opportunities. Many of these professional organizations offer membership to students at very low rates. Membership in such organizations can provide students, especially juniors and seniors, with wonderful opportunities including internships, scholarships, and networking. Most academic departments can provide a list of related professional organizations as well as information on local student chapters.

Finally, several involvement opportunities are usually available to students who have achieved a certain level of outstanding academic performance. There are usually certain criteria that must be met for admission, which might be by invitation only.

Visit www.cengagebrain.com to find the companion website containing links to:

- Alpha Lambda Delta, a freshman honor society
- Phi Beta Kappa, a national academic honor society
- National Society of Leadership and Success

HONORS SOCIETIES   These can be campus, regional, or national groups and usually require a certain GPA for admission. Depending on the sponsoring group, information would be available at a campus department or a national office. Honors societies can also be focused on a certain population, such as freshmen or seniors, or they might be open to students in a certain discipline, such as environmental studies or a foreign language. Some honors societies, such as Phi Beta Kappa, are nationally recognized. Often, honors societies have some kind of induction ceremony as well as annual fees or dues. Benefits include access to conferences, publications, and networking opportunities for alumni. To check the legitimacy of an offer you have received, visit the Association of College Honors Societies at www.achsnatl.org.

HONORS PROGRAMS   These are usually academic programs run by a college or major department and require a certain level of participation and excellence in order to participate. Often, certain benefits are offered such as priority enrollment, special events, and higher levels of access to university resources such as the library or computer labs. Some programs are designed to be an acknowledgment for achievement, and participants receive admission and benefits based on maintaining a certain GPA. Other programs are designed to be an additional experience and may have requirements for certain courses or a certain number of honors sections to "complete" the program on graduation.

HONORS AT GRADUATION   This is an academic acknowledgment bestowed by the university and is based on the performance of the senior class. There are usually three levels that reflect placement in the highest percentages (based on GPA) of the senior class as a whole:

- Honors, also known as cum laude
- High honors, also known as magna cum laude
- Highest honors, also known summa cum laude

Students do not apply for these honors but rather receive them from the university at graduation. These levels are usually indicated on the diploma and may be noted in commencement programs or by special regalia to be worn by students during commencement.

Because this honor is based on an individual student's placement in comparison to the senior class, exact GPAs for qualification cannot be determined, as these change with each group of students. However, a university usually keeps records of the results each year, so a student could learn the general level of accomplishment that will be required. It is important to note that participation in honors programs and societies is usually *not* related to honors at graduation, although there will be a certain overlap among the students who qualify for them. Many students who completed an honors program are confused and disappointed that this did not earn them honors at graduation.

You have the unique option to seek out and participate in academic opportunities such as the ones described in this section. Each one has a different focus but all are designed to help you experience deeper levels of scholarship and intellectual engagement. Review your campus website and other documents such as your college brochure and general catalog to find at least three curricular opportunities that interest you. Note them below, along with the office or department to contact to gain more information:

1.

2.

3.

Major departments can also award special honors to graduating seniors in various forms. There may be prestigious awards presented to students as well as departmental honors based on academic performance. These vary by department; an academic advisor can usually provide more information.

Cocurricular Opportunities

In addition to the academic, or curricular, aspect of a university education, there are ways to get involved in cocurricular opportunities. While these are outside of the academic arena, they can provide a plethora of opportunities to gain valuable experience and skills that can prepare students for post-graduation possibilities.

Most graduate schools and employers are looking for students who have developed more than just their transcripts—they are looking for students who have experience working with others, possess good communication and leadership skills, and conduct themselves in mature and professional ways. Cocurricular opportunities can provide opportunities to develop all of these and also can help prepare students for a wide range of future careers, especially those not affiliated with research and academia. See "Tricia's Story from the Path."

Each of these options may be housed in, or affiliated with, a different campus program, so consult your campus website or student handbook for information. Also, most universities have an office of student life or campus activities, which would be a natural place to begin your search for cocurricular opportunities. Table 8.2 provides an overview of common cocurricular opportunities and possible requirements for participation. Check off those that interest you.

STUDENT GOVERNMENT   Most universities have some form of student government in which students get elected to represent their peers in campus issues. There are more positions to which a student can be elected than students experienced in high school. In addition to elected positions, many student governments provide a range of other opportunities, such as serving on boards and committees that work on certain issues (e.g., environment, use of student fees, gender/ethnic equality, social programming) as well as student services that are run by students for students. Depending on the position, these opportunities can prepare you for political and policy-making careers as well as careers that focus on specific issues, such as the environment. In addition, there may be other forms of student government, affiliated with a residence hall or campus facility, in which students govern programming and use of student fees.

CLUBS AND ORGANIZATIONS   According to the 2009 national Your First College Year (YFCY) study on freshmen, 63 percent of students participate in student clubs or groups (Ruiz, et al., 2010). Most clubs and organizations are created and run by students, which allows for the organizations to change and evolve as students' needs change and evolve. It is usually easy to start a new club or organization, so students are empowered to create the involvement opportunities that interest them most. These can run the gamut from academic

TRICIA'S STORY FROM THE PATH

Upon entering college, campus involvement was the furthest thing from my mind. I spent the first half of my freshman year adjusting to residence hall life, memorizing the campus map, and learning how to balance classes and a part-time job. However, I soon began to feel that something was missing. I felt a sense of disconnection from my university and a desire to connect with my peers on a more personal level. The answer to my dilemma came through my eventual role as a student leader.

My journey toward student leadership began with my attendance at a leadership retreat sponsored by the university's Office of Student Life. At the retreat, I found myself surrounded by students who both recognized themselves as leaders and wished to develop the skills and abilities they brought to the clubs and organizations to which they belonged. We were there for a common purpose and each brought unique examples of involvement in the campus community. I saw the relationship they had with the campus through their involvement and knew that was what I was seeking as well. When the retreat came to an end, I not only felt I had grown in my understanding of what student leadership was but was eager to begin my campus involvement.

The next three years were a time of incredible growth and personal development. I applied for and was selected for the student summer orientation staff. The next year, I was promoted to the coordinator position and I hired, trained, and supervised the student staff along with my coordinator. As an orientation leader and student coordinator, I developed skills in diplomacy, professional conduct, and organization. I worked with a large group of incredible student leaders who all had an appreciation for their school and wished to help new students develop the same feeling.

That same year, I applied for the Walter Capps Leadership intern position with the Office of Student Life and helped coordinate our campus's leadership program. The year I spent in this position introduced me to event planning, public speaking, and communication with a variety of groups (students, faculty, and staff). Involvement that I had with student government gave me a better understanding of the power students have over their education and the importance of the student voice. My senior year, I was able to work in the Office of the Vice Chancellor for Student Affairs. Not only was I developing close relationships with peers and mentors through my involvement, but I was learning lessons that I knew would be beneficial in my professional career.

All of these positions taught me that I wanted to continue working in higher education where I plan to play an active role in encouraging student involvement and helping students recognize the leaders within themselves. Upon graduation, I went on to complete a master's degree in higher education and student affairs at the University of Vermont. My undergraduate experience would not have been the same if I had failed to pursue campus involvement or to believe in my ability to be a leader. Through these experiences I formed long-lasting friendships and found mentors who continue to serve as role models in my life today.

TABLE 8.2 OVERVIEW OF COCURRICULAR OPPORTUNITIES

OPPORTUNITY	POSSIBLE REQUIREMENTS	INTERESTS YOU
Student government	Application, election	
Clubs and organizations	—	
Greek life	Rush, selection, fee	
Athletics and recreation	Tryouts, selection, fee	
Religious groups	Service, fee	
Performing groups	Audition, selection	
Peer advisors	Selection	
Committee appointments	Appointment	
Volunteering	—	

and career-focused to hobbies and personal interest to ethnic and religious identity. Following is a sample of the types of clubs or organizations you might find on a typical university campus:

+ Academic: Environmental Studies Students Association, Communications Association, Los Ingenieros
+ Career focus: Pre-Med Association, Accounting Association, Society of Women Engineers
+ Community service: Habitat for Humanity, Feeding the Homeless
+ Cultural: Chinese Student Union, Hermanos Unidos, Israeli Club, Irish Students Association, Gay and Lesbian Student Alliance
+ Environmental: Rainforest Alliance, Students to Reduce Global Warming, The Organic Food Club
+ Ethnic: Black Student Union, Korean Student Association
+ Health: Students Against Drunk Drivers, Safer Sex Peer Educators
+ Hobbies: Chess Club, Japanese Anime Association
+ Honorary: Alpha Lambda Delta, Mortar Board, Mensa Society
+ Ideological/political: Campus Democrats, College Republicans, El Congreso, National Organization of Women
+ Recreational: Billiard Club, Swing and Ballroom Dance Club, Mountain Bike Club
+ Religious: Asian American Christian Fellowship, Muslim Student Association, Hillel, Nichiren Buddhists, United Methodist Student Movement, Real Life
+ Social: Friday Night Film Fanciers, Hip Hop Club
+ Special interest: National Society of Leadership and Success, Disabled Students Advocacy Union, Club Britain

GREEK LIFE   According to the national YFCY study on freshmen, 12 percent of freshmen joined a sorority or fraternity in their first year (Ruiz, et al., 2010). There are many forms of Greek life on campus these days, and they are becoming less and less like the "animal house" stereotype of years past. Risk management has forced universities and national organizations to crack down on excessive drinking and hazing, which have been the negative and dangerous sides of the Greek community. In addition, many campuses have a wide range of involvement opportunities, so Greek life is no longer the only, or most popular, option for students, and this has contributed to major reforms as well.

There are many benefits to Greek life, such as the opportunity to meet people through shared interests and experiences, the opportunity to hold leadership positions, and the experience of performing community service. There are still the traditional sorority and fraternities that have national organizations and in which a group of men or women live together in a "house." In addition, there are Greek organizations for different academic and career fields as well as ones that focus on certain cultural or spiritual heritages. There are certain times of the year that students can apply to join a Greek organization, known as recruitment or "rush"; consult with your campus office of Greek affairs to learn more.

ATHLETIC AND RECREATIONAL EVENTS   There are usually many opportunities to get involved in athletic and recreational events at a university campus. In 2009, 41 percent of freshmen participated in club, intramural, or recreational sports, and 55 percent did so for three or more hours per week, as reported by the Your First College Year study (Ruiz, et al., 2010). In addition, 15 percent stated that they participated in intercollegiate athletics.

Talented and motivated athletes can usually pursue competitive opportunities through university-sponsored teams and club sports. University-sponsored teams play in division and national leagues and are supported financially by the university. Club sports are not officially sponsored or supported by the university but also compete at divisional and national levels.

Walk-on spots are often available to talented individuals who were not recruited, but tryouts might be required. It's important to note that collegiate competitive sports require a lot of practice and training time, which can affect a student's academic performance.

For the less serious athlete, intramural sports can be a great way to get involved. There are usually different levels of competitiveness, so this can be an option for the beginner as well as the expert (although they would never compete in the same league). You will find traditional sports like basketball and soccer as well as the unusual like innertube waterpolo or broomball. In addition, there may be opportunities to take classes, from beginner to expert levels, in a variety of sports and recreational activities.

Finally, if a campus has a popular athletic team, such as football or basketball, there will be opportunities to get involved with the pep squad, marching band, and cheer or dance squad. Consult your campus gym or recreational facility for more information.

RELIGIOUS AND SPIRITUAL GROUPS   In any community where people gather, there will be ways to express religious and spiritual beliefs. This is certainly true in a university community as well. According to a national study on spirituality of college students by the Higher Education Research Institute (2007), 40 percent of college students believed that it is essential or very important to follow religious teachings in everyday life. In addition, 81 percent attended religious services occasionally or frequently, and 69 percent said that they pray.

Many students choose to join a place of worship in the local community surrounding their campus; these can be found by looking in a local telephone directory. Many students choose to participate in religious/spiritual student organizations or groups that focus more on the needs and experiences of young adults in college. These often are registered as campus clubs and provide opportunities for learning, worshiping in community, addressing the challenges of maintaining spirituality in college, and performing community service. The office that coordinates student clubs and activities should be able to provide you with a list of options at or near your campus.

PERFORMING GROUPS   Many college students have a developed interest or talent in one of the performing arts, such as music, dance, drama, or art. While serious performers will most likely choose to pursue one of these fields as a major, many more students perform just for fun. Most campuses have opportunities for students to fulfill this interest through informal and formal performance groups. There might be already established ensembles and groups that students can audition to join, and there are most likely opportunities that are open to all who are interested, such as student choirs and swing dance clubs. These opportunities are most likely affiliated with the academic departments in the arts, but you can also check the student clubs as well as general fliers posted around the campus and local community.

PEER ADVISING FOR NONACADEMIC DEPARTMENTS   Many nonacademic departments and services utilize undergraduate students in peer-advising positions. These are a wonderful way to get involved around a particular issue and also gain valuable training and preprofessional experience, as most provide extensive training. There are many peer positions on campus that can focus on topics such as stress management, peer health topics such as sexual health or body image/eating disorders, athletics, career advising, diversity issues such as ethnicity and sexual orientation, leadership training, and summer orientation. In addition, if your campus has university-owned living environments, there will be resident assistant or coordinator positions, which are great opportunities to explore whether a career in counseling or higher education would be for you.

CAMPUS COMMITTEE APPOINTMENTS   Every year, campus committees that include faculty, staff, and student members address many important campus issues. These committees meet regularly to discuss and provide recommendations on a particular issue like graduation requirements or green business practices. There are usually one or two student spots on these committees, and they are excellent ways for students to get involved. Student members participate in the actual workings of a university and gain valuable experience working in a team environment with a wide range of people. In addition, they become very familiar with the committee's topic so students should choose one that interests them or might be relevant to their future career. Most academic departments and college offices would be able to point you to the office where these committees are coordinated.

VOLUNTEERING AND SERVICE LEARNING   According to the national YFCY study on freshmen in 2009, 58 percent of students participated in volunteer or community service (Ruiz, et al., 2010). Volunteerism is very important and is highly valued by future employers and graduate programs. It is also a way in which the campus community, particularly students, can give back to the local community. Students can contact local organizations directly to find out whether there is a need for volunteers, or there might be an office on your campus that coordinates such efforts.

Some campuses require students to participate in service learning programs as part of their degree requirements. **Service learning** differs from volunteerism in two key ways: first, it is performed in connection with an academic course, and second, it focuses on the concept of serving others, in other words, to be in the service of bettering another's situation or experience. For example, a student might work weekly at a homeless shelter or coordinate a community event to raise awareness about racism. Researchers at the Higher Education Research Institute found that service learning had several key benefits over volunteerism. Specifically, "participating in service-learning courses during college appears to have positive effects on nine key outcomes: civic leadership, working with communities, volunteerism, charitable giving, general political engagement and its four subfactors: political activism, political expression, commitment to political/social change, and voting behavior" (Astin, et al., 2006).

Other Exciting Options

Most of the activities listed above occur during the academic year and are based on or near your campus. However, several exciting opportunities also exist off your campus that you might find very valuable.

SUMMER OPPORTUNITIES   Many universities have exciting summer opportunities for students, both on the campus and in the students' home communities. Most universities host summer conferences for national and international organizations, and there are often student positions available with these programs. Your university might also host a summer academic program for high school students in which positions are available. Of course, there will be some kind of orientation for new students and their families that requires the assistance of current students. There might also be an alumni vacation program that utilizes students to coordinate and host activities for alumni and their children. The campus activities or student life office can most likely help you find information about all of these options. Finally, most universities can help you find an exciting summer internship in your home community and even internationally. These internships can be great ways to build your preprofessional skills as well as a way to earn some money. Contact the career advisors to learn more about summer internships.

INTERNSHIPS IN THE NATION'S OR STATE CAPITAL   Our nation's capital has a long history of utilizing college students as interns in every kind of office from the White House to the Smithsonian Institution to national nonprofit organizations. Students, usually juniors and seniors, from all over the United States can spend a term in Washington, DC, interning at an office. Many universities even offer academic credit for this experience and host students in group living environments with local mentors for guidance and support. A similar internship program might be available in your state's capital. These internships provide truly exciting opportunities and help students prepare for their future careers.

@*myU* SO HOW DOES THIS AFFECT YOU?

In addition to your academic experiences, you have a plethora of options for developing your personal and professional interests through cocurricular opportunities. These can help you prepare for a career as well as deepen your personal values and provide opportunities for fun and social connections—all part of a balanced student life. Review your campus website to find at least three cocurricular opportunities that interest you. Note them below, along with the office or department to contact to gain more information:

1.

2.

3.

SEMESTER AT SEA   This unique program is run out of the University of Virginia; your university might or might not have a formal relationship with it. The program conducts a university term on a cruise ship that travels the world. Students live and study on the ship, and take regular classes while the ship is at sea. When the ship docks in a port, the students, faculty, and staff have a few days to disembark and travel in the country on either prearranged trips or ones of their own planning. There is a spring and a fall voyage, each lasting approximately three and a half months, and a shorter summer voyage lasting one month. The fall voyage leaves from the West Coast and travels to Japan, China, Vietnam, Singapore, India, South Africa, Ghana, Morocco, and Spain, ending on the East Coast. The spring voyage leaves from the East Coast and repeats the trip in the other direction with a few changes in destinations to include Dominica and Brazil. The summer voyage often travels through the Mediterranean countries or along the coast of Central and South America. Even if not all of the classes transfer, this amazing experience is not to be missed. Most students utilize their tuition and rent savings to afford the program and financial aid is also available. To learn more, visit www.semesteratsea.org.

SERVING IN A LEADERSHIP ROLE

Once you find opportunities you enjoy and you have participated for a while, you can begin to explore how you might move into a leadership role in that organization. Serving in leadership roles is very important because these roles allow you to gain very valuable leadership skills that will make you more desirable for both graduate programs and employers.

There are many kinds of leadership roles, both formal and informal. Formal roles will have some kind of official title or set of responsibilities, such as vice president of an organization, chair of recruitment for a sorority, captain of an athletic team, resident assistant, or coleader for a freshman seminar, to name a few. Some of these positions are highly competitive and require some type of selection or election process while others require the interest of a committed person who is willing to serve. Informal roles do not have a specific title or set of responsibilities yet play a vital part in the successful running of the group or organization. These are often a reflection of the individual person's leadership skills and abilities, and people in informal roles sometimes lead more effectively than those in formal ones do.

This highlights the importance of leadership skills. It is really the development of genuine leadership skills, not a title or position, that makes a person an effective leader. Although you will certainly want to apply for and hold leadership positions, it is more important to focus on developing leadership skills and serving as an effective leader.

Developing Important Leadership Skills

While 51 percent of the students in the 2009 Your First College Year survey indicated that they were "above average" or in the "highest 10 percent" in terms of leadership ability, many students realize that college offers a wonderful opportunity to improve their leadership skills. In fact, 20 percent of freshmen participated in leadership during their first year (Ruiz, et al., 2010). A search on the Internet will lead you to hundreds of websites about leadership skills. Leadership skills are often very specific to a certain position or context; for example, the skills that are necessary to be successful as a leader in the military might be different from those needed to be an entrepreneur or an elementary school teacher. For this reason, this section will focus on the leadership skills that are most often needed by university students, although many of these will certainly translate to other settings. It is important to maintain your status as a successful scholar while adding leadership roles to your university experience. You will need to find a balance and not forsake one for the other.

Some of these leadership skills will come through experience, but all of them can be learned and sharpened with some focused effort. There will probably be opportunities on your campus to take classes or workshops on these skills/topics. In addition, the community surrounding your campus will most likely have similar programs available for local businesses and organizations. Finally, there are hundreds of books and websites on these topics. The point is that any person who is serious about developing leadership skills will take the time to study, learn, practice, and improve his/her skills as often as possible. If you are lucky enough to have a leadership development program on your campus, take advantage of its resources as early in your college career as possible.

All of the skills discussed in the following section refer to the needs of a "group" or "members" as well as an "organization"—no matter what kind of leadership position you hold, most likely your position will influence the actions and behaviors of others. Table 8.3 provides an overview of student leadership skills, where you can rate your level of competency and write in campus resources.

COMMUNICATION SKILLS

Teaching and Training

Connected to time management and delegation is a leader's ability to teach and train others. In the process of delegating, the leader might need to provide information and/or skills to others so that they can perform the duties successfully. This is especially relevant for student leaders because student organizations often have high turnover each year when students graduate. A strong leader makes sure that she or he is training and developing the next generation of leaders by giving them opportunities to learn and develop leadership skills.

Communication

Every leader needs strong communication skills—written, verbal, and nonverbal. Communication is the primary way in which a leader leads. There are different communication styles, and a strong leader can adjust his or her style to the needs of the group and when interacting with different individuals. In addition, a leader needs to ascertain when to utilize passive, assertive, and aggressive communication styles as needed for the situation.

Public Speaking

While not every leadership role requires a person to give speeches in front of large audiences, most leaders do find that they are required to speak at various gatherings pretty frequently. A leader is often seen as the primary representative of a group, so it is not uncommon for a student leader to be asked to speak at a meeting, event, or assembly. In addition, leaders will find that they have to speak in front of their group often and also might need to speak in public in the process of recruiting new members. Depending on the situation, skills in dialogue or debate are needed as well. Public speaking is a skill that can be improved with practice, especially because the biggest challenge for most people is dealing with nerves. Public speaking classes and organizations such as Toastmasters are great ways to work on this important skill.

TABLE **8.3** **OVERVIEW OF STUDENT LEADERSHIP SKILLS**

Fill out this table by ranking yourself for your level of competence in that particular area. Use a scale of 1 to 5, with 1 being "no experience" and 5 being "extremely competent." Also, do some research about what is available on your campus to help you develop these skills.

SKILL/AREA	YOUR RATING	CAMPUS SUPPORT AVAILABLE
Communication Skills:		
Teaching and training		
Communication		
Public speaking		
Group Skills:		
Interpersonal skills		
Collaboration and coalition building		
Conflict management		
Motivating and inspiring others		
Management Skills:		
Time management		
Delegation		
Organizational skills		
New member recruiting		
Event planning		
Marketing and advertising		
Budget management		

GROUP SKILLS

Interpersonal Skills

This has to do with how well a person can interact with a wide range of people who may differ in terms of personality, age, gender, ethnicity, spirituality, political ideology, sexual orientation, physical disability, and other dimensions. It is important for a leader to have the ability to listen, as that will be a primary way to learn how best to connect with others. Furthermore, a leader might need to gain cultural competence or understand various aspects of diversity.

Collaboration and Coalition Building

This skill focuses on working well with others. Obviously leaders are going to encourage collaboration among the members of their group, but it is also important to collaborate with other groups. Nowadays, most student groups can accomplish more when they collaborate with other campus entities, such as the administration, various departments or services, and other student groups. A strong leader can help members collaborate with each other by helping them see and appreciate each person's strengths (as opposed to competing with each other). In addition, a good leader maximizes the effectiveness of the group by matching each member's strengths to a need of the organization in terms of roles and responsibilities.

Many student organizations utilize a form of collaboration called coalition building. Coalitions are formed when several groups have an interest in a certain outcome but cannot achieve that outcome single-handedly. This might take the form of lobbying together for a certain campus change, cosponsoring events in ways that create a bigger event than could be achieved by a single group, or sharing resources in a way that serves all of them better.

Conflict Management

All groups experience conflict, which is one of the natural stages of group development. A good leader recognizes this and is not afraid of conflict. In addition, strong leaders are able to assist the group in moving through conflict smoothly in ways that strengthen, rather than splinter, the group. Training in mediation or conflict resolution is especially helpful to most leaders.

Motivating and Inspiring Others

This skill speaks to the leader's ability to work well with followers. When the leader can work with members to cocreate a vision and/or a mission statement, then followers are more likely to take ownership of the success of the group and not leave it to the leader to make this happen. Leaders who are able to motivate and inspire others have an easier time delegating and dealing with conflict in the group.

MANAGEMENT SKILLS

Time Management

This is a mandatory skill for leaders to master, as their success will depend on their ability to balance their academic and cocurricular involvements, as well as meet their obligations on time. Student leaders often take on too many commitments, which results in either a poor performance or sacrificing their personal well-being by losing sleep or skipping meals to meet a deadline. Strong leaders are able to meet their commitments at a high level of performance while also maintaining a calm and well-balanced personal life. This also includes the ability to say no when appropriate.

Delegation

This skill goes hand-in-hand with time management. Delegation requires the leader to be, first, willing to let go of some duties and responsibilities and, second, able to pass those duties on to another in a way that is not bossy or dictatorial. Delegation requires the leader to share the workload with others so that she or he is not too overwhelmed with work and to allow other members to learn and grow.

Organizational Skills

This skill has to do with keeping clear and organized records. Student leaders are often responsible for a wide range of information and activities. It is important for leaders to keep detailed records of all information related to the position, from memos and conversation notes to receipts and meeting agendas. This is especially true when money is involved. Students are held to high standards of fiscal responsibility, and accurate record keeping is a must. Keeping an organized file or notebook allows leaders to be more effective and efficient in performing their duties, as it provides a central location in which to find all relevant information. In addition, these documents can be shared with others and passed on to the next generation of leaders.

New Member Recruiting

On a more practical level, many student organizations need to keep their organization running so that it continues to exist and function in the future. This includes recruiting new members so there are future leaders who can take over when the current leaders graduate. New member recruitment requires a leader to be able to identify potential new members and communicate with them in a way that encourages interest in, and eventual commitment to, the group. Because students are busy, recruitment can be challenging and requires a leader who is able to make connections between the group's mission and the potential member's personal goals and aspirations.

Event Planning

In addition, many student groups organize events as away to fulfill their group's mission. If a group holds events occasionally, such as rallies, dances, performances, or blood drives, someone will need to be strong in event planning. Event planning first requires strong organizational skills, as there will be many records to keep. A crucial tool for event planners is an accurate and detailed timeline of what needs to be accomplished by when. In addition, the leader will need to know how to reserve various campus facilities and order services such as sound and public address systems, tables and chairs, and refreshments. There might also be a need for security guards and ticket sellers.

Marketing and Advertising

For the activities of a group to be successful, people need to know about them. You will need the ability to craft a message that accurately describes and motivates people to attend your program. Then you need to disseminate your marketing. This will require a knowledge of desktop publishing and writing skills as well as knowledge of campus policies regarding posting, and avenues for advertising (both paid and free) through campus and local media.

Budget Management

Many campus organizations operate within a budget, and money is getting tighter and tighter. Managing budgets and being fiscally responsible are important skills. Student leaders should learn about various sources of funding and the methods for applying for them. There might also be a need to engage in fundraising by hosting events, selling products, or seeking individual sponsors.

It would be a challenge for any one student leader to be strong in all of the areas discussed above, yet every one of them is needed for the overall success of an organization, whether student or professional. In any organization, there will most likely be a group of leaders, each of whom has different levels of these skills, who come together to ensure a group's success. Whether they hold formal or informal positions, each person will serve in an important leadership role. Over time, they can learn from one another through observation and experience. Ideally, they will be able to cross-train and gain skills in each of the areas. All of these skills are very helpful to the success of any organization, and your office of student activities or campus life might offer training or information on these topics. See "Point of Interest: Becoming a Leader."

...OMING A LEADER   Consider the devel-...nt of your leadership skills to be as impor-...tant as the requirements for your bachelor's degree. While you can certainly graduate without leadership skills, your future opportunities are expanded considerably if you have paid attention to developing them. Also, don't be intimidated. You don't have to be an outgoing person who enjoys speaking in public to be an amazing leader. Leadership takes all forms, and you will want to find your own special style. Most universities provide for the leadership development of their students through a range of support services. First will be the various ways in which students can get involved on their campus or hold a leadership position, as mentioned in this chapter. Get started early on joining so that there will be time for you to move into leadership positions. Second, you will find educational workshops, talks, and even classes that focus on leadership skills. You can piece these together to create your own curriculum for leadership development. Don't forget options that are not affiliated with your campus. Many communities have workshops and seminars on leadership topics for local business owners and leaders of organizations. Contact the Chamber of Commerce in the town in which you attend college to find out more. Third, you might even have a formal campus leadership program that includes classes, retreats, conferences, workshops, and mandatory service in a leadership role. If such a program exists, enroll early and participate often.

THEORIES OF LEADERSHIP

The concept of leadership has been researched over the years as people have tried to ascertain the qualities that make a good leader and the kinds of behaviors that strong leaders perform. There are many theories on different leadership styles and strategies, some of which are based on empirical studies and others that stem from business practices in the corporate world. Two that are useful to college students are Kouzes and Posner's (1995a) Five Practices of Exemplary Leadership and Hersey and Blanchard's (1993) Situational Leadership Theory. An understanding of these theories will allow you step into a leadership role with more clarity and help you be more effective.

Kouzes and Posner's Five Practices of Exemplary Leadership

This model ties closely to Dr. Claudine Michel's thoughts about the responsibility students have to become leaders and better the experience of others. James Kouzes and Barry Posner's **Five Practices of Exemplary Leadership** grew out of the Transformational Leadership Model, which looks at leaders in terms of the influence that they have on followers. Transformational leaders share a variety of qualities, including the ability to create and promote desirable visions of the organization, generate creative solutions to problems, and facilitate the emergence of other leaders within organizations; transformational leaders are concerned with "doing the right thing" (Andreatta, 2010).

Kouzes and Posner further developed this model after they interviewed thousands of managers in corporations and businesses. They discovered that successful leaders consistently utilized five practices, which they described in their book *The Leadership Challenge* (1995a). They later did research on student leaders and found that student leaders also utilized these five practices. Kouzes and Posner also developed the Student Leadership Practices Inventory (1995b), which allows students to assess their skills in the five practices, and they identified some strategies that students can use to develop their skills. The five practices are as follows.

CHALLENGING THE PROCESS   This practice has to do with "thinking outside the box." Kouzes and Posner found that good leaders are pioneers who are willing to take risks and experiment to create better solutions. They are willing to question the status quo and commonly accepted ways of doing things. Leaders who utilize this practice actively seek out possibilities for change and view mistakes as opportunities for growth. Some student strategies include the following:

+ Make lists of tasks you perform and identify ways in which they can be significantly improved.
+ Read about people who were pioneers in their field to learn about their experience. Don't forget your faculty as possibilities.
+ Sign up for an outdoor adventure program or a creative problem-solving class.

INSPIRING A SHARED VISION   This practice is about how leaders look to the future. Successful leaders dream about what *could* be and have a long-term vision for the development of the organization. Leaders are able to involve others in the organization in both creating the vision and bringing it into reality. This vision ultimately gives direction and purpose to all the members, thereby creating more commitment and pride. Some student strategies include the following:

+ Change your everyday language to be positive; for example, say, "will" instead of "try."
+ Read about or interview people who inspire others and look for how they convey their vision.
+ Create a motto, logo, or slogan for your values and vision, or create a collage vision board of images and phrases that represent your dreams.

ENABLING OTHERS TO ACT   Kouzes and Posner found that successful leaders realize that they cannot do it alone and therefore work from a belief of cooperation and collaboration. They are able to create an atmosphere of mutual trust and respect within their organization by designing opportunities for others to do work that matters to the organization. This also helps members grow and develop as future leaders, thus preparing the next generation and ensuring the long-term success of the organization. Some strategies are the following:

+ Take a class or workshop on team building or effective communication skills.
+ Ask for volunteers to take on tasks and give people choices about what they are assigned to do.
+ Study a social movement and find out how the leaders motivated others to get involved.

MODELING THE WAY   This practice has to do with "walking your talk" and reflects the consistency between the leader's words and actions. Strong leaders are guided by a personal set of standards and values that they communicate to others, and to which they consistently adhere. Leaders serve as role models for others, and their word is their most important asset, as people follow leaders they trust. Successful leaders also help others see what is possible, thus creating opportunities for success. Student strategies include the following:

+ Visit a store or business that has been complimented for its customer service. Observe what employees do to create this reputation.
+ Develop a personal mission statement about your values and principles. Let your choices be strongly guided by them.
+ Allow less experienced members to "shadow" you for a day so that they can observe how you do your work.

ENCOURAGING THE HEART   This final practice is about encouraging others to contribute. Leaders accomplish this by having high expectations for themselves and others and then giving clear directions, providing strong encouragement and personal attention, and giving meaningful feedback to help others grow. Good leaders also express their pride in what individuals and the team accomplish through acknowledging both small and big milestones and achievements. Some strategies include the following:

+ Celebrate your organization's accomplishments and acknowledge people's contributions.
+ Find someone who you believe is good at encouraging the heart. Interview this person and ask for advice or coaching to improve your own skills.
+ Ask everyone in your organization how they like to be recognized. Make a list of the information and honor their requests.

THE SCENIC ROUTE

Visit www.cengagebrain.com to find the companion website containing links to:

- Student Leadership Practices Inventory by Jim Kouzes and Barry Posner
- Situational leadership courses and products by Paul Hersey
- National leadership society and training for college students

Whether or not you serve in a formal leadership position, your college experience will provide you with many opportunities to utilize the Five Practices of Exemplary Leadership. These are excellent skills to develop for your future after college as well. Review your abilities in each of the five practices and identify areas for growth. Utilize campus services and involvement opportunities to further hone your skills. If you have the opportunity, attend trainings in the five practices. Visit www.leadershipchallenge.com for more information.

Hersey and Blanchard's Situational Leadership Theory

Another useful leadership theory is Paul Hersey and Ken Blanchard's **Situational Leadership Theory** (1993). These authors argue that there is no one best style of leadership; rather, "Successful leaders are those who can adapt their behavior to meet the demands of their own unique situation." This means that leaders can intentionally make choices that increase the effectiveness of their leadership by correctly assessing and responding to a specific situation.

Their theory identifies three primary factors in any situation that a leader must assess in order to make good choices. This model is illustrated in Figure 8.1. The first is **task behavior,** which is information the leader needs to provide the followers in order for them to know how to accomplish their tasks. This is often achieved through one-way communication and includes information on where, when, and how the followers are to do the specific tasks. The second factor is **relationship behavior** and is about how the leader interacts with the followers through two-way communication. This focuses on the leader providing emotional support to the followers, which creates positive relationships and good feelings about the organization. Leaders provide support, engage in active listening, and help the followers have a positive experience.

Hersey and Blanchard argue that leaders are always engaging in both the task and relationship behaviors, but the amount of each changes depending on the situation. They have identified four possible combinations: high task and low relationship, high task and high relationship, low task and high relationship, and low task and low relationship. The correct combination depends on the third factor: the **follower readiness.** Readiness, in this instance, refers to the followers' capacity to set high but attainable goals, their willingness and ability to take responsibility, and their education and/or experience for the task at hand. In other words, the leader must assess whether the followers are willing and able to perform the required tasks and have the confidence to do so.

Hersey and Blanchard believe that the leader's choices of task and relationship behavior should be based on first assessing the readiness of the followers. When followers are new or have low readiness, the leader should engage in more task behavior to provide instructions and supervise performance. This is also known as the *directing* phase. As the level of readiness increases, the leader should maintain high-task behavior and increase relationship behavior by explaining decisions and allowing the group to ask questions—also known as *coaching.* Next, the leader would maintain high-relationship behavior but decrease task behavior as the group becomes more skilled and needs less instruction. The leader shares

FIGURE 8.1 Situational Leadership Model

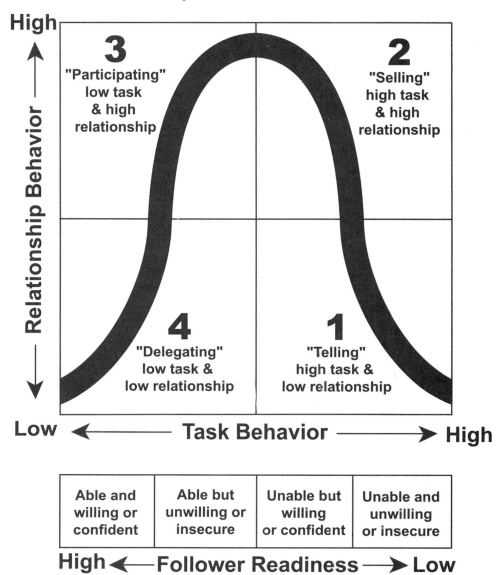

ideas and includes the group in decision making. This stage is called *supporting*. Finally, when the group is very ready, the leader moves to both low-task and low-relationship behavior because the group is essentially capable of performing without the leader's guidance. The leader turns over responsibility to the group in the phase known as *delegating* (Blanchard, Zigarmi & Zigarmi, 1985).

Hersey and Blanchard believe that good leaders are able to develop both their task and relationship behaviors and then use them accurately to guide the group to the highest level of performance and cohesion. A strong leader is skilled in assessing the readiness of the group and adjusting his or her behaviors to that particular situation.

@myU SO HOW DOES THIS AFFECT YOU?

Earlier in this chapter, you read about specific skills and abilities that student leaders often need in their roles with organizations. You will discover that they relate in some way to one or both of these theories. For example, leadership can be especially challenging in student organizations because members are constantly coming into and leaving the organization. This means that members are rarely all at the same stage of readiness, as new members will need more task behavior than more advanced members. Student leaders have to make decisions in this very complex environment, perhaps adapting their behaviors to meet the needs of subgroups of followers instead of using the same strategies with the entire group. Based on what you just read, rank your experience, from 1 (no experience) to 5 (lots of experience), with the following leadership behaviors and identify ones that you'd like to focus on this year:

Challenging the Process

Inspiring a Shared Vision

Enabling Others to Act

Modeling the Way

Encouraging the Heart

Assessing Follower Readiness

Directing

Coaching

Supporting

Delegating

AWARDS AND OTHER FORMS OF RECOGNITION

Most universities acknowledge outstanding student leaders with formal awards. Some of these are scholastic in nature; others are focused on cocurricular involvements. Scholastic awards can be given by a department, program, college, or university, and are based on the student's academic performance. This may be based on overall GPA or may reflect outstanding research or writing in a particular area. Cocurricular awards usually focus on the contributions a student has made to his or her organization or campus. Some have minimum GPA requirements, and some do not.

While all universities will have awards for graduating seniors, many also have class-based awards for every year as well as awards for student groups. In addition, there are annual national competitions and awards for which students can enter or be nominated.

To illustrate this variety, Table 8.4 lists some awards that are granted to graduating seniors at various research universities around the United States. Write in awards at your campus that you might want to qualify for during your time there.

Needless to say, a student's record is improved by the achievement of an award or honor. It is in your best interest to learn about opportunities for which you might qualify. Find out what awards exist on your campus and how they are determined. Read about past winners to discover the kinds of efforts that have been deemed as worthy. By gathering this information early in your university career, you can make informed choices about how to ensure that you will qualify for consideration. Although it is always nice to have someone recognize your talents and nominate you, this doesn't always happen. Every year, truly deserving students are accidentally not considered because the staff and faculty who knew them thought others were submitting their names. It is perfectly appropriate for you to utilize the following strategies to ensure that you will be considered.

TABLE 8.4 SAMPLE OF AWARDS FROM RESEARCH UNIVERSITIES	
UNIVERSITIES	AWARDS
University of Alabama, Birmingham	Dean's Leadership and Service Award Cecile Clardy Satterfield Award for Humanism in Health Care
University of Maine	Outstanding International Student Award Young Women's Social Justice Award
New Mexico State University, Main Campus	American Indian Program Outstanding Senior Award Outstanding Undergraduate Student Award
Texas A&M University	Charles Gordone Writing Award Senior Merit Award
Virginia Commonwealth University	Outstanding Judaic Studies Award Excellence in Spanish Award
Your University	

Some awards are based on rigid criteria, and the students who meet those criteria are automatically considered. For example, at one university, the Mortar Board Award is given to the graduating senior with the highest GPA. Every spring, the records of all the graduating seniors with a 4.0 GPA are reviewed (you would be surprised by how many there are!). Most never even know that they are under consideration. The award is given to the student with the most A-pluses on his or her transcript, and she or he is notified a couple of weeks before commencement. Students cannot apply for this award, although any student who really wanted to receive it could have learned about it as a first-year student and worked hard to earn only As and A-pluses.

Other awards have an application process that is advertised to students. Students apply by the deadline and are considered along with the other applicants. Students can make choices that make them more eligible or more competitive depending on the criteria for the award. In addition, the student who marks the deadline and takes ample time to submit a professional application will have better chances than those who submit a mediocre application or who miss the deadline entirely.

There are also a host of awards that have a nomination process. If self-nominations are allowed, then obviously a student can nominate himself or herself, but I recommend finding out whether self-nominations are given the same credence as others. In some cases, they are; in other cases, they are not. If not, then you will want to find someone to nominate you. Some awards might allow students to nominate other students. In this case, you can probably ask a friend and even nominate each other. Just be sure that this person knows enough about you to describe your qualifications accurately.

Some awards, usually the most prestigious ones, allow nominations only from faculty and staff. While faculty and staff try very hard to nominate all the students who qualify, this doesn't always happen. It is acceptable behavior for a student to communicate with faculty and staff about potential awards to ensure that you will be considered. See "Point of Interest: Securing the Nomination."

SECURING THE NOMINATION If you find an award for which you believe you qualify, I strongly recommend that you bring it to the attention of a faculty or staff member whom you have gotten to know. I suggest approaching this in the following way (this can be done either in writing or in person). Print out the award information and the nomination form. Give it to the person along with a note that says something like the following:

Dear [name],

I recently came across information for the [award's title or name] award. I believe I may qualify for it but I wanted your opinion. Please read the attached information and let me know whether you think I might qualify and whether I would be competitive. I would love to hear back from you by [date], since the deadline is [date]. Thank you so much for your time.

Sincerely,

[your name]

[your e-mail address and phone number]

If the person does not believe that you qualify, she or he will probably tell you why. Sometimes there are certain stipulations that might not be clear in the materials. If the person does think you qualify, you might get a response like "Yes, I agree with you. It sounds like you meet the criteria for consideration." This will allow you to write back and ask whether she or he will nominate you. The person also might be able to give you a better sense of how competitive the award is and how strong your chances might be. Or you might get a response such as "Yes, you do. I was already planning on nominating you and will get the form in by the deadline. I hope that you get it."

I am never offended if a student approaches me in this way. In fact, I am grateful! I always want to nominate my deserving students for awards, but frankly, there are so many different awards that I cannot always keep track. I would rather a student approach me than find out later that I missed an important deadline. As with every other aspect of university life, students are responsible for making sure they are appropriately qualified for awards they wish to receive.

Developing your leadership skills can only enhance your educational experience and future opportunities. Give attention to your leadership development and utilize your campus's resources to help you. If there are courses on leadership theories or skills, definitely enroll in them. Likewise, you will see many workshops and presentations on your campus about a variety of leadership skills—attend them. Your campus will also host many special engagements for current leaders in politics, medicine, economy, arts, science, and world affairs. Even if they cost money to attend, they will be well worth your time, and you might find that a special event has been arranged for students to interact with the speaker. Don't miss these! Your campus might also have a leadership conference or retreat where you can gain valuable skills. To find out about your options, visit the office of student life or campus activities and make plans to participate in as many events and programs as possible. As you participate, you may become eligible for various honors and awards that acknowledge your skills.

RELATED MATERIALS

For Scenic Route websites, more Stories from the Path, glossary, and student activities, access the study tools for *Navigating the Research University* at www.cengagebrain.com.

REFERENCES

Andreatta, B. (2010, January 25). *Transformational leadership.* Lecture presented at Education 173, University of California, Santa Barbara.

Astin, A. W., Vogelgesang, L. J., Misa, K., Anderson, J., Denson, N., Jayakumar, U., Saenz, V., & Yamamura, E. (2006). *Understanding the effects of service-learning: A study of students and faculty.* Retrieved from http://www.heri.ucla.edu/PDFs/pubs/reports/UnderstandingTheEffectsOfServiceLearning_FinalReport.pdf.

Blanchard, K., Zigarmi, P., & Zigarmi, D. (1985). *Leadership and the one minute manager: Increasing effectiveness through situational leadership.* New York: William Morrow.

DeAngelo, L., Hurtado, S. H., Pryor, J. H., Kelly, K. R., Santos, J. L., & Korn, W. S. (2009). *The American college teacher: National norms for the 2007–2008 HERI faculty survey.* Retrieved from http://www.heri.ucla.edu/publications-brp.php.

Florio, M., Mudd, D., Peosay, T., Peosay, S. (Producers), & Peosay, T. (Director). (2002). *Tibet: Cry of the snow lion* [Motion Picture]. (Available from New Yorker Films, 85 Fifth Avenue, 11th Floor, New York, NY 10003.)

Hersey, P., & Blanchard, K. (1993). *Management of organizational behavior: Utilizing human resources* (6th ed.). Englewood Cliffs, NJ: Prentice-Hall.

Higher Education Research Institute. (2007). *The spiritual life of college students: A national study of college students' search for meaning and purpose.* Retrieved from http://www.spirituality.ucla.edu/publications/research-reports/.

Invisible Children, Inc. (2010). *Media kit.* Retrieved from http://www.invisiblechildren.com/media/assets/file/online_media_kit.pdf.

Kopp, W. (2003). *One day, all children ... The unlikely triumph of Teach For America and what I learned along the way.* Cambridge, MA: PublicAffairs.

Kouzes, J. M., & Posner, B. Z. (1995a). *The leadership challenge* (2nd ed.). San Francisco: Jossey-Bass.

Kouzes, J. M., & Posner, B. Z. (1995b). *Student leadership practices inventory: Student workbook.* San Francisco: Jossey-Bass.

Michel, C. (2004, March 11). *Making the most of your college experience.* Lecture for Interdisciplinary 20, Introduction to the research university. University of California, Santa Barbara.

Mortenson, G. (2009). *Stones into schools: Promoting peace with books, not bombs, in Afghanistan and Pakistan.* New York: Viking Press.

Mortenson, G., & Relin, D. (2007). *Three cups of tea: One man's mission to promote peace ... one school at a time.* New York: Penguin Books.

Ruiz, S., Sharkness, J., Kelly, K., DeAngelo, L., & Pryor, J. (2010). *Findings from the 2009 administration of Your First College Year (YFCY): National aggregates.* Retrieved from http://www.heri.ucla.edu/publications-brp.php.

Semester at Sea. (2010). Retrieved from http://www.semesteratsea.org.

Teach For America. (2010). *What we do.* Retrieved from http://www.teachforamerica.org/what-we-do/.

Three Cups of Tea. (2010). *About Greg Mortenson.* Retrieved from http://www.threecupsoftea.com/greg-mortenson-bio-and-professional-photo/.

CHAPTER **9**

Planning for Your Future

Virginia Commonwealth University

Photo by Tom Kojcsich, VCU Creative Services

  This book has focused on many of the experiences first-year students have during their enrollment at a research university. I hope you have found it informative and illuminating. The goal of this chapter is to help you take what you learned to improve your remaining educational experiences, both for your college degree and beyond. While this chapter could certainly be placed earlier in this text, it is placed here because I want to encourage you to reflect on your experiences during and after your first year as a freshman or transfer student. On the basis of this reflection, you will be invited to set specific objectives for the next years of your university attendance through graduation. You will also be provided with tips and strategies to set goals that support your academic, social, and personal success.

REFLECTING ON YOUR FIRST YEAR

As you go through and eventually finish your first year at a research university, it is important to reflect on your experiences. Each experience you have, academic and social, provides you with valuable information that can allow you to improve your future experiences. Positive experiences can lead you to repeat certain actions and behaviors, and negative ones can assist you in making changes to avoid repeating the same experiences. You will be gaining valuable lessons in two areas. One is the university itself and all it entails, including expectations of faculty, policies, departments and services, overall climate, the student body in general, and so on. The other is yourself and the many things you will learn about your values, your preferences, your skills and abilities, and your strengths and weaknesses. Together, these can inform your future choices so that you can navigate the university environment with ease and success.

One way you can learn from your experiences is to review what has happened during your first term or first year of university life. An in-depth review of your academic and social experiences can provide you with valuable insight for shaping your future goals. Take some time to reflect on the following questions. You can also do this with a partner.

1. What have you learned about the academic environment of the campus?

2. What have you learned about the social environment of the campus?

3. What have you learned about your academic strengths? And weaknesses?

4. What have you learned about your social strengths? And weaknesses?

5. What were the things that contributed to your academic successes?

6. What were the things that hindered your academic successes?

7. What were the things that contributed to your social successes?

8. What were the things that hindered your social successes?

9. What things from your first term or first year should you definitely try to continue or repeat in the future?

10. What things from your first term or first year should you definitely try to change or avoid in the future?

11. What are some new opportunities or experiences that you would like to participate in during college?

12. What are the qualities that you believe a person should possess to be a successful adult? (Consider the whole picture: career, family, health, spirituality, interests, community, etc.)

13. How can you utilize your college experience to become that person?

14. Are there any other questions you should ask yourself?

After engaging in this reflection, use these insights to set concrete goals for the remainder of your college experience. While these goals are not set in stone and will likely change over the years as you learn more, it is good to start with a clear set of goals and then review every term and adjust accordingly. The following sections will help you create more specific and measurable goals that will guide you during the remainder of your college experience.

GOALS FOR FOUR YEARS OF COLLEGE

There are many theories that explore the development of young adults through the college years, including stages of development in various areas, but all lead to a more mature and functioning adult who is ready to step into the world in many roles, such as a leader, an employee, a community member, or a parent. You should pay attention to your academics, personal growth, social experience, and career preparation. Think about the two to four years you have to maximize your growth and take advantage of all the opportunities you have. Our academic, career, and personal counselors outlined a general set of guidelines for development during each of the four years of college, focusing on the four major areas areas of academic, personal, social, and career development (UCSB Career Services, 2010). It has been edited to be appropriate for almost any university experience. Explore this plan of action and see how and where your own insights from the prior exercise might fit in.

A Plan of Action

Each year of your time in college will be marked by challenges and opportunities as you learn more about yourself and make choices about your future. The keys to success are planning ahead, using your time well, taking advantage of campus and community resources, and being proactive. Every student's experience is different, but the following plan of action can help you become the person you would like to be by graduation.

FRESHMAN YEAR: EXPLORING The focus of this year should be about exploring the four areas. Check off these activities as you accomplish them, and add others that interest you.

Academics: Explore the University	Personal: Self-Understanding
• Read the general catalog and other campus materials • See an academic advisor • Meet many professors and go to office hours • Attend workshops on study skills, test taking, time management, etc. • Develop and hone your academic success skills • Explore general education requirements and electives to discover your interests • Enroll in freshman seminars • Explore the honors programs • Other: • Other:	• Develop a group of friends • Take a personality test (e.g., Myers-Briggs Type Indicator©) • Do values clarification exercises • Identify fears of college life and address them • Explore individual counseling • Redefine your relationship with family • Other: • Other:
Social: Initiate Relationships	Career: Explore Career Areas
• Join residence hall government or committees • Join an activity, club, or organization • Make summer travel plans; nurture hobbies • Develop a peer group • Seek out volunteer opportunities • Other: • Other:	• Attend a choosing-a-major workshop • Talk with parents, friends, professors, and career advisors • Do career testing by trying out jobs through volunteering • Identify the following: past accomplishments, skills and abilities, hobbies, personality style, career values • Explore summer internships • Other: • Other:

SOPHOMORE YEAR: DEFINING The focus of this year should be about defining your ideas and goals in all four areas. Check off these activities as you accomplish them, and add others that interest you.

Academics: Gain Specific Information	Personal: Explore New Roles
• Seek academic advice from teaching assistants, professors, and advisors • Talk to many professors about academic and career goals • Establish a personal GPA goal • Choose a major and talk with people in your major • See a career advisor • Develop an academic plan with an academic advisor • Explore study abroad programs to become eligible • Explore summer school and summer internships • Other: • Other:	• Learn about cultural diversity through events • Join a counseling growth group • Explore your family dynamics • Clarify your values • Assess which friendships best support your goals and aspirations • Find a mentor who can offer support • Other: • Other:
Social: Increase Involvement	**Career: Collect More Information**
• Work on a project for a club/organization • Serve on student committees • Volunteer in the community • Join intramural sports teams • Attend campus events (e.g., films, lectures, performances) • Other: • Other:	• Read about careers • Talk with professionals in several careers (do an information interview) • Make short-term goals • Look for a summer internship • Volunteer to "shadow" a professional for a day • Talk with career advisors • Explore career resources such as books and websites • Attend career workshops • Other: • Other:

JUNIOR/TRANSFER YEAR: RESEARCHING The focus of this year should be about researching your post-graduate options in all four areas. Check off these activities as you accomplish them, and add others that interest you.

Academics: Make Initial Choices	Personal: Risk Personal Openness
• Take mock GRE, MCAT, or LSAT exams • Attend seminars/conferences that relate to your major • Request a junior progress report from your college • Find an academic mentor • Participate in a faculty research project • Apply for internships • Participate in study abroad or Washington, DC, internship programs • Explore summer school and summer internships • Other: • Other:	• Seek out sources of support • Help others with their problems • Continue discussions with a mentor • Test ideas through discussion groups • Disagree with an authority • Other: • Other:
Social: Exercise New Skills	**Career: Increase Experience**
• Start a small business • Get involved in student government • Apply for a peer advisor position with the residence halls, colleges, or other campus departments • Volunteer in the community • Mentor younger students • Other: • Other:	• Find interesting internships • Make preliminary career choices • Attend grad school or career fairs • Attend resume-writing workshops • Do more information interviews • Develop awareness of career options in many areas • Talk with a career advisor • Take career-preparation courses or workshops • Other: • Other:

SENIOR YEAR: IMPLEMENTING   The focus of this year should be on implementing your post-graduate plan in all four areas. Check off these activities as you accomplish them, and add others that interest you.

Academics: Long-Term Decisions	Personal: Make Commitments
• Prepare grad school applications • Apply for awards • Present at scholarly meetings • Do a senior thesis project • Develop an independent study project or a directed reading with a professor • Request a senior progress check • Investigate senior honors program or seminars • Take a graduate course • Attend a national conference in your field • Other: • Other:	• Prepare for your chosen lifestyle • Attend stress management workshops • Talk about your first year after graduation • Make a list of your firm decisions • Write down three life goals • Other: • Other:
Social: Demonstrate Leadership	**Career: First Career Choice**
• Lead a group or club • Supervise a few student projects • Join a professional organization • Tutor high school students • Take leadership classes and workshops • Join a public speaking club • Other: • Other:	• Attend workshops on: job searches, interviewing, recruiting, mock interviews, resume writing, applying to grad school, etc. • Establish life goals • Develop a contact list for career networking • Interview for jobs • Develop a budget for job or grad school • Check job listings • Other: • Other:

ACHIEVING YOUR GOALS

Most people would agree that setting and achieving goals is a path to success. Goal setting is a way for a person to clearly state what she or he hopes to achieve; it creates focus and direction, and inevitably guides thoughts, actions, and behaviors. However, goal setting can be a bit more

RAVEN'S STORY FROM THE PATH

When I first started college, the only goal I had was not to flunk out. I knew I wanted to graduate and then pursue a career, but that was as far as my "plan" went. I stuck with that "plan" for most of my first semester, but I realized only too late that I was not making the grades I wanted. Things not related to school that I planned to do—like getting in better shape—were not happening for me, either. I could not figure out what I needed to do or to change to make my life go the way I wanted it to go. After learning about goal setting in my Success Strategies class, I realized my problem: I was not *properly* setting goals for myself.

Once I knew my problem, I knew how to fix it. I went home and made a list of everything I wanted to accomplish in my life. It was the first time I had written down anything from that "plan" in my head. Then, I concentrated on the things on my list that I was capable of accomplishing in the near future, and narrowed my list to those items. I also made sure that my goals were really specific; so, instead of saying, "I want to make good grades," I stated what grade I wanted to get in each class, and listed strategies I needed to use to earn those grades. I kept the list saved on my computer so that I could go back and look at it whenever I needed to check where I was toward meeting my goals. In the end, I was able to turn my semester around—but I know I could have done even better if I had followed these guidelines from the beginning.

I am now a lot better about setting goals for myself. I make a list of goals at the beginning of every semester, and I include both personal and academic goals. I still keep my list saved on my computer, but I also print a copy to hang on my wall. That way, I see them every day and am reminded of what I want to accomplish and how to go about doing it. If I do not accomplish a goal in the time period I set for myself, I do not beat myself up about it—I just realize that I have to adjust my approach or my expectations, and I add the same goal (with the new changes) to the next semester's list. I feel like setting realistic goals for myself each semester has helped make my life more purposeful.

complex than some people might think. It is easy to say, "I'll have a 4.0 GPA," but this statement lacks many things that are essential to good goal setting and the ultimate success of achieving them. See "Raven's Story from the Path."

SMART Goals

One technique that is espoused by many is known as the **SMART goal** technique. According to Dr. Cherie Carter-Scott (2000) from her book *If Success Is a Game, These Are the Rules*, the SMART technique states that goals should have the following five qualities: **S**pecific, **M**easurable, **A**ction-oriented, **R**ealistic, and **T**imely. In addition, you will outline the smaller steps needed to achieve the larger goal.

SPECIFIC   The goal needs to be very specific so that it is clearly defined and achievable. For example, "I'll have a 4.0 GPA" is a bit general. The goal "I will earn straight As in the four classes I am taking spring term" is much more specific. Another general goal might be phrased as "I'll be thinner by summer." Again, this is too general—what does thinner mean? When, exactly, is summer? A specific goal would be "I will lose a half-inch each from my waist, hips, and thighs by the end of finals week." Another example of a general goal might be "I will get involved on campus my second year." A better goal would be "During the fall term, I will attend three club meetings and join the one I like the most." This is much more specific, and it will be easier to recognize whether you are on track. Try to include information on who, what, where, how, and why.

MEASURABLE   This quality also has to do with specificity and reflects how you know whether you have achieved the goal or not. The goal "I will feel better about school" is not measurable. By what criteria can you measure that? You need to set goals that have some kind of measurable benchmark. These might be inherently available in the goal (e.g., GPA points, pounds, inches), or you might have to create a benchmark, such as a scale of 1 to 10. For example, "On a scale of 1 to 10, I'm currently at a 3 in terms of liking my college experience. I would like to increase that to at least a 6 by June."

TABLE 9.1   SAMPLE OF GOALS WRITTEN AS SMART GOALS WITH SPECIFIC STEPS

General Goal	General Goal	General Goal
To be more involved	To do better academically	To get along better with roommates
SMART Goal	**SMART Goal**	**SMART Goal**
During my second year, I will attend three club meetings and join the club I like the most.	I will earn straight As in the four classes I am taking spring term.	This term, I will improve my relationship with roommates so that my enjoyment of my living situation goes from a 3 to at least a 7 (on a scale of 1–10).
Specific Steps	**Specific Steps**	**Specific Steps**
• I will get a list of all of the clubs and organizations at the university. By Oct. 1. • I will review the list and select five that sound interesting to me. By Oct. 15. • I will contact officers for those five clubs and find out more about the organization, including when they meet. By Nov. 1. • I will select the three that sound the most interesting and attend their next meeting. By Dec. 1. • If I need to, I will attend a second meeting. By Feb. 1 (earlier if finals and break do not interfere). • I will officially join the organization of my choice and make a commitment to attend at least two meetings per month. By Feb. 15.	• I will review my previous term's grades and assignments so that I can see what I did wrong last term. By Jan. 10. • I will meet with an academic skills advisor to create a plan for improvement. By Jan. 15. • Every other week, I will attend office hours for each of my classes to ensure that I am on track. By Jan. 15, Feb. 1, Feb. 15, Mar. 1, Mar. 15, April 1. • Each week, I will use a scheduling grid and assignment planner to ensure that I have made accurate time to finish all of my studying. Will review every Sunday. • I will start each paper as soon as it is given to me and do no fewer than three drafts before handing them in. TBA. • If I am struggling, I will hire a tutor to work with me until I feel more confident. As needed.	• I will read over the roommate handbook provided by our housing department. By Sept. 15. • I will meet with my resident advisor to get suggestions about how to improve our living situation. By Sept. 15. • I will go to lunch with each of my roommates (one-on-one) and ask them how they think we can make our situation better. I will also share my request to have them not eat my food without asking and to use earphones for music after 11 P.M. on weeknights. By Oct. 15. • On the basis of the previous meetings, I will set specific goals to improve in the areas determined. By Nov. 1. • I will do at least one social thing with my roommates every week. • I will meet with my roommates again to see how things are coming along. By Jan. 1 and adjust accordingly.

THE SCENIC ROUTE

Visit www.cengagebrain.com to find the companion website containing links to:

- Idaho State University's goal setting for freshmen
- Information on vision boards and other tools
- An iPhone app that tracks your goals

ACTION-ORIENTED   This is the quality that empowers you to be in control. Set goals that allow *you* to take some specific actions to achieve them. The goal "I want to be liked by more people" is not action-oriented; it is based on the actions of others. However, the goal "I will meet at least ten new people by the end of the term" is action-oriented, as is the goal "I will ask my roommates two things I can change to be a better roommate." You want your goals to have some action in them so that you can be proactive in achieving them. This is especially important to remember in relationships. You cannot control the behavior of others, so having a goal of getting more flowers from your boyfriend is not a good idea. However, you certainly can set a goal for telling him that flowers are important to you and for requesting that he give you flowers more often. You can even have a goal regarding how you will handle the situation if he does not honor your request. These are all the things for which you can control the action.

REALISTIC   It's very important that goals be realistic; otherwise, you set yourself up for failure. While you might wish to lose 20 pounds in 2 weeks, this is not a realistic goal. Neither is earning straight As the next term if you are currently flunking your classes. You can certainly improve and bring your GPA up, but it may not be realistic to expect perfect grades if you have not mastered average grades yet. You have to be able to envision yourself accomplishing the goal and believing that you can do it—otherwise, you won't.

TIMELY   This is where you address the "when" of your goal. Each goal needs to have a target date for completion; otherwise, it is too easy to put it off. It's important to get specific about when you will accomplish something because this holds you accountable for taking action. However, it's also important to be realistic about the time frame—setting the deadline too far away will not be very motivating, and too close can be discouraging.

Once you have a clear goal that has all of the SMART qualities, break each goal into smaller steps that will lead to the achievement of that goal. Each smaller step should also have a specific deadline, and the smaller steps should lead to accomplishing the SMART goal by its stated time frame. (See Table 9.1.)

Obstacles to Success

Setting goals can be fairly easy, but achieving them can be another matter. If achieving goals were easy, then everyone would have exactly what they want. People could set goals and then just achieve them—there would be no disappointed or unhappy students on campuses. Unfortunately, the best intentions are not always carried out easily. Most students who are doing poorly genuinely want to earn better grades, and they may set SMART goals to help them do better. However, as you try to achieve your goals, you might find that you have some obstacles in your way. These might be unforeseen challenges, such as becoming sick with H1N1 flu or discovering that you have no talent for physics, or there might be a lack of resources or motivation. If you are knocked off track by an unforeseen situation, such as becoming ill, you might have to adjust your timeline accordingly. You want to be reasonable with yourself and know when flexibility is appropriate.

In the case of doing poorly at physics, that might not be something you can change. There are certain things you can control, such as how much time you devote to studying and using resources like office hours and tutoring groups. But if after your best effort, physics continues to be a challenge, you might need to rethink your dream of being an astrophysicist. Goals aren't always achievable even with your best efforts, and it's prudent to know when to move on and set different goals.

Other obstacles might be more emotional, such as realizing that you are majoring in something only to please your parents but that you have no real interest in it. Another common problem is setting a goal of a certain career because it pays well. Often, if we set goals to please others in some way, we might not have the personal motivation to succeed. People often set goals because they feel that they should—the "shoulds" undermine people's success because, without the personal motivation, the difficult or challenging circumstances can stop someone's forward movement. If you discover that you are not making progress on a goal, look at whether it is something *you* really want. If not, look at why you think you should have that goal. Has someone made a specific request of you, such as parents who have said you must major in the sciences? Or have you assumed that you should for some reason, such as thinking you will be happier if you have a job that would allow you to afford a sporty car? If you can identify why you set that goal in the first place, it can help you evaluate whether or not you want to keep the goal. If you decide to keep it, you will need to find your own personal reasons for wanting that goal so that you have the motivation to succeed.

You might even discover some hidden obstacle that you didn't know existed such as an internal emotional conflict. Sometimes we discover that we have more complex emotions at work underneath the experiences, ones that might have to do with our past and might require meeting with a professional counselor to work through. See "Tasha's Story from the Path."

TASHA'S STORY FROM THE PATH

In my junior year, I really wanted to lose weight and become thinner. I had gained the "Freshman fifteen" and had added the "Sophomore seven" as well. I met with the campus nutritionist who helped me create a great plan for eating healthy and exercising that would fit with my college life. It really seemed doable so I set my goals for losing 20 pounds and getting in shape. However, I just kept struggling with these goals. While I wanted to lose weight, I was completely unmotivated to work out and every tempting snack messed up my food plan. Each week, I would start fresh with every intention of sticking to it, and every week, I would blow it. This went on for the whole semester.

I got really frustrated with myself and my lack of self-control. I just couldn't understand why I couldn't achieve this relatively simple goal. I finally saw a campus counselor and she really helped me get to the bottom of it. I discovered that I was actually in conflict with myself about becoming thinner. I have two older brothers, and growing up, I would always overhear them talk about girls they thought were hot and how they wanted to have sex with them. I know it was just guys' crude talk but it made me feel that if I was thin, then a guy would only be interested in having sex with me and not care about me for myself.

This internal conflict kept sabotaging my goals because, down deep, I wasn't really sure that I wanted to be thin. I worked with my counselor to feel more empowered about my body and my relationship with men in general. Once I worked through that, it was easy for me to achieve my goals and I lost the 20 pounds.

Using Resources and Seeking Support

To overcome these obstacles, it is important to utilize all the campus resources available to you. You are already paying for them in your tuition, and they are there for your benefit. As mentioned earlier, many of the staff and faculty on your campus have years of training and experience in helping students be successful. While you can certainly go it alone, that's not necessarily the best use of your time and energy, not to mention your tuition. You don't win any prizes for suffering through challenges alone—the prize comes in achieving the goal, whether you needed support or not. So use your resources with abandon. These resources include workshops, educational programs, one-on-one advising, courses, and websites, to name a few. If you don't find exactly what you need, don't hesitate to look beyond your specific campus to another college nearby or other businesses and services, both local and Web-based. There are also many great books available on topics that affect college students. Check out your campus bookstore regularly for possibilities, as well as local and Web-based bookstores.

Think about it this way: Everyone has the ability to cut their own hair—all they need is a pair of scissors, and they can snip away. But most people recognize that there is more to a good haircut than simply cutting hair with scissors. With this is mind, they hire a professional, someone who is trained in cutting hair and who knows how hair lies and how best to cut different types of hair. Think of the services on your campus as a "success salon" and the staff and faculty as trained professionals who know useful tricks and strategies to turn your college experience into the vision you have dreamed of.

In addition to utilizing the services provided at your campus, it's always a good idea to also have a support team in place. The purpose of a support team is to help you achieve your goals, especially when you hit an obstacle. They are people who either can give you specific assistance or are there to encourage you when the going gets a little rough. These should be people whom you can count on and whom you trust. Sometimes people are automatically on your support team; for example, most academic advisors can be counted on for giving you sound and accurate advice to lead you to successful completion of your college degree. Others might need to be asked or informed that you would like them on your team.

It's always a good idea to tell someone what kind of support you would like from him or her; this gives you a much better chance of getting exactly what you need when you need it. Your request might go something like this: "I'm calling because you have always been really helpful to me in the past. Right now, I am working on a specific goal, and I'd like your help.

@myU SO HOW DOES THIS AFFECT YOU?

It is ultimately your responsibility to make the most of your university experience. You need to ensure that you are not only making progress toward your degree, but also preparing for your life after college. There is no prescription for how this should look, which gives you a lot of freedom for designing your college years in ways that you both enjoy and get the most from. Be actively engaged in the process. Seek advice from faculty and staff, use campus resources and services, learn from your mistakes, set goals, and meet them. Take a moment to outline some goals for the next 12 months.

General Goal	General Goal	General Goal
SMART Goal	SMART Goal	SMART Goal
Specific Steps	Specific Steps	Specific Steps

The goal is (fill in here), and what I'd like from you is (fill in here)." Your request could range from asking for specific advice, to listening to you vent when something is hard, to reminding you of your strengths and that you can do it, to giving you brutally honest feedback, and so on. A good support team for a college student would include family members, friends (both at home and at school), counselors, advisors, mentors, and advocates.

Mentors and advocates are very important. A **mentor** is someone who has a bit more experience than you in the particular area on which you are focusing. She or he should have achieved some level of success that you are hoping to emulate. This mentor will share his or her own story with you and can provide you with advice about how to achieve your goal. You can have different mentors for different parts of your life, and they should change with time as you achieve a certain level of success and need a new mentor for the next level you wish to achieve. Look for people who could serve as mentors to you and then approach them. Most people are quite flattered to be told that they are looked up to and to be asked to be a mentor. If they do not have the time to serve as a mentor, they might be able to connect you to other people who are available.

Advocates are different from mentors in that advocates do not need to have achieved anything in the area in which you have set goals. The only thing they need to do is to care about you and believe in your ability to achieve your goals. Advocates are like cheerleaders—when the going gets rough, they enthusiastically remind you that you said you wanted this goal and that you absolutely can achieve it. You can never have too many advocates, but be sure that they are on board for believing in you for that particular goal. A person who is a strong ally in supporting your goal to get good grades might not be the best ally for career planning if this person really doesn't want you to move across the country. His or her personal preferences might get in the way of supporting you completely. So choose your advocates carefully, be explicit about what you want them to support you on, and even give them guidance about how best to support you when the going gets rough.

ONE FINAL THOUGHT

Attending a premier research university is an amazing opportunity. You are one of a small group of lucky individuals who gets to live and learn in this special environment. Earning your college degree can, and should, be more than satisfying your requirements and being handed your diploma. It's a time to discover who you are, what you value, and what you are meant to contribute to this world. These answers might come easily for some of you, but most of you will need to explore and experiment to gain more clarity. As you progress through college, you will learn and grow in ways that will shape your sense of yourself and your future. Be open to this process and embrace it fully. Set goals and make plans, but also be flexible enough to change them as new experiences influence your path. Finally, be proactive about making your university years all that you had hoped for and more.

RELATED MATERIALS

For Scenic Route websites, more Stories from the Path, glossary, and student activities, access the study tools for *Navigating the Research University* at www.cengagebrain.com.

REFERENCES

Carter-Scott, C. (2000). *If success is a game, these are the rules: Ten rules for a fulfilling life.* New York: Random House.

UCSB Career Services (2010). A plan of action. In the *2010 UCSB Kiosk student handbook.* Retrieved from http://kiosk.ucsb.edu/Citizenship/ActionPlan.aspx.

Index